Sister Republics

SISTER REPUBLICS

Security Relations between America and France

David G. Haglund

Louisiana State University Press

Baton Rouge

Published by Louisiana State University Press
lsupress.org

Manufactured in the United States of America
First printing

Designer: Andrew Shurtz
Typefaces: Fournier MT, Futura PT, Le Jeune

Library of Congress Cataloging-in-Publication Data

Names: Haglund, David G., author.
Title: Sister republics : security relations between America
    and France / David G. Haglund.
Other titles: Security relations between America and France
Description: Baton Rouge : Louisiana State University Press, 2023.
    | Includes index.
Identifiers: LCCN 2022032181 (print) | LCCN 2022032182 (ebook)
    | ISBN 978-0-8071-7901-7 (cloth) | ISBN 978-0-8071-7968-0 (pdf)
    | ISBN 978-0-8071-7967-3 (epub)
Subjects: LCSH: United States—Relations—France. | France—
    Relations—United States. | National security—United States—
    History. | National security—France—History. | Strategic
    culture—United States. | Strategic culture—France.
Classification: LCC E183.8.F8 H169 2023 (print) | LCC E183.8.F8
    (ebook) | DDC 327.73044—dc23/eng/20220912
LC record available at https://lccn.loc.gov/2022032181
LC ebook record available at https://lccn.loc.gov/2022032182

Contents

Preface and Acknowledgments vii

I. The *Problématique*

1. A Franco-American Special Relationship? 3

2. The Role of "Strategic Culture" in Understanding
   Franco-American Relations 35

II. Cultural Analysis

3. Historical Context:
   From Erbfeindschaft to Relational Realism 73

4. "Ethnicization" and Foreign Policy:
   The Duroselle-Tardieu Thesis Revisited 113

5. *Vive la différence?*
   Cognitive "Antinomies" of a Special Relationship 150

III. Culture and Individual "Agency"

6. Do Leaders Matter?
   Individuals and Their Relationship to Strategic Culture 199

Conclusion 221

Notes 227
Index 287

Preface and Acknowledgments

The past little while has constituted an especially tumultuous period in the life of the venerable transatlantic alliance. The Donald Trump years represented for NATO watchers what psychedelically oriented members of the forty-fifth president's own boomer generation might have called, back in the 1960s, a "real trip." Although President Trump did not invent the category of intra-alliance fractiousness, he certainly seemed to take great delight in his role as the alliance's disruptor in chief.[1] Nor did the new Biden administration, prior to the Russian invasion of Ukraine in early 2022, augur any significant improvement in the tenor of intra-alliance relations. In large measure, early skepticism regarding the therapeutic impact of President Biden was a function of how he carried out the policy of his predecessor in withdrawing precipitously from Afghanistan during the summer of 2021, evoking for many of the allies a depressing sense of déjà vu.[2] Nor was it lost on too many that American voters just might, three years hence, choose to send Donald Trump back to the White House.

But the anxiety caused by Biden's Afghanistan missteps and the specter of Trump becoming another Grover Cleveland, troubling as each was, represented less a departure from a long-standing alliance pattern than simply the latest chapters in a saga replete with tales of intra-alliance disharmony. The truth is that for as long as there has been a NATO, there has also been discord among the allies, to such an extent that Squabbles "R" Us might as well have been registered as the alliance's trademark. Yet a mere half year after the chaotic Afghan withdrawal, Russian president Vladimir Putin launched his boneheaded (and catastrophic) invasion of Ukraine, and in the process injected a new and welcome note of harmony in intra-alliance relations. Although no one can predict the long-term implications of Putin's recklessness, either for transatlantic or global security, one short-term consequence of the Russian dictator's thuggery has been to replenish the cooperative reservoirs of the Western alliance, awakening a feeling of resolve among the member states that few would have imagined possible just a short time earlier, to such an extent that it would be hard to detect a syllable of hyperbole in claims highlighting how, "in a few frantic days, the West threw out the standard playbook that it had used for decades and instead marshaled a stunning show of unity."[3]

There had, of course, been previous moments during its existence of more than seven decades when NATO had briefly witnessed outbursts, stunning or otherwise, of unity. Mostly these occurred during its first half century, coinciding with the first Cold War. None of those eras of good intra-alliance feeling proved lasting; neither, however, did the allies' tendency toward disputatiousness turn out to be particularly damaging. They frequently quarreled, yet their alliance endured, even taking on new membership once the ideological contest with the Soviet Union ended upon the latter's disappearance in 1991.

Thus, we might take it as given that no matter how Putin's so-called special military operation ends, the renewal of alliance solidarity it has occasioned will not prove to be of long duration and will be followed by a return to the default pattern—that "standard playbook"—in which intra-alliance disputatiousness is again the familiar background noise of transatlantic security and defense relations. It should also be taken as given that the most relevant fault line within NATO in the future will resemble the one of the past, when America and France so often found themselves on different sides of important debates.

Ever since the formation of NATO in 1949, the two countries have cut for themselves distinctive figures within the arena of transatlantic security and defense. Occasionally, albeit very rarely, they have stood shoulder to shoulder in solidarity when facing a crisis. Most of the time, though, they have appeared more to be at daggers drawn than to be wrapped in any comradely embrace. While it may be tempting, and many have sought, to lay the blame for this state of affairs solely on France, the challenge of achieving *coopération renforcée* between them really has been a two-sided affair. Each country has left its own distinctive marks, for reasons that, in important ways, can be traced to certain of their "cultural" attributes. Some might even claim that the responsibility for the pair not getting on better than they have can chiefly be laid at America's doorstep, due to a historic inability to develop a coherent grand strategy that French policymakers might find congenial to their own strategic tastes.

This is another way of stating that Americans themselves have been and remain split over the task of trying to figure out what should be their country's optimal grand strategy—or even whether they should bother cultivating such an ambitious vision at all![4] What has been said about intra-alliance discord might also be said about discord within the US itself on the question of grand strategy; the debate goes on, in puzzling fashion. And though French observers can and do have such difficulty figuring out which American grand strategy might be best for *their* interests, so too do Americans wrestle with the chore of developing a strategy that might best advance *America's* interests. Some of the participants in the American debate over which grand strategy is ideal for the US have regarded the country's alliance networks—NATO, first and foremost—as being of such obvious net benefit as to constitute nothing other than the veritable "shields of the republic" (to cite the title of one recent book).[5] But many other participants have worried that allies are a costly and possibly dangerous burden to the US, and some even conclude that allies should be jettisoned altogether.

None of this is new. At the usual risk of overgeneralizing things, America's alliance watchers, prior to the current Ukraine war with its temporary forging of something approaching a bipartisan consensus in the US, could have been disaggregated into a trio of clusters, arrayed along a continuum of policy advocacies. At one extreme were to be found those whose version of security and defense nirvana inhered in America's assuming the lowest level of involvement with other states as it could possibly get away with doing. At the opposite extreme were those calling for maximalist involvement in the security of others. Somewhere in the middle were the advocates of security and defense cooperation with only some states, chosen for reasons of their importance to America.

Over time, labels got attached to the three clusters. Policy actors and analysts with minimal enthusiasm for security and defense commitments to others have in recent years been associated with a posture of "restraint"—a posture that in an earlier era was often synonymous with a strategic perspective known as isolationism.[6] In some important contrast have stood those championing a middling perspective on strategic interdependence that has lodged within the rubric of "selective engagement" and has lately been termed "offshore balancing."[7] Finally, at the maximalist position on the continuum are enthusiasts for a "primacy" that has sometimes borne the name of liberal (or benign) hegemony.[8]

No matter which of these three strategic postures was under discussion, France had managed never to be very far from the center of debate. As I will demonstrate in this book, France had installed itself as an important fixture in the security and defense affairs of Americans even before an independent United States had ever come into existence. It contributed mightily, albeit unintentionally, to the growing sense of an American national identity in the eighteenth century, by serving as Americans' adversarial "significant Other" during long decades of intercolonial strife between Britain and France in North America. It became the first country with which an independent America allied itself, just as it was the first country from which an independent America would seek and obtain a strategic separation.

More than a century after that estrangement, France would be a country with which America would once again, if only briefly, become allied, through America's participation in combat at the side of the Entente Powers in 1917 and 1918. And France would develop into one of the most important (or "vital") security interests imaginable to policymakers in Washington following the Second World War, a time when the perception of French debility vis-à-vis the Soviet threat contributed to spurring America's constructing, in close cooperation with Britain and Canada, the multilateral North Atlantic alliance.

A great deal of the story of their bilateral relationship has been characterized by debates about the risks and benefits of alliance between America and France, and their various alliances have been the institutional stage upon which so many of the acts of these two sister republics have played themselves out. While it would be wrong, and it is certainly not my purpose, to attempt to situate Franco-American security and defense interaction *entirely* within an alliance context, it has been the institutional defense framework that has endowed their bilateral relationship with its quality of empirical "specialness." Simply put, the two countries have related to each other *in their roles as allies* in a manner in which neither quite relates to any of its other allies.

Sometimes this point gets overlooked, as for instance in accounts of the post-1945 Western security and defense order that lay heavy emphasis upon the notion of America's "benign hegemony," said to have been a security dispensation that was widely acceptable to, and fairly uncontroversial among, the members of the transatlantic alliance. Not only was this post-1945 dispensation regarded as legitimate and beneficial to all Western countries, but also it constituted, according to this perspective, "a sort of rudimentary political system—a liberal hegemonic order. It had organizing principles, authority relations, functional roles, shared expectations, and settled practices through which states did business with each other. Led by the United States, it existed inside the larger Cold War bipolar order. . . . At its core it was a political community dominated by the advanced liberal democracies."[9] This sanctified core comprised the transatlantic membership of NATO.

This *tout va bien* picture painted by John Ikenberry, of a liberal, essentially Western paradise lost, is not completely or perhaps even mostly inaccurate. Nor is he the only observer to diagnose, in the metastasizing of globalization over the past quarter century, a chief cause of that loss, as new illiberal challengers set out to revise a status quo that had—cruel irony!—fueled the very increase in the revisionists' economic (and therefore military) capability that would prove so troubling. For globalization was facilitated by what we now know to have been a woefully misguided faith in the pacifying and democratizing impact of enhanced economic interdependence, accompanied by an equally misguided belief that the logic of absolute gains must always and everywhere trump that of relative gains.[10]

Nevertheless, Ikenberry's account *is* misleading to the extent that it glosses over very real tensions that existed within and among the Western community of states prior to the age of hyperglobalization, when intra-allied relations were supposed to have been at their most paradisiacal. Regularly during those years, with occasional but important exceptions, tensions within the transatlantic community could be traced back to Franco-American disagreements. To say this is simply to utter a truism about life in the transatlantic alliance since its inception.

If in these pages I were only attempting to restate the obvious, there would be little point in making the effort. Few students of transatlantic affairs would wish to stake their scholarly reputation on the argument that the Franco-American relationship has represented the alliance's paramount success story or has otherwise constituted its exemplar of seamless bilateral cooperation in security and defense matters. Still, in some very important ways, it has been, in its own right, a "special relationship," controversial as that claim might strike those who think that the category of special relationship should be restricted to pairs of states that are demonstrably "good friends." France and the United States may not be good friends, but they are allies, and all things considered, their relationship is not such a terrible one. Yet it is a strange and special one, whose qualities can and should, to some important degree, be ascribed to this thing we call "culture."

It is, of course, not an original thought that Franco-American interaction must somehow bear the strong impress of cultural influences.[11] My challenge is to try to show how and why culture has accounted for this special relationship's qualities in the realm of security and defense policy. As is often noted, those who sup with the devil are well-advised to use a long spoon. This caution especially applies to scholars reckless enough to make culture a central engine for propelling their accounts of why things happen in security and defense relations between states. Culture truly is one of the most devilish of concepts possible to invoke in the analysis of international relations, being at one and the same time both indispensable and yet maddeningly resistant to construal in a manner that easily permits its "operationalization." What goes for culture goes even more so for the modified variant I rely upon in this book, the rubric of "strategic culture."

In examining the pattern of Franco-American relations through a lens provided by strategic culture, I am responding to a challenge put to me nearly a quarter century ago by a German colleague who clearly understood that I was growing more interested in Franco-American relations. What was less clear to her, though, was what particular analytical angle (or lens) I proposed to adopt in contemplating a strategic dyad that certainly had never suffered from a lack of scholarly attention. "What," she asked, "do you intend to do that has not already been done by so many others?" It was a simple yet a great question, one to which I had no immediate response other than to mutter something about chronicling the relationship's growing importance in light of the shifting strategic sands of the late 1980s and early 1990s.

Indeed, ever since the renewed onset of "declinist" theorizing about the United States during the last phase of the first Cold War, in the 1980s,[12] it had been the expectation of some students of transatlantic relations that a re-equilibration of NATO would have to be effected if the alliance was to survive, and that France was going to have to be centrally involved in the rebalancing. This expectation of transatlantic relations evolving, in the words of one author, "beyond American hegemony,"[13] prompted my initial scholarly foray into French security and defense policy matters and provided the research focus of my first sabbatical in 1989–1990. I spent that sabbatical in

Strasbourg, France, researching a book on what at the time was being regarded by some as an emergent Franco-German "axis" within the alliance.

What had seemed to me, prior to leaving for Europe, to be a promising notion appeared, on closer look, to be more problematic than I had realized. My developing skepticism regarding the solidity of that so-called axis revealed itself in the book that resulted from my research year.[14] Over the ensuing two decades, transatlantic security and defense relations continued to be at the center of my research. During that period I managed to spend three more sabbatical years in Europe (Germany in 1996–1997, then France in 2002–2003 and again in 2009–2010), such that while I thought I knew a thing or two about the intricacies of defense cooperation within Europe and between Europe and the United States (as well as Canada), I was still groping my way to a satisfactory answer to my German colleague's question. As well, my geographical focus within the transatlantic world was shifting away from continental Europe and becoming more riveted upon the Anglo-American relationship.

But I did retain a working brief on matters appertaining to France and the United States, publishing during those years a series of journal articles and writing several conference papers. Not until the middle of the decade of the aughts, however, would I begin to develop a sustained interest in strategic culture, the rubric that some years later would seem to provide the framework I needed if I was ever to get around to producing the book on France and the US.

I hesitate to brand that developing interest in strategic culture as a loving, or even as a particularly affectionate, one. In fact, the more I read about this confounding notion, the less sure I became that it was going to be able to help me say anything worth saying about Franco-American relations. I found my esteem for strategic culture starting to take on a worrisome resemblance to the "esteem" Gertrude Stein evinced for her quondam hometown of Oakland, California. I never could completely shake off the fear that when it came to the employment of strategic culture as an explanatory device, what she had so memorably said of Oakland might also be said of my core construct: "There is no there there."

To the extent there *is* some there there, it owes a great deal to colleagues who whetted my original interest in strategic culture. I have to single out for my appreciation Professor Stéphane Roussel of the École nationale d'administration publique in Montreal, spearheading a research project on Canadian strategic culture with which I had been involved some dozen and a half years ago. That venture constituted the first step on my journey of inquiry along the tortuous highways and byways of this rubric. Another colleague who kindly invited my participation in his own scholarly projects on strategic culture is Jeffery Lantis of the College of Wooster, in Ohio. To both Stéphane and Jeff go my hearty thanks for bringing this particular realist in from the cold, so that he might sit down and warm his scholarly bones in the comforting radiance of their social-constructivist hearthstones.

The earlier Roussel collaboration had been funded in part by the Social Sciences and Humanities Research Council of Canada, and it was to this same federal funding agency that I made application, in 2017, for financial support of the project that would eventually lead to this book. I very much enjoyed working on that grant application with Adrian Kelly of Queen's Research Services, and if I did not always, to Adrian's consternation, follow his advice, I always appreciated the enthusiasm with which he tendered it, as well as the skill with which he guided my application through the grant submission process. Among other activities made possible by that council funding was my participation in some prepandemic scholarly collaborations involving colleagues from France and the United States, including and especially conferences and publications organized by French colleagues Maud Quessard-Salvaing, Maya Kandel, and Frédéric Heurtebize, as well as Canadian colleague Frédérick Gagnon. I am grateful to them all for involving me in their research endeavors.

Although the material in this book reflects matters about which I have been thinking and writing at intermittent stretches over the past couple of decades, putting everything together into one manuscript really did require a sustained block of relatively unmolested time. Happily, this latter was supplied by the Queen's University Faculty of Arts and Science grant to me of a six-month sabbatical leave in the first half of 2021, which proved indispensable for my completion of the book. My deep appreciation goes to Dean Barbara Crow and colleagues in the Faculty office. On a less happy note, I have to say that the coronavirus pandemic also contributed to freeing up a great deal of time that might otherwise have gone to international travel for the purposes of research collaboration. With little to do but to stay put and write, I found my laptop to be a close and constant companion from the beginning of January through the ending of the summer of 2021. While in-person scholarly collaboration proved difficult to the point of impossibility for me during this period, needed research materials remained always available, digitally as well as in hard copy, thanks to the unstinting efforts of the staff at Queen's Stauffer Library. I am grateful to them, and especially to Gillian Akenson, the Stauffer liaison officer with my own Department of Political Studies. I also warmly acknowledge the technical support provided by Natasja Diab of the Queen's Department of Political Studies in preparing the manuscript for submission.

Finally, words cannot capture my loving appreciation for all that my wife, Susan Murphy, has contributed, both to this undertaking and to everything else in which I have been involved, inside and outside of academe, for close to half a century. It is to Susan that I dedicate this book.

I

THE *PROBLÉMATIQUE*

1

A Franco-American Special Relationship?

On the Edge of a Macronian Precipice

The late autumn of 2019 was a season in which it was still possible for the transatlantic world's leaders to reflect upon what they believed to be the most serious policy challenges they and their citizenry were likely to be facing in the immediate future. That period of time was once generically referred to as the "foreseeable future," until the novel coronavirus pandemic of early 2020 served once more to remind us of something that should never be forgotten: whatever else the future is, it tends not to be easily, if at all, foreseeable. In the particular realm of transatlantic security and defense policy, it was naturally assumed that for policymakers in many of the twenty-nine (soon to be thirty) member states of the North Atlantic Treaty Organization, what would continue to keep them awake at night was not a pandemic but rather anxiety over the current state and future prospects of their venerable alliance, about to step gingerly into the eighth decade of its existence.[1]

With some rare exceptions, thoughts about NATO's future prospects were becoming increasingly gloomy ones, well prior to the heightening of the Russian–Ukrainian crisis and subsequent war, in early 2022. The gloomy mood testified to how far the transatlantic community of states had traveled from those headier times, some three decades earlier, when the future appeared to be so much brighter. Back in 1989, nearly everyone had been certain that authoritarianism just about everywhere was on its last legs, and that liberal democracy, fortified in no small degree by the calming presence and probable looming expansion of Western institutions such as NATO, was well and truly launched on an unstoppable march guaranteeing that the coming twenty-first century would be a far happier one than the expiring twentieth century had been.

This interlude of good feeling lasted but a dozen or so years.[2] The infant century had not even had a chance to sprout baby teeth before familiar forebodings began to replace those earlier, effervescent visions of the 1990s, the celebrated "post–Cold War" decade that had once been so full of the promise of a world, and a Europe, that really *could* move from one success to another. Already, by the middle of the first decade of the new century (and millennium), a more sobering normal was beginning to intrude upon the collective consciousness of policy elites in the transatlantic community. Commencing as a result of difficulties and strains associated with nation-building in the Greater Middle East, and accelerating with the 2008 financial crisis that would so catalyze swelling populist sentiment within several precincts of the Western world, pessimism emerged as the default perspective of a growing legion of commentators and policymakers alike.[3]

Nor has pessimism easily been avoided even by such well-known champions of the liberal international order as John Ikenberry, who agrees that the "old Western-led liberal order looks more troubled today than at any time since the 1930s. . . . Across the Western world, something fundamental seems to have been lost: a sense of possibility, a belief that the future can be made better. Decline, decay, and backsliding are the new catchphrases of the old order."[4]

To capture this restive mood, some began to speak of "Westlessness."[5] Troubles in the Western liberal international order mounted, and solutions were hardly anywhere to be glimpsed.[6] Perhaps most worrisome of all, in late 2019, more than two years prior to Vladimir Putin's launch of his assault on both common sense and common decency, it was becoming possible to descry the return of great power armed conflict in an international system from which, not too long before, such conflict had been authoritatively declared to have been banished.[7]

Nothing better symbolized this general funk than the imagery employed by one well-known commentator on US foreign policy, warning of a "jungle" threatening to overgrow the increasingly neglected "garden" of the transatlantic security community, the cynosure and principal buttress of the post–Second World War liberal order.[8] As had happened on several previous occasions, the West was again being regarded as in fundamental, possibly even terminal, decline.[9] Growing numbers of questioners were wondering whether we had finally come to the end of a long era in which transnational amity had made possible the construction and preservation of an amazingly successful security community spanning the transatlantic world.

As had happened so often in the past, a French leader would again be venturing a strategic prognosis guaranteed to get the attention of policymakers and other attentive publics throughout alliance countries. It was not so much what was being said by that leader, Emmanuel Macron, in November 2019; it was *how* it was being said that garnered for him such attention. After all, as hinted earlier, squabbling had become second nature to alliance member states, for as long as anyone could remember. In the words of one seasoned NATO watcher, "throughout NATO's history, the alliance has been said to be moving from one 'crisis' to another, and its demise has frequently been projected by scholars and officials alike."[10] Without a doubt, by the late autumn of 2019, nearly all of America's traditional allies had grown disenchanted with the quality of the "leadership" the chaotic Trump administration was providing the alliance.[11] So while those traditional allies might nervously agree that France's well-known, and oft-expressed, skepticism about American fealty just might turn out to be warranted this time, none of their leaders would have verbalized the problem with the words chosen by France's youthful president when he agreed to sit for an interview with an editorialist for the *Economist*.

If there could be little new or startling in Macron's message regarding NATO's current state of disarray, he really did raise eyebrows by the manner in which he depicted the problem to his interviewer from the journal that had been, by far, his most exuberant and unabashed cheerleader in the two and a half years that had elapsed since his election to the French presidency. Now, just a few short weeks prior to the first cases of coronavirus infection being identified, and initially hushed up, in Wuhan, China, Macron was unburdening himself on his sympathetic listener. Grave peril was facing a Europe whose integrative juices had been steadily desiccated by the myriad economic, political, and demographic challenges it had been confronting for more than a decade, to such an extent that the European Union now looked to some to be in danger of falling apart.[12] Yet something just as bad, maybe even worse, loomed: Europe itself risked being left to its own devices by an

America that had, ever since the Second World War, installed itself as an omnipresent fixture in its regional security but was now appearing eager to decamp from the Old Continent.

Nor was this latter prospect solely the result of America's election three years previous, which had brought to power a chief executive so unlike any recent—and possibly any not-so-recent—predecessor. To put it mildly, Donald Trump turned out to be not very popular among Western Europeans. Even so, his predecessor, Barack Obama, although widely (some say wildly) liked by European publics, also had caused many of France's policy elites to question the durability of America's commitment to European security. They thought him too fixated on parts of the world other than Europe, or simply too fixated on "nation-building" at home.[13] As one French commentator astutely observed, apropos the growing disenchantment of Americans with international leadership so evident during the 2016 campaign, there was a common thread linking such otherwise disparate members of America's political class as Donald Trump, Ted Cruz, Bernie Sanders, and yes, even Barack Obama: all had been promoting the idea that America's role in the world needed to be reduced.[14]

Three or so years into the Trump era, Macron seemed certain that the project begun under Obama was being recklessly accelerated by Trump, to such an extent as to render it likely that America's deliberate self-distancing from its traditional transatlantic allies might result in NATO's disappearance. It was in this context that Macron made his widely quoted comment about the alliance suffering from "brain-death," coupling this unflattering diagnosis with a call for Europeans to become much more serious than heretofore about *autonomously* building their own security and defense structures, because, as he put it to his friendly interlocutor, Europe was sitting "on the edge of a precipice" and needed above all to "reassess the reality of what NATO is in light of the commitment of the United States."[15]

Many of France's European allies, otherwise in general accord that the consequences limned by Macron could be dire, nevertheless blanched at his blunt manner of characterizing NATO. Germany's chancellor, Angela Merkel, was particularly unsettled by what she took to be a gratuitously cruel description of NATO's current status, since more than one German defense analyst will insist that the alliance remains the "indispensable guarantor of German, European, and transatlantic security."[16] Thus, it was scarcely surprising to find it reported that the chancellor had become "uncharacteristically furious" with her French counterpart, a reaction that a few commentators alarmingly (if prematurely) took as heralding an unstoppable deterioration in the level of Franco-German cooperation.[17]

Elsewhere in the alliance, others were grumbling about Macron's choice of imagery. Even President Trump, who had himself earlier in his mandate never shied away from heaping dispraise upon an alliance he liked to claim was "obsolete," saw fit to use Macron's word choice as an opportunity to *defend* NATO. According to Trump, not only had the alliance ceased being obsolete—thanks, as the president saw it, to his own enlightened leadership—but also it now served "a great purpose," and thus it was unfairly being targeted with the "very, very nasty" term of opprobrium Macron had hurled in its direction.[18]

Irrespective of what this episode may have revealed about the geo-neurological health of the Western alliance, the Macron interview and the Trump reaction thereto certainly spoke volumes about the geo-psychological tenor of Franco-American relations. For reasons that I will elucidate, the two countries actually *have* had a behaviorally "special" relationship over the years, with each frequently going out of its way to try to demonstrate how misguided the other has been, and remains, on matters relating to security and defense policy. Nowhere have the most noteworthy qualities of this relationship revealed themselves more than in the manner in which the countries have comported themselves in their roles as allies, although these qualities also were in evidence during periods when the two had not been allied, and thus they can in some ways be said to be the direct legacy of a much longer pattern of bilateral comportment that predates, by centuries, their coexistence as security and defense partners.

That comportment might profitably be examined with the aid of the conceptual framework known as "strategic culture." In chapter 2, I will flesh out what I take this ambiguous concept to mean and will provide clues as to how it might be of service in helping us better comprehend the bilateral relationship between France and the US. Subsequent chapters will systematically pursue those clues down a variety of cultural alleyways, starting with claims predicated upon assumptions of hereditary enmity of a decidedly "ethnic" kind, assessed in chapter 3. That chapter concludes on a note less somber than the one on which it began, suggesting that "historical context" might better be assayed as an instance of path-dependent sequences that culminate in chronic—yet not dangerous—disgruntlement, rather than being understood as an acute, lasting form of animosity triggered by hereditary enmity. Chapters 4 and 5 continue the investigation into postulated cultural sources of bilateral discord, examining in turn sociodemographic characteristics, inclinations toward heterostereotyping, concerns for ontological security, anxieties about status, ideological differences, and disputes about the symbolic structure of the international system. Throughout, the recurring objective will be to try to understand why and how culture might have inhibited the cultivation of more "optimal" patterns of bilateral cooperation.

In this introductory chapter, though, I want to approach my *problématique* from a different perspective and ask not what the mooted cultural sources of their strategic interaction might be. Instead, I want to pose a different, albeit related question, one that might seem to some to be either flippant or, especially in light of the current crisis engendered by Putin's war on Ukraine, deranged: Why should anyone really care about the quality of Franco-American strategic interaction, however that latter might be gauged? My answer to *that* perhaps diplomatically obtuse question will be prefaced by asking a second, possibly even more startling, question: Is it possible to conceive of the pattern of Franco-American security and defense interaction, with its many valleys and occasional peaks, being somehow representative of a special relationship?

The burden of the chapters following this one will be to seek to explicate what I take to be the omnipresent existential reality of Franco-American strategic interaction. That reality can be summarized thusly: *for whatever reasons*, the two countries seem to have had an uncanny ability repeatedly to get under each other's skin, and this is what sets them apart and makes them special in a behavioral sense. Each deals with the other in a way that neither consistently deals with any other Western security and defense partner. The aberration of the Trump presidency, which certainly *did* constitute a case sui generis in American and transatlantic history, might offer the seductive thought that discordant relations between Paris and Washington can simply be chalked up to the personality foibles of leaders. But succumbing to this temptation, however comforting, would be unwise. The Franco-American problem is more deeply rooted—and the French actually were relatively less troubled by Trump than were publics and governments in other allied lands. This is because for a very long time, France and the United States have gotten used to being mutual irritants—not *always* so, but much more often than not—acting and reacting toward each other in such a fashion as to lead one observer of the tandem to refer to them, unflatteringly though not unfairly, as the "feuding hillbillies" of the West.[19]

Their behavior toward each other—the "acts" upon which these two "sister" republics have been engaged—can be conceptualized as representing "suboptimality" in bilateral cooperation, a quality I analyze in some detail in the next section. If there is and remains one existential quality of the Franco-American relationship, then suboptimality in cooperation is that quality. While they are hardly in the business of adopting toward each other what Michael Doyle terms "assumptions of enmity," neither are they noticeably prone to displaying behavioral qualities that he insists typify relations between liberal democratic allies, founded upon "assumptions of amity."[20]

And because of the way in which Franco-American relations stray from these latter assumptions, it is easy to see why some scholars believe that to construe Franco-American interaction as suggestive of a special relationship is so oxymoronic as to be nothing short of, well, *moronic*. For these scholars, a special relationship axiomatically must mean that the two countries involved get on exceedingly well diplomatically; they cooperate successfully and routinely on matters of security and defense, without much hassle and backbiting. In short, they share assumptions of amity. But these scholars would be wrong in so judging, for their strictures miss the point about what it is that qualifies a bilateral relationship as somehow being a special one.

Why Can't We Speak of a Franco-American "Special Relationship"?

Determining why we can't speak of a Franco-American "special relationship" begins with an investigation of what it is that scholars and policymakers alike believe must be entailed in the idea of a pair of states experiencing a particular cast of relations between themselves that is unlike any that they have with any other states—a cast that, in a word, deserves to be considered special. Traditionally, international relations (IR) scholars have tended to give a wide berth to the supposition that states might actually be, or become, "friends,"[21] and since many routinely consider amicability to be the most relevant marker of "specialness," they take *it* to be the obvious core of the construct, special relationship. Therefore, since few of sound mind would wish to claim that amicable diplomatic relations have represented the secular norm in Franco-American security and defense interaction, it must follow that this bilateral relationship should be considered as anything *but* a special one.

Are these scholars correct in so arguing? They are certainly accurate in assessing friendship to be an anomalous category, but does this necessarily imply that for a relationship to be a special one it must also be a regularly amicable one? While countries can certainly have cordial relations with any number of other countries, and might even be considered "friends" with some of these, amicability in and of itself does *not* a special relationship make. Something else is involved in this business of identifying and analyzing special relationships. But what is it?

The question is more complicated than it seems, for the meaning of specialness is anything but self-evident. This is so, whether the term is made to apply in demotic usage or in the specifically delimited context in these pages, where it is brought to bear upon dyadic interstate relations in the arena of security and defense. And while, in this latter context, a few scholars *have* been bold enough to make the case for (possibly) construing the France–US dyad as a special relationship, they really are a minuscule group.[22] Much larger, by orders of magnitude, is the community of scholars and policy analysts who concentrate upon what truly *does* rank as the platinum standard for interstate dyadic interactions within the transatlantic policy setting, the geostrategic institution we know of as the "Anglo-American special relationship." This institution is usually, and not incorrectly, said to have received its baptism in a March 1946 speech delivered by Britain's former (and future) prime minister, Winston Churchill, in Fulton, Missouri, though its origins lay in a more distant past.[23]

This contrast, in large part, accounts for the reaction sometimes experienced when analysts dare to nominate Franco-American bilateral ties as somehow deserving of "special relationship" consideration, because for most observers of transatlantic security, there seems to be something fundamentally wrongheaded about positing *any* significant parallelism between Anglo-American and Franco-American relations.[24] Others even go so far as to take the equating to be not merely wrong but actually insulting, normatively as well as empirically; to them, the roles traditionally played by America's two long-standing transatlantic allies could not be more dissimilar, with the

United Kingdom more often than not seen to be a very helpful fixer while France is regularly styled as being the most rebarbative of all US allies.[25]

Notwithstanding the abundant attention lavished, understandably so, upon the US–UK tandem, it bears emphasizing that it hardly represents the only relationship said to connect America with another country in a manner so singular as to merit employment of the adjective *special*. This is so in the transatlantic arena, as elsewhere.[26] In the late 1980s, a time when Germany's pending reunification was prompting President George H. W. Bush to anoint it America's emergent "partner in leadership," there were quite a few observers who imagined that the solidity of the bond between Bonn and Washington was well on the way to eclipsing the robustness of the more celebrated London–Washington pairing. Underlying this assumption was the belief that an enlarging Germany was going to become a more influential Germany, not just in transatlantic security relations but also, by extension, in global ones as well.[27] Few, during the Trump years, would have wished to wager too heavily on Berlin–Washington replacing London–Washington as the "ne plus ultra"[28] of special partnerships—unless of course their understanding of the meaning of the word *special* was almost entirely a pejorative one, such were the depths to which the once-promising diplomatic coupling with Germany had tumbled during the administration of the forty-fifth president.[29] And while it is obvious that under President Biden there has been a greatly improved quality to German–American cooperation, few imagine their ties will blossom into anything remotely resembling the first President Bush's partnership "vision thing."

Apart from the UK and Germany, other countries have variously been nominated as special security partners of the US in recent decades. The list would include Canada, Australia, New Zealand, the Netherlands, and Israel—and this is hardly an exhaustive list.[30] But before we can begin to make heads or tails of what such a qualitatively distinctive partnership must entail, we need to tarry a bit more over the employment of the adjective *special*. On this matter, we can take instruction from a fictional setting, the "imagined community" conjured up in George Orwell's famous satire on revolutionary dictatorships.[31] For as it was said of the pigs of *Animal Farm*, so might it be said of a country's (in our case, America's) alliance network ever since the early post–Second World War years: all allies may be equal, but some allies are more equal than others. As noted, however, there really *is* one bilateral relationship that has to be deemed special because of the way it has distinguished itself among the universe of America's relations with its transatlantic allies. It is the Franco-American relationship, which clearly has been and remains "more equal" than those other dyadic combinations within the alliance, in some important and obvious ways.

Consider the standard dictionary definitions of the adjective *special*. It can be understood as referring to a particular quality that sets whatever is being assessed apart descriptively from other cases, including from some cases that might initially have been taken to be reasonably comparable. Here, the emphasis is placed upon observable *behavioral* differences among cases. In the helpful words of a leading British expert on this kind of relationship, "'special' is an obvious marker of something beyond the ordinary; the mundane is elevated discursively to a higher significance."[32] Alternatively, and often, *special* can be understood as conveying a *normative* judgment, usually positive (as in, he is my special—that is, "best"—friend), though at rare times the normative value being connoted by the distinction can be negative (for instance, in the highly tenable claim that Hitler and Putin have been special kinds of fiends). Each sense of our word *special* has been implicated in discussions of the France–US relationship, with its Orwellian comparative aspects relating to both the behavioral and the normative sides of a diplomatic ledger in which the entries of greatest interest to us are those concerning the quality of the two countries' cooperation in the realm of security and defense.

It would be comforting to some to identify the essential qualities of Franco-American relations as being rooted primarily, if not exclusively, in the normative and *positive* understanding of the word *special*. In this understanding, the countries are imagined as having been friends—even great ones—for a very long time and this is precisely what sets their bilateral relationship apart from any other such relationship that either of them has. This is what Jean-Baptiste Duroselle must have had in mind when, at the end of his magisterial history of Franco-American diplomatic interaction, he suggested that there was an "old fund of affection" that characterized ties between the two peoples and made those ties special in their own right.[33]

This thought has regularly surfaced over the years, and never more so than when bilateral relations have been plunged into such a trough of despond as to cry out for the kind of remediation that only a "proper" recollection of that old fund of affection can provide. One especially poignant invocation of this recollection came in the immediate aftermath of the most serious strategic disagreement France and the US have had so far in the twenty-first century, triggered during the months leading up to the Iraq war of early 2003 by the two countries' radically differing assessments of the desirability of ousting Iraq's leader, Saddam Hussein. It is no secret that France had for many years been suspected as being the most prominent of America's critics within its circle of allies, to such a degree that it was routinely being taken as the ring-leader, and possibly even the generator, of the judgmental political tropism that falls under the rubric of "anti-Americanism" in alliance, if not in global, politics.[34] (We will return to this matter in chapter 5.)

Normally, French criticisms of America, of the sort that we will encounter in later chapters, have been regularly sloughed off by American decision-makers and public opinion alike, inured as they had become during the twentieth century to barbs hurled in their direction from the other side of the Atlantic. Americans may not have liked what it was that French public intellectuals and even policymakers were so often saying about them, but for the most part they could discount the criticisms as being simply annoying rather than endangering. In the apt words of one American expert on France–US diplomatic relations, his fellow citizens did not know very much about France, but what little they did know "tends to annoy, intrigue, or amuse them. Since World War II the operative word is annoy."[35] Still, annoyance with France could be kept in check by a calm recognition of the greater national interest, so it was never very difficult for counsels of forbearance to prevail, not least because "we have our own mental disorders to cope with without being too much concerned with those of France."[36]

The criticisms, then, could easily get written off as just another collection of things that "went with the territory" for a country (America) that was clearly on the rise in the international hierarchy. Not only was it a continually ascendant power in that hierarchy but also it was one that would, consistently from the early 1940s on, become an ongoing and major presence in European security and defense affairs. Thus, it was a country whose insertion into the European balance of power would be bound to stimulate resentment in France, for multiple reasons, often having their roots in concerns about "identity" (or what today is called by some IR scholars "ontological security").[37] By the early 1990s, notes André Kaspi, anti-Americanism was once more bubbling over in France. "In a word, anti-Americanism is one of our country's core values," he claimed. "Whether we realize it or not, it permeates our words and our thoughts. It constitutes one of the pillars of French culture."[38]

Writing at the same time as Kaspi, in a period when the Kosovo war was stirring tension anew between France and the US,[39] one German specialist on French foreign policy summarized the traditional pattern in which brickbats had been regularly flying westward across the Atlantic since the end of the Second World War, noting that "whether for good or ill, there *is* a French fixation with America that simply is not reciprocated by a big brother who often does not even notice it."[40] However, by the run-up to the Iraq war, three years after the Kosovo war, big brother *was* starting to take alarmed notice. For between the Kosovo intervention and late 2002, Americans were becoming painfully aware of how anti-Americanism might endanger their physical security. They were also becoming a great deal more sensitive, as one commentator has noted, "to anything approaching candid criticism of their country."[41] The September 11, 2001, attacks on New York and Washington, DC, made Americans much less willing to accept, with the traditional rolling of eyes and shrugging of shoulders, incoming verbal fusillades from *any* direction, but above all from reputed friends and allies.

With respect to this phenomenon, which was being dubbed "friendly fire" anti-Americanism,[42] one ally stood out. It was France, partly because unlike other NATO allies that opposed the Iraq war—Belgium, Canada, Germany, and Luxembourg—France occupied a permanent seat on the UN Security Council and was more than willing to exploit that status in a bid to prevent the US (and the UK) from obtaining the council's blessing for military action against Iraq. President Jacques Chirac made it clear he intended to do so, shortly before the invasion of Iraq was launched, in an extraordinary interview aired on Monday night, March 10, 2003, by two of the country's leading television networks, France 2 and TF1.[43]

Through its veto threat, France may have been able to prevent the Security Council from giving its stamp of approval to the impending invasion; it could not, however, prevent the invasion, which began nine days after Chirac's warning. What the French president did accomplish was to uncork a volcano of "Francophobia" in the US, with feelings of animosity unleashed toward France at a level of intensity not witnessed since the colonial era predating America's independence from Britain.[44]

It was not simply, or even chiefly, France's status as one of the "permanent five" veto possessors on the Security Council that made it stand out. Two other permanent members also disapproved of a military strike against Iraq. Russia verbalized its own disquiet, while China preferred to hold its tongue, sitting things out on the sidelines, with little interest at that time in presenting itself as an object of vituperation to an America with which it was becoming, to Beijing's self-acknowledged benefit, more and more economically interdependent. Yet it was France, of all the war's major power opponents, that most enraged Americans, so much so that for a brief period before, during, and after the fighting against Saddam Hussein, the hottest heads in Washington became fixated on France and France alone. As the mantra had it, shortly after the toppling of Saddam Hussein in April 2003, the US should forgive Russia, forget Germany, but *punish* France.[45]

Americans could understand that Russia, given its tradition of security rivalry with America over so many decades, might naturally have been reluctant to approve military action against Saddam Hussein. It could be forgiven. As for Germany? Well, considering that it happened to be *the* one foreign country responsible for killing more American soldiers than any other in the country's history, its opposition might not have been totally unexpected; nevertheless, it was no longer considered to be important enough militarily to bother worrying about. It could safely be forgotten. But France? France was not only supposed to be a dependable ally, it also was the country's "oldest" ally—the country of the sainted Lafayette.[46] It was supposed to be America's "go-to" ally, the partner that despite all the chronic frictions, nevertheless could always be counted upon when the chips were really down. Maybe it was not, like the UK, America's constant friend, but it definitely seemed to be its "foul-weather" one, to use imagery waggishly suggested at the time of the Kosovo war by Michel Fortmann and Hélène Viau.[47] That France, of all countries—America's very own sister republic—should now, in 2002 and 2003, be standing so defiantly in the way was regarded by American leaders and public opinion alike as nothing short of betrayal.[48] Betrayal requires punishment.

Gradually, the passions aroused by the onset of the Iraq war would subside in both countries. In France, there surfaced a preoccupation with domestic socioeconomic problems, reflective of a long-running (in fact, neverending) malaise within public opinion, troubled as it was by levels of persistently high unemployment and increasing immigration from the Muslim world.[49] Illustratively, one poll published in the spring of 2008 found that nearly half the respondents (47 percent) thought they themselves might someday end up homeless.[50] In America, the public soon began to entertain the possibility that Jacques Chirac might actually have had a good point or two in opposing the rush to war back in 2003. And though America's history, like that of other countries, has featured a set of states and societies against whom it has been possible to craft enduring "enemy images," it has been a very long time, as we will see in chapter 3, since Americans could seriously entertain the thought that France might actually be their foe.[51] A mere three years after the onset of the Iraq war, Gallup found that nearly one-third (31 percent) of Americans considered Iran be the chief enemy of the US, while at the other end of the scale, only 1 percent chose France—the same percentage that adjudged the US *itself* to be America's single most important adversary.[52]

The results of this poll illustrated how quickly the damage of the Iraq war would be repaired. It turned out that France was going to be neither punished nor forgotten, In fact, it was not only going to be forgiven but also was shortly going to be wrapped in a loving embrace. Remarked one American journalist, on the occasion of a visit paid to New York late in 2006 by a leading contender for the French presidency, Nicolas Sarkozy, should the visitor gain the Élysée in the coming May's balloting, and should Tony Blair step down as Britain's prime minister (both of which *did* transpire in 2007), then, irony of ironies, America's own leader, George W. Bush, could "find himself ending his term with his staunchest European ally in Paris. Which," concluded Roger Cohen, "is the way the US–French myth tells us it was always meant to be."[53] Seconding this observation were a pair of British analysts, commenting that Sarkozy "succeeded Tony Blair in 2008 as Washington's favourite European."[54]

Sarkozy again visited America, six months after winning the presidency in May 2007. This time he came on a state visit to Washington, where the American political elite could hardly contain their exuberance in playing host to a French leader not named Jacques Chirac (or, to use the insult hurled at him by detractors during the recent war, "Jacques *Iraq*"). So warmly was Sarkozy being feted in Congress and the White House alike that it was hard to believe that anyone in America could have ever found fault with the old ally they had been so feverishly castigating back in 2003 and 2004. Here, in the flesh, had come America's best friend in the heart of a region that only a few years before had been getting written off, with a snarl, as the irrelevant "Old Europe."[55] Nor, a few years later, in January 2011, did Barack Obama fail to sense the radically altered tenor of Franco-American relations when, much to the irritation of British tabloid newsrooms, he remarked, "We don't have a stronger friend and stronger ally than Nicolas Sarkozy and the French people."[56]

That the American mood toward France could have shifted so dramatically in such a few years reminds us that perhaps Duroselle's comment about that "old fund of affection" needs to be taken more seriously than it usually has been. This does not mean that the two countries should be styled as friends, as happens so often when one speaks of the Anglo-American special relationship. But it does mean that there is an unmistakable *emotional* quality about the Franco-American relationship; the two states interact toward each other in ways that differ from the ways in which either interacts with other states, and certainly with other allies. This emotional quality, in turn, generates an empirically special pattern in their bilateral relationship—a pattern marked neither by consistent amicability nor by consistent loathing, for both emotions have been on intermittent display in this transatlantic relationship, captured in this perceptive comment of the French sociologist André Siegfried during the interwar period: "France occupies a special place in Americans' feelings: no other country, at certain moments, is as intensively loved; none, at other times, is as severely criticized."[57]

But there is *one* quality, "cultural" in origin and consequence, that *has* been a consistent default setting of the relationship. It has been a quality in the two states' decision-making regarding security and defense interaction that, in chapter 2, will be labeled "suboptimality." It will be a quality that, as we will see, is going to carry a hefty load in the story I tell in these pages.

There are two principal ways in which the story might be told. The first of these would betray more than a whiff of urgency and would insist upon attributing great policy significance to Franco-American security and defense interaction. As such, it would present the reader with an argument, breathless at times, intended to provide suggestions for improving the quality of the interaction, not just for the sake of the two countries most immediately involved but also for that broader transatlantic community of which they each are such important components. Something, according to this manner of framing the issue, *must* be done to improve—that is to say, to "optimize"—the quality of bilateral cooperation. And it is the duty of scholars to find out just what this ameliorative formula is, and to demonstrate how it might be implemented.

I do happen to believe that there must be *some* policy import attributable to this bilateral relationship, and the current emergency triggered by Putin's invasion of Ukraine, providing as it does the "geopolitical equivalent of CPR for NATO,"[58] merely underscores the obvious: at times of collective peril, unity of action is at a premium. That said, teasing out this import, and recommending policy changes, is not a "duty" I embrace here. I happily disavow the role of Monsieur Bricole (Mister Fix-It). Instead, what whets my curiosity is the more mundane prospect of utilizing the Franco-American special relationship to prosecute a different kind of case, a scholarly one, probing whether and how culture, properly understood, might come to bear upon strategic interaction. I find this more "academic" pursuit to be fascinating enough in its own right.

Since the remaining chapters of this book deemphasize policy significance in favor of empirical analysis, I will reserve what remains of this introductory chapter to commenting upon the mooted policy significance that so typically hogs the limelight in studies of Franco-American relations. Even if one might reasonably query whether Franco-American relations today really *are* as important to either country as they once may have been,[59] there can be no question that, at various junctures in the past, those relations have lain at or close to the very heart of either country's "grand" strategizing. Because of their centrality in this regard, each country can be considered to have a been a very significant strategic Other, helping it, nolens volens, to frame policy issues and responses such that in order fully to understand what it, itself, was doing and why it was doing it, one country depended upon knowledge of what the other country was up to, and why. So let's take a look at what those policy implications have been thought to be, over the span of many years.

Why Should Anyone Care About the Policy Significance of Franco-American Relations?

More than four decades ago, political scientist James Rosenau instructed students and others trying to understand the complexities of foreign policy that they should always begin by asking, apropos the object of their curiosity, "Of what is it an instance?"[60] For Rosenau, first and foremost among the talents necessary for sound scholarship is contextual (or situational) awareness. In the case of the France–US relationship, one regular response has been to imagine that such awareness comes through highlighting the ongoing importance of this bilateral relationship, not just to the two countries most immediately involved in it but also to others, regionally and at times even globally. At the extreme, this way of answering the Rosenauvian question showcases the Franco-American special relationship as being of absolutely critical importance to the very future of the West. Inordinate security policy significance within an alliance context, then, is construed as the "instance" of which the France–US relationship is part and parcel.

Link this last thought with the broadly based apprehension many had been feeling about the spread of "anti-American" sentiment worldwide over much of the past few decades—a sentiment that survey data shows was exacerbated in most allied countries during the Trump era[61]—and it is easy to imagine that re-cementing the France–US relationship could be a first step in the restoration of an American ability to offer global leadership on a variety of fronts relevant to security and defense. This assumes that America actually seeks to perpetuate such leadership, something President Biden has indicated he wishes to do and something that the Ukraine war has, for the moment, enabled him to do. Indeed, one highly creative interpretation of Emmanuel Macron's "brain-death" interview would not conceive the comments as being primarily intended to *distance* European countries from America by getting them to take more seriously their own security and defense imperatives, but rather would see the remarks as having been cleverly aimed at Biden's predecessor, on the assumption that if a French leader happened to say one thing, then an American president would likely affirm the opposite of whatever that thing happened to be. If it truly was Macron's intent, in that interview, to emulate tactics adopted by Br'er Rabbit (as recounted by Joel Chandler Harris), then the stratagem worked like a charm, resulting, as we saw, in President Trump coming out stoutly in support of an alliance he had so often, and recently, been denigrating as a geostrategic briar patch.

Macron, whatever else he may be, is no Charles de Gaulle, and few serious students of transatlantic relations imagine that the current French leader slakes his ontological thirst at any anti-American watering holes. Just the opposite, some consider him to be one of the most "Atlanticist" (and thus, by implication, pro-American) leaders the country has ever had.[62] In chapter 5, we will return to this question of whether the French have been particularly anti-American over the years, and if so, why. It is an important question, one that will be contextualized with reference to strategic culture. For the moment, though, let us leave aside the source(s) of French anti-Americanism (if that is what it is) and turn our attention toward the *consequences* of Franco-American tension in the sphere of transatlantic security and defense policy.

It goes without saying that once the US became a direct (though initially only temporary) presence in the European balance of power, in 1917, it would begin to figure much more importantly than heretofore in French policymakers' conceptualizations of their country's vital interests; this really did mark the onset, insofar as French strategic assessments were concerned, of the country's "time of the Americans,"[63] which has endured to the present day. By the same token, when Europe (re)emerged as the cynosure of America's grand strategy, following the country's interwar experience with isolation, France would obviously rank as a very important, at times even "vital," American interest. And if, with the passage of years during the postwar decades, France became relatively less important to American interests than America was to French ones, it still remained that, from the perspective of security and defense policy, the two states continued to matter a lot to each other, even if not in equal measure.

Let us focus upon an assessment of their interaction since the moment they became allies on a continuing basis, concentrating upon their strategic interaction after the formation of NATO in 1949. How have the two countries mattered a great deal to each other in the area of security and defense policy over this span of more than seventy years? From the French perspective, we could argue without too much fear of contradiction that the primary objective of policymakers has always been to identify and secure a "Goldilocks" solution to their American problem. That solution entails arranging just *enough* of an American presence in European security to calm French fears about a resurgence of intra- or extra-European warfare, without inviting in too *much* of an American presence, so as to threaten France's identity and its "way of life." From the American perspective, there has also been a Goldilocks aspect to strategic thinking, but to nothing like the degree evident in France. Washington, over the past several decades, has never been able to figure out whether France was too weak to be relied upon, and thus in need of being built up, or too strong to be reliable, and thus requiring to be cut down to size. Somehow, perhaps, France's geopolitical heft could be sized "just right" for America's purposes?

These respective concerns with finding some golden (or Goldilocks) mean in the relationship have dominated the two countries' strategic interaction ever since they became enduring allies in 1949. Even before that year, for France at least, Goldilocks had been a strategic presence, one dating back to the First World War and its immediate aftermath. Never lying too far from the center of the post-1949 discussion has been the supposition that somehow getting the France–US relationship just right has been the key to "fixing" the West.[64] Thus it is easy to see how important the *Who cares?* question has been to numerous analysts and policymakers alike, who really *do* believe that the quality of this bilateral relationship carries with it portentous implications for the future of not just Franco-American relations but also the broader transatlantic community.

In subsequent chapters I will be addressing the question of France's *America* policy in greater detail. As the less powerful partner in the relationship for at least a century, France naturally has had more at stake than the US in bilateral security and defense ties, and thus it has had greater need to ponder what America means to it than Americans have had need to ponder what France means to them. This is not anything particularly new, nor is it anything that could be laid at the doorstep of Donald Trump. It predates not only the Trump era but even NATO, having its origins in that moment during the early twentieth century when it became obvious that America's military prowess eclipsed that of France. We can probably date this to 1918, by which time America had more soldiers deployed on France's soil than France itself had, the American Expeditionary Force having by autumn of that year swollen to some 2 million troops, with another 2 million scheduled to be deployed in the event the war dragged on through 1919.[65] America's economic predominance over France is of an even earlier vintage, dating back to the early post–Civil War period, by which time America's gross domestic product was nearly half again as large as France's.[66]

For understandable reasons there is a long-standing tradition among French policy analysts, when they contemplate America, to style US presidents and the country they lead as presenting significant policy challenges in need of careful management. Although in hindsight it might be thought that the presidency of Bill Clinton was an exception to the rule, even appearing to have been a decidedly pro-French and pro-European administration, it hardly looked this way at the time. Opinion polls conducted in France toward the end of 1996 revealed that more people had an unfavorable view of Clinton's America than a favorable one.[67] Obviously, in retrospect and compared with that of his successor George W. Bush, Clinton's image in France improved, Bush having easily stepped into the role of bête noire for so many French defense and security commentators.[68] By contrast, it has not been difficult for American policy analysts, impressed by constantly growing asymmetries in power between the two countries, to downplay France's significance and to query whether it deserves any longer to be regarded as much of a foreign policy interest at all to Washington.[69]

Nor has it just been America's policy elites who could question France's strategic significance, especially once the first Cold War had become history; so too did the man and woman on the street. Four years after the demise of the Soviet Union, polling conducted by the Chicago Council on Foreign Relations found that while 69 percent of the American public believed their country had a vital interest in the UK, only 39 percent thought similarly of France. Moreover, when asked which country Americans considered to be their country's closest ally, the UK ranked second only to Canada, while France trailed in sixth place, behind Germany as well as Italy and Mexico.[70]

Despite such survey data, it is also true that in the US there has never been any shortage of policy analysts prepared to make the case for ongoing French centrality to American interests. This was so even in the aftermath of the first Cold War, when one American expert on France argued that notwithstanding the disappearance of the Soviet Union, "understanding contemporary French views about security is important for Americans. The construction of a new security order in Europe and around the world is dependent on the convergence of—or at least compromise between—the many national positions involved, and no completely satisfactory arrangements can be reached in the absence of Franco-American cooperation."[71] Traces of Francocentrism among American analysts remain, even today, and may well become more pronounced pari passu with the unfolding second Cold War.

But it was really during and immediately following the last of the twentieth century's two global conflagrations that Washington came to regard France as of utmost significance to America's own security interests.[72] Historians and political scientists continue to debate just how much the national security argument figured in the American decision to go to war in 1917.[73] There have even been echoes of that debate, albeit muted ones, with respect to the US entry into war in December 1941, though most scholars would argue that in the latter contest America's physical security was obviously endangered and that France's position during and after that conflict led to its emergence as a much more "vital" US interest than it earlier had been.

Unlike after 1918, after 1945 there would be no American disengagement from the European balance of power. But if France emerged as a central element in post-1945 American strategic thought, it was hardly because the country was regarded as being a *strong* ally of America's. Just the opposite: France mattered to Americans because of its debility following the Second World War and throughout the dozen-year lifetime of the Fourth Republic (from 1946 to 1958). Insofar as Washington was concerned, the objective following the war must closely resemble what it had been *during* the war: keeping France from going over to (or, otherwise, retrieving it from) the adversary's side—that of the Germans, in the first instance, and then of the Soviets.

Interestingly, a succession of governments during the Fourth Republic knew how to exploit Washington's fear of their collapse and were able to extract from their powerful American ally concessions associated with what one European analyst has dubbed the "tyranny of the weak."[74] By the midpoint of the twentieth century, France truly did possess special standing in American eyes, owing largely to the perception that it was dangerously weak, and not, as had been the case at the start of the century, that it was one of the great powers and deserved to be treated accordingly.[75] Moreover, this special standing was due to one empirical quality of the bilateral relationship, outlined in 1956 by Arnold Wolfers, who wrote that from Washington's perspective, "relations with no other country presented issues quite so disturbing and paradoxical" as did those with France.[76]

The thesis that France counted precisely because it was so enfeebled was the core claim of political journalist David Schoenbrun, who toward the tail end of the Fourth Republic decreed France to be the single most important Western European country for US foreign policy, at a time when Western Europe was the region of greatest relevance to American grand strategy. France was, figuratively and literally, the keystone to the arch of European, and by extension global, security. Thus, there had been great strategic wisdom, said Schoenbrun, in Washington selecting France to host the headquarters of the North Atlantic Treaty Organization, "because geographically, politically and strategically France is the linchpin of any Continental coalition." France was "sick" beyond dispute; that is what made it so important. Washington's inability to keep France from becoming wrapped in a totalitarian strategic hug would signify nothing less than its inability to safeguard America's *own* political and civil liberties on the home front, because combating a Soviet empire that included France would require the establishment in America of a virtual garrison state for as far into the future as anyone dared to glimpse. Thus, concluded Schoenbrun, "as France goes, so go the plans and hopes of many other nations, for the case of France is a case of world concern."[77]

It has been a long while since American observers have waxed so melodramatically about an anemic France's existential meaning for them, and even at the time Schoenbrun was proclaiming the country's debility, it was beginning to appear to many that he was exaggerating the matter. Still, the image of France as weakling had been easy enough for those observers to entertain a decade earlier, at the beginning of the Fourth Republic. One French authority on the Fourth Republic captured the American mood of anxiety in early 1947, as the first Cold War was beginning to assume its unmistakable form: "The American analysis of the situation in France was summed up by [Dean] Acheson on 22 February thus: with four Communists in the government, one holding the vital Defence portfolio [François Billoux]; with one-third of the electorate voting for the PCF [Parti communiste français, France's communist party]; with the trade unions, factories, and military either controlled or infiltrated by the Communists; and with a worsening economic and social climate—a Soviet takeover could occur at any moment."[78]

In the Western Europe of the late 1940s, only Italy was considered to be more susceptible to Soviet subversion than France, but because France was the region's geographic heart, it had to be regarded as its most important country from the standpoint of America's strategic interests.[79] France, then, was simply too important for American post-1945 interests to be allowed to become destabilized by developments, in Europe or elsewhere, thought to be linked with Soviet expansionism, though this might occur not through overt military means but through political subversion associated with the specter of what by the mid-1970s would eventually be baptized as "Eurocommunism."[80]

In less than two decades, however, the optics would change fundamentally. Starting in the mid-1960s, American eyes would gaze upon a portrait of France not as the West's sick man but rather as the rowdiest participant in a transatlantic alliance it was determined to sabotage. Over the past two decades, some in France have been only too eager to concede that their country really *is* the sick man of the European Union, stewing in a collective funk described by one scholar as "one of *déclinisme* or *sinistrose,* pessimism about the future and a sinister sense of an irreversible decline unfolding in the present."[81] If so, it hardly follows that France's infirmity (such as it is) must have calamitous consequences for the United States. In fact, insofar as many American (and other) observers of transatlantic security at the onset of the twenty-first century were concerned, it might not have been such a bad thing for France to be cut down a peg or two. Quite unlike the situation of the 1940s and 1950s, in later decades France began to stir up disquiet in some transatlantic quarters because it was acting once more as if it truly *was* a great power, one moreover that often propounded an interest (rhetorical if nothing else) in hacking America down a couple of notches, through the wonder-working properties thought to be associated with "multipolarity" and "soft balancing."[82]

This reversal in the perceived strength of the French ally had a great deal to do with Charles de Gaulle's policies toward America and the other transatlantic allies. During de Gaulle's decade as president (1959 to 1969), a constant refrain in alliance circles had been "What's the matter with France?" Already by the early 1960s, a few analysts in the United States were foreseeing the impending "end" of the alliance.[83] But even for the majority of NATO watchers, who thought the alliance still had much life left in it (there *did* remain a Soviet threat to parry), the burden to be shouldered by a France that de Gaulle had taken out of NATO's integrated military command continued to be an open question. The country was variously styled during ensuing decades as a "reluctant" ally and "guarded friend" in what had degenerated into a "cold alliance."[84]

NATO managed to ride out the tensions between Paris and Washington during the first Cold War, so much so that the bipolar conflict's fortuitous outcome might have led to the conclusion that Franco-American strife, all things considered, had proved to be largely irrelevant to the functioning of the transatlantic alliance and to the broader community known as the West. This, however, is not how observers of the bilateral relationship tended to regard the issue once the Soviet Union disappeared and new security challenges began to crop up. Surprisingly, in this altered global security environment, many said that the consequences of France–US tension were even more pernicious than they had been during the era of superpower rivalry, if for no other reason than that the Cold War had constituted such a credible basis for holding the allies together.[85] In the words of one scholar, writing at a time during the early 1980s when transatlantic discord was percolating once again (mainly over "regional détente"), intra-allied squabbles were of no great significance, "largely because the Alliance *cannot* break up."[86] But with that superpower rivalry having ended, the transatlantic allies would presumably be tempted to go their separate ways, and worst of all, from Washington's perspective, France looked only too eager to shepherd them on their pilgrimage.

Thus, by the early 1990s a more acerbic tone was becoming discernible in what passed for transatlantic dialogue, and to some, France appeared to have gone on a footing of permanent opposition to the United States, as reflected in President François Mitterrand's not entirely facetious assertion that "we are at war against America."[87] In this increasingly bilious atmosphere, it should have surprised no one that America's top diplomat could in 1992 bluntly put to his French counterpart the very undiplomatic question "Is France for us or against us?"[88] Paris, suspect in Washington's (and several other NATO capitals') thinking for so many years, now grew even more worrisome, to the point that Thierry de Montbrial would exaggerate only slightly when he concluded in that same year that his country had apparently emerged as America's new "public enemy number one."[89]

Particularly bothersome, for those who continued to take inspiration from a common set of Atlanticist values held to incarnate liberal democracy's creedal and normative foundations, was the suspicion, solidifying during the 1990s and into the new century, that France had defected from universalistic Western undertakings it had once espoused and henceforth was going to throw itself wholly into the project of building an exclusionary Europe.[90] This Europe, once constructed, would be bound to widen the distance separating France from America. As one British scholar of strong Atlanticist proclivities explained, the ending of the first Cold War had, from this ontological perspective, unsettled Europe much more than it had the US. The latter did not have to flagellate itself over its identity; its leaders at that time knew what the country was and what it stood for, and they certainly felt no compulsion to "build America." That compulsion was still several years in the future.

Things were otherwise for the Western Europeans, so many of whom were (and still are) caught up in the belief that Europe needed building, even if they were not quite sure for and against *what* they were building it. There was, warned Timothy Garton Ash, a very thin line separating the ontological entity called "not-America" from one that resembled "anti-America," so thin that Americans might fail altogether to notice it. Because there was an unmistakable "Euro-Gaullist" model being flaunted on the continent's ideational construction site, "Americans have not been wrong to see in France the political leader of Europe as Not-America."[91]

One contemporary term of art best summed up this new, French-conceived Europe: "autonomy." It was hardly necessary in France (at times, to British dismay)[92] to identify the "significant Other" for the envisioned autonomous Europe. It was, and *had* to be, the United States, at a time when it was not easy to imagine a resurgence of the Russian threat. Nor were French analysts hesitant about making explicit the American referent, should the occasion call for it.[93] By the close of the 1990s, such occasions were becoming more frequent and, for many observers in the US, more worrisome than ever.[94]

One of those observers was the Harvard professor Samuel Huntington, who only a few years earlier, in the first part of the 1990s, had been arguing that the West, as a civilizational grouping distinct from the world's other major such groupings, could and did constitute a fairly coherent ideational entity, one that might even be said to be capable of "civilization rallying" in moments of crisis. To those skeptics who, midway through the decade, believed the West to be in terminal decline, Huntington had even offered the uplifting rebuttal that "if North America and Europe renew their moral life, build on their cultural commonality, and develop close forms of economic and political integration to supplement their security collaboration in NATO, they could generate a third Euroamerican phase of Western economic affluence and political influence."[95]

Just a few years later, however, Pollyanna would turn into Cassandra, Huntington himself recanting his recently expressed faith in a rallying civilization.[96] Now the solidity of Western civilization itself was under dire threat, only this time it was not the "rest" from beyond the pale who were the problem. Far worse, the source of the trouble was internal. All the evidence, according to Huntington, pointed in France's direction. The French, he claimed, were hell-bent on forging an "antihegemonic" coalition intended to balance American power. Whether they would succeed in this objective depended upon their ability to entice Germany to slip from its traditional pro-NATO, pro-Washington moorings. The stakes could not be higher, Huntington warned. The future of world order depended upon which way Europe would lean, for at a time when it was still possible to miss the geostrategic significance of China's rise, and to dismiss Russia as yesterday's problem, only Europe was said to be capable of making or breaking the dispensation known to some as American hegemony. This hegemony, to function, required others to want to follow US leadership—exactly the thing that France was contesting. To Huntington, the way to preserve hegemony, and thereby to stave off the loneliness of America's "superpowerdom," was obvious. France would have to be blocked from winning Germany over to its side, because "given the pro- and anti-American outlooks of Britain and France, respectively, America's relations with Germany are central to its relations with Europe."[97]

Thus did the immediate post–Cold War decade, a time otherwise supposed to be so full of geopolitical promise, appear to not just Huntington but also many other American students of transatlantic relations. Divorce had finally arrived in the household of the family that had stuck together through the thick and thin of the first Cold War, which now had become a thing of the past. France, which in the late 1940s owed its importance to its weakness, and in the 1960s cut a separate figure because of de Gaulle and Gaullism, had become, *after* the first Cold War, more relevant to America than it was during it, because of its disposition to denigrate and reject American claims to leadership. As a result, some were quick to pronounce bilateral relations as being at the point of rupture.[98] On its own, France might continue to count for little in the global balance of power, but if it could organize Europe according to its own lights, then the consequences could be momentous, enabling Paris to utilize the collective strength of its European partners as a "force multiplier" for its own objectives.[99]

What those objectives might be, no one could say for sure, but for more than a few observers of transatlantic affairs, developments in the transformation of Western European power were much more likely to result in a "systemic change"—i.e., an alteration of the distribution of power within the international state system—than was any apprehended rise of an Asian state (read: China) as a potential peer competitor of the US, much less any return of Russian revisionism. Shortly before the onset of the Iraq war, Charles Kupchan sounded a quasi-Huntingtonian note in announcing the impending demise of the West and proclaiming that "the coming clash of civilization will not be between the West and the rest but within a West divided against itself."[100] Nor was it easy to dismiss, in the incredibly strained atmosphere of late 2002 and early 2003, the possibility that Iraq would prove to be the decisive, and final, crisis of the West.

From Rupture to Rapture and Back Again?

The war in Iraq hardly constituted a tonic for the Western alliance. All the same, it really did not turn out to be that mother of all crises many feared it was destined to become. Far from representing, as one policy observer put it, NATO's "near-death" experience,[101] the war gave the appearance of nearly sounding the death knell for Europe itself. It did so because the European Union, America's ostensible peer challenger, in the opinion of some analysts at the time, witnessed its many member states, to say nothing of the numerous aspirants to membership, falling out over whether to back the Anglo-American coalition or the Franco-German "axis." Not surprisingly, except to those who still believed in the willingness of Europeans to follow a French lead,[102] the overwhelming majority of the European Union members and would-be members (though not necessarily their publics) opted for the Anglo-American picture of the transatlantic future, warts and all.

In retrospect, although no one at the time could possibly have made this argument, the Franco-American falling out over Iraq might be more accurately conceptualized as a "therapeutic crisis."[103] These crises recur occasionally in bilateral relationships, and they are valuable because they can give policymakers that rarest of opportunities: to catch a glimpse into a future that they should wish at all cost to avoid. They are the geostrategic equivalent of Charles Dickens's Ghost of Christmas Yet to Come.[104] The most commented-upon therapeutic crisis ever to occur in transatlantic security affairs was the ghostly apparition of Anglo-American war in late 1895. This geopolitical wraith made its appearance to British and American observers during a brief, bitter, and bizarre dispute over a boundary separating Venezuela from Britain's colony of British Guiana. Although Washington was indifferent about where the boundary line was to be drawn, it was adamant that the dispute be taken to arbitration and not resolved unilaterally by British might. America's status demanded nothing less than this British deference to its claim to preeminence in the Western hemisphere.

By the end of the nineteenth century, a more powerful America was putting greater stock than ever in the long-established Monroe Doctrine and was basically arrogating to itself the right to lay down the international law in the hemisphere, south of the Rio Grande.[105] For a short period toward the end of 1895, it almost looked as if the two English-speaking powers would come to blows over the issue. But cooler heads prevailed, leading many to argue ever since that the menace of a "fratricidal" war provided policymakers on either side of the Atlantic with precious insight into a possible future reality—armed conflict between their two countries—that they should urgently strive to keep from ever becoming a *genuine* reality. For this reason, the 1895 crisis has been hailed by some students of the Anglo-American special relationship as the "contingent" moment in their bilateral security and defense interaction, providing the impetus for fostering their "great rapprochement" by century's end.[106]

So, too, might we conceptualize the Franco-American dispute over Iraq. Rather than splitting them apart, it had the opposite effect, of stimulating a reciprocal desire to improve what had admittedly become very strained bilateral relations since the early 1990s. It was left to Paris to take the first step toward rapprochement, something it did in the summer of 2003, when it mounted a peculiar publicity campaign aimed at winning over American hearts and minds. It was not that the aspiration was in any way peculiar; after all, there had been several tenuous moments throughout previous decades when French leaders saw reason to court American public opinion, just as Americans had understood, from time to time, the need to "seduce" French opinion.[107] The aspiration itself could have appeared unobjectionable, at least to those who imbibed their history only in small drafts: Paris was seeking that summer to remind Americans of how good things once had been between the two old allies—and presumably could, and should, speedily become again.

However, the messengers, and the manner in which they made their pitch, did strike some as being unusual. To get its call for rapprochement across, Paris engaged the services of a handful of American celebrities, all of whom spoke glowingly of the bilateral relationship in a videotaped infomercial for distribution to travel agents in the United States. One of those celebrities was director and quondam film star Woody Allen, whose popularity in France at the time was decidedly much higher than it was at home, a judgment reflected in the catty remark of one critic of the cinematic celebrity, who posed this question: "Want to see a truly long line for the movies, check the next showing on the Champs Élysées of any new film by classic New York shlub Woody Allen."[108] Even more surprising than Allen being tapped as the chief message bearer was the message itself. The video, entitled "Let's Fall in Love Again," featured him making some sentimental but historically daft remarks, the most striking of which was the declaration that the United States and France "have been great friends and great, great allies going back many, many years."[109]

What was daft about this declaration? Mostly, it was the flagrant manner in which it clashed with empirical reality. "Going back many, many years" does, it is true, reveal a certain pattern of bilateral relations. But it was the sort of pattern one would not expect to see on the part of "great friends and great, great allies." It was, instead, a pattern of chronic perturbation in bilateral relations. For reasons to be addressed in subsequent chapters, falling in love was really not the kind of activity that routinely characterized the Franco-American couple.

Yes, there had been periods in which marked improvement in bilateral ties took place. One such would occur a few years after the 2003 airing of the infomercial, though for reasons unrelated to it. That improvement commenced, as we saw above, with Nicolas Sarkozy's election as French president, which took place while George W. Bush still occupied the Oval Office.[110] It seemed for a while as if the warming trend might continue uninterrupted for some time to come, as Sarkozy's election was followed a year and a half later by that of Barack Obama, who proved to be very popular with French and other European public opinion. In July 2009, the German Marshall Fund found that 77 percent of Europeans (as opposed to 57 percent of Americans) had a favorable opinion of the president, even if some disquiet was beginning to be expressed about the new administration's foreign policy.[111] Although French political elites and other pundits would shortly begin to worry even more about Obama's continued willingness to backstop European security, the public seemed happy enough with America's forty-fourth president, whom they took to be much more congenial than so many of his predecessors.

Exemplifying the reconciliatory mood of the decade from 2007 to 2017 was the reappearance of the "oldest allies" imagery whenever American and French leaders got together. President Obama, on a trip to Europe in the spring of 2009, welcomed France's "return" to NATO by appealing spe-cifically to this venerable cliché.[112] So, too, did his secretary of state, John Kerry, four years later—a comment made in gratitude for support shown by President François Hollande, and one that was being interpreted as a "not so subtle dig" at the British for their refusal to endorse a military strike against Syria that Obama had (reluctantly) been thinking of mounting in retaliation for Damascus's use of poison gas against Syrian opposition forces on August 21, 2013.[113] Nor was it obvious at the outset of the Trump administration that the era of good bilateral feelings would soon screech to a halt. In something of a surprise, given the forty-fifth president's normal desire to distance him-self from anything his immediate predecessor in the Oval Office had ever said, done, or apparently even *thought* of doing, was Trump's parroting of Obama's invocation of the old-ally symbolism, when he arrived in Paris for a Bastille Day visit in July 2017.[114]

So while there can be no question that European publics, in France as elsewhere, had a favorable opinion of Barack Obama, never more so than when he was contrasted with George W. Bush, it is less well appreciated that the thaw in the bilateral relationship, as we saw, had begun while Bush was still in the White House. Comments made a decade apart by Robert Kagan exemplify how the French image would change so significantly in the eyes of American analysts of transatlantic and global security. During the Iraq war, Kagan had established for himself in France a somewhat sinister repu-tation, as a running dog for American primacy in a "unipolar" era that was causing heartburn for legions of French analysts and policymakers alike. He had made himself a target to French critics through the publication of a small and widely discussed book entitled *Of Paradise and Power*. This 2003 tract is mostly recollected today for some planetary imagery evocative of the West's structural predicament at the dawn of the new millennium, which Kagan ar-gued was a result of Europe's (including France's) choice to live in a Kantian posthistorical "paradise" at a time when the US remained stuck in a defiantly Hobbesian phase of history and was showing itself very determined to wield its enormous power in defense of its interests. "Americans," wrote Kagan so memorably, "are from Mars and Europeans are from Venus: They agree on little and understand one another less and less."[115]

Yet a mere decade later, it appeared even to their author as if those words had never been written. In the wake of the French decision to intervene against Islamic terrorists in Mali in January 2013, Kagan lavished praise upon the country that had recently been the target of his and so many other Americans' wrath. To Steven Erlanger, Paris bureau chief of the *New York Times*, Kagan confessed his admiration for his erstwhile French adversaries and offered an innovative comment on leadership within the alliance. "I have a new philosophy," he said. "If the French are ready to go, we should go."[116] Forgotten were those moments, a dozen years earlier, when it was commonplace in Washington to hear these same French being caricatured as a nation of "surrender monkeys."[117] Now, to Kagan and quite a few other Americans, France was demonstrating that it was the country with the guts, and was willing to do what America was too timid to do—use military means to spread liberal democracy. Whatever else it was supposed to mean, the grand strategy of the Obama administration, or if one prefers, the "Obama Doctrine,"[118] was showing itself to be, in the minds of many analysts in France and elsewhere, too diffident when it came to this business of mounting interventions that Europeans regarded as necessary.

Once more, Goldilocks was proving to be elusive for those in France trying to divine and help design the American foreign policy that would best work to support France's interests. Where George W. Bush had caused consternation because of a zeal to deploy American military assets unilaterally, Barack Obama's administration, as "multilateral" as any American president's was ever likely to be, was considered to lack the requisite appetite for deploying American military assets at moments when leaders in France and possibly some other European countries would have desired a greater show of American muscle in support of causes they were promoting. Especially worrisome was the apparent shortage of enthusiasm in Washington for mounting interventions in countries at Europe's southern doorstep, such as Syria or Libya, to cite the two most conspicuous errors of omission (as many European security analysts took these to be), on the part of an administration whose announced "pivot to Asia," they worried, betokened a possible withdrawal from Europe altogether.[119]

Then Donald Trump strutted onto the transatlantic stage, and his doing so quickly made manifest the worst nightmare of analysts in other parts of Western Europe—the nightmare of the sundering of alliance.[120] Whatever else Trump's administration meant for the ongoing bilateral relationship with France, it had the undeniable effect of reminding all students of this peculiarly special relationship how significant can be the impact of "culture," properly construed, upon diplomacy. It is the task of chapter 2 to establish what I take such a "proper" construal of strategic culture to be. The chapter will establish the analytical framework for parts 2 and 3, in which I put to work a select number of cultural variables in a bid to explicate *le différend franco-américain*.

2

The Role of "Strategic Culture" in Understanding Franco-American Relations

A Matter of Temperament

In Year XIII of the French Republic (1805), François Marie Perrin du Lac published an account of his recent experiences visiting the North American heartland, under the title *Voyage dans les deux Louisianes et chez les régions sauvages du Missouri.*[1] Not for the first time, and certainly not for the last, would an accomplished French observer traveling in the New World be able to get a close-up look at the American people. Perrin du Lac had been a French colonial administrator who, for reasons both political and geopolitical, found himself stranded in the New World from 1789 until 1803, when he was finally able to return home. Along with many other well-heeled French political figures of the period who considered the country in which they chose to find safe haven to be very much a cultural backwater, he represented an "esthetic anti-Americanism" that would, by the twentieth century, evolve into a full-throated "cultural anti-Americanism" in France.[2]

By the time of his American sabbatical, signs of tension between the two "first allies" had already become too manifest to be ignored, and what Perrin wrote about at the onset of the nineteenth century—divergent behavioral patterns within and between collectivities—would become a dominant characteristic of the bilateral relationship throughout the ensuing years, so much so that, toward the end of the twentieth century, one prominent NATO watcher from France could pronounce that the "most acute transatlantic antagonisms" had been, still were, and likely would always be, those between the French and the Americans. Alfred Grosser's assessment certainly contained more than a grain of truth, but it was not completely accurate, as a better way to capture the bilateral relationship would be to describe it as the "most unsteady . . . of all the long-standing connections between allies in the Western world."[3] In fact, Grosser might more precisely have qualified those antagonisms as chronic rather than acute, for when it came to transatlantic tensions of an unmistakably "acute" (as in, hostile) nature, nothing in the twentieth century had ever been able to hold a candle to the record of *German*–American discord during its first half.[4]

Still, Grosser's comment was an apt enough reflection on the quality of transatlantic disputatiousness once the Germans and the Americans had outgrown the practice of fighting each other, which allowed chronic Franco-American wrangling to occupy center stage in transatlantic strategic melodramas for almost the entirety of the century's second half, as well as into the early decades of the twenty-first century. Apropos of that wrangling, Perrin du Lac's long-ago observation goes some way to helping us understand why this relationship should be so consistently suboptimal. Perrin understood the source of the Franco-American problem to be cultural in nature, and he summed things up with the pithy observation that "the guiding principle of Americans seems to be never to do anything as we do."[5]

More than a hundred years later, André Tardieu would second that cultural diagnosis when, taking the measure of the rapidly and worrisomely deteriorating relationship between France and the US shortly after the ending of the First World War, he insisted that "instinct" had kept, and would continue to keep, the two sister republics ensnared in a dysfunctional embrace. Things could never be improved, Tardieu cautioned, until such time as policy elites in both countries abandoned the destructive fiction that common republican institutions somehow enshrined healthy bilateral cooperation between putatively like-minded entities and recognized the obvious—that the two societies were fundamentally dissimilar, and were so for reasons rooted in their respective cultures.

As Tardieu saw matters, nothing could be better guaranteed to ensure continued turmoil in the relationship than the mistaken belief that the two countries somehow should be acting much more harmoniously, in accordance with a shared collective identity born of institutional similarity. Though they were "sister Democracies, both equally Republics—as the parrot-like exponents of the alleged identity of French and American institutions keep on repeating"—these qualities had hardly anything to do with the fundamental reality of the bilateral relationship. "If we rely on alleged identity for ease of mutual understanding, surely we rely in vain!" he wrote. Instead, it was and would remain the *temperament* of two fundamentally distinct societies, reflective of basal cultural divergence rather than political isomorphism, that would set the tone of bilateral relations in the future, just as it had assuredly done so in the past.[6] Only after accepting that their two countries were not really alike could leaders in both begin to take the steps necessary to improve the relationship.

It has been a long time since analysts of international relations and foreign policy have made either "instinct" or "temperament" a leading explanatory category, or at least have explicitly done so under either of those labels. These days, while it may be common enough to accept the general thrust of an assessment like Tardieu's, very few analysts would employ its terminology. Instead, they might refer to "emotion," an omnibus construct that is much in vogue among international relations scholars, particularly those who spend time exploring the various social-psychological phenomena that could be said to result in, or otherwise "cause," the selection of certain foreign policy outputs.[7]

Though the lexicon might be different, the strategic syntax has remained unchanged ever since Tardieu's, and even Perrin's, time. Is it possible, many continue to wonder, to establish reliable causal linkages between culturally conditioned social attributes and state behavior in the sphere of security and defense? A generation of social scientists earlier than our own but later than Tardieu's, writing in the era of the Second World War, expended enormous intellectual resources attempting to establish just such linkages, discerning in the category known as "national character" the underpinnings of state behavior. Although the era of the Second World War constituted, as we will see, the salad days for those who trafficked in this category, it had far deeper intellectual roots in American soil, extending down to the era preceding the Civil War, when, as one scholar reminds us, there were "few things . . . more characteristic of the eighteen twenties, thirties and forties than the absorption with what was called the national character."[8] Today, foreign policy behavior, especially when it involves matters of national security and grand strategy, gets garbed in a different conceptual raiment, one frequently held to be synonymous with an approach that over the past few decades has come to be known as "strategic culture."[9] As we will see, there are many similarities between the older rubric of national character and the more recent one of strategic culture.

In this book I rely on this latter conceptual and perhaps even theoretical perspective, strategic culture, which constitutes a sustained inquiry into Perrin du Lac's observation and asks whether it might, after all these years, remain highly revelatory of the quality of Franco-American strategic interaction, and if so, why? Bringing strategic culture to bear upon the analysis of the bilateral relationship necessitates, as an important preliminary step, an explanation of what I think the concept might imply—and possibly even mean. This is a necessary task, though by no means a simple one, as will be obvious in this chapter, which for the most part is an extended conceptual and theoretical essay on strategic culture as a general approach in foreign policy analysis. The remaining chapters will be reserved for applying what I take to be the most germane elements of culture to the specific case of Franco-American interaction in the realm of security and defense policy.

But before we plunge into the thickets of conceptual analysis as these relate to strategic culture, a further preliminary chore is in order: to specify what exactly *is* the problem for which strategic culture is supposed to provide some hermeneutical guidance. What, to use the fitting terms of André Kaspi and Simon Serfaty, *is* this familiar and recurring "différend franco-américain," this "querelle permanente"?[10] Why is it that in a world such as ours, with 193 sovereign states belonging to the United Nations, some observers can assert, with little risk of exposing themselves to ridicule, that the Franco-American tandem "may well be the most perverse relationship in modern global relations"?[11] As I suggested in chapter 1, the answer can be summed in one word: suboptimality.

The Problem of Franco-American Suboptimality

We begin with a bit of history, and rely once more upon André Tardieu, who provides some valuable contextualizing for this behavioral disposition known as suboptimality. Barely remembered today, even in France, Tardieu once was a tremendously important member of his country's political class during the first three decades of the twentieth century. He represented

Premier Georges Clemenceau as special commissioner in the United States during the latter stage of the First World War, following which he was a principal drafter of French positions at the Paris peace talks. Eventually he become a cabinet member in a succession of governments of the 1920s and 1930s, twice serving as prime minister (technically, président du Conseil). He was also a gifted political journalist and an undisputed opinion leader of his era. In the words of one biographer, Tardieu was "an intellectual colossus [who] strode through a third of a century of history wielding more power over the Republic than its constitution-makers had ever dreamed of."[12] Another commentator said of him that he was the "bright hope of the French moderate Right: alone in a group of fusty, used-up politicians, he seemed to represent the new postwar world."[13]

Tardieu was hardly ill-disposed, in principle, toward the United States; if anything, he had been reputed, early in the twentieth century, to be quite pro-American.[14] However, he had grown increasingly disenchanted with American foreign policy following the First World War, and it showed—so much so that Philippe Roger could later quip, "With pro-Americans like this, who had any need of anti-Americans?"[15] Writing in 1927, at a time when America had been in existence as an independent state for nearly 150 years, Tardieu observed that for all the talk of Franco-American amity going back to the era of Lafayette, there had in reality been only a dozen or so years since the forging of the first Franco-American alliance, in 1778, that warranted being taken as evidence of genuine friendship.[16] Close to a century after he made this observation, we can probably tack another twenty years or so on to Tardieu's list, meaning that in its history since 1778, the Franco-American tandem has experienced a bit more than three decades' worth of something approximating cordiality, interspersed throughout some two centuries of mainly mediocre and sometimes just plain rotten relations.[17]

This, of course, does not take into account the pattern of interaction between France and what would become the United States in the eight decades *preceding* American independence, a potentially critical formative period that we will examine in detail in chapter 3. For the moment, all that needs saying about that pre-independence period in America's history is that its security setting bore a striking similarity to what scholars, in more recent times, have taken to labeling "ethnic conflict." In light of that awful historical legacy, there was absolutely nothing hyperbolic in Crane Brinton's observation that prior to the emergence of the Soviet nuclear threat in the 1950s, no country in the Old World had *ever* presented more of an existential threat to American "homeland security" than had France, during the years 1689 to 1763.[18] It was a far greater existential threat to the homeland than even that posed by Germany during the two world wars.

Because American policy elites and leaders alike, as Walter Russell Mead reminds us, often know little and care even less about the history of their country's foreign policy, there has been allowed to grow up the fiction of enduring harmony between America and the country with which it was briefly allied between 1778 and the ending of the eighteenth century.[19] I emphasize *briefly* allied, because their collective-defense agreement had effectively become a dead letter during the decade following the termination of hostilities between Great Britain and its rebellious American colonies. Some even say that the alliance's demise was sealed as early as the Paris peace conference of 1783, when, in Walter McDougall's evocative term, American emissaries "double-crossed" the French and negotiated a separate peace with Britain.[20] Others maintain that it was the French, through their indifference to America's request for assistance in getting the British to vacate their forts south of the Great Lakes, who triggered the unraveling of the pact. In this view, France's inaction rendered the alliance moribund, even if it would require a few more years for it to come face to face with its memento mori, in the form of President George Washington's proclamation of neutrality in 1793 and his acceptance of the Jay Treaty the following year.[21]

Both actions indicated a diplomatic tilt toward the recent enemy, Britain, and away from the current ally, France, at a time when the two European powers were once again fighting each other tooth and nail, first in the wars triggered by the French Revolution, then in their continuation under Napoleon.[22] Much worse, from the perspective of Franco-American friendship, was that a scant sixteen years after their fraternity in arms had prevailed at Yorktown, the two erstwhile allies became engaged in an undeclared, but real, naval war against *each other*.[23] Ironically, though still a nominal ally, France was the first country against which an independent America ever entered into combat. The 1778 alliance received its death certificate with the 1800 Treaty of Mortefontaine, and if in the short-term future there would be brief moments, such as between 1812 and 1814, when the two countries found themselves fighting the same (British) enemy as cobelligerents, they assuredly did not do so as allies.[24] And when, a century later, they again became allies in deed if not in name, their collective-defense arrangement proved to be very short-lived, lapsing soon after the defeat of the Central Powers in 1918.[25]

It would not be until 1949 that the two old "friends" once more became de jure allies, with the Washington treaty and the formation of NATO. In the meantime, for most of the intervening years between the world wars, French society would more often than not demonstrate a chronic anti-Americanism that on occasion, most notably during the 1930s, could come back to haunt France, reinforcing an American opposition to intervening in the European balance of power.[26]

But even without the goad of anti-Americanism, majority opinion in the US during this same interwar period was hardly showing France much love, with the notable exception of America's "countercultural" minority, for whom Paris loomed as a mecca.[27] Insofar as the majority of that same public was concerned, however, one of the newly unearthed "truths" of their country's interwar revisionism was the conclusion that France not only may have been culpable of having caused the war in the first place [!] but also, through its wrongheaded policy toward Weimar Germany, was embarked on a course guaranteed to result in a new European conflict.[28] By the late 1920s, opinion in the US looked once more to be warming toward Germany and cooling toward France, such that it was hard to tell which of the two European countries Americans liked—or perhaps more to the point, *dis*-liked—the most.[29]

The French, stung by the increasing acerbity of the American critique, and particularly disenchanted by their former security partner's dogged insistence upon being repaid for loans made to it during the war, responded during the second half of the 1920s and into the 1930s with a growing crescendo of anti-American commentary, something hardly guaranteed to make the American public, and those who would lead it during the coming years, wax romantically about France's being America's natural friend among the Western European countries.[30] One American with widespread experience of life in France at the time admitted her surprise that the tenor of French criticism of America was not even harsher than it was, "considering that for the past ten years they have seen us through one of the worst phases of our prosperity—which consisted of thousands of our tourists informing them that we were the richest country in the world, that they should pay their debts, that we had made the world safe for democracy, that we were the most generous people in the world, that they should pay their debts, and that we were the richest country in the world."[31]

Although some scholars would later claim that a collective-defense pact between France, Britain, and the Soviet Union—the so-called alliance that never was[32]—might have averted the Second World War, the more conspicuous institutional absentee in this period was an alliance among the West's leading democracies of the transatlantic world—the US, the UK, and France. In the regnant mood of the 1930s, such an alliance could not reasonably have been expected to form.[33]

Nor did the experience of the Second World War fundamentally erase the long-standing discord between the US and France. In fact, many tell us that it was the frictions and animosities that had arisen between American and (Free) French authorities during the war itself that so poisoned the postwar atmosphere, resulting in those chronic, and apparently indelible, tensions of the second half of the twentieth century that Grosser and so many others have discerned. According to this version of Franco-American reality, to be revisited in chapter 6, bilateral relations took an unnecessary turn for the worse following the conflict, and did so for reasons intimately related either to the singular manner in which Franklin D. Roosevelt had treated, "dissed" really, the champion of Free France, Charles de Gaulle, while the fighting was going on[34] or to the counterproductive "intransigence" of de Gaulle, which would bear the responsibility for "sow[ing] the seeds for modern-day American Francophobia, with its endless jokes about cheese-eating capitulators and bumbling Clouseaus."[35] Had wartime relations between the two leaders been more amicable, goes the argument, the course of Franco-American postwar cooperation would have been much more "optimal," in contrast to what in fact transpired, and never more so than during de Gaulle's decade as president of the Fifth Republic, from 1959 to 1969.[36] Who can say, but perhaps with Western unity bolstered by Franco-American cordiality instead of bickering, the first Cold War might have turned out to have had its happy ending sooner, and at much less cost, and post–Cold War difficulties, in Iraq and elsewhere, might have been averted altogether.

But for this undoubted wartime bad blood to have truly represented a setback in the quality of bilateral cooperation, there must have been some balmier moments of Franco-American cordiality prior to the war, so many such moments as to have constituted the behavioral norm from which wartime tensions represented the sad departure. The problem with this depiction is that apart from some surprisingly good relations between the two countries during the administration of Theodore Roosevelt,[37] coupled with the short and on occasion bliss-filled interlude of their being wartime allies in 1917 and 1918,[38] there really had not been much in the twentieth century worth boasting about, for those who championed Franco-American amity. The norm was as tediously depressing as it was empirically special: underachieving in the effectuation of cooperation between the two states, even and especially when it should otherwise have made plain sense for leaders in each country to try to work together more fruitfully.

And this is what makes suboptimality such a compelling way of categorizing the "essence" of the Franco-American relationship. After all, and notwithstanding the brutality of the colonial period's frequent episodes of ethnic conflict, there really have been few occasions since the ending of the Seven Years' War on which Americans and French actually have fought against each other. These occasions can be tallied on a hand the majority of whose digits have been bitten off by a ferret. The first, as we have seen, was the Quasi-War. The second instance of Franco-American bloodletting in combat would not come for nearly another century and a half, occurring with Operation Torch in November 1942, when Vichy French officials in North Africa orchestrated a short but stout resistance to allied invasion forces in Morocco and Algeria, taking the lives of 663 American and other soldiers before agreeing to suspend opposition to the landings.[39]

This brief record of martial interaction stands in sharp contrast to the pattern of Anglo-American strife, given the centrality, and the savagery, of the two wars the Americans and the British fought against each other (the American Revolution and the War of 1812), to say nothing of the distressing regularity with which London and Washington crossed diplomatic swords throughout most of what remained of the nineteenth century, usually as a result of British desire to "contain" America's territorial expansion.[40] It is for this reason that Charles Campbell could remark that for Americans, the most serious foreign policy challenges between 1775 and the closing years of the nineteenth century all emanated from Britain.[41] During the first half of the twentieth century, Germany supplanted Britain as the European country that most negatively affected American security interests, prior to being succeeded in this tenebrous category by the Soviet Union following the Second World War.

All of this is to recognize that in light of the kind of difficulty that can most seriously plunge a bilateral relationship into deep trouble—the two states waging war against each other—Franco-American diplomatic discord has tended comparatively to be rather small beer. Because of the anodyne record of Franco-American bellicosity, I have chosen an equally anodyne concept, suboptimality, to help us take the measure of the Franco-American special relationship. Contained within the bland notion of suboptimality is an expectation that, all things being equal, the two countries should naturally have been more cooperative and less competitive in their dealings with each other—or at least more cordially competitive than was the case. This, in turn, presupposes that "rational action" should otherwise have been more regularly the order of the day in Franco-American interaction, and yet somehow was not.

Thierry Maulnier seized on this point nearly a half century ago, when he reflected on the absurdity of two countries having, objectively, so little reason to stand in opposition to each other yet continuing to act as if each was the other's principal adversary.[42] Suboptimality thus carries with it the implication that "healthy" (or at least healthier) cooperation should be the natural default setting for Franco-American interaction in security and defense policy, and it raises the obvious question about this bilateral relationship: Why was it always so difficult for the two countries to hit the "reset button" that could restore this putative default setting?

It is not that Paris and Washington have never cooperated very much over the years, dating back to the Americans' winning of independence from Britain, with abundant French help, in 1783.[43] To the contrary, they have cooperated on many occasions. It is just that the kind of cooperation in which they have so regularly engaged has typically not reflected a pattern of faithful adherence to the apparent dictates of rational action, interpreted here as "action . . . presumed to be consequential, to be connected consciously and meaningfully to knowledge about personal goals and future outcomes, to be controlled by personal intention."[44] Those dictates can and do vary according to the tastes of scholars keeping track, but usually this kind of "action" presupposes a preference for utility maximization, a belief in the possibility of rank-ordering preferences in a transitive fashion, a conviction that when all is said and done, individuals must be the relevant maximizing agents, and a faith in the "homogeneity" of rationality, such that it is not the possession of any group in particular but is a generic psychological attribute of the human condition.[45] Had Franco-American interaction more consistently adhered to such tenets, the assumption goes, its payoff would have been greater for both of the cooperating countries, and thus more "optimal." But it did not, and suboptimality became the rule rather than the exception to the rule, never more so than during the course of the decades that followed the Second World War.

Once they became formal allies again, following the onset of the first Cold War, it might have been expected that the dictates of rational action would result in the interchanges among policymakers in both capitals being guided by a reasonably accurate calculus of the costs and benefits of various policy options confronting them on matters relating to how best to deal with each other in a threatening strategic environment. Accordingly, they should have assessed the trade-offs between costs and benefits of any given course of action in conformity with the dictates of culture-blind, and presumably dispassionate, "right reasoning." As a result, healthy (or optimal) cooperation should have manifested itself more consistently, through what some game theorists might term a positive-sum set of interactions, in which one side's gain does not have to translate into another side's loss.

True, other game theorists could point to the dynamics of the Prisoner's Dilemma as a reminder that even value-maximizing actors might, for reasons quite independent of culture, act in such a way as to foreclose positive-sum "payoffs"—that is, to generate suboptimal results of interaction.[46] But the Prisoner's Dilemma is a problem caused by lack of information about the thinking of the partner, and after 1945 it had to be reliably assumed, both in Washington and in Paris, that each knew what was on the other's mind when it came to the Soviet threat. Ergo, with both countries sharing a perception of threat, both would presumably be similarly motivated to enhance their security vis-à-vis that threat.

With the decision-makers being so guided by common purpose, it follows that the road illumined by right reasoning should have led to a consistently more harmonious relationship than to the bumpy path the two countries have so often traveled over the decades since NATO's creation. There always would have been conflicting interests that would manifest as the occasional diplomatic pothole, even on that illuminated roadway. But there also should have been absolutely no reason, with both countries at the time *apparently* having become established liberal democracies,[47] for France and the United States to stand out among the other liberal democratic dyads of the West. As John Ikenberry strongly implies, what went for America's relations with fellow liberal democratic allies in the West should also have gone for the relationship with its French ally. France, too, participating in a "liberal hegemonic order,"[48] should have understood and followed the rules of the road. Therefore, with respect to its great ally, America, France should have behaved in a manner not that different from the manner in which the other liberal democratic allies behaved.

If it did all this, there should have been no noteworthy empirical distinctiveness attached to the Franco-American relationship, thus making it impossible for Alfred Grosser or anyone else to remark that the cooperative quality of their interaction stood out from the pattern of bilateral interchange between the US and its other NATO allies. Behaviorally speaking, there should have been *no* special relationship between the two. Yet there *has* been such a distinctiveness in the Franco-American case, a distinction that was thrown into high relief after 1949, notwithstanding the countries having a common adversary.

Indeed, as Raymond Aron observed toward the end of the Fourth Republic (before Charles de Gaulle reassumed the reins of power in France in late 1958), it was precisely because of this alliance-generated growth in the two countries' security and defense interdependence that bilateral relations soured rather than soared. "In certain respects," he wrote in 1957, "the two peoples have liked each other less and less as they have come to know each other better. As things are today, the average American and the average Frenchman do not seem to get on together."[49] The other liberal democratic allies, despite also having differing interests, as well as moments of friction and annoyance with each other, nevertheless seemed able to cooperate more or less uneventfully—or at least uneventfully enough to not draw unflattering attention to themselves or invite comparisons with "feuding hillbillies" and other such chronically dysfunctional pairings.[50] But as we saw in chapter 1, relations between America and France *have* invited those sorts of comparisons, both behaviorally and normatively, so much so that the special trajectory of the France–US relationship has stood apart from the universe of other bilateral relations between the US and Western allies.

Strategic culture might help us understand why this has been, and will continue to be, the case. It might help us understand the ongoing existence of the behaviorally special Franco-American relationship by shining light on a pattern of behavior that seems only partly rational.[51] This pattern need not have been "irrational" in the sense of having been totally or even largely divorced from the sort of efficient cost-benefit calculations we have discussed—though it must be said that some students of culture do cite the manner in which culture draws our attention to the "complexity, chronic non-rationality, and diversity inherent in the human condition."[52] Despite numerous claims to the contrary, there need be no incompatibility between rational choice and cultural analysis, approaches that have been considered by some to be "complementary rather than mutually exclusive and antagonistic."[53] Still, we can take strategic culture as suggesting that decision-makers act with less than total attentiveness to the job of efficiently balancing inputs (preferences) and outputs (actions).[54] Thus, we might consider strategic culture to represent not irrationality or even nonrationality but rather a form of "bounded" rationality, to use a label popularized by Herbert A. Simon more than sixty years ago.[55]

I have been hinting so far that in the Franco-American relationship, rationality has tended to be more bounded than in any other bilateral pairing between the US and a Western ally. I will try to show why this has been so and what culture might have had to do with making it so. First, however, we need to plunge more deeply into a conceptual analysis of strategic culture, not only to try to determine what it means but also to ask how it might be put to the service of analyzing foreign policy behavior.

Strategic Culture and Its Discontents

In an important policy address delivered at the Sorbonne in late September 2017, Emmanuel Macron announced his desire to "re-Europeanize" France's grand strategy. In a televised New Year's address to the French public a little more than three months later, he restated this aim, asserting that 2018 would be a decisive year for Europe. "We must rediscover our European ambition," he told the nationwide audience, "because Europe has been good for France. We have to stand fast against the nationalists and the Euro-skeptics, and to do this I am going to need your support." In making his case on the two occasions, as well as at other times, the French president indicated that Europe would simply have to develop a strategic culture.[56]

Macron's remarks obviously are significant for France (and others), given the long-standing tension within French security and defense policy between certain precepts of "Gaullism," with the precepts promoting autonomy said to be standing in uneasy correspondence with those promoting Europeanization.[57] But Macron's remarks do something else. They provide a wonderful illustration of one of the epistemological discontents surrounding usage of the concept of strategic culture. If it is what social scientists, more than historians, like to call a variable, should it be an independent or a dependent one? That is, should it be a cause of something or an effect?

The idea that Europe, which in this case means the European Union, needs to develop a strategic culture is certainly not original with Emmanuel Macron; any number of analysts have been making a similar argument for a good many years.[58] In this usage, "culture" enters into the realm of security and defense policy as a consequence rather than a cause of some prior action. Strategic culture, by inference, becomes the output—invariably the *desired* output—of a process of national and transnational policy formulation intended, in this instance, to enhance the security and defense capabilities of an institution, the European Union. Culture, in this construe, owes its significance to being that output rather than being the output's cause (or, as some might put it more grandiosely, it is the *explanandum* instead of the *explanans*).[59]

Now, one does not have to be a European political leader like Macron to feel comfortable invoking strategic culture as an explanandum. Consider Robert Kagan's widely discussed book that appeared at the time of the Franco-American brouhaha over the invasion of Iraq in 2003. To Kagan, strategic culture certainly may exist, but it stands for effect not cause, being entirely explicable in terms of something else: relative capability. Thus, when he advanced his binary metaphorical distinction between an America that was from Mars and a Europe that was from Venus, what Kagan was really saying was that strategic culture is a consequence of relative capability, or "power." To make his point, he employed some further dichotomous imagery, citing the famous observation that when you have a hammer, all problems look like nails. To this, Kagan offered the riposte that when you are like so many European leaders and you lack a hammer, "you don't want anything to look like a nail."[60]

There is nothing wrong with conscripting strategic culture as a means to a greater end, which in the Macronian context is the fashioning of the European

Union into that "more perfect union" it is often imagined it should—and to some, *will*—someday become. However laudatory the aim, especially in light of the Russian aggression against Ukraine, it is not so easy to see what the explanatory role of culture is supposed to be if strategic culture is employed as consequence. To develop a strategic culture is to admit that some other forces—presumably other than culture itself, whatever that might mean—must bear the responsibility for creating the strategic culture; otherwise, we would have a perfectly tautological situation in which culture produces culture. Those wishing to avoid this problem of tautology need to make of culture a forensic afterthought. Rather than using it to help account for *why* things occur, it simply serves as a vocabulary expander, providing a synonym for more familiar notions, such as the generic grand strategy we encountered earlier or the specific European security and defense policy (formerly known as the European security and defense identity) that has been making the rhetorical rounds for close to a quarter century.[61]

Admittedly, for many analysts, strategic culture does have a certain charm to it, lending cachet to whatever objective happens to be desired in the realm of national or regional security and defense policy. Its undoubted cosmetic allure notwithstanding, I do not intend to splash on strategic culture as a kind of conceptual/theoretical cologne. Instead, I want to see if culture can be put to work more as an explanans than as an explanandum. Rather than construing strategic culture as being the result of forces that may, in and of themselves, have next to nothing to do with culture, I seek to develop coherent claims that start with this thing we call culture and then lead to those aforementioned suboptimal consequences for the quality of Franco-American interaction in the realm of security and defense. I am going to try to take culture seriously as a *determinant* of strategic interaction rather than as simply another word for a policy orientation. That argument will begin to take shape as I present three categories of culture—historical context, ethnicity, and ideas—as potential generators of suboptimal cooperative interaction. Before we leave the present discussion of strategic culture and its discontents, however, a further question beckons us: What do we mean when we invoke culture as an explanans?

This question opens up the Pandora's box of conceptual analysis and operationalization. Is it even possible, as some scholars desire, that a working definition of strategic culture could gain widespread acceptance? To many analysts, it is a matter of considerable regret that, so far, definitional consensus has proved elusive. In the wonderfully understated words of one of them, the "idea of strategic culture is intriguing, but there is a significant amount of work to be done before the concept completely matters within security studies."[62] Indeed there is. The place to begin this work is with Oscar Wilde's description of fox-hunting gentry in England as "the unspeakable in full pursuit of the uneatable."[63] Mutatis mutandis, it might be remarked that those of us who are tempted to analyze political developments through the prism of strategic culture resemble nothing so much as the unintelligible in pursuit of the incomprehensible as we speed off in search of our conceptual quarry.

The problem of how to define the terms upon which we rely is hardly limited to those who take strategic culture as their point of departure; the problem is endemic throughout the social (or human) sciences. But recognizing the widespread nature of the problem is no reason to abstain from the obligation to say what we think the concept means, at least for those who would employ strategic culture as a dependent variable, for if we cannot establish what it is that we are trying to explicate, we will be very hard-pressed to come up with any explanation at all. Counterintuitively, the definitional problem is somewhat less grave for those whose embrace of strategic culture is as an explanans, for reasons that will become clearer toward the end of this chapter.

Jeffrey Lantis is one scholarly enthusiast who has highlighted both the potential and the pitfalls of reliance upon strategic culture for the generation of policy insight. In his case, this is not a means of gaining insight into the Franco-American special relationship but rather is a tool for comprehending the manner in which America's adversaries think about weapons of mass destruction. Lantis, whose research has been part of a broader project related to such weapons, conducted under the aegis of the Defense Threat Reduction Agency in Washington,[64] laments not only weapons proliferation but also the proliferation of definitions of strategic culture. He hopes that if scholars are given enough time, they will be able to develop "a common definition of strategic culture [so as] to build theoretically progressive models," which in turn can be put in the service of guiding policymakers.[65] The goal is perhaps admirable. The likelihood of it ever being attained, however, is slender. Colin Gray grasped part of the reason for this, when he remarked that "scholarship on strategic culture . . . is bound to fail when it ventures far beyond our culture-bound common sense and positivistically seeks a certain general wisdom."[66]

Strategic culture might not be a metaconcept in the way that, say, "power" is, but there is value in the comparison. Consider that power is supposed to be one of the key notions for those in international relations and foreign policy analysis who are inclined to wax theoretical, and yet what strikes the student of power analysis is how much basic disagreement there can be over this word's meaning. If power is nothing other than aggregate capability, as many structural realists insist it is,[67] then it becomes possible to make certain claims about the "structure" of the international system. Among the most important of such claims is that we can discern a systemic pecking order predicated upon "relative capability," enabling us in turn to develop such other important concepts as unipolarity, bipolarity, or multipolarity in a bid to describe and comprehend that system. But if we follow the injunction to regard "power" as simply another way of saying "influence," then all descriptive—to say nothing of predictive—bets are off, and theories about how and why states act become increasingly complicated because of their dependence upon myriad situationally specific contexts, mostly comprehended only after they have played themselves out.[68]

The point is not that there is something abnormal about the way the debate rages over the metaconcept of power. To the contrary, the debate is completely normal, and indeed necessary, for unless there is healthy and substantial scholarly divisiveness about concepts, there can be no advance of theoretical knowledge in social science.[69] This is what Stanley Hoffmann had in mind when he wrote, with regard to the birth of IR as a social science, that "sound and fury are good for creative scholarship."[70] And while it is perhaps possible to imagine a political concept whose definition elicits neither sound nor fury, the cases when such occurs must be rare, and a concept about which we can say there exists fundamental agreement is probably not a very important tool for anyone's use.

Thus, if the normal trajectory of political concepts is to be followed by strategic culture—which, it bears noting, should be considered still to be in the pre-gouty stages of middle age, having been apparently first employed under that name only in the late 1970s[71]—then we can expect not only that debates about its meaning will be ceaseless but also that the concept will be prone to expansion, as are all concepts. Churchill's witticism about democracy being the worst form of government except for all the rest serves as a useful reminder about how unexceptional conceptual discord really is. And conceptual expansion is no less exceptional, even though one might wish it were otherwise.[72]

It is possible that our concept still has some expansion ahead of it as it shuffles from midlife into old age. But its two "parental" elements, strategy and culture, both truly venerable, have spent a good deal of time on the stretching rack, such that our concept comes to us with a much longer family history of conceptual confusion, one that has left its mark. Studying that genealogy can provide insight into the definitional problems afflicting strategic culture and can offer some clues regarding its possible utility for analyzing the Franco-American special relationship.

The Genealogy of Strategic Culture

It is no mystery why there should be such discord surrounding the meaning of strategic culture, for you can tell a lot about offspring by studying their parents. Ample foretaste of the definitional angst attending strategic culture was supplied in earlier discussions about unadorned culture as a social variable. As Raymond Williams has noted, the word *culture* ranks as one of the two or three most difficult in the English language (and, he could have added, in any other language).[73] If things were not opaque enough as a result of the nominative half of our concept, what shall we say of its modifier, *strategic?* Put this adjective and this noun together and you get a sense of why Alastair Iain Johnston should have complained about how "remarkably undefined" is the concept of strategic culture.[74]

How could it be otherwise, in view of the parental elements' own definitional promiscuity? Take for starters the modifier, *strategic*, as it is probably the less wayward progenitor. Although many seem to think that the root formation of strategic, *strategy*, must be about things martial—and by extension, so too must strategic culture[75]—this does not have to be the case. Yes, strategy can be about military matters, and it often is, but those who insist it must *always* be called to the colors do it, and us, a disservice. The term actually connotes much more; used commonly, it simply seeks to establish a "rational" link between ends and means. Thus, to think or act strategically is to attempt to correlate, in a manner that can pass basic cost-benefit muster, one's goals with the resources at one's disposal to meet those goals, and vice versa. As John Lewis Gaddis explains, "by 'strategy,' I mean quite simply the process by which ends are related to means, intentions to capabilities, objectives to resources."[76]

Things begin to get more complex when we couple the adjective with its noun, for unless we know what is meant by culture, we are at a complete loss to determine its relationship to strategy. To be sure, culture has become a very popular notion in the human (or social) sciences, never more so than since the ending of the first Cold War. It has been more than a quarter century since two sociologists told us that, now that culture's ship has come in, the time is ripe for social scientists to do an "inventory of its cargo."[77] But before we can take a peek inside the cargo hold, we first must locate its hatch, meaning that we need to come to some understanding of the basic structure of this vessel called culture. This is all the more necessary because the concept's earlier career had led to it being branded, with reason, a "semantic monstrosity."[78]

If it had stood for anything consistently since Giovanni Andres introduced it in 1782, under the name *coltura* (by which he meant to imply the conditions of human attainment preserved in writing), it was the notion of extension, or growth.[79] And grow it did. In less than a century, the term was expanded from the written to all other forms of tabulating the achievements of humanity, so that the anthropologist Edward B. Tylor, in a seminal 1865 work, could conceive of culture as "that complex whole which includes knowledge, belief, art, morals, law, custom, and any other capabilities and habits acquired by man as a member of society."[80]

Culture did not possess importance only as a register of civilization's noblest accomplishments (its "high," or capital-C, variant); it also was beginning to take on an epistemological function, helping those who engaged in studying collective life to develop ways of thinking about what was important in group cognition. History was one early discipline to feel the effects of culture's epistemological role. The "new history" of the late nineteenth and early twentieth centuries stood out against dominant perspectives associated with Leopold von Ranke's "scientific" approach to history and Edward Freeman's notion of history as merely being the record of "past politics."[81]

That "new history" faced an uphill climb in the early decades of the twentieth century, especially in America, where the conventional historiographical wisdom held it to be downright antediluvian to argue against the hardheaded economic interpretation of history propagated by the Progressive (or Wisconsin) school, for whom class interests provided the most elegant and satisfactory answer to the large questions about America's past. But following the Second World War, it became not just possible but well-nigh obligatory for American history and politics to be examined under a brightly shining cultural lamp—one that illuminated such heretofore overlooked collective categories as ethnicity (including race) and social-psychological propensities toward irrationality and antinomy.[82]

Though it might not have been easy at midcentury to identify what culture *was*, it was more than possible to signal two areas of enquiry that properly belonged to the new cultural history. The first was *ideas*, such that, generically, culture could come to stand, as one student of US foreign policy explains, for "any set of interlocking values, beliefs, and assumptions that are held collectively by a given group and passed on through socialization."[83] The second was *ethnicity*. Thus, intellectual history and ethnocultural studies began to emerge as important subdisciplines in their own right, each subsumed under the broader rubric of "culture."[84] We will encounter each of these constituent elements of culture in part 2 of this book, where they appear in the form of the sometimes overlapping categories of "context" and "cognition," disaggregated for analytical (if somewhat arbitrary) convenience under the three broad headings of historical context (chapter 3), ethnicity (chapter 4), and ideas associated with heterostereotyping (chapter 5).

What had been occurring in the historical discipline was also taking place in most of the other human sciences, with anthropologists among the most noteworthy contributors. And if no one could define culture to everyone's satisfaction, the name of one anthropologist in particular was becoming a consensus repeater on most "must read" lists. This was Clifford Geertz, whose 1973 collection of essays, *The Interpretation of Cultures,* quickly established itself as the locus classicus in the field of cultural studies.[85] What Geertz did in this book, which has rightly been adjudged "phenomenally influential,"[86] was to propose that we regard culture as "socially established structures of meaning in terms of which people do . . . things."[87]

By so proposing, Geertz not only contributed to culture's growing popularity in social sciences beyond anthropology (with economics and psychology being, for a time, notable holdouts) but also provided the opportunity for later analysts of international security with a fascination for the emerging notion of strategic culture to contemplate actually *defining* their concept. As

I noted in the previous section, definitional consensus would continuously prove to be missing in action, but some scholars began taking their cues from the cognitive instructions implicit in Geertz's work. More and more, and again following Geertz, culture was being conceived as a system of symbols by which collectivities transmit knowledge across time and space. As William Sewell put it, culture was nothing other than the "semiotic dimension of human social practice in general."[88]

Alastair Iain Johnston seized upon this recognition of the symbolic content of culture to offer what has been, to date, the most ambitious and sophisticated attempt at defining strategic culture. Its Geertzian pedigree is obvious, for as Johnston defines it, strategic culture consists of "an integrated system of symbols (i.e., argumentation structures, languages, analogies, metaphors, etc.) that acts to establish pervasive and long-lasting grand strategic preferences by formulating concepts of the role and efficacy of military force in interstate political affairs, and by clothing these conceptions with such an aura of factuality that the strategic preferences seem uniquely realistic and efficacious." Lest it be thought that his reference to "military force" makes his construe a narrowly restricted one, akin to military culture, Johnston goes on to stipulate that the "grand strategic preferences" at whose service strategic culture must be placed entail more than purely military considerations and include all those economic, political, and military aspects of national power that must be brought to bear upon the task of accomplishing "national goals."[89] In short, just about everything qualifies, so long as a credible linkage can be made between those aspects and the strategic preferences.

This omnium-gatherum aspect of Johnston's definition can pose operational challenges, unless one takes care to discriminate. To his credit, Johnston was careful to do just that, discriminating in favor of one cultural datum, symbolism.[90] In so doing, Johnston was following in the footsteps of an earlier generation that had explored a cognate field, "political culture." He took such care to discriminate because on his target list were scholars who minimized, or dismissed outright, ideational factors when they theorized "explanatory" variables in international security. Most visible in his crosshairs was the group he and so many others unfortunately call the "neorealists"—structural realists, who he insists are oblivious of the role of culture and history when they conceive the basis of state action. There is clearly something to the allegation, and even if it was Kenneth Waltz who primarily served to inspire his critique,

Johnston's admonition could apply equally well to the more recent invocations (such as by Macron or Kagan) of strategic culture as a quintessentially dependent variable.

The structural realists may have been Johnston's principal objects of pursuit, but they were not his only quarry. He was also concerned with improving upon the work of what he took to be the two prior generations of strategic culturalists. In particular, he chided the "first generation" of strategic culturalists, chiefly area-studies specialists of the first Cold War period with an interest in the Soviet Union, for their indifference to specifying their variables; and the "second generation," Gramscians of the late Cold War/early post–Cold War period, for what he claimed was their laziness in tracing the manner in which they would link their causes and effects.[91] The constructivist Johnston is himself a good exemplar of the "third generation" of strategic culturalists, and if the cultural turn was animated by a number of developments,[92] the most important of these was the ending of the age of bipolarity, upon the demise of the Soviet Union.

This development obviously made life more complicated for structuralists who had assimilated what Kenneth Waltz had had to say about the basic stability of the systemic structure known as bipolarity, given that within a decade of his vaunting of that system's "stability," bipolarity collapsed in ruins. Although not everyone within the vaguely composed "school" of IR realism had seen eye to eye with Waltz during the Cold War,[93] many in the nonrealist precincts of the professoriate assumed that the sudden and unexpected derailing of structural realism à la Waltz meant the end of the so-called realist dominance in international relations.[94]

Hence, the "turn" that the discipline was ostensibly in the process of making concerned not only levels of analysis but also IR paradigms, with realism beating a headlong retreat in the face of the onslaught mounted by adherents to Johnston's preferred body of theory, constructivism.[95] In this new environment, where culture was a word tripping easily off everyone's tongues, it naturally could seem to the constructivists that strategic culture must be their conceptual *chasse gardée*.[96] Were they right, so to assume?[97] Not exactly, and to understand why constructivism does not have a monopoly on strategic culture, we need to focus our genealogical search upon the aforementioned generations, but with a slight twist with regards to that postulated first generation of strategic culturalists.

When Alastair Iain Johnston criticized what he termed this ostensive first-generation's inability or unwillingness, or both, to distinguish between cause and effect, he touched an epistemological nerve. Colin Gray's rebuttal of the charge constituted something of a *tu quoque*, for Gray presumed to tar Johnston with the same "positivist" allegation Johnston had brought to bear against those "ahistorical, aculturalist" structuralists (read: realists) who had spurred him to action. Gray's rejoinder made two significant points. First, not all realists, in whose ranks Gray justifiably included himself, were ahistorical or aculturalist. Second, it was wrong to assume that strategic culture could be an independent variable; the best that could be hoped for was to conceive of it as "context," a category transcending both cause and effect. Gray essayed his own concise definition of the concept: "Strategic culture is the world of mind, feeling, and *habit in behaviour*" (emphasis in original).[98]

In sum, Gray took strategic culture to be much more of an explanandum than an explanans, though to him, and to the consternation of his critics, it was a bit of both. In his response to Johnston, Gray was staking out his own position on an important epistemological dispute within IR. This was the debate between scholars who favored what they took to be "explanation" and those who placed their chips on the heuristic payoff they believed to be associated with "understanding." Esoteric as this dispute might otherwise seem, it goes to the core of the problem that Lantis and others have raised regarding strategic culture, specifically that "discontent" associated with the distinction between independent and dependent variables.

For Gray and many others who rejected the promise of strategic culture's wielding any explanatory—much less predictive—prowess,[99] the best to be hoped for from strategic culture was that it would serve to "contextualize" thinking about policy issues in the realm of security and defense. What Gray was chiefly articulating was an approach to strategic culture with affinities to what has been called the "intuitive" school of history, whose adherents would buttress analytical rigor through the "exemplification of the intentions or motives of intelligent purposeful agents."[100] In short, Gray was siding with a perspective that some philosophers of science might label "idealism," but one that might better be referred to as "hermeneutics." For his part, Johnston's construe of strategic culture arrayed him alongside the "positivists."

The battle between idealists and positivists is a long-running one in the social and human sciences, and the combat ranges far beyond the theater of strategic culture. It is an epistemological struggle over perspectives that the German philosopher Johann Gustav Droysen long ago labeled *Verstehen* and *Erklären*, with *Verstehen* being said (by him) to be the method of the historical sciences and *Erklären* that of the natural sciences.[101]

Thus, the Johnston–Gray tussle over the definition of strategic culture reflects an old epistemological division between social scientists, who never can seem to decide whether they should follow Émile Durkheim down the path of positivism or stroll alongside Max Weber on the trail of interpretivism. This debate has possibly outlived its usefulness, as more than one philosopher of science is prepared to tell us that the distinction between explanation and understanding can be overdrawn,[102] and perhaps should be laid to rest, in favor of agreement that what we are really trying to generate, or must at least content ourselves with, is some modicum of "explicative understanding."[103]

This is the thought that will guide my own application of strategic culture to the problem of Franco-American suboptimality in part 2, where I will be relying upon both Gray's preference for strategic culture as a contextualizing vehicle and Johnston's preference for strategic culture as a cognitive construct. In the case of both context and cognition, the aim will be to inventory the Franco-American cultural vessel's "cargo hold"—save that, unlike Gray, my own use of context will situate it closer to the explanans pole of the epistemological spectrum than to the explanandum pole. But before we get around to inventorying the cultural context and content of Franco-American suboptimality, there are two more chores to get out of the way. First, we must pay a visit to the *real* first generation of strategic culturalists; second, we must inquire further into what it actually means when "context" is invoked in discussions of strategic culture.

From National Character to Political Culture: Strategic Culture's First Generation

Strategic culture as a mode of thought in IR has actually been around for longer than is often realized. Though the term dates from Jack Snyder's 1977 RAND study, the ideas underpinning it had been animating policy discussions for some time before then. Revisiting the generations (or waves) of strategic-cultural research brings this into sharper perspective. It also provides useful clues to enhance the explicative understanding of the suboptimality of Franco-American security and defense relations.

Culture and security likely have been intermeshed for as long as there has been strife among social (and thus, cultural) groupings, but the systematic, scientific study of the relationship between culture and warfare really only began to take off during the Second World War, stimulated by funding provided by an American government eager to acquire operational insight into the national (strategic-cultural) character of its Axis enemies. To this end, theory was essential. Thus, while Johnston's three generations might have been accurately enough enumerated for discussions of strategic culturalists so *named*, it is apparent, as Michael Desch has shown, that there was at least one highly significant generation of "culturalists" who pioneered the terrain of strategic culture.[104] Like Molière's Monsieur Jourdain, this generation was speaking prose—the prose of strategic culture—without realizing it, and thus they deserve to be considered the real first generation in the field of strategic culture. Leading their ranks were cultural anthropologists such as Ruth Benedict and her colleagues, who worked so diligently in the 1940s to try to demonstrate how "national character" had an impact upon an adversarial state's development of strategic will.[105]

In other words, and quite unlike so many later scholars interested in strategic culture, this early group was employing culture in a most energetic sense, out of a conviction that the stakes could not be higher. Not for them was the relegation of such an important aspect of the human condition as culture to the explicative sidelines, as a mere dependent variable; instead, they wanted to establish what it was about the adversary's culture (Japan's, in Benedict's case) that made it fight in certain ways. This belief in the security policy benefits to be accrued from careful cultural analysis persisted into the postwar period, with the object of study no longer being the wartime adversary but rather the postwar "reconstruction" project of beaten foes. Anthropologist David Rodnick expressed this optimistic expectation when, apropos of the recently defeated German adversary, he asserted that "greater understanding of human motivations and culturally learned behavior is essential today if social scientists are to bring to the field of human relationships knowledge at all comparable to that which physical and natural scientists have developed through their studies of the animate and inanimate world."[106]

This first generation was nothing if not bold in its quest to link culture with security and defense outcomes. But partly because of their direct and vigorous insertion of culture into the strategic debates of their times, national character would soon develop an unsavory reputation among many schol-ars—a reputation that would prove durable. Indicative of this durability were the harshly dismissive words of one writer who, in the late 1990s, saw fit to disparage the "once-popular, but now discredited, pseudo-scientific game of trying to identify what used to be called 'national character,' traits by which it was thought possible to distinguish between Frenchmen, English-men, Germans, Spaniards, Italians, Russians, and so on."[107] To its critics, national character suffered from the vice of "essentialism," which they said sustained and was sustained by a second, even more pernicious vice, that of heterostereotyping.

Following a peak of interest in the concept during the early postwar de-cades, national character came close to disappearing altogether from the re-search agendas of analysts interested in security studies, even though these analysts might have needed no prodding to concede that ideational factors, including and especially ones appertaining to national idiosyncrasies, de-served to be taken with the utmost seriousness by those expressing an interest in security policy.[108] For reasons not too difficult to detail, even if they are somewhat less easy to comprehend, national character began to take on a very bad odor, especially to those who (quite erroneously) insisted upon link-ing it to the kind of heterostereotyping that had so characterized the recent past and had even caused, or so it was claimed, any number of international catastrophes, not least of these being the First World War.[109] Hamilton Fyfe had led this particular charge with his 1940 polemic *The Illusion of National Character*, in which he argued that national character was the principal source of nationalism, and that nationalism was the principal cause of war.[110]

Others piled on, resulting in national character developing, among certain analysts, a sinister profile it never could or did shake. Still, the concept had a few defenders. One of the most exuberant of them was Dean Peabody, who questioned, a bit acerbically, why it was that if someone were to express a scholarly interest in national character, he or she ran the risk of being dubbed muddleheaded, likely even "somehow fascistic," yet if someone else chose to dabble in an equally problematic and confusing category of analysis—such as, for instance "social class"—then he or she would be heralded as rather sharp, both epistemologically and ethically.[111]

Peabody's spirited retort had considerable merit to it, but it also revealed a second, much more difficult problem that confronted those who would employ the concept of national character: it was far from easy to define and therefore to "operationalize." Disagreement surfaced regarding whether national character was best defined as practically synonymous with culture (that is, as learned cultural behavior) or as something else, a "modal personality" (that is, as a statistical notion for expressing personality traits appearing with great frequency within a society). It did not take too long for the latter understanding to nudge out the former, given that it foretold an apparently greater prospect for attaining social-scientific rigor, if for no other reason than that means could, in theory at least, be devised for taking its measure.[112]

But this embrace of modal personality as the essence of national character could not solve that second, definitional problem, for even if scholars could agree on this statistical abstraction as the most appropriate signifier of national character (as many began to do), it was far from obvious how they were to *take* that measure. Here the issue turned on whether character was to be revealed through systematic exploration of those presumed group behavioral traits (possibly through survey techniques) or character would become apparent in other, albeit less direct ways by focusing upon a social entity's (in our case, a nation's) cultural products. These products could include such items as the collectivity's "institutions, its collective achievements and its public policy."[113] Needless to say, the repertoire of such products was virtually limitless, and relying upon them to tease out a national character was not an enterprise for the faint of heart. Some even dared to suggest that this sort of enterprise could not be entrusted at all to the likes of mere political scientists, who instead should be filling their days with the study of government and governing while leaving national character to those who actually possessed the necessary expertise to grapple with it.

And just who *were* those fortunate experts? They were none other than the scholars whose professional comfort zones situated them within the confines of the "personality-in-culture" approach near and dear to social psychologists, some other psychologists, and even a few psychiatrists. This was the rather blunt judgment of Bernard Hennessy, who would permit political scientists into this conceptual sandbox only when national character could be shown to have an impact upon the making of foreign policy. Such an impact, he hastened to add, was unlikely to be detected very often, if ever, since in his view foreign policies "are made largely by cosmopolitan elite groups who appear to be on the whole little affected by national character or modal personality trends. And they [the policies] are based, for the most part, on 'hard' facts of geography, economics, historical traditions, and on more-or-less rationally calculated factors of power and prestige."[114]

Hennessy's was quite an indictment, apparently much more damaging to the attempt to conceive of strategic culture with reference to national character than Fyfe's condemnation of the concept of national character, on normative grounds, had been two decades earlier. Where Fyfe imagined reliance upon national character to be dangerous, Hennessy saw it as being futile—or more accurately, irrelevant. To him, foreign policymaking was a culture-free zone. Yet even Hennessy's critique, despite its author's intent, contained strong hints about how one might actually bring national character into the discussion of strategic culture in general, as well as in the specific context of Franco-American relations, and do so with the assistance of those political scientists whom Hennessy would wish to ban.

There were two hints, the first of which was contained in his catalog of the "hard" facts that shape foreign policy, including calculations of power and prestige. It turns out these facts really are not so "hard," after all.[115] As was briefly mentioned earlier, many scholars of foreign policy believe that prestige (or status) can be a highly significant reason why states get into conflict with each other, and in their various analyses of the phenomenon, these scholars explore conceptual terrain that decidedly does provide a solid footing for political scientists—terrain we will revisit in chapter 5.[116]

The second hint was embedded in Hennessy's invocation of the social psychologists as the experts best equipped to say anything sensible about national character. Again, as with prestige/status, so it has been with the personality-in-culture approach in recent decades. There has been a veritable invasion of this turf by political scientists interested in how group psychology can play an important role in IR and foreign policy analysis, matters that we take up in chapter 3 and, especially, chapter 4.[117]

The difference between then and now, of course, is that "national character" is as much out of scholarly fashion as that much older category of "temperament," with which this chapter began. But what animated the first generation (properly tallied) continues to animate scholars today, save that the referent object of the adjective "national" has been switched from character to identity. So, even if they do not quite put it in this fashion, researchers really want to know the answer to this question: What components of a collectivity's (in our case, a nation's) identity can be held to have important causal significance for its foreign policy and strategic choices?

This thought gets us to the last of Johnston's enumerated generations, the "third" one that, for him, really *was* the exclusive preserve of him and his fellow constructivists. But he was wrong in thinking realism had no room for strategic culture. One of the core precepts of constructivism is the notion that identity prefigures interests. It may be true that structural realists have to disagree on this point, as Michael Desch has so unmistakably done in remarking that the best that could be hoped for from strategic culturalists is that they might supplement a realism that they can never supplant.[118] But for a classical realist such as, for instance, Colin Gray, there was absolutely nothing off-putting in the claim about identity's preponderant role in security and defense policy.

Nor was Gray the only classical realist to understand how identity and the "national interest" could be so closely correlated. Although Samuel Huntington could more reasonably be pigeonholed among the specialists in comparative politics than among those in IR, he was assuredly a classical realist, at least as this breed of analyst can be known through a declared passion to try to identify and defend something called the "national interest."[119] Consider what Huntington wrote in his final book: "National interests derive from national identity. We have to know who we are before we can know what our interests are."[120] Many contemporary realist theorists, who regard themselves as neoclassical realists, would concur with this thought.[121]

Clearly, it is no easy matter to figure out what any country's national interest is considered to be; entire libraries are filled with published journeys of discovery into this important but elusive construct.[122] It is even more of a challenge to figure out what national identity might mean, and how it might differ from national character. This is owing in no small measure to the ambiguous nature of the concept of character, for whatever semantic difficulties plagued it are eerily similar to those that have plagued identity.[123] This is no reason to throw up our hands and conclude that the quest for conceptual clarity is fruitless. It is surely challenging, but some guidance has been supplied by scholars who also worked during the era of what I have been calling the real first generation of strategic culture. Unlike the national-character scholars, however, this other group of researchers into the impact of culture upon behavior labored in a different field of social science; they were political scientists whose disciplinary subfield was not IR but comparative politics, and whose concept of choice was "political culture."

It is obvious that Alastair Iain Johnston's definition of strategic culture owes a great deal to Clifford Geertz. Less obvious is what it also owes to students of political culture. Although few strategic culturalists, Johnston excepted, seem to recognize the debt, the older notion of "political culture" has served to blaze the trail for strategic culture, just as much as the old notion of national character has. This is especially so when it comes to scholars such as Johnston, whose definition of strategic culture is suffused with ideation. The career of political culture demonstrates that it had to slay (or at least confront) the same definitional dragon whose breath would subsequently heat up the debate over strategic culture.

Strategic culture is subject to a variety of definitions, just as political culture used to be. One student of political culture whimsically observed that there were almost as many different meanings of it as there were political scientists professing an interest in it.[124] When it first burst on the scene in political science during the 1930s and 1940s, it was as a result of the same interdisciplinary transfusion process that would bring culture into the purview of those who later contemplated strategy, and it was again the anthropologists who were making the initial running. What happened in the subfield of IR also occurred in the discipline of political science more broadly: culture was often equated with "character" in the early days, but the more character was dissected, the more it grew suspect as a useful category.

By 1956, some two decades earlier than in the case of strategic culture, "political culture" got its name, yet even though Gabriel Almond told us what we should call it, he could not decree what it meant. Debate continued about whether it was to signify the generalized personality of a people, or the collectivity's history, or something else altogether. By the late 1960s, political culture was well on the way to the conceptual dust heap.[125] Then it caught an epistemological break and managed to become, once again, one of the important concepts in the subfield of comparative politics.

Political culture's rebound owed a bit to those exogenous changes we encountered earlier, associated with the ending of the first Cold War, but it was primarily some analysts' discontent with rational choice modeling and game theory that endowed the concept with its new lease on life in the 1980s and 1990s.[126] The concept might have taken a nose-dive in the late 1960s and early

1970s, but its core question—how to tap the subjective orientations of societies' members so as to account for political differences cross-nationally—had never gone out of fashion.[127] What had changed in the period between the decline and the reemergence of political culture was that a new element had been injected into the discussions of political scientists when they pondered how to assess "culture." That new element was symbolism.

Symbolism helped resuscitate political culture in two ways. First, it solved the "level-of-analysis" problem hobbling political culture. Much of the early work by Almond and his associates relied upon survey data that, while it might indicate much of value about the perceptions and psychological state of individuals, seemed incapable of generating usable knowledge about the cognitive patterns of collectivities. Individuals, after all, had personalities, but only collectivities could be said to possess cultures, and the trick was to find a way to go from the individual to the collective level of analysis if culture was to mean anything. Symbolism provided the answer, enabling theorists to explore the social ideas of individuals.[128]

Symbolism could do this because of its second major contribution, which was to draw us to the cognitive devices upon which social groupings rely, as Lowell Dittmer phrased it, to "transmit meanings from person to person despite vast distances of space and time." Dittmer invited us to think of those devices, which include but are not limited to imagery and metaphor, as being identical to what the poet T. S. Eliot called "objective correlatives," or mechanisms for the efficient expression of feelings. In this regard, symbols become a "depository of widespread interest and feeling." For Dittmer, the task of those who would employ political culture must be nothing other than the systematic, scientific analysis of society's key symbols.[129] Or as Michael Walzer so nicely put the same thought, symbols and images tell us "more than we can easily repeat."[130]

It is apparent that Johnston's definition of strategic culture, so reliant on Clifford Geertz's own understanding of the meaning of culture, also reveals strong affinities with the renascent concept of political culture. And we could do much worse, when we seek to apply strategic culture in the guise of an explanans, than to put the emphasis upon those aspects of cognition so closely linked to symbolism, especially ones that lend themselves easily to heterostereotyping. Even if strategic culture proves incapable of serving as anyone's independent variable, it can still render valuable scientific service as a "specifying," or conditioning element, in explicative understandings of strategic choice, just as political culture supplies a conditioning element in political choice.[131] Analysts whose interest in strategic culture is situated primarily in the cognitive category might, for instance, be tempted to follow in Johnston's footsteps and concentrate their efforts at explicating strategic choice through the study of such nonliteral forms of communication as myth and metaphor, to take just the two most obvious such examples.[132]

But this is not the only way to try to employ strategic culture as a speci-fying element in the elaboration of security and defense policy; there is also Colin Gray's preferred use of strategic culture as *context*. There are enough similarities between strategic culture as cognition and strategic culture as context to dissuade anyone from making too big a fuss about their analytical separability.[133] That said, there is at least one difference worth noting, and it speaks to the very core of the explicative enterprise. Recall the thrust of Johnston's criticism of Gray, that Gray's use of strategic culture was hope-lessly muddled because it so blurred the distinction between independent and dependent variables as to eliminate any prospect of strategic culture being of anyone's use in trying to sort cause from effect.

I have hinted that this criticism has merit only to the extent that one is committed to the notion of reliable causality. The more Laodicean the analyst is regarding the attainability of such causality, the less problematic becomes strategic culture as context. After all, and heretical though it might sound to some, if taxonomy and the kind of systematic understanding conveyed through interpretation are themselves part of the explicative enterprise, then even culture as context can serve us profitably, by helping us see things in foreign policy we might otherwise have missed. But what is implied when we take strategic culture to mean context, as Gray so ardently wished us to do?

"Context" and Strategic Culture: Ethnicity, Path Dependence, or Something Else?

If strategic culture owes an enormous intellectual debt to earlier cohorts of anthropologists, political scientists, and even psychologists, it is no less de-pendent on the contributions of historians and historical sociologists. My account of Franco-American strategic interaction in parts 2 and 3 will be influenced by the latter two disciplines. I will invoke historians and historical sociologists to give operational substance to the two categories I hold to be most useful for unpacking strategic culture. We have just encountered one of those strategic-cultural categories, the one I called cognition. We will be returning to cognition in chapter 5, when the symbolic ideation of Franco-American strategic interaction will be probed for its explanatory significance, with a few particular ideas (or "myths") capturing our attention, including "Anglo-Saxonism," anti-Americanism, liberalism, and multipolarity. The other category is "context." Chapters 3 and 4 will lean heavily upon this category, so only a brief introduction of what context means and how it might work to enable us better to grasp suboptimality in bilateral strategic interaction is necessary here.

Broadly, there are two ways in which strategic culture conceived as context can be put to work in the explication of security and defense policy choices. We might ask it to help us explain those choices in terms of how our two particular states have acted toward each other in the past, on the assumption that their established patterns of behavior might tell us something important about their current, and even future, interactions in the realm of security and defense policy. Alternatively, but not totally distinct from this, their pattern of interaction might be powerfully conditioned by the way they "happen to be," which is to say that something associated with their national identity can yield important clues about policy choices they have made in the past and are likely to make in the future.

Analysts who employ strategic culture as a means of accounting for the impact of past behavior upon the present and the future often turn to historical sociology for guidance. Those who prefer to put the emphasis upon conceptions attending identity also avail themselves of approaches with a long-established pedigree, initially subsumed, as we have seen, under the rubric of national character. Both approaches are similar in having originated in earlier eras, but a difference worth noting is that historical sociology has regained scholarly respectability after having been for some years in eclipse,[134] whereas national-character studies, under that label, remain controversial, though when they are rebranded as national-identity studies they appear to be more than legitimate.[135]

Whatever else might divide them, strategic culturalists are almost always dissatisfied with structuralist accounts of foreign policy behavior that take their cues from assessments of relative capability (there is an exception of note, to be discussed in chapter 5). Strategic culturalists may or may not be in agreement as to the attainability of reliable causality, which was the real bone of contention between Johnston and Gray. In that dispute, the ostensibly positivist (and emphatically constructivist) Johnston was parrying with the interpretivist (yet defiantly self-proclaimed realist) Gray, the gravamen turning on how one should deal with this thing called "context." Gray, it has often been said, preferred a descriptive rather than explanatory construe of strategic culture, whereas Johnston intended to vest culture with the kinds of causal properties associated with independent variables, and he did not think there was very much utility in the notion of context, which simply muddied the waters. As one scholar whose sympathies resided much more with Gray than with Johnston explained, the debate "illustrates the futility of thinking about strategic culture in terms of causal explanations and falsifiable theory, whilst confirming the potential of a contextual or constitutive framework."[136]

In this rendering, the contextual side of the house is typically construed as an antipositivist lodgment as well, with positivism here being said to represent the will-o'-the-wisp of reliable causality (otherwise known as explanation). As we saw earlier, some contextualists hold this epistemology to be vastly inferior to the more modest but honest quest for interpreting (or understanding) social reality. Yet there is another way of looking at it, and it involves not only how one regards history but also how the pattern of relations between states can itself come to assume explanatory potency, a point to which we shall return in chapter 3. Odd as it may seem to some, it is possible to be at one and the same time both a contextualist *and* a positivist, if by "positivist" we mean to suggest that one subscribes to the business of explaining.

Take, for instance, the case of Paul Pierson, a political scientist whose areas of interest and expertise are neither strategic culture nor IR but rather comparative and domestic US politics. What Pierson has to say, both about how history might be taken to "matter," and especially about the importance of context, should comfort even the most hard-bitten antipositivist, notwithstanding that Pierson himself dances to a different epistemological beat and very much aspires to establish reliable causality.

Context, acknowledges Pierson, has become a "bad word" among many social scientists. He refers to these folk, and not in a way that flatters them, as "decontextualizers." These theorists often tend to take a very dim view of historical context, regarding it as so much factual clutter drifting between the observer and the object of the observer's curiosity—chaff confusing their radar screen. Now, if all that historical context represented was the mindless amassing of ever-increasing details about past events, the critics might have a point. But of course, they do not, for they caricature the historical enterprise and in so doing fail to notice that context has a powerful, theoretically pregnant, signification: it concerns those things that surround and therefore define matters of great interest to social scientists. Seen in this light, Pierson says, it becomes nothing short of a "scientific disaster" to effect the "removal of defining locational information," as the decontextualizers wish to do.[137]

For Pierson and many others, including and especially historical sociologists, "placing politics in time" can best, and perhaps only, be done by adhering to the logic of path dependence. Although this is hardly a straightforward or uncontested logic, it should appeal to strategic culturalists who are discontented with structural explanations of foreign policy behavior, such as the sort that ascribes policy outputs to variables like relative capability (power) or cumulative wealth—testifying, in short, to a conviction that large causes should result in commensurately large outcomes.[138] In contradistinction to this, path dependence implies that the process itself through which history unfolds takes on causal importance, in what some scholars refer to as "narrative positivism," and others call "emplotment."[139]

It is, of course, one thing to invoke path dependence as the mechanism by which history can be said to continue to matter in the shaping of foreign (including security) policy, with applicability (in our case) to the Franco-American relationship. For instance, there is the commonsense observation that choices made long in the past can go on limiting policy options in the future.[140] Yet it is quite another thing actually to winkle out, or trace, the process(es) by which path dependence manages to become *itself* a causal, as well as cultural, variable. In this regard, a concept intimately associated with path dependence becomes extremely important. This is the notion of contingency, suggestive as it is of a break point after which the ability of postulated initial conditions to shape the future is substantially altered.[141] Those who employ this notion see it as setting in train a new inertia, one in which the path leads either to the efficient reproduction of cooperation (sometimes called "self-reinforcing sequences") or to the reverse, the efficient reproduction of conflict and discord (called "reactive sequences").[142]

So one application of contextual analysis to the Franco-American relationship will have us canvassing the historical record in search of that turning point in bilateral affairs after which relations between the two states could never be what, presumably, they once had been. But that is not all that context can bring to the task of comprehending Franco-American suboptimality. There is also the question of national character (identity), which as we are about to discover, can and does make appeal to what is arguably the most eminently cultural marker of them all—the marker we know as "ethnicity."

In part 2, the investigation of Franco-American suboptimality will unfold against the backdrop of the context/cognition binary introduced here. Chapter 3 starts by portraying context in the guise of interactions strongly stamped with the impress of ethnicity as posited in assessments of national character, and finishes by suggesting reasons for downplaying the enduring significance of such assessments, supplementing if not replacing them outright with relational analysis heavily impregnated with assumptions about path dependence. In short, chapter 3 may start on the terrain of initial conditions thought to be imbued with ancestral hatreds (what the Germans call *Erbfeindschaft*), but it strays into the domain of contingency. Chapter 4 will continue, mainly, to nestle in a contextual mold, and if it too explores how culture as ethnicity might inform strategic interaction, it does so within a decidedly less "essentialist" frame than the Erbfeindschaft of chapter 3—a frame that elides easily into other, nonethnic elements of heterostereotyping in the France–US relationship, such as the generic category of anti-Americanism, to be covered in chapter 5.

In that final chapter of part 2, we will alter the analytical focus from context to cognition, with the symbolic objects of curiosity being the myths, images, and metaphors held to endow the bilateral relationship with its operational guideposts at moments of international systemic change. The aim in the chapter will be to demonstrate the impact of cultural antinomies upon the quality of bilateral cooperation in security and defense policy.

II
CULTURAL ANALYSIS

3

Historical Context

From Erbfeindschaft to Relational Realism

Does the Venom Truly "Go Deep"?

We saw in chapter 2 that "history" frequently gets invoked by scholars interested in strategic culture. To many of these scholars, the cultural turn in the human sciences (including international relations) has also been a historical turn. What is not so obvious is *how* history gets brought into their discussions, especially when those doing the discussing happen to be political scientists, for there is an epistemological, and some say aesthetic, divide that can sometimes degrade interdisciplinary dialogue between them and their historian colleagues. While in recent decades there has been a growing recognition on the part of many scholars that mutually beneficial collaboration is a sensible way forward, there remain pockets of resistance to the idea of breaking down disciplinary silos.[1]

It is well known that political scientists sometimes adopt a supercilious air when reflecting upon historians' contributions to IR, deeming them to be so focused upon individual trees as to be incapable of comprehending the meaning of a forest. And historians have not been shy about returning fire, often sensing that political scientists are so addicted to theorizing reality as to be unable to recognize it when they see it.[2] To more than a few historians, political scientists can appear to be a bunch of sloppy, bafflegabbing pretenders who suffer from an added defect that stems from a proclivity to apply history to the contemplation of contemporary problems—a proclivity sometimes denounced as "presentism," "historicism," or, much worse, "Whiggism."[3] There are two manners of construing Whiggism. In one usage, past events are analyzed from the vantage point not of their own era but of the present; in another, the present is construed as the unavoidable outcome of past events, with the normative imputation that history connotes the notion of an unstoppable march of progress.[4]

In addition to this epistemological/aesthetic divide, there is a second disciplinary fault line that has grown up within the social and human sciences, over the issue of historical context. It is a line setting some sociologists of a historical bent apart from both historians and political scientists. On one side of this line we find scholars and other analysts who focus on the initial conditions that they believe bear most of the causal weight for policy outcomes, while on the other side are those who see history as representing a path-dependent iteration and reiteration of behavioral patterns that take on a determinative life of their own, at some remove from those initial conditions.[5] For some of those on one side of this line, the initial conditions as applied to the Franco-American relationship can be located within a decidedly ethnic conceptual framework, testifying to the explicative richness of national character. For those on the other side, historical context can mean something quite different, representing as it does a pattern of "institutionalized" interaction that, over time, assumes such an autonomous presence of its own as to render those initial conditions suspect, possibly even useless, for the purpose of grasping contemporary realities. And, they say, this interactive pattern need not have any basis in national character (though, of course, it may have such a basis).

This is an important epistemological divide, as we will discover in this chapter's initial effort to tease out one of the most salient cultural referents imaginable when considering the chronic pattern of Franco-American suboptimality in security and defense policy: ethnicity. Although this is hardly a normal starting point for those seeking insight into the peculiar qualities of the contemporary Franco-American special relationship, ethnicity might nevertheless provide a useful springboard for diving into contextual analysis.

If one insists that culture must somehow play a role in generating strategic choice, as opposed merely to being a product of such choice—that is, if we take culture to be more of an active (independent) and less of a reactive (dependent) variable—there may be reasons for invoking ethnicity as the initial condition from which, at least according to some scholars, inexorably stems the chronic malaise that has plagued the Franco-American special relationship. Two reasons for this insistence come to mind. The first is the tight semantic connection between culture and ethnicity. As we saw in chapter 2, the cultural turn in many disciplines of the human sciences (including and especially history) featured a renewed scholarly fascination with the intertwined concepts of ideas and ethnicity, both of which remain core features of an American foreign policy that is "based as much on ideas as ethnicity." America, says Joseph Nye, "has long seen itself as a cause as well as a country."[6]

The investigation in this chapter will start with the latter of Nye's two cultural referents, ethnicity, before veering off into a quite different way of examining historical context, one associated with historical-sociological notions of path dependence as the source of whatever causal force "historical context" wields. Later, chapter 5 will concentrate upon the cognitive domain of culture, ideas. In between, chapter 4 will serve as a bridge connecting historical context with ideas (thus, cognition) by focusing upon how the "ethnicization" of foreign policy has been said to affect the quality of Franco-American relations. Obviously, the distinction drawn between the two cultural rubrics in chapter 2—that is, between context and cognition—must be somewhat arbitrary. Nevertheless, the distinction can be a useful one for an inquiry into the cultural sources of Franco-American strategic interaction.

Robert Kelley reminds us that, for his profession, the cultural turn generated an explosion of scholarship in the fields of intellectual history and ethnocultural studies.[7] Much the same can be said for IR and other organized fields of scholarly investigation. Indeed, in some ways the cultural turn simply amplified a trend that had begun decades earlier; by the time Kelley was writing (1979), ethnocultural studies had already become, for some students of American foreign policy, a familiar and fertile source of hypotheses about decision-making. For scholars pioneering this frontier, ethnicity became virtually a synonym for culture.

This trend began to gain serious traction during the era of the First World War, with the publication of a path-breaking series of essays by Horace M. Kallen, covering various facets of ethnicity's mooted impact upon American domestic and, especially, foreign policy. They were reproduced in a volume Kallen published following the war, which he intended to stand as a solid rebuttal of claims made by the Ku Klux Klan and other nativist groups about the adverse consequences of immigration for American national identity. In the America of the 1920s, as in later decades, there was a good deal of opposition to political entities that would eventually come to grouped under the rubric of "ethnic diasporas," seen by the nativists as being antithetical to, and corrosive of, their ideal of "one hundred percent Americanism."[8]

The title of Kallen's volume said it all: *Culture and Democracy in the United States: Studies in the Group Psychology of the American Peoples.* As the author understood the term, the "American peoples"—at least the white ones, for he was silent regarding the country's African Americans, to say nothing of its Indigenous and Chicano populations[9]—were discrete ethnic constituencies of European origin. They were not, as the nativists insisted, legatees of "old-stock" Americans of British descent. To Kallen, and to so many others over the ensuing decades, culture meant ethnicity and ethnicity meant culture; failing to understand the connection between the two was to fail to understand contemporary America. In this view, the American story was imbued with "cultural pluralism," having been written with pens held in the hands of a multitude of European immigrants and their descendants; it was not simply the narrative construction of the so-called Anglo-Saxon settlers.[10]

Kallen's insistence upon the enduring and inexpungible meaning of America's ethnic heritage was memorialized in his book's most memorable, if gendered, passage: "Men may change their clothes, their politics, their wives, their religion, their philosophies, to a greater or lesser extent: they cannot change their grandfathers."[11] Nor was Kallen's by any means a solitary voice in considering America's ethnic mix to be absolutely central to its national identity and political culture. Observers abroad, in France and elsewhere, also had been detecting a tight correspondence between the concepts of ethnicity and culture.[12] The term Kallen preferred to use to depict America's demographic reality was "cultural pluralism," a precursor to what in our own day is usually called multiculturalism. Like the earlier term, the later one is synonymous with multiethnicity.[13]

To be sure, there can exist any number of cultural markers in domestic and international society, but nothing seems to pack as much of a cognitive and affective punch as ethnicity, and never more so than when it is understood to subsume race.[14] On the score of its obvious importance alone, ethnicity would look to be a sensible enough jumping-off place for an inquiry such as ours, into the impact of culture upon the Franco-American special relationship. But there is more to it.

The other reason for beginning our inquiry with the concept of ethnicity is that it invites and even compels us to challenge the veracity of that familiar trope of Franco-American strategic interaction, the one holding them to be such "old allies," and by inference, "great, great friends." Might it turn out that the "old fund of affection"[15] conjured up by Duroselle and a few others represents something else altogether, a fund of *disaffection* handed down by a horrific past that had been blotted with a sanguinary, presumably inexpiable, record of ethnic conflict between French and Americans? Testifying to the existence of such a past is the trenchant assertion made by one American analyst of the bilateral relationship, at the time of that bitter Franco-American clash over Iraq: "The venom and the grudges go deep."[16]

There can be little doubt that bilateral ties have been heavily seasoned by the spice of emotionalism, yet it may well be that the frequently invoked image of Lafayette as a symbol of abiding Franco-American comradeship and solidarity conjures up a very misleading emotion, empirically.[17] Perhaps, some suggest, the affective tone of the Franco-American special relationship is better captured in the dysthymic German word *Erbfeindschaft*, meaning traditional or hereditary enmity. Maybe ethnicity tells us something important about how history is supposed to exert such a lasting impact upon a Franco-American relationship made "special" only because of its horrid past. In this reading of the past, the fate of the relationship was sealed in a very early and bloody phase of the two countries' historical interaction. That interaction, some think, established the initial conditions that henceforth would continue to weigh heavily upon the manner in which the relationship was to evolve.

Few, in our own troubled times, would disagree with William Faulkner's oft-quoted claim about the inextinguishable presence of history: "The past is never dead. It's not even past."[18] But what *is* this undead past?[19] And how, if at all, might the notion of an enduring past be imported into the discussion of the cultural source(s) of Franco-American suboptimality in matters of security and defense?

Here, and to a somewhat lesser extent in chapter 4, ethnicity is going to be tasked with the burden of shedding light on the bilateral relationship. The inquiry starts off with what we can consider to be a massive, maybe even excessive, dose of ethnicity. In these early pages, our aim will be to see whether—and if so, how—the historical legacy that presumably has such enduring impact upon the present is nothing other than the residue of enmity spawned by former ethnic conflict between French and Americans (though they were English, politically, at the time). Is *this* the "meaning" of history for today's Franco-American special relationship? The idea seems, on the face of it, more than a bit odd, yet some scholars do argue that historical enmity has left an indelible trace on the bilateral relationship, down to the present.

It is sometimes said that history "constitutes" national identity, or what I have alternatively called national character. To know who you are now, you must have some idea about what you think you once were, and hence you must canvass the past for clues. But in doing so, you import into that very past ideas, and often desires, about contemporary realities. You sift through that past in a bid to discover the most "usable" history for your present purposes, retrofitting past events in such a way as to render them meaningful for articulating and advancing current desires.[20] In this fashion, as Jonathan Friedman explains, history matters because "making history is a way of producing identity." Put differently, "history is an imprinting of the present onto the past."[21]

Here we find expressed one means of interpreting historical context in a Faulknerian sense: history creates contemporary social meaning because it is the forge upon which the contours of national character and national identity are shaped, even though those contours may be shrouded in myth (not necessarily to be confused with falsehoods).[22] It cannot stay dead because we need it to be alive. Not only this—or, better, *because* of this—the Faulknerian message can often be fortified by the derivative assumption that history does not simply exercise continuing influence on the *present* because of its power to constitute identity but also provides invaluable "lessons" for the *future*.[23]

There is the familiar warning that those who do not remember the past are condemned to repeat it. According to this vision, history's most important meaning is to be gleaned from its lessons, especially as these get absorbed and operationalized by policymakers.[24] Yes, there have been some skeptics, Henry Adams prominent among them, who have been known to scoff that the only thing one can learn from history is that one cannot learn from history. Although the skeptics may well be on to something, I am going to proceed on the assumption that historical context must be of *some* significance to the quality of contemporary Franco-American relations, and that historical context itself deserves to be construed as an aspect of culture. My challenge will be to try to figure out just what that context might be and why some scholars insist that it is inextricably linked to culture, conceived as ethnicity.

What is to be made of the claim that the past has stamped upon the Franco-American present (and future) some lasting and unshakeable behavioral constraints? The first set of these constraints is of a deeply ethnic provenance, rooted in events that took place in the century preceding American independence. For those who adopt this perspective on the Franco-American special relationship, the era in bilateral relations known as the period of the "intercolonial wars" (1689 to 1763) continues to resonate with political significance and thus can be interpreted as representing nothing so much as that kind of Faulknerian past that has never managed to die. Accordingly, we will explore the theoretical and empirical basis of the Erbfeindschaft thesis, which basically holds that the two countries have not been friends but rather foes, and have been so over the long sweep of time. Hence, if they do get on suboptimally today, it has almost everything to do with that deep and ineradicable historical legacy, dating from those intercolonial wars, and especially from the first two of them, King William's War and Queen Anne's War.

In this perspective, those two wars, far from having been marginal to either contemporary American political life or the country's evolving relations with France, have in fact been central and *lasting* cultural shapers of that Franco-American special relationship. They constitute the initial conditions from which subsequent Franco-American strategic interaction can never be totally liberated. These initial conditions were both imported and important, and in the words of one chronicler of the bilateral relationship from nearly a century ago, they were the inevitable outcome of "generations of European rivalry [that] had fixed in the consciousness of the Anglo-Saxon and Gaul a pattern of dislike and distrust. . . . It appeared natural to continue in America quarrels begun on the continent."[25]

Following this initial historical examination of the more distant Franco-American past, we return once more to theory, only this time with a different purpose in mind. We will try to determine whether history "matters" less because of what it might tell us about initial conditions and more because of how it reveals the ability of path dependency to allow for outcomes different from the ones "predicted" by those conditions. History, according to this alternative manner of construing context, really *does* matter, only not in the way the initial-conditions theorists imagine it should. I call this second group of contextualists "relational realists," and their approach to comprehending the Franco-American relationship rounds out this chapter's discussion of historical context.

Specifically, I ask whether historical sociologists might have something important to tell us about strategic culture, as the latter can be assessed through the *iterative* mutual acts of the sister republics, such that those dreadful initial conditions born of the hereditary, terrible enmity of the Erbfeindschaft thesis might have become effaced, thanks to "contingent" developments that managed to set the Franco-American relationship upon a different, less dismal, trajectory. This chapter's final section queries whether there have existed obvious moments of historical inflection so powerful as to have altered the path upon which the relationship had hitherto been traveling and to have set it upon a different one, in which the element of ethnicity, although continuing to have a presence, would cede central position to some other prepotent vector(s) of cultural causality.

History Matters:
Probing that Deep Franco-American Past

As noted earlier, historians have been known to get agitated when they discover political scientists encroaching upon their epistemological and empirical turf. There are many reasons for this, some more valid than others. Among the least valid of the reasons is a lingering suspicion that political scientists are too addicted to theorizing reality and not concentrated enough upon the task of understanding reality through a careful examination of the record of the past. The corollary assumption is that historians are averse to theory, which of course they are not. The historians' employment of theory, relative to that of political scientists, may be more inductive than deductive, expressing more affinity with "idiographic" than with "nomothetic" perspectives, but it is theoretical, nonetheless.[26] In addition, there is that other, more damning allegation of "presentism," which is the scholarly equivalent of the criminal lawyer's hot pursuit of the paddy wagon, save that in the case of the political scientist it is not the undignified hunt for a potential client that attracts the disdain of some historians but rather the attempt to apply history to the contemplation of contemporary problems.

As with so much else in life, there is a good side and a not so good side to presentism, even the kind on display by international relations specialists from the discipline of political science, who profess an interest in what some of them call "applied history." Prior to the return of the Russian "problem" in European and global security, the most keenly debated application of history to contemporary policy was the question of China's much-discussed "rise." For some scholars, Graham Allison foremost among them, so many historical analogies can be mustered from a reading of former instances of "power transition" that it generates distressing probability assessments of future great power war. Such a war would be triggered by those presumably eternal dilemmas that surface at moments when the top-ranking state in the system finds itself close to being matched in "power" by a rising challenger.

Allison's own work pays homage to lessons Thucydides is said to have imparted in his historical account of the Peloponnesian War.[27] The most important of these lessons, Allison believes, is the two-pronged danger of hubris on the part of the rising power, propelling it to undertake risky expansionist policies, and of paranoia on the part of the challenged power, before whose eyes dangles the temptation of waging a preventive war, on the logic that any delay in starting a war will only strengthen the capabilities of the challenger. Allison has labeled this dynamic Thucydides's Trap.[28]

Allison has been charged by critics with misreading the "lessons" of the Peloponnesian past, and of even somehow promoting the inevitability of a future Sino-American war.[29] Some IR scholars, echoing Henry Adams's skepticism about history's ability to impart lessons, go so far as to urge colleagues who are inclined to ponder the contemporary meaning of that ancient war between Athens and Sparta to take a page from the book of Tony Soprano rather than Thucydides and "fuggedaboutit."[30] Yet others, even if they are not directly hitching their pedagogical ponies to any Allisonian cart, believe that there are important lessons for contemporary security policy to be gleaned from past episodes of great power conflict, although they are more inclined to analogize not with the Greece of the fifth century BCE but with the Europe of 1914.[31]

Although the rise of China, with its problematic impact upon the Sino-American relationship, demonstrates how history might be applied to the investigation of current challenges in international relations, this is far from being the only dyadic relationship susceptible to having history applied to it. The special Franco-American relationship hardly lacks for analysts who similarly take guidance from the past, even if they refrain from couching their historical analyses explicitly within a power-transition theoretical framework. *Something* in that Franco-American past, they are certain, yields invaluable clues concerning the Franco-American present and even future.

To discover what that something might be, let us revisit an argument briefly encountered in chapter 1, where some authors looked to the deep past in trying to explain the very contemporary bilateral tensions that had arisen over the Iraq war. We recall that pressure had been building within the bilateral relationship throughout the 1990s, as French suspicions about American policy behavior in the post–Cold War decade reinforced older critical tendencies among many in Paris, prompting them to wonder whether France itself would be bound to suffer in an era suddenly characterized by "unipolarity."

The growing French critique of America, gathering strength during the Clinton years, became greatly exacerbated during the first administration of George W. Bush, when Franco-American clashes over the best means of dealing with Saddam Hussein brought things to the boiling point. In this ebullient emotional context, a book appeared with a title, *Our Oldest Enemy*, that showcased the Erbfeindschaft thesis adumbrated by Elizabeth Brett White three-quarters of a century earlier. As far as the book's authors, John J. Miller and Mark Molesky, were concerned, the only way to comprehend the contemporary crisis of Franco-American relations was to return to the initial conditions of Franco-American interaction. Theirs was a decidedly Faulknerian past from which escape never could be an option, as was becoming obvious in the bitterness engendered by the Iraq imbroglio. It was not just that history had a strong grip upon the Franco-American present, though that was bad enough. Even worse, the historical hand that gripped the present was dripping with the blood of ethnic hatred.

Americans, Miller and Molesky charged, might delude themselves into thinking happy thoughts about France being a friend, as a result of its having aided them in obtaining their independence from Britain. But they were wrong; their view of history suffered badly from myopia. In particular, it could not reveal the obvious reality that Franco-American strategic interaction did not begin in the months following the Battle of Saratoga in autumn 1777 and the onset of the (short-lived) bilateral alliance the following year. Instead, the history of the two countries' relationship was an older one, best conceptualized as a preexisting condition without cure, which would continuously redound to the ill health of their interaction. "The tale of Franco-American harmony is a long-standing and pernicious myth," declared the two authors. "The French attitude toward the United States consistently has been one of cultural suspicion and political dislike, bordering at times on raw hatred . . . that occasionally erupted into violent hostility. France is not America's oldest ally, but its oldest enemy."[32]

Here, in a nutshell, we find the starkest exposition imaginable of the Erbfeindschaft thesis. Here, as well, is presentism with a vengeance. The roots of hostility not only stretched down far into the Franco-American past but also were buried in soil made toxic through the ugliest possible expression of cultural politics, which in more recent times has come to be conceptualized through the social-scientific category "ethnic conflict." To take the proper measure of a bilateral relationship Miller and Molesky knew to be destructively and irremediably dysfunctional, one must dig deeply into that poisoned past. "The true story of Franco-American relations begins many years before the American Revolution, during the French and Indian Wars. . . . French military officers used massacres as weapons of imperial terror against the hardy men, women, and children who settled the frontier. . . . America's first authentic sense of self was born not in a revolt against Britain, but in a struggle with France."[33]

Startling words, perhaps, but what the two authors were claiming apropos of those "French and Indian Wars" was not, empirically, really very controversial. At least, it was not controversial to those who knew their North American colonial history and were under no illusions that nearly a century of Franco-American interaction prior to 1778 could be, at best, written off as being of no account and, at worst, distorted so as to represent some kind of interlude of antique geopolitical bliss.[34] To the contrary, as we saw in chapter 2, an excellent case can be made that no foreign country has *ever*, to this very day, posed a greater existential threat to Americans' physical security in their homeland than France. Moreover, if we employ the contemporary label of ethnic conflict to capture the significance of that long era of Franco-American strife, we get a better sense of what was at stake in that strife, and how it unfolded.

But does it follow that there continues to exist meaningful policy relevance derived from a past so demonstrably replete with awful happenings? It is not that those incidents were anything other than gruesome; no informed student of the era of intercolonial warfare argues otherwise. What is disputable, however, is the contention that today's Americans remember enough (if anything) about that distant past that it would be capable of shaping their country's contemporary policy toward France.

In this regard, it would be difficult to improve upon Gore Vidal's characterization of Americans' historical consciousness: "We are permanently the United States of Amnesia. We learn nothing because we remember nothing."[35] Others have harbored similar views about Americans as not being a people much given to historical introspection. At the close of the 1990s, the American Council of Trustees and Alumni commissioned a survey of fifty-five of the country's elite postsecondary institutions to determine how historically literate current undergraduates were. The study, conducted by the Center for Survey Research and Analysis at the University of Connecticut, produced some disturbing findings, the most important of which was that "our future leaders are graduating with an alarming ignorance of their heritage—a kind of collective amnesia—and a profound historical illiteracy which bodes ill for the future of the republic." Had the center's exercise taken the form of one of their classroom exams rather than a commissioned survey, fully two-thirds of the students would have flunked, with only 2 percent managing an A.

All respondents seemed to know well enough who Snoop Doggy Dogg was, and even who Beavis and Butthead were, but confusion reigned when topics of lesser importance to their lives were broached. A majority thought it was Ulysses S. Grant rather than George Washington who received the surrender of Britain's General Cornwallis at Yorktown. A third of them believed the Battle of the Bulge had taken place in the First World War. And so their answers went, leading the study's disconsolate commissioners to query, "Beavis and Butthead instead of Washington and Madison; Snoop Doggy Dogg instead of Lincoln? How did it come to this?"[36]

We might reasonably conclude that during the two ensuing decades since this survey was conducted, Americans' historical consciousness has become even more dulled, given what Shoshana Zuboff rightly terms the "epistemic chaos" inflicted upon the public mind by "antisocial media" that is responsible for the distressing dumbing down of civic discourse.[37] At least we might so conclude with respect to foreign policy. But defective memorization skills do not necessarily imply the absence of a sense of the past, for when it comes to *domestic* politics, as witnessed by the renewed focus upon the country's racial divisions, America certainly seems to be a land in which the Faulknerian past lives on, and on, and on—even though anything remotely approaching a fact-based understanding of that past continues to be so elusive and controversial. Nor is America alone in this respect; there are any number of countries that have a tough time shaking off history when it comes to their domestic politics.

But what about the foreign policy implications, which really is what Vidal had in mind in his condemnatory comments about deficient historical memory? Might it be that his commentary, despite his intent, actually reflects a positive rather than a negative attribute, at least insofar as it concerns the foreign policy implications of past ethnic conflict, the focus of this chapter's analysis? There are a great number of countries, in fact far too many, about which it can be said that the historical legacy of past ethnic animosity continues to agitate passions, with powerful implications for contemporary foreign policy. So while Vidal might be right in detecting historical amnesia, he may be wrong in holding this necessarily to be a bad thing. In foreign policy, sometimes a little forgetfulness can go a long way to assist the cause of peace. And when the topic being forgotten is the record of past ethnic hatred, amnesia could be just what the doctor ordered. There is a reason, after all, that a leading global nongovernmental organization, dedicated to the promotion of human rights, has chosen to call itself Amnesty International.

Anyone tempted to believe that keen historical memories constitute an unalloyed good for international relations should contemplate the Balkans, a region populated by Faulknerians with a viselike grip on a past they persist in keeping alive, many of whom cannot and will not concede that a battle that took place on June 23, 1389[!], should cease to animate current and future political fantasies.[38] Perhaps even more pertinent is the deranged behavior of Vladimir Putin, who is giving every impression that as far as he is concerned, the Battle of Poltava took place the day before yesterday rather than back in 1709, and the memory of that fight inspires (in his mind, at least) the idea that Russians and Ukrainians are one and the same, thus supporting the perverse logic of his bludgeoning the latter in his misbegotten 2022 war.[39]

These cases might provide reason to believe that perhaps the "oldest enemy" imagery of Miller and Molesky is not so misguided after all. The North American deep historical context to which the two authors make reference is a lot closer to our own times than are the deeds that transpired at Kosovo Polje in 1389, and Poltava was more or less contemporaneous with the events they describe. The crux of their Erbfeindschaft thesis is to be found in the thought that states can and do have hereditary foes, and that for the US,

France empirically *has* to be styled as just such a foe. Some scholars go a bit further and tell us that states not only have such foes but even *need* to have them, if for no other reason than that their citizenry may know who they, themselves, are.[40] If this is so as a general aspect of interstate relations, why should it not also have applicability to the question of Franco-American strategic interaction? Perhaps, then, Miller and Molesky are not so wrong to assess this bilateral relationship from the perspective of hereditary ethnic enmity.

Perhaps. But there are reasons to doubt they are right. One reason we encountered already. Americans appear to lack any "granular" recollection of the past, to put it charitably, when it comes to foreign policy.[41] Another reason is that the ancestral enmity trope seems to contradict traditional understandings of the nature and meaning of nationalism as it has developed in both the United States and France, ever since the countries' respective revolutions of the late eighteenth century. Both countries have often been heralded as embodying, in every fiber of their respective constitutional fabrics, the very antithesis of a politics of ethnicity, at least when it is domestic policy that is being shaped. In particular, each in its own way is said to represent the rejection of that disreputable conceptual accompaniment of ethnicity known as ethnonationalism. Instead, we are instructed, if the two states stand for nationalism at all, it is in the different, and benign, sense connoted by the label "civic" nationalism.[42] This variant of nationalism has even been heralded as constituting the best that Western civilization offers the world, a set of political ordering principles "based upon the belief in the equal rights of all, irrespective of religion, ancestry, or class; upon the concern for the dignity and humanity of every individual; and upon the right to intellectual and political opposition and criticism."[43]

Surely, then, it is more than a bit perverse to suggest that ethnicity might play—or at least, might have played—a part in undermining cooperative relations between two such paragons of enlightened republicanism as the United States and France.[44] They, of all countries, deserve to be exempted from the suspicion that ethnic hatreds could possibly have left lasting contaminating traces upon their bilateral relationship, for, whatever their differences, the pair remain what they have been for more than two centuries: exemplars of republican (and therefore civic) virtue. They are the world's most important and accomplished "sister republics."[45] Nor is this all that might be said to be odd about attempting to examine their bilateral relationship through the conceptual lenses of ethnicity and ethnic conflict, because for some scholars, the concept of ethnicity is nothing if not hazy, and the concept of ethnic conflict makes so little sense as to be virtually meaningless when applied to any relationship—and is veritably absurd when associated with the Franco-American one.

Still, it may be that the critics overshoot the mark and that their strictures regarding the Erbfeindschaft hypothesis are misplaced. At the very least, we can speculate that if history truly is supposed to matter, in foreign as well as in domestic policy, then it might be worthwhile to plumb the initial conditions of Franco-American strategic interaction, and to do so from the coign of vantage of ethnic conflict. The value in doing this presumably exists, even though so very few today can recall those initial conditions. It is, after all, possible that policymakers themselves might sense a great deal more staying power in the historical record than the vast majority of their citizenry understand—so much so as to render irrelevant the defective collective memory. The policymakers may not know the difference between Beavis and Butthead, but we can be confident that they can distinguish Grant from Washington. In the next section, then, we will explore those Franco-American initial conditions from a perspective that begins with social-scientific conceptualizations about ethnic conflict.

"Ethnic Conflict" in Franco-American Relations

Among social scientists who study the perplexing phenomenon of ethnicity (and its spawn, ethnic conflict) in global politics, there tends to be a strict demarcation between a majority who take their concept(s) to be fundamentally ideational and a minority who are suspected of wanting to invest ethnicity with "essential" qualities. Of these latter, it is charitably said that they fail to realize that reality is socially constructed. Less charitably, they are taxed with being "primordialists" who read too much meaning into such ostensible markers of ethnicity as language or skin color, or both, and not enough into the realm of ideas and ideology. As a result, they fail to recognize the more or less optional nature of identity, which can be adopted and shed with surprising ease, as the occasion warrants.[46]

In so many ways, this distinction can be said to be more apparent than real. Is there anyone, anywhere, who would dispute that social reality is, and has to be, what observers tend to make of it? As one leading scholar of ethnicity comments, "Real-world primordialists and constructivists agree that identities are constructed . . . during some identifiable period in history, that their symbolic content can vary to some degree over time, and that there is at least some variation in the intensity or nature of group identification across members."[47] Nor is this a particularly new and original manner of grasping the distinction, which did not spring into view only in the 1960s, with Peter Berger and Thomas Luckmann's seminal work on the "social construction of reality."[48] Indeed, as far back as 1919 the great French historian Lucien Febvre was instructing his students that the "spirit" of history was and had to be idealist, because "all . . . social facts, are facts of belief and opinion. Are not wealth, work and money not 'things' but human ideas, representations and judgements of things?"[49] One could go back to well before Febvre's time, for instance to the end of the seventeenth century, and recall John Locke's similar observation about meaning being "arbitrary, the result of social convention."[50]

It does not follow from this that social actors are immune or otherwise resistant to fashioning their identity largely out of primordialist bricks and mortar; to the contrary, this is a fairly regular activity on their construction sites.[51] One of those sites might even happen to be the place where the foundation of the Franco-American relationship has been laid. For this reason, ethnic identity has sometimes been said to be the single most relevant clue for solving the puzzle of that relationship's suboptimality. Ethnic conflict, in this view, is not just something applicable to fairly recent developments in the post-Soviet space or in what used to be called the Third World, before we began to speak of the Global South. It is something as old as human history, and it is as unrestricted in its geographic settings as in its temporal ones. In North America, it had a particularly bloody run within the strip of frontier separating the French and British empires.

To speak of that continental strip as the site of ethnic conflict can be jarring, because if ethnicity is a contested concept in social science,[52] the notion of ethnic conflict is even more contested. Ethnic conflict is interpreted in two major ways, each linked to the distinction between the constructivists and the primordialists. While the primordialists have little difficulty believing that animosities between culturally distinct groups can—and will continue to— spill over into violent clashes precisely *because* of those cultural differences,[53] many constructivists want to put the causal emphasis elsewhere, such as upon the deliberate manipulation of sentimentality by unscrupulous or even criminal agitators, so that what often is trumpeted as ethnic conflict really turns out to be something much different. In the words of one who is skeptical that the notion adds very much to our understanding of reality, if "ethnic war" is supposed to connote a kind of Hobbesian struggle of "all against all and neighbor against neighbor, [then] ethnic war essentially does not exist." Instead, what is often mistakenly identified as pent-up communal hatred finally getting uncorked is "something far more banal: the creation of communities of criminal violence and pillage," inspired by nonideological thugs.[54]

There even are some scholars who would have us abandon altogether the category of ethnic conflict, which they dismiss as little more than a conceptual "holding pen for a herd of disparate descriptive events,"[55] if not an outright myth.[56] The abolitionists' case primarily centers upon causality, and those who make the argument seem to prefer trying to situate the locus of conflict elsewhere than in behavioral responses associated with perceptions of ethnic difference. There may be merit in the argument that we should restrict, if not eliminate altogether, the concept of ethnic conflict, but if so, it cannot rest entirely (if at all) on the belief that some other causal agent than ethnicity can be more credibly implicated in the onset of violence, given the aleatory nature of the search for reliable causality, irrespective of whatever "independent variable" happens to be spurring that search. At the risk of siding with an essentialism that appears decidedly old-fashioned, I will begin this inquiry by asking whether the controversial notion of ethnic conflict might tell us something about the state of relations between our two sister republics, possibly even down to the present time.

Should we pose the question thusly, we could turn to two groups of scholars to help us frame our investigation: psychologists and historians. Let us start with the psychologists, to see how they might help us make a connection between present and past. For those who study the collectivity's impact upon the individual's consciousness, particularly the social psychologists, Erbfeindschaft turns out to be less an outcome of specific patterns of culturally mediated behavior than a generalized predicament of collectivities anywhere, best subsumed under the broader concept of ethnocentrism.[57] They might agree that the modern pattern of suboptimal cooperation between France and America has its origins in the past, but they would certainly not express much surprise about this. Instead, they would see the two collectivities (the French and the Americans) as having gotten off on the wrong foot, less out of design than out of circumstance—in this case, the circumstance of their happening to have been neighbors at an unfortunate historical moment, when the North American continent could still be characterized as a "dominion of war" rather than as the "zone of peace" that it eventually became.[58]

Propinquity in any part of the world can easily be related to conflict, given that neighbors have not always tended to act in any noticeably "neighborly" way toward each other, a reality that Ukrainians are only the latest people to so tragically confront. Far too many neighbors, even today, continue to bristle at the thought of interacting peaceably with the folk across the line. Why should anyone expect things to have been different for the French and the Americans in the early years of their North American cohabitation, especially considering that the Americans were a mere extension of the people who truly *were* France's hereditary foes? Those were France's near neighbor in Europe: the English.[59]

Throw into the mix the currently voguish and unavoidably cultural category of identity, and it might even appear as if the social science case for Erbfeindschaft becomes overdetermined. Admittedly, by the time they began to bump up against each other in the New World, the French and the Americans were at radically different stages of their own national identity formation. In fact, the French were so far along in the process of figuring out who they were that they had little need for a next-door, and hostile, Other in North America to serve as a handy means of cultivating a sense of themselves.[60]

This is not to say that introspection about the real meaning of Frenchness ceased after the formation of the modern French state, during what some label the "beautiful" sixteenth century. To the contrary, trying to uncover the essential core of French ethnic identity—was it the Gauls? the Romans? the Franks? the Trojans?—continued to be a popular pastime well into the nineteenth century and even beyond.[61] And as time went on, this voyage of discovery would increasingly pivot around the notion of an Anglo-Saxon counter identity against which could be constructed a French political identity, even if not a totally essentialist, ethnic, one.[62] So if only by dint of being a large representative of those Anglo-Saxons, Americans have of late (as we will discover in chapters 4 and 5) been known to stimulate anxiety in France, stemming from concerns about French identity.

But things were different for the Americans, and here is where the social psychologists have some thoughts to offer regarding Erbfeindschaft. For them, the French were very significant (and dangerous) Others from the earliest stages of their existence as a territorially embedded collectivity. As we saw, there are theorists who emphasize the cognitive necessity for budding collectivities to possess an enemy; if they are correct, then it is far from difficult to comprehend the service provided willy-nilly by France in the construction of American identity. According to this understanding of identity building, all national groupings, no matter where (or when) they have emerged, have been greatly influenced by the presence of their significant Other, some "nation or ethnic group that is territorially close to, or indeed within, the national community and threatens, or rather is perceived to threaten, its ethnic and/or cultural purity and/or its independence."[63] Thus, one's own national consciousness takes shape, necessarily, because of the contributions of another, who might not even have willed, much less desired, such an outcome.

Nor do social psychologists have the field of Erbfeindschaft all to themselves. For their part, the historians rely less on theories about collectivities and identity formation and much more on actual happenings when they come to grips with the postulated hereditary enmity in relations between the French and the Americans. It is not that they must be indifferent or even opposed to the notion that one's own national identity can often be coaxed into being by the existence of a significant Other able to stand as an *a contrario* testament to one's own self-consciousness, to say nothing of one's self-valorization. Indeed, some historians openly accept the vital if unintended impact of France upon the formation of American political culture.[64]

But more important than the theory are the facts on the ground. Those facts are the cumulation of bellicose events that turned so much of the territory separating the respective heartlands of the French and British holdings in North America into a killing ground for nearly three-quarters of a century. They are the evidentiary foundation of an inductive, narrative-based account that establishes ethnic conflict, and therefore Erbfeindschaft, as a legitimate—indeed necessary—element in the history of the Franco-American special relationship. Contrary to the assertions of Miller and Molesky, among others, this does not mean that the ancestral hatred somehow continues to inspire foreign policy behavior. But it does mean that a fuller understanding of how the bilateral relationship has evolved requires the recognition that if there ever were such things as initial conditions in Franco-American relations, Erbfeindschaft points us in the direction of deciphering them.

So let us take a look at those facts on the ground through the conceptual prism of ethnic conflict, which is taken to suggest "a sense of incompatible vital interests [that] generates hostility; and that this hostility, if sufficiently intense, finds expression, under specifiable circumstances . . . in deadly attacks of members of the opposing group."[65] We begin with what might be said to be the two defining qualities of such conflict. First, it features violence directed at civilian populations of a differing ethnicity, who are regarded as being not only legitimate but also choice targets of brutal attack, a principal aim thereof being to sow terror. Second, a major objective of ethnic conflict is the purging of specified ethnic communities from geographically defined territories—the "cleansing" of such communities from these regions. On both counts, it is apparent that if we are to use the disputed category of ethnic conflict anywhere and at any time, then the frontier separating French and English holdings on the North American continent during the seventeenth and eighteenth centuries more than fills the bill as a setting for such contestation.[66]

We can make three observations about the conflict between the French and the Anglo-Americans during the formative decades of their not-so-peaceful coexistence: the conflict was frequent; it was bloody, more in terms of relative than absolute numbers of casualties, but also in the brutal manner in which the casualties were incurred; and it did result in territorial cleansing of ethnic groups, either via their mass transfer from territories in which they had already settled or by preventing them from settling in the first place.

With respect to the frequency of strife between Americans and their French neighbors in North America, it has to be said that hardly had Britain and France begun to establish a toehold on the North American continent than they began to fight each other. For instance, in 1613 Captain Samuel Argall attacked Acadia; in 1629 the French Huguenot David Kirke took Quebec for England and held it for three years, until it was handed back in the Treaty of Saint-Germain-en-Laye; and in 1654 Oliver Cromwell ordered Robert Sedgwick of Boston to take Port Royal and other sites on the Bay of Fundy, only to have these returned to France in 1667 with the Treaty of Breda, which ended the Second Anglo-Dutch War.[67]

To be sure, those earliest military operations do not warrant being branded instances of ethnic conflict. Instead, they featured small-scale and fairly mild applications of force, according to traditional European norms of warfare, and as a result they had little in common with what was to come in

North America, later in the seventeenth century and into the eighteenth. Besides, territories seized in these initial skirmishes, far from being "cleansed" of their possessors, were routinely handed back to them. It would not be until the onset of the first of the colonial wars—called variously in Europe the War of the League of Augsburg, the Nine Years' War, or the Palatinate War but remembered in North America (to the extent it is recalled at all) more commonly as King William's War—that the era of ethnic conflict between the French and the Americans would begin in earnest.

There had been instances of ethnic strife in North America prior to the outbreak of the intercolonial wars, but these did not directly pit French against English. To the extent that the continent's European inhabitants were involved in them at all, these earlier episodes featured sanguinary struggles in which both French and English fought, separately, against their respective Indigenous adversaries. For the French, this meant the Iroquois, with whom a long conflict commenced in 1609 and reached its crescendo of brutality with the raid on Lachine, eighty years later, in August 1689, costing more than one hundred French inhabitants their lives.[68] For those Americans who were the immediate neighbors of the French on the continent, primarily the New Englanders, the fighting began with the short war of 1637 against the Pequots, only to reignite in the vastly more deadly King Philip's War of 1675–1676.[69]

King Philip's War pitted the New England colonies of Plymouth, Massachusetts Bay, Rhode Island, and Connecticut, alongside Indigenous allies— the Pequots and Mohegans, and to the west of the embattled region, the Mohawks, who were cobelligerents if not exactly allies—against a coalition led by Philip (also known as Metacom, sometimes Metacomet) and his Wampanoags, supported by fellow Algonquians—the Nipmucks, Pocumtucks, Narragansetts, and Abenakis.[70] The war was noteworthy in foreshadowing the ethnic conflict that would lie ahead for the region, in both its brutality and its costliness. For each coalition, it could and did appear to be a fight to the finish, nothing short of a "war of extermination," to determine who would preside over, or even get to live in, the disputed territory.[71] In the words of one historian, not since the early (or "beachhead") years of settlement on the continent had the English come so close to being driven from North America as they had in 1676.[72]

On a per capita basis (that is, the rate of casualties suffered by the total population, both combatant and noncombatant), this short war is generally remembered, when it is remembered at all, as the bloodiest in American history, not excluding even the Civil War. More than half of the English settlements (fifty-two out of a total of ninety) were attacked during the year of fighting, with thirteen being destroyed, while some 10 percent of the combat-eligible English males ended up as casualties. High though the rate of casualties may have been among the English, it paled in comparison with the losses sustained by their Native adversaries (both combatant and noncombatant). At the start of the war, Philip's army counted 2,900 combatants out of a total Indigenous population of 11,000; within a year, some 2,430 combatants and noncombatants had been killed or captured, and most of the Algonquian survivors had fled the region.[73] The question as to who would dominate the region—English or Algonquian—looked to have been finally settled.

Those appearances might well have translated into reality had not a new existential challenge—for a while, greater even than that pitting settler against Indigenous inhabitant—appeared in the aftermath of King Philip's War. This challenge was posed by none other than the transatlantic world's most powerful state, France, which had established a presence in lands to the north and, increasingly as time went by, to the west of the frontiers of English settlement. By the time of King Philip's War, some in New England already were convinced (wrongly) that a French hand had been orchestrating the Algonquian military campaign. Shortly after the war's end, it was becoming understood, correctly this time, that France would be an ever-growing menace to American interests, so much so that at times the specter of English settlement being pushed into the sea loomed large. It was not a specter that sober calculation of power balances on the North American continent should have nourished, given that at the time of King Philip's War, English inhabitants of the continent outnumbered the French by a margin of more than twenty to one—a margin that never would diminish over the course of the next century.

Still, the English were characterized by nothing so much as their disunity, making their real military capability much less than the sum of their fractious parts. In addition, only half of the English (around 100,000) lived in New England and New York, the provinces most at risk when the colonial contests began. In theory, France should be able to vastly upgrade its own military presence on the continent, being at the time indisputably Europe's ranking military power, with a homeland population that stood at 20 million, nearly six times that of its British enemy.[74]

For good measure, France also could tap into a network of effective Native alliances, something New England could hardly do after the carnage of 1675–1676, which all but depopulated the region of its original inhabitants. While New York may have been able to seek support from the Iroquois, the latter were careful to pick the wars in which they would join, meaning that there were considerable stretches after the "great peace" of 1701 with the French during which the Iroquois opted for neutrality rather than alliance with the English.[75] To the English, therefore, the threat seemed real enough in their northernmost zones of settlement on the continent, where in the decades following 1676, "French influence among the more remote tribes was increasing, giving a dark hint as to the nature of coming wars."[76]

This is why it is so wrong to misconstrue the early wars of the intercolonial period as being either of no great significance or as having been conflicts inflicted upon the inhabitants of England's and France's North American holdings by the imperial powers. This is the approach of Andrew Bacevich, for instance, when he notes that many of America's wars have largely dimmed in collective consciousness, with some of them being "altogether forgotten," including the "several wars fought against the French at England's behest prior to 1776." He is correct to note that those wars have largely slipped from memory but incorrect to imply that in the first three of the intercolonial wars, Americans were fighting not for their own interests but for those of London.[77]

French scholar Maya Kandel writes that these wars, and especially the first two of them, set the standard for the earliest American military culture, stamped as it was by a need to crush the enemy, whose very presence constituted an existential threat.[78] She could have said the same with respect to the military culture of New France. In French, this period is often styled as the *petite guerre,* but there was nothing small about its consequences for those who lived the daily reality of the period of ethnic conflict that spanned nearly a quarter century, from 1689 until 1713, with few interludes of peace.[79]

It may well have been that the two wars constituted a sideshow for the metropolitan powers back in Europe, but that is not what they looked like to those living on or near the killing fields of the frontier. For the inhabitants of the frontier, the first two wars provided a traumatic glimpse of life, which often turned out to be, in Thomas Hobbes's famous formulation, "nasty, brutish, and short."[80] Though it was published at the end of the nineteenth century, Samuel Adams Drake's assessment of the two wars' existential meaning has stood the test of time. "A twenty-years' war, practically contin-uous," he asserted, "would certainly constitute a critical period in the history of any people, but to one only just beginning to take firm root in the soil, and to stretch out a few feeble branches into the wilderness, it was really a ques-tion of life or death. It was the strategy of the enraged enemy to lop off these branches and thus prevent the growth of, if not finally kill, the tree itself."[81]

That these wars merit being deemed ethnic conflicts has everything to do with the tactical and strategic qualities of such conflicts: brutal attacks on soft targets intended to terrorize civilian populations, with the objective being to rid a territory of a particular ethnic group or to keep it empty of such a population, or both. In the first of the wars, King William's (1689–1697), the brunt of the fighting that ensued after the Lachine raid (which was really an episode in the long-standing conflict between Iroquois and French, before it became the spark that touched off the first of the intercolonial contests) was borne by settlers on the New York frontier, as well as those in northern New England. The major raids of that war took place early against civilian targets in frontier communities—in February 1690 in New York's Mohawk Val-ley, against Schenectady;[82] the following month in New Hampshire, against Salmon Falls; and then in May in Maine, against Casco. The raids left some one hundred settlers dead, contributing mightily to sowing terror along the frontier and thus to deterring further English settlement.

Though the casualty toll might seem slight when registered in absolute numbers, its impact upon the collective psyche was anything but slight, with the fighting on the northern frontier being "frighteningly reminiscent of the opening of King Philip's War" and constituting one more sign that "God had manifestly turned His countenance from a people unworthy to be chosen as He had once chosen them."[83] This mood, some scholars suggest, was respon-sible for generating the hysteria that swept through the Massachusetts village of Salem during the winter of 1691–1692, where it was easy for inhabitants to give credence to conspiracy theories about Satan's accomplices.

In all, during that first war, it is likely that 650 Anglo-Americans (mostly New Englanders) were either killed in raids or died in captivity, while the French suffered about 300 dead, with their Native allies losing a further 100. The Iroquois bore the heaviest relative burden of all, with some 650 lives lost, a toll that contributed directly to their deciding to sit out the next two colonial wars.[84] To put the Anglo-American and French losses in perspective, around one in every 230 inhabitants perished, or some .0043 of the European population in the English and French parts of North America. Projected onto current population levels in North America, this would be comparable to Canada losing 140,000 in a war, or the United States losing 1.35 million.

Although the absolute death toll was lighter during the second of these two existential clashes, Queen Anne's War (1702–1713), this conflict, known in Europe as the War of the Spanish Succession, did provide a more long-lived symbolic touchstone for Erbfeindschaft: the Deerfield raid of February 29, 1704. Deerfield, a settlement in the western reaches of Massachusetts, was not a strategically important place. Nor was the attack on it any new depar- ture in ethnic cleansing, being a virtual reproduction of the Schenectady raid of the earlier war, save that this time the attacking force was much larger (at 250 French and Natives), as were the numbers of young children slain in the attack, though the overall death toll among the defenders (about 50) was ac- tually about a dozen fewer than at Schenectady. In fact, it was far from having been the first time that the village's inhabitants had experienced the horrors of ethnic conflict, as it had been a site of battle during King Philip's War and had even known sporadic fighting years prior to that struggle.[85]

Until the raid slipped from memory, future generations would mostly re- call Deerfield as a scene of infamy—the Pearl Harbor or 9/11 of its day—and not just because of the numbers slain or even because of the grisly manner in which they met their ends. Once again, a surprise attack launched from a great distance and in the dead of winter had laid waste a sleeping town, whose inhabitants would come face to face with the "terrifying brutality" of guerrilla warfare with a depressingly familiar North American flavor.[86] However, it was mainly the fate of the 112 captives taken back to New France to live among their irreligious or—nearly as bad—Roman Catholic captors that caught the attention of contemporaneous New Englanders. This was due, in no small measure, to the 1707 publication of *The Redeemed Captive Returning to Zion*, the account written by the Reverend John Williams, the most celebrated former hostage seized at Deerfield.[87]

Deerfield notwithstanding, there were fewer deaths in the second colonial war than in the first, even though it lasted three years longer than the earlier contest. Following the end of Queen Anne's War, an uneasy peace, punctu- ated by intermittent raiding, would prevail along the frontier separating New

England from New France for another generation.[88] That pinchbeck peace came to an end with the outbreak of the third, and in one ironic way, most relevant of the intercolonial wars, from the Erbfeindschaft perspective. King George's War (1743–1748), known in Europe as the War of the Austrian Succession, was important not so much because it was the same kind of existential struggle for New Englanders as had been the two earlier wars. It was not that kind of struggle, for by this time the demographic imbalance was weighing even more heavily in favor of the English and against the French, with around 1.5 million living in Britain's colonies, compared with a population of New France that was sluggishly approaching 60,000. Instead, this third intercolonial conflict, sometimes later known in North America as the Old French War, was important because it signaled the potential for the start of a new and different era in what would become Franco-American relations—an era that would, contrary to the Erbfeindschaft thesis, open up the possibility for a new historical path to emerge in relations between the French and Americans, though no one alive at the time would have been able to sense this.

Historical Context as Relational Realism?

It is not difficult to understand why the Erbfeindschaft thesis ultimately cannot be adjudged a persuasive one, notwithstanding that it—like so many theories in the human sciences—can boast of some considerable store of forensic evidence, as we saw in the previous section's historical discussion. But to generalize from that evidence, as some have been tempted to do, and to use it as the basis for an "explanation" of the peculiar and *ongoing* qualities of the Franco-American relationship really is an imaginative leap of death-defying dimensions. Indeed, it is just as absurd to focus on the "oldest enemy" imagery as it is to wax enthusiastic about the reverse trope of "old allies, great friends."

If the only charge against the Erbfeindschaft thesis were the one contained in Gore Vidal's indictment of Americans as amnesiacs, that would be grave enough. After all, how can the citizenry's nationalist blood be brought to the boil by agonizing memories of past indignities if the public has no recollection of that past to begin with? But even assuming a more refined collective understanding of that past, it still would be necessary to take into consideration other aspects of the historical record, including and especially those that speak to a different quality of relations from that of enmity. Insofar as contemporary Americans are concerned, amnesiacs or not, it is simply ludicrous to imagine that there exists a sizable contingent of French haters among them. Whether we can say that there is a similarly tiny component of the population of contemporary France prepared to harbor sinister thoughts about the *ennemi américain*[89] remains a very different question, which will be more fully addressed in chapter 5.

So if America and France are neither old enemies nor old friends, what are they? In the previous chapters, I indicated that they constitute a special behavioral category within the network of each other's transatlantic cohort of states, a dyad that can and does experience cooperative comportment, though not on so regular or satisfactory a basis as either enjoys with respect to most, if not all, of their other cooperating partners. This is, in the deft expression of André Kaspi, the "différend franco-américain."[90] America and France are neither the fish of enemies nor the fowl of good buddies. They get along, as I explained in part 1, in a cooperative manner that could be worse but also could be better. It is a manner of cooperation, to reiterate, that is known by and through its suboptimality. Moreover, the source of this cooperative manner can be found somewhere in the multifarious dimensions of culture.

To the extent that historical context can be held to represent one of those cultural dimensions, and thus to be freighted with some portion of responsibility for this suboptimality, it has to account for dispositions other than those highlighted by the Erbfeindschaft thesis. This is so, irrespective of whether we believe that historical context must be otherwise informed by the cultural attribute we know of as ethnicity (a prospect to which we return in chapter 4). In a word, if we are going to insist, as so many strategic culturalists would do, that history "matters," then perhaps we might find it worthwhile to turn our gaze for a while away from both the psychologists and the historians and direct it toward the historical sociologists. We already met some of them at the end of chapter 2, when discussion focused on the distinction between scholars who extrapolated from initial conditions, which is what the Erbfeindschaft theorists do, and those who understand history's "mattering" to be a function of path dependence.

Among the latter is a historical sociologist whom we did not encounter in the previous chapter, Margaret Somers. From her I have borrowed the notion of "relational realism," an exceptionally well-chosen rubric for assessing how historical context, stripped of its initial-conditions presuppositions, might account for the quality of suboptimality in the Franco-American relationship. She was, I hasten to add, hardly seeking to make any claims whatsoever about that special relationship, and even had she sought to do this, it would assuredly not have been from any paradigmatic perch in the tree of international relations theory. As with Paul Pierson, whom we did encounter in chapter 2, Margaret Somers's main scholarly focus has been on topics leagues removed from either IR theory or foreign policy analysis—in her case topics associated with political economy, social change, and historical epistemology, all of which she approaches from an academic discipline different from Pierson's own political science realm.

Somers is a sociologist, yet what she has to say about historical epistemology speaks volumes about Franco-American suboptimality, and does so from a perspective that might even, with a bit of conceptual adjustment, be argued to be a strategic-cultural one. Her claims were advanced in a skillful critique of two fellow sociologists, testimony to the wisdom contained in the old saw regarding turnabout being fair play. The critique appeared toward the end of the 1990s, in the *American Journal of Sociology*, which was featuring a forum on rational choice theory in the sociology profession. The object of Somers's attention was an article written by Edgar Kiser and Michael Hechter, defending rational choice as the epitome of proper sociology, construed from the point of view of proper science.[91]

Somers skewered the two self-proclaimed positivists not only for engaging in metaphysics rather than proper science but also for not even being good positivists, given the causal prowess they were assigning to variables that were empirically unobservable. In particular, she focused on their core concept of rationally motivated action, something that they asserted as the theoretical explanation for decision-making but never actually substantiated as such. Precisely because the two scholars were essentially taking matters of primordial explanatory importance on faith, she said, "they are . . . forcefully *antipositivist* in their commitment to rational choice's *theory-driven* logic of social analysis and causal mechanism. . . . Kiser and Hechter's ontology of agents-as-mechanisms invokes a world populated by 'angels'—ontological entities that, implicitly, are not of this social world. . . . A world of angels may be parsimonious and convenient to theorize, but—disappointing, to be sure—we're no angels."[92]

Against what she termed Kiser's and Hechter's "theoretical realism" (in a philosophical rather than any traditional IR sense of the paradigm),[93] Somers advanced a different extrapolation of philosophical realism, which she called "relational realism." Her explanation of what this other realist variant implies is compelling. Like Kiser and Hechter, she is convinced that reliable causality can be established; unlike them, however, she insists that history, understood as the process through which events unfold, must be central, not peripheral, to the quest. Relational realists, she tells us, acknowledge their debt to historians, for it is the historians' method of representing "the nature of that to be known," through narratives capable of revealing the unfolding of historical sequences, that refute claims about "essences" devoid of any relational context. Reality, in a word, is socially constructed and therefore necessarily a relational matter. "In place of a language of essences and inherent causal properties," she writes, "a relational realism substitutes a language of networks and relationships that are not predetermined but made the indeterminate objects of investigation. Relational subjects are not related to each other in the weak sense of being only empirically contiguous; they are ontologically related such that an identity can only be deciphered by virtue of its 'place' in relationship to other identities in its web."[94]

We recognize, from discussion of culture as context in chapter 2, some familiar themes in this passage from Somers, related to how strategic culture can be enriched by some borrowings from path dependency and "narrative causation." One of those borrowed items is the notion of contingency. Another, less evident, contextual element, also discussed in chapter 2 and critiqued in the Somers article, is the essentialism that figures so largely in analyses predicated upon national character, updated as those analyses now may be by the substitution of identity for character.

Ironically, Somers's relational realism can tell us a lot about national character/national identity as a cultural variable with significance to Franco-American suboptimality. The place to begin discerning how it might do this is not where chapter 2 left off but rather where it began, with François Marie Perrin du Lac's 1805 quip that "the guiding principle of Americans seems to be never to do anything as we do."[95] As I noted in that chapter, some have interpreted Perrin's comment as evidence of the temperamental aspect of Franco-American relations, and thus as an essentialist component of one side's character (to Perrin, the Americans' side, because he was convinced that the French were eminently rational). But what it really tells us is more than that, for it speaks to the unavoidably relational meaning of national character/identity when it is employed as a cultural variable in foreign policy analysis.

What this means is that scholars who have zeroed in on the discretely "national" dimension(s) of character may have been missing their target all along. It is not so much the cultural traits of the individual states grasped in isolation that should capture our attention if we are bent upon trying to employ strategic culture in an explanatory manner, important as these traits may be. Instead, it is the dyadic package of interactions to which we should turn for guidance in understanding culture's impact. The relationship, not the individual components, can even be considered to be the carrier of culture, a proposition suggested more than a quarter century ago by one student of Franco-American relations, who argued that improving transatlantic relations could only come about through changing "the *culture* of US–French relations, because a history of mutual dislike among much of the elite and general public is not without its effect on relations between the two states" (emphasis added).[96]

Some might think that using the container rather than the contents as the referent object for culture is, at the very least, counterintuitive. But is it? Consider what one scholar of national character had to say, at a time when it was still possible to employ the concept in its original version rather than the updated one of national identity: "Predicting how two nations will interact by knowing the national character of only one of the nations will probably be as inexact as trying to predict the interaction between two chemical elements when the character of only one is known."[97]

We are going to see in a subsequent chapter just how "relational" an item Franco-American suboptimality can turn out to be. If scholars happen to believe that the French and the Americans have a tendency to get on each other's nerves, there may be good reasons for this—reasons that I will explore in chapter 5. But before we get into those next stages of our inquiry, we need to round off the discussion of historical context, by returning to the manner in which path dependence can and does become imbricated in strategic culture.

To pursue this line of inquiry, recall what was remarked during the conceptual analysis of strategic culture in chapter 2, the key thought that contingency is the mechanism by which path dependence might alter the course of the future in a direction different from the one that has presumably been foreordained by the initial conditions. That new course, or path, could be one in which cooperative outcomes would stem from institutional "lock-in" of cooperative gains already made; in effect, the relevant actors would catch a glimpse of the "shadow of the future"[98] and be able to arrange their interrelations in such a way as to ensure continued mutually beneficial (optimal) cooperation. The processes that yield this benign reproduction of cooperation are sometimes labeled "self-reinforcing sequences." At other times, however, path dependence results in the reproduction not of benign cooperation but of discord, generated by what are called "reactive sequences."[99]

Since suboptimality is the defining quality of the Franco-American special relationship (or so I maintain here), it appears obvious that insofar as path dependence can tell us anything about the bilateral relationship, it places us closer to the domain of reactive sequences than of self-reinforcing ones. The quality of their cooperation seems to be captured less by beneficent shadows of the future than by dark clouds lowering overhead, these clouds being the legacy (or the context) of their historical interactions. But—and this is important—it is *not* a legacy of unexpiated hatred. To carry on a bit further with this theme of culture as context, and context as history, if we must cast aside the utility of Erbfeindschaft, for reasons already given, where then should we look in "history," once the initial conditions of ethnic enmity are ruled out of bounds? Perhaps the answer is to be found in the notion of contingency. At least, this would seem to be our first investigatory port of call.

If it is, we would hardly find ourselves lacking for company on the port visit. In recent years, many political scientists who specialize in IR have developed a fascination with contingent events, those historical moments during which it is believed the course of the future was altered. Consider that if path dependence is to mean anything at all, it must mean that somewhere along the "causal chain" (in our case, the chain of Franco-American interaction in security and defense) there appeared a break point, after which the ability of those so-called initial conditions to shape the future began to weaken significantly. Typically, this break point is called contingency (or sometimes "critical junctures"), to represent what it was that enabled events to henceforth travel a path different from the one on which they had apparently been heading.

That, at least, is the theoretical gist. However, as many commentators have noted, pinpointing contingency is no easy matter, for it requires analysts to have confidence in their ability to identify those critical junctures that give contingency its meaning. This is a difficult task. In fact, it may well be an impossible undertaking, given that one scholar's contingent moment often can be just another's factoid. So some analysts have sought to try to separate the ore of contingency from the gangue of historical trivia by resorting to counterfactual analysis. In the words of two scholars who have studied critical junctures, the "reconstruction of plausible counterfactual scenarios, based on theoretically informed expectations and narrative reconstruction of the decision-making process supported by empirical evidence, is therefore key in this kind of analysis."[100] In short, asking different questions about a historical episode opens up the possibility of examining causal assumptions under a new and possibly better light.[101]

Louisbourg: Americans' Vimy Ridge?

In this section, following Jack Levy's advice, I am going to ask new questions about a historical episode, and in doing so draw to an end the discussion of historical context as somehow providing the key that unlocks the door leading from strategic culture to suboptimality in Franco-American defense and security cooperation. We turn once more from theoretical gist to empirical background, canvasing that very "deep" Franco-American past, with the goal of deriving some heuristic benefit by employing contingency, informed as it has to be by a bit of counterfactual analysis.

If we do go down this counterfactual route to establishing historical context, then at the very least we might be tempted to argue that the alliance of 1778 really *did* represent a fundamental turning point in what had previously been a pretty dismal relationship between the French and the Americans. In Levy's terms, we could even posit a counterfactual in which we take the *absence* of that first alliance as being the necessary condition (the "counterfactual antecedent") of the counterfactual past and then ask what bilateral relations might have looked like without the alliance. Doing this, we would be on solid enough ground for supposing that those initial conditions assumed by Erbfeindschaft theorists would have continued to exert their baneful influence into some indeterminate future. Our use of Levy's formulation "if not x, then not y" should lead us to the conclusion that enmity would have continued to be the default position of Franco-American interaction, had the alliance never been struck. The nonexistence of alliance, presumably, would have guaranteed the non-expunging of Erbfeindschaft.

Therefore, armed with equal parts hindsight and counterfactual reasoning, we might easily detect contingency's heavy hand in changing the course of the Franco-American future; it was the great transformation of 1778 that represented that heavy hand. There can be no question about the strategic significance of that year's alliance. While it would be difficult for anyone to take seriously the idea that American independence could never have been achieved without diplomatic, financial, and military support from France, it would be just as difficult to claim that independence could have been achieved so quickly in its absence.

However, there is a problem in regarding 1778 as *the* contingent moment, *the* critical juncture. Indeed, it raises as many questions as it answers. For starters, we would want to ask why the two erstwhile enemies decided, and were able, to alter their relationship in such a fundamental way when they did. The simple response, of course, would be that it was in the "interests" of each to do just this. America needed French support in its independence war against Britain, and France wanted to avenge itself against its European rival, which had recently bested it in another war, the Seven Years' War, which ended in 1763.[102] The American victory at Saratoga in the early autumn of 1777 provided the French with the evidence they needed to justify gambling on the American cause.

The more complicated answer, if we really were committed to unearthing contingency, would require us to establish how things had come to such a pass in the American relationship with Britain to make possible such a transformation in America's relationship with *France*. If interests are in no small way prefigured by identity, Americans must have considered themselves, some time prior to their declaration of independence on July 4, 1776, to have been growing less English, and to the extent they did so, it presumably rendered increasingly brittle the ethnic foundation of Erbfeindschaft, at least insofar as this had been predicated on age-old strife between English and French, as many maintain it had been.

This is why placing overweening importance on 1778 as the critical juncture leads us to overlook an equally important (some say, more important) development on the path to an altered Franco-American future. Metaphorically speaking, 1778 is low-hanging fruit for the contingency harvesters. Tantalizing as it may be pick it, our search for contingency should take us to other temporal orchards. Since an American alliance with France would have been a logical absurdity in the absence of an American separation from Britain, the occurrence of such a separation must have betokened an unbridgeable ontological rift between the two English-speaking communities. It follows, then, that the place to look for the onset of contingency is in the emergence of a significant identity shift among politically aware Americans. This thought obliges us to return to the era of the intercolonial wars, with our focus now, since we are in pursuit of contingency, being not on the first two conflicts, because those merely "ratified" the initial conditions of Franco-American ethnic animosity, but on the latter two. These were the game changers.

On this short list of the usual suspects for changing the game, one looms largest of all: the Seven Years' War. Of the four intercolonial wars, it is usually only the last, the Seven Years' War (in North America, this is often called the French and Indian War, as if the other three wars had nothing to do with either the French or the Indigenous peoples), that captures our attention as being *the* decisive moment in North American geopolitics.[103] It was decisive, the argument goes, because in removing the existential French threat from the quotidian anxieties of Americans, it freed up the Americans to flex their ontological muscles with respect to the protector (Britain) whose services could now be dispensed with, particularly since British governments were beginning to lean on the colonies to pay more taxes to London for protective services rendered. In short, it made their American identity much more relevant to them than their English identity. This American identity was primarily to be taken as an extrapolation of the New England consciousness, for in the words of one historian, the "westward movement of New England was to continue until her sons and institutions were to be found in a continuous chain of communities from Portland on the Atlantic to Portland on the Pacific, and the influence of New England thought upon the life of the nation cannot be overestimated."[104] Thus, on grounds of both national character and physical security, this final intercolonial conflict marked the parting of the ways for Americans and Britons.

But maybe the contingent moment actually arrived prior to 1763. The idea, on the face of it, seems odd. Yet a case can and should be made for seeking contingency in the relatively neglected conflict that preceded the Seven Years' War. Why look to King George's War in our bid to locate the "real" critical juncture? Answering this requires a very slight detour through time and space, one in which we fast-forward the analysis from the eighteenth to the twentieth century. This section's subheading invokes what to most American and French readers must seem an enigmatic referent, Vimy Ridge. I bring up this battle from the First World War to make a claim regarding a battle from King George's War. That claim concerns the impact that successful martial feats can have upon the development of national consciousness on the part of the "colonial" entities that have accomplished those feats. The April 1917 Canadian victory over well-dug-in German forces who had rebuffed earlier attempts by allied armies to dislodge them is often said, with reason, to have been a major step in the transformation of Canada's political status within the British Empire (soon to be called the Commonwealth, following the Anglo-Irish treaty of 1921).

Canadians, the Vimy story goes, succeeded where others had failed, and in so doing they learned something about their own merits. Of course, as with all symbols, Vimy's meaning can be contested, sometimes hotly; thus, while it is fair to say that most Canadians put great stock in its contribution to national identity, not everyone does.[105] But for the majority, the Canadian Corps' victory is held to have generated a burst of national pride back home (at least among English Canadians),[106] bolstered by the knowledge of great deeds having been accomplished in common with other Canadians. They see it as having marked the most significant step on Canada's road to eventual political independence, a critical juncture if ever there was one in the country's sovereign development. Some even say that Canada's own Fourth of July moment came on April 12, 1917, the day of the battle's triumphant end. For those who subscribe to this view, the point is that although it was the Germans that the Canadians bested in combat, sovereignty would be extracted from Britain.[107]

The meaning of Vimy, therefore, is that victory in battle can lead to alterations in national identity. The reason it is so easy for some analysts to assume the transformation of American identity must have taken place in the Seven Years' War, as mentioned, has a lot to do with the removal of threat. Neglected in this account of contingency, however, is the Vimy phenomenon, or the impact of military victory upon identity through its infusion of collective pride and enhancement of collective self-esteem. Clearly, there were notable victories in the Seven Years' War, otherwise the outcome for the British side would have been far different. Its side obviously won the war. However, unlike the intercolonial war immediately preceding it, the Seven Years' War was a contest in which it could legitimately be said that the *em-*

pire had been victorious; it was British forces that won the decisive battles in North America, culminating with Wolfe's victory over Montcalm on Quebec City's Plains of Abraham, in September 1759.

While it is also true that British imperial interests had prevailed (though in a less clear-cut manner) in the War of the Austrian Succession, or King George's War, those British victories occurred primarily in the European theater. In North America, the most significant military accomplishment had been registered not by imperial forces but by the colonials. This is why, although it was not the traumatic experience for New England (and New York) that the first two wars had been, the third war would prove to be a major step in the formation of an American national character/identity. It is obvious that by the 1770s, Americans had begun to see themselves less as Anglo-Americans, or even as simply English, and more as Americans; their identity was "shifting." But it had to have begun doing so prior to the onset of the Revolution, and therefore it had to have preceded the 1778 alliance. This much is usually taken for granted by historians of the period. But when did the shift get under way, and why?

As we saw above, many seem to think that the juncture must have been the fourth intercolonial war. If this is correct, then that war would constitute the crucial step on the path to the different kind of Franco-American future anticipated by path dependence theory. But maybe the shift began earlier, with the third intercolonial war. For this third conflict to have constituted the critical juncture of greatest importance to the future of the Franco-American relationship, it must be seen to have played an important role in the shaping of a new American identity from which the older, Anglo, significance would become deemphasized. This is exactly what it did.

It is sometimes overlooked how "re-anglicized" New England had been growing toward the end of the seventeenth century as a result of the effects of warfare on the collective consciousness—warfare waged initially, as we have seen, against the Indigenous populations of the region but subsequently against the French and their Indigenous allies. Recall Stephen Saunders Webb's thesis about how close to extinction the English presence in North America had grown by 1676. This thesis is conveyed in the otherwise incongruous subtitle he chose for his book, advertising that year as marking the "end of American independence," a full century before the year that most Americans believe was the *beginning* of their independence.[108] What Webb is implying is that as time went on during the seventeenth century and security threats mounted, the political status of New England altered in favor of imperial interests and in opposition to colonial ones, with the Crown taking a much greater responsibility for the governance of the affairs of the northern colonists than heretofore, leading to the creation, in 1686, of the short-lived Dominion of New England (which also embraced New York).

And while the Glorious Revolution in the mother country might have brought an end to the dominion, it did not bring any cessation to the security-driven "anglicization" of New England that had been under way since King Philip's War.[109] France's contribution to this strengthening of English identity among the Americans was substantial. As one expert on the era explained, "New England needed the strong central authority of the English crown both for internal stability and for external protection from rampaging French and Indian enemies who, by 1702, were engaged in yet another war for New World dominion."[110] Although Queen Anne's War was followed by three decades of what some called peace, the northern frontier of New England remained a site of intermittent violence.

In 1745, trouble returned with a vengeance, and France was again at war with England. For the New Englanders, there were two tremendously important events associated with King George's War. One was a stunning victory in combat. The other was a staggering diplomatic defeat. Each involved the same object, the New World "Gibraltar" of the French empire, the seemingly impregnable Fortress of Louisbourg on Cape Breton Island (part of today's province of Nova Scotia). Louisbourg was key to the security concerns of the New Englanders, for whom the principal objective of the war effort would be to achieve the impossible and conquer that bastion.

To this end, a force of 4,500 soldiers and sailors was assembled in early 1745, recruited from Massachusetts and Connecticut. Never before had such a strong contingent of colonials been mustered to bring the combat to France's holdings. By late June 1745, the French garrison surrendered. In early July, news reached Boston that the "impossible had been achieved. With no assistance from England, New England troops had humbled one of the most powerful French fortresses in the New World and fixed their self-image as a divinely assisted people of war."[111]

Greater than the jubilation experienced upon the receipt of this joyous news from Louisbourg would be the keening greeting another piece of news three years later, that the fortress was being restored to France as a result of peace deliberations at Aix-la-Chapelle, which brought the war to an end. Although it is possible to interpret this third war as continuing, if not strengthening, the identification of Americans with Britain,[112] a more compelling description has it marking the beginning of a new era in North American security, one in which Americans would increasingly come to differentiate their country from the mother country, which had, they believed, callously betrayed them by returning Louisbourg to France in exchange for favorable concessions from France in the European theater.[113] "For New Englanders who had fought and suffered to capture the fort," notes one chronicler of this era, "the treaty signified insensitivity and betrayal. Even more than the impressment riots, the return of Louisbourg created suspicions about English good will that would not disappear."[114]

When all is said and done, this discussion about identity shift leading to political rupture really "proves" nothing other than the Janus-faced nature of contingency, a notion that is of undeniable relevance to path-dependent construes of historical context, while also being undeniably ambiguous. I have been plumping for dating the critical juncture in Franco-American relations of this deep past to 1745. Others, as we have observed, seize upon different moments as marking that juncture, with 1763 and the definitive ouster of France from the continent probably representing the consensus choice on the matter, if there is such a thing. No matter which date one happens to choose, it remains that the path-dependent understanding of historical context stands at odds with the heavily ethnic construe of Erbfeindschaft. For whatever else it managed to do, the short-lived alliance of 1778 did have the effect of nullifying the initial conditions of ethnic hatred between those people who became Americans and their French adversaries of the previous seventy-five years.

From the perspective of relational realism, as we are going to discover in chapter 5, alliance turns out to be a very big conceptual deal. This does not mean, however, that the alliance of 1778 somehow came to constitute the "new" initial condition [sic] of Franco-American cooperation, from that point onward ratifying what Woody Allen and other panegyrists of the "old allies" myth make them out to be, the very best of friends. It may well have driven the final nail into the coffin of the Erbfeindschaft thesis, but in doing so it did not usher in any discernibly bright new future in Franco-American relations.

Obviously, those bilateral relations became better than they had once been, but they did not become particularly effervescent. France–US interactions would remain, throughout almost the entirety of the nineteenth century, relatively uninspiring to those in pursuit of evidence of bilateral amity.[115] The best that could be said of that relationship during that century, empirically, is that it looked less troubled than did America's more important transatlantic relationship with Britain. Save for two brief flurries of martial excitement, during the Andrew Jackson years and again shortly following the Civil War,[116] nothing in the Franco-American relationship throughout the nineteenth century came close to approximating the danger of armed conflict that existed in America's fraught relations with Britain during that same century, down to 1895. That year's war scare over Venezuela punctuated a lengthy series of sharp Anglo-American disagreements before serving as a goad to rapprochement at century's end.

Nevertheless, as we will see, the status of France and America as allies really is fundamental to the issue of suboptimality in their relationship, and it was clearly 1778 that started that dynamic in motion, even if it would soon be profoundly interrupted. Though their first alliance expired after some two decades later, the *fact* of alliance would later come to represent what has been, for more than seventy years now, the single most important touchstone of the Franco-American special relationship. Alliance membership emerges as a central "institutional" and attitudinal feature of this bilateral relationship, notwithstanding that for most of the time over the centuries in which the two peoples have interacted historically, they have emphatically not done so as allies.

But then, when they were not allies, they really did not have much call to cooperate a great deal with each other, rendering the quality of their (mostly nonexistent) cooperation a moot point, especially for an America that took pride in eschewing security interdependence with any power in the Old World. Had the United States and France never become, after 1949, allies once more, there would be little reason for me or anyone else today to posit suboptimal cooperation as an empirically distinguishable trait of the bilateral security and defense relationship, for the good reason that their not being allies would have stripped away the objective correlative ("bounded rationality") of their behaviorally special relationship. But they *are* allies, and bounded rationality governs their interactions. And therein lies the problem:

allies are expected to behave toward each other in a manner different from the way that non-allies behave toward each other. Cooperation is assumed to be a normal behavioral trait of interaction between allies, which naturally leads to inquiries, on the part of policymakers and scholars alike, about the quality of the cooperation between the US and France.

Erbfeindschaft, it turns out, has it all wrong, at least since the era of the intercolonial wars faded into history. The puzzle is not why the two countries have not warred against each other more often. Rather, it is why they have not done a better job of cooperating with each other, when there would seem to have been, and to continue to be, every interest-based reason for them to seek more fruitful cooperation. In the next two chapters, the challenge will be to demonstrate what else it may be about "culture" that could account for the bounded rationality that governs the two states' interactions. Significantly, and despite those scholarly legions that insist that realism cannot coexist comfortably with "culturalist" accounts of foreign policy behavior, the analysis in those chapters, especially in chapter 5, will be informed by assumptions rooted in relational realism.

4

"Ethnicization" and Foreign Policy

The Duroselle-Tardieu Thesis Revisited

The Duroselle-Tardieu Thesis

This chapter will be the second in which that quintessentially cultural category of ethnicity is presented as a potentially important clue for solving the puzzle of Franco-American suboptimal cooperation in security and defense policy. However, unlike the discussion in chapter 3, which had ethnicity being administered in heaping tablespoons of Erbfeindschaft, the dosing in this chapter will be accomplished with the more rounded teaspoons associated with ethnic diasporas. So while it will feature a continued (if diminished) role for this cultural referent in bilateral relations, the manner in which ethnicity is contextualized will part company from the Erbfeindschaft thesis conception of history as presentism, and of France as America's abiding "enemy," themes we saw to be suspect in important ways.

In addition, this chapter's contextualizing will mostly be silent regarding that other, more credible manner in which history was glimpsed in chapter 3, which presented it through a relational-realist lens. That lens invites an appreciation of the special character of the Franco-American relationship by representing it as the inevitable consequence of a path-dependent "reactive sequence" of suboptimal interactions in security and defense matters, in which cooperation never could yield its fullest bounty, for reasons stemming from the very culture of the relationship itself. The Franco-American special relationship, in this rendering, is a behavioral cage, the bars of which have been forged by successive iterations of frustrating cooperation, decreed by the dynamics of path dependence.

Where the first few sections of chapter 3 placed emphasis upon a historical context that largely took its meaning from the Erbfeindschaft thesis, the analysis here will leave behind history conceived as presentism and instead isolate a different cultural, contextual referent, demography, which is sometimes said to have possessed, and even to continue to possess, considerable influence upon the pattern of Franco-American strategic interaction. This chapter will critically explore this putative influence.

The discussion will branch out into a new cluster of referents associated with American cultural pluralism and will adjust our temporal focus from a distant past to a more recent one. We will mainly be interested in figuring out how America's demographic mix has been assessed by French observers, with our attention upon the currently popular social science rubric of "ethnic diasporas." Of late, these demographic entities have been said to be attaining mounting importance in international relations, in no small part because of their assumed prominence in the shaping of American foreign policy.

The analysis here will be guided by conceptual and theoretical issues, interwoven with empirical demonstrations of what concept and theory can be taken to portend. We will begin with a framework enabling us to see a bit more clearly why anyone in France could possibly have thought, or might even continue to think, that American demographic qualities can meaningfully be connected with their country's security and defense interests. After this foray into concept and theory appertaining to ethnic diasporas' mooted influence in the shaping of foreign policy, we proceed to the empirical presentation and evaluation of what the theory might be expected to tell us regarding the impact of American demography upon French interests. As always, the goal is to try to insert cultural variables into the "causal" saga of Franco-American suboptimal cooperation, weighing these in light of both logic and evidence.

The overall intellectual thrust here owes a great deal to two familiar students of Franco-American relations: Jean-Baptiste Duroselle and André Tardieu. Together, the two are responsible for what I have elsewhere labeled the Duroselle-Tardieu thesis.[1] This refers to the conviction held by these two eponymous figures, and many other analysts, that there must be something about America's particular demographic mix that has redounded poorly for French interests in the past, and perhaps still does. As a result, that demographic mix has functioned to prevent bilateral cooperation from flourishing as much as it might otherwise have done. At least, that is how the matter is typically framed, and our task is to determine whether there really is something to the thesis, and if so, what it was (and may still be).

Although this thesis (though not its name) dates from developments in the latter third of the nineteenth and the first half of the twentieth centuries, one variant of it continues to possess a surprising amount of vitality. French observers may no longer worry about America-based ethnic diasporas, but they have been known to express strong opinions about the ongoing meaning of American demography—to *France*. There recently has been a debate heating up over whether ideas percolating in America's multicultural society are "invading" France and threatening the very future of the country's republican institutions, with obvious and sinister implications for its foreign policy interests as well.

The idea is not as odd as it might seem at first encounter, but it certainly is an old one. In France, many have long assumed that the very sociological and political meaning of America contains potential for menacing French interests at home as well as abroad. It even predates America's emergence as a great power, as exemplified by an observation of Gilbert Chinard about French perceptions during the late eighteenth and early nineteenth centuries, when "any American shortcoming, any failure to fulfill the mission the young country had assumed, was felt by the French as if it had directly affected their national life and their own possibilities of changing their own order."[2]

This theme, so famously enunciated more than ninety years ago by Georges Duhamel,[3] continues to echo down to the present, even if it is true that America as "menace" does not constitute, and never has constituted, a universal judgment on the part of France's America watchers. But America, not least because of certain of its demographic features, does possess an uncanny ability to continue stirring passions in France. Consider the startling words reported by one American journalist writing early in 2021 about a threatening challenge many in France, including its president, have found their country to be encountering. "The threat," relates Norimitsu Onishi, "is said to be existential. It fuels secessionism. Gnaws at national unity. Abets Islamism. Attacks France's intellectual and cultural heritage."

What exactly was this threat, and by whom was it being articulated? By none other than France's president, Emmanuel Macron, who saw grave peril in "certain social science theories" entirely of American origin. Macron had in mind theories bubbling up from the American culture wars that, prior to the *real* war touched off by Vladimir Putin in 2022, came close to monopolizing debate in France—theories about race, gender, and postcolonialism. This sinister reproduction of America-sourced social ideas, Macron fretted, was being aided and abetted by France's own universities, where "ethnicization of the social question" raised the real prospect of "breaking the republic in two."[4]

It is possible, though doubtful, that this America-engendered "ethnicization" to which Macron draws our attention represents something novel in France's *domestic* politics.[5] But there can be no question that when it comes to French foreign policy interests, including security and defense policy, the French president's forebodings about American cultural pluralism have a lengthy pedigree, predating Macron by many generations. I am not alluding here to the Erbfeindschaft hypothesis; rather, I am suggesting that when our thoughts turn from France's domestic to its foreign affairs, there had for a considerable period of time existed an important "ethnicization" of the country's policy debate. That ethnicization was also fixated upon America's multicultural population, invariably regarded as presaging little good, and much harm, for French interests. We will look at these earlier manifestations of ethnicization before expanding our object of inquiry from diasporas to heterostereotyping, the concept that will do so much to establish a framework for the analysis in chapter 5.

We start the investigation with Duroselle and Tardieu because both of these celebrated experts on Franco-American relations made it a point to explicitly highlight US-based ethnic diasporas as being of considerable relevance to France's strategic interests, and therefore to the quality of the bilateral special relationship. Writing about those strategic interests, both men asserted that France had been disadvantaged in great power competition because it lacked a diaspora in the United States that was able and willing to go to bat for it and to champion France's foreign policy interests in the pluralistic American political arena. Duroselle went so far as to remark that France was unique among the major European powers in the early twentieth century in being the only one not represented in the United States by a diaspora of any size. This, he added, had had a negative impact upon the quality of France's relationship with America, and by extension, with France's broader interests in global security.[6]

It was a claim that Tardieu had memorably made before him, in his important treatise on the sorry state into which Franco-American relations had tumbled during the 1920s. One symptom of the distressing tenor of the bilateral relationship in that postwar decade was the well-advertised discovery that many American soldiers stationed in the Rhineland between 1918 and 1923 preferred the company of their recent foes, the Germans, to that of their recent allies, the French. Writes Jennifer Keene, "When some American troops began to say in conversations and letters home that 'we fought the war on the wrong side,' US Army officials realized they had a serious problem on their hands. The relatively comfortable life American soldiers found in Germany increased their disdain for the impoverished and miserly French."[7]

Tardieu was among many observers in France who sensed, and regretted, this symptomatic preference, something he knew was hardly limited to those Americans who wore uniforms and liked to fraternize with Germans. Instead, the cause of this preference had deep roots in American society, where it was traceable to the simple fact that too few French had ever chosen to settle down in the United States, whereas too many Germans had, and were invariably making their voices heard in ways that Tardieu and others in France took to be antithetical to French interests.[8] As a result, Americans knew and liked Germans, whereas the French remained foreign to Americans' experience. It was hardly a surprise, he thought, that young Americans should find it so difficult to warm to "the only country which has given them no schoolmates. . . . France has contributed nothing to the melting-pot. France has not woven itself into American life by immigration."[9]

Admittedly, few French observers today continue to adhere to the foreign policy variant of the Duroselle-Tardieu thesis as originally propounded. Among the many things about America that might cause them consternation when they ponder their country's security and defense interests, the absence of a diaspora to call their own in the United States no longer has much salience. While Macron's remarks demonstrate that American demography continues to resonate in France, none would today cloak that demographic variable in the garb of "diasporic lobbying." But when Tardieu was writing, and even later, when Duroselle was, American ethnic diasporas were assumed to be matters of obvious concern to observers in France. That this is no longer the case is a result of important developments in both American and global politics during the twentieth century.

The first reason why the Duroselle-Tardieu thesis has ceased being regarded by French observers to be of significance to their country's security policy interests had little to do with the war Tardieu had recently lived through and everything to do with the war that was to break out, a dozen years after the publication of his book. The outcome of the Second World War managed to extinguish France's own "German problem," presumably for all time.[10] It may not have done so immediately, but the extinguishing was accomplished fairly soon after the war. This effect can be glimpsed in Alfred Grosser's comment on the short existence of the French Fourth Republic, born in 1946, at a time when, as he so memorably put it, the watchword was "no enemy, except for Germany," and expiring a dozen years later, when it could be said of France that it had "no friend, except for Germany."[11]

Once France no longer had to confront the sobering prospect of a future conflict with Germany, it ceased to matter how few French lived in the US, or how many Germans did. But during the years when Tardieu was active in politics, France did face obvious challenges to its security from its neighbor across the Rhine—challenges that had not been resolved by the "successful" outcome of the First World War.[12] So there was nothing really unusual about Tardieu and other French analysts paying close attention to those aspects of America's demography that they were sure served to complicate their country's security situation, all the more so because they understood only too well the geostrategic consequences of their country's chronic demographic inferiority vis-à-vis Germany, a key aspect of the long-running angst about France's "decadence."[13] Those consequences, and the indirect American dimension thereof, had been apparent since the turn of the century, if not earlier.

The first two decades of the twentieth century were a period when America's cultural pluralism was beginning to intrude, more than it ever had before (or ever would again), upon debates regarding the policy it should adopt toward the European balance of power. Testifying to the growing importance of the demographic variable in the framing of that policy was a remarkable—there is no other word for it—warning that President Woodrow Wilson issued to Americans shortly after the outbreak of war in Europe in August 1914. In reacting to the distressing news emanating from the European killing fields, Americans had a duty, said their president, to remain "neutral in thought as well as in action."[14] For a people defiantly stamped with their constitutional right to freedom of expression, being told that they should police not only their speech but also their *thoughts* really did come as something wildly out of the ordinary.

That the president could even have imparted such advice had a great deal to do with the country's demographic makeup. As the home to millions of European-descended inhabitants whose kin states were now at each other's throats, the US might expect to witness the European conflict playing out in its own cities. At least, that is how many historians have assessed Wilson's instruction. To one of those, Ernest May, the president's enjoinder to the strictest neutrality imaginable—*cognitive* neutrality—was predicated on the assumption that "the nation could never take part on either side without bringing on a civil war at home."[15]

French observers who contemplated those same demographic realities were concerned with something other than potential domestic turmoil in the United States; that was Wilson's problem. Their own problem was encapsulated, then and later, in a different worry: the fear that America's large German diaspora would become mobilized on behalf of Germany's strategic interests in a manner bound to damage those of France. Were they wrong to have this worry?

To address this, we must resort to concept and theory to try to determine whether anything associated with the very recent, and lively, scholarly debates over the postulated role of ethnic diasporas in the making of America's foreign and security policies might be "retrofitted" to help us contextualize those earlier French worries of the first few decades of the twentieth century. Following upon this injection of concept and theory, we move on to presenting and assessing the Duroselle-Tardieu thesis in the light of historical evidence.

Concept and Theory: Ethnic Diasporas and American Foreign Policy
The ending of the first Cold War occasioned a spate of scholarly publications on the role that ethnic diasporas might play in international security, and by extension American foreign policy.[16] The new interest in these demographic entities was stimulated by two apparent realities. The first was America's enhanced power in a world suddenly become "unipolar." The second was the country's constitutional order, which lent itself to the politics of "lobbying," a practice sometimes referred to as the "fourth branch" of government in the United States, embedded as it has been in the First Amendment right of the people to petition their rulers for a redress of grievances.[17]

But if the first Cold War's ending served to turbocharge scholarly curiosity about diasporas' political activities, it did not *create* that curiosity in the first place. Over many decades, there had already existed a tradition of scholarship on US foreign policy that explored the potential impact of ethnicity upon American interests and actions in the world—a tradition that had itself been nourished by frequent policy debates associated with ethnic-diasporic militancy during the early twentieth century.[18] As we will see, it was to those early twentieth-century policy debates that French analysts turned their attention when pondering the meaning of American demography for their country's security interests.

Before we address that empirical record, however, two conceptual and theoretical matters require airing: What are these entities called ethnic diasporas, and why have so many analysts attributed to them such significant (many say, outsized) influence over the shaping of American foreign policy? Let's begin by trying to define the concept of diaspora. The origins of the concept are to be found in the sixth-century BCE dispersal of ethnic Greeks who had voluntarily left their city-states in search of opportunity around the Mediterranean basin. And so it has gone for many other groups throughout the ages. They have departed their place of origin, sometimes voluntarily and sometimes anything but voluntarily, and resumed their lives elsewhere.

Whether one has left one's birthplace willingly or otherwise is irrelevant to the meaning of diaspora as a term of analysis, and no one has done a better job of explicating that meaning than Rogers Brubaker. He is definitely no fan of "conceptual stretching."[19] Nor is he very fond of the proliferation of diaspora analyses conducted by battalions of social scientists and social activists after 1990. To those scholars of diaspora who seem bent upon ceaselessly expanding their concept, Brubaker offers the caution that if they failed to operationalize their concept effectively, they would doom it to irrelevance. "The problem with this latitudinarian, 'let-a-thousand-diasporas bloom' approach is that the category becomes stretched to the point of uselessness. . . . If everyone is diasporic, then no one is distinctively so. The term loses its discriminating power—its ability to pick out phenomena, to make distinctions."[20]

To preserve the concept's analytical and theoretical utility, we must carefully limn the concept's distinguishing characteristics. These, Brubaker finds to be threefold. First, the group in question must have been dispersed from its original homeland. Second, it must retain a strong homeland orientation.

And third, there must exist some social "boundaries" setting it apart from others in the new host state(s) in which it has become established.[21] There is much worth pondering in Brubaker's critique. Although it is not exactly clear whether dispersal requires, as some scholars insist it must, the distribution of a diasporic group to two or more host states, it is obvious that there exist some ethnic groups that are so exclusively concentrated in only one host state that it would seem odd in the extreme for them to be excluded a priori from consideration within the diasporic set.

The second of Brubaker's denotative qualities is that diasporas must retain a strong orientation toward the homeland. Usually, this gets expressed positively, captured in the anxieties Woodrow Wilson revealed in discussing those American diasporic dilemmas at the outset of the First World War, when he spoke of immigrant communities' "ancient affections."[22] Sometimes those affections have been extended toward the notional ancestral homeland but definitely *not* toward its current government, as in the case of the Cuban diaspora in the US. Typically, however, the affective significance of homeland orientation runs in a direction leading more toward affinity than disdain for the kin country's governing elite. The point remains that the members of the diaspora must, one way or the other, care deeply about the fortunes of the land they or their forebears have left behind.

Brubaker's third defining quality of diasporas is that they maintain "boundaries" between themselves and the dominant demographic/identity group(s) in the host state, which is simply another way of saying that the diasporic group cannot become so assimilated into the host state's culture as to lose a sense of itself as being, in a nonnegligible fashion, a separate community. A very good—perhaps the best—example of how an ethnic group can cease to be a politically relevant diaspora is the group about which French analysts in the era of the world wars expressed the greatest concern: the very large German American diaspora. As we will see, this group stopped militating in favor of the German kin state during the 1930s and thereafter, so much so that some have regarded it as even ceasing to be a diaspora as Brubaker understands the concept. For instance, Michael Lind has suggestively, if somewhat brusquely, dismissed this ethnic enclave for having turned itself into the sociological equivalent of "at best, . . . television sets, receiving transmissions from the mother country but unable to transmit messages in return. At worst, they are mere curiosity shops."[23]

We will reexamine, with a critical eye, Brubaker's third defining condition of diasporas, because it is going to reveal, surprisingly, something significant regarding the other reason (apart from the extinction of the German problem of yore) why the Duroselle-Tardieu thesis no longer retains any grip on the imaginations of French observers of American demography. For the time being, though, let's limit our curiosity to trying to understand the theoretical and logical assumptions that would have, however implicitly, informed the Duroselle-Tardieu thesis. Why have these two scholars, along with so many other analysts, taken so seriously the claim that diasporas must wield a great deal of clout in shaping American foreign policy?

The United States is considered to be peculiarly susceptible to having its foreign policy degenerate into a free-for-all in which numerous participants strain all of their energies to attain influence over decision-making. This is one of the major reasons why many IR realists consider lobbying by special interests to be so detrimental to the making of sensible policy; these interests are said to distort, and often pervert, the national interest in pursuit of their own "parochial" aims.[24] The problem is held to be particularly acute when the lobbying is done by ethnic groups. There are, naturally, those who take a different view and see America's multiethnic demography as being very much a useful diplomatic tool, as it gives Washington a voice and a presence across a broader range of countries than it presumably would have were it a monoethnic society. Thus, they say, ethnic-diasporic politicking improves rather than degrades foreign policy.[25]

Both sides of the debate manage to agree on one thing: the "ancestral homeland," usually taken as synonymous with the kin state, has a way of exercising an affective claim on diasporas located in the host state, who are stimulated to action on its behalf. Hence the logic behind the theory: a country with a significant demographic footprint in the US is in much better shape than those countries without such a footprint. Such a country can tap into the diaspora to help it achieve influence over the shaping of America's policy toward not only itself but also its adversaries.

There are two principal ways through which diasporas have been known to seek to support their kin country. One of these is a decidedly nonconstitutional practice representing a particularly "kinetic" form of political activity. It inheres in diaspora-based entities employing force to obtain desired kin country outcomes, doing so either within the United States (through, for instance, domestic terrorism) or, much more typically, outside the US but launched from American territory. In the annals of American foreign policy, by far the premier instances of kinetic influence seeking took place in the years before and immediately following the Civil War, when it was not uncommon for neighbors of the United States to experience incursions mounted from its territory by what some political scientists today call "nonstate armed actors,"[26] and which in the 1850s began to be referred to as "filibusterers." This latter name has nothing to do with the custom of American senators to impede legislation through vast eructations, actual or virtual, of hot air; instead, it comes to us directly from the Spanish word for "freebooter," *filibustero*.[27] Fascinating as are the exploits of those kinetic elements, they were never the reason why French observers turned their attention to America's ethnic diasporas during the first half of the twentieth century.

Instead, our focus shifts to the damage that might be inflicted by America-based diasporas participating in completely legal and constitutional lobbying activities. These activities would endow an adversary of France (or Britain) with a troubling degree of influence over the making of American foreign policy, or so it was thought. Two ethnic diasporas were especially worrisome to the French (and the British) by the time of the First World War, that of the Irish Americans and the German Americans, although the anxieties these groups stirred up did not arise at the same exact time or in the same exact way. French observers of American political developments were slower than British observers had been to detect menace in the activism of Irish America; eventually, Irish America came to be seen, in French eyes, as a perhaps unwitting accomplice of the far more disturbing German American diaspora, which they took to be acting as cat's-paws of their own principal rival, Germany.

Though I have been employing the generic category of diasporic "lobbying" to describe this variant of influence seeking, I do so (with apologies to both Sartori and Brubaker) in an expansive sense, in which the notion of lobbying is seen to constitute those legal and constitutionally protected activities that embrace not just the right to petition government but also—and more importantly—the right to exercise the vote to change the government or otherwise influence its foreign policies. Both aspects of this expansive sense of lobbying have been invoked by scholars and others interested in exploring how ethnic diasporas are able to exploit the legal channels available to them in the American political system in their bids to achieve leverage over the crafting of US foreign policy initiatives that might, directly or indirectly, affect the interests of the kin state.

To reiterate: America's constitutional order invites such influence attempts, and its demographic makeup virtually compels them. At least, this is what many believe now and believed a century or so ago. Of these two legal means, it is the "ethnic vote" that has attracted the greatest attention, from both scholars and worried foreign observers, on the assumption that certain large or otherwise well-situated ethnic groups can and do possess the ability to sway the outcome of American elections and as a result gain control over foreign policy decision-making.[28] As Melvin Small relates, while the US may only be one among many lands possessed of a multiethnic democracy, it is the "only one among them that lacks the ability to suppress the cacophony of voices from electorally powerful ethnic groups."[29]

Though it is true that the US has, over the past century and a half, often been a site of influence attempts mounted (whether successfully or not) by ethnic diasporas, it is not true that it has only been in the past three decades that ethnic lobbying attained this purported prominence in US foreign policy debates. The claim that it did suffers from two problems. One is its curiously ahistorical aspect. The other is the related assumption that because ethnic diasporas have at times been so evidently active since the ending of the first Cold War, they must also, by sheer dint of that activity, have been "influential." It is one thing, as Trevor Rubenzer reminds us, to ascribe foreign policy influence to ethnic diasporas; it is a much more difficult thing actually to demonstrate it.[30]

So let's for the moment leave concept and theory behind us and turn in the next two sections to the historical record. We want to take a close look at that supposed impact of American demography upon France's strategic interests in the first half of the twentieth century. In particular, we want to assess the crux of the Duroselle-Tardieu thesis, conveyed in the belief that if only America's ethnic mix had been other than it was, French interests would have been better served and Franco-American strategic interaction would have benefited accordingly, with implications that this presumably would have been beneficial for the future quality of Franco-American cooperation in security and defense.

"Hooray for Old Pruss":
The Duroselle-Tardieu Thesis in Historical Context

The first two decades of the twentieth century saw a veritable explosion of interest, unmatched to this day, in the apparent meaning of ethnic diasporas for American foreign policy. That interest continued, diminuendo, over subsequent decades, spanning the period from the ending of the First World War to the conclusion of the first Cold War, after which scholarly interest in diasporas again accelerated. But even before the twentieth century had begun, European observers of America began to wonder whether US-based ethnic entities might prove troublesome for their own country's strategic interests.

True, for most of this earlier period, it was not in France but in Britain that one would most likely confront such fears, based on the objective reality of America's having become home to an unusually large, and unusually nationalistic, Irish diaspora, which by definition was bound to be antagonistic to British interests.[31] As a result, the "Irish Question" would be a constant refrain among officials in London and Washington who were charged with managing the always tenuous yet increasingly important bilateral relationship between the UK and the US during the latter part of the nineteenth century and into the twentieth. American policymakers were under constant pressure from militant groups in the Irish diaspora to try to convince British counterparts that changing the political status quo in Ireland was essential if diplomatic accord was ever going to be achieved between the two great English-speaking powers of the world. And the British felt equally pressured by the need to deprive Irish oppositional elements (and not just those given to violent political change) of the manifold advantages offered to them by their American host state. In British eyes, there very much was a "Greater Ireland" across the seas, and it was not a comforting vista.

This anxiety found clear expression in the views of Sir William Harcourt, who served as home secretary of the Gladstone government in the early 1880s. These were years during which Ireland, so chronically unsettled politically, was in a particularly "fierce stage of revolution,"[32] associated with widespread agrarian unrest (the Land War of 1879–1882) and an urban terrorism campaign featuring dynamite attacks on British cities; many of these attacks had been planned, financed, and outfitted from the United States.[33] Harcourt acerbically, though accurately, noted that "in former Irish rebellions, the Irish were in *Ireland* . . . Now there is an Irish nation in the United States, equally hostile, with plenty of money, absolutely beyond our reach and yet within ten days' sail of our shores."[34] To another British observer, commenting during this same tense time, "the Irish in America were, in fact, an *imperium in imperio*—a great and powerful nation with unlimited resources by sea and land, and ready and willing to give important material aid, and troops and arms, with the connivance, or even in spite, of the United States government. . . . Looking across the Atlantic to what is sometimes called Greater Ireland, we see a vast population of Irish, divided into sections among themselves, but united as one body in their desire to inflict injury on England."[35]

Compared with such British worries about American diasporas, the French anxieties that had begun to materialize were initially trivial, but they would soon cease to be so, in direct proportion to the growth in French security concerns about Germany. Once its neighbor across the Rhine supplanted Britain as France's most important security problem, the German presence in the United States, which was even larger than the sizable Irish diaspora that so disturbed British officials, became an object of concern to policymakers in Paris.[36] It is not that those policymakers worried about violent attacks on French assets being mounted by German American filibustering. There was no German American equivalent of the Fenians poised to pounce on nearby French territory or to dynamite French cities. Rather, the concern was over a different form of combat, the struggle for the hearts and minds of Americans. Should France find itself fighting a war against Germany, it would be the Germans who would deploy the heaviest artillery on the battlefields of American public opinion. This is because the Germans had the largest continental European diaspora of them all in the United States, while the French believed they had nothing with which to compete. In fact, so large and apparently politically influential was America's German community that some have said of it that it "invented" the concept of ethnicity in American society.[37]

A foretaste of these French anxieties came shortly after the ending of the Civil War, which had severely strained relations between certain European governments and the victorious North.[38] Although the transatlantic discord engendered by that conflict was greatest in the sphere of Anglo-American relations, Franco-American ties also suffered, and for the same reason: the victorious Union deeply resented the diplomatic support that had been offered the Confederacy by the French government, almost as much as it had resented the support offered by the British government. Nor did it help matters that France chose to try to "contain" America and stick a finger in its eye by meddling in Mexican affairs, to the extent of installing a European monarch, Maximilian, on the "throne" in Mexico City in 1864.[39]

For Paris, the consequences of this ill feeling became glaringly obvious, a mere half decade following the South's surrender at Appomattox Courthouse, when war broke out between France and Prussia.[40] The conflict with Prussia was to alter radically the security context of France for generations to come. Not only did France spectacularly lose the war but also it had to witness, in its own capital no less, the humiliating spectacle of triumphant Prussians unifying most of the rest of Europe's German speakers into a new Reich, within whose boundaries would be situated the two formerly French provinces of Alsace and Lorraine.[41] France also had to contemplate American satisfaction with these results, for there can be no question that Washington took great solace from the Prussian victory. Nevertheless, notwithstanding the large size of the German diaspora in America at the time of this war as well as the reality that many members of the diaspora had been moved to contribute what they could to the war effort (some even enlisting in the Prussian forces), it would be hard for anyone to make the case that the German diaspora had in any meaningful way "influenced" the American government's diplomatic tilt toward Berlin.

How could diasporic activism at that time have played much of a part in this tilt, given that by 1870 there was so little love lost in the US for the country's so-called oldest ally? There was no need for German diasporic efforts to try to induce American support for Germany because such diplomatic support was predetermined—indeed, one could say *overdetermined.* [42] Moreover, this pro-German tilt predated the Franco-Prussian conflict. There were many reasons for Americans' greater affection for Germany than for France, not all of which could be directly traced to the Civil War tensions, with or without the extra aggravation of Maximilian, who died at the hands of a Mexican firing squad in 1867. Still, those recent tensions did rankle, and in 1870 it was easily recalled that Prussia had stood out as one of the rare Europeans states that had supported the North. (Russia was another one.)[43]

In the circumstances, it was also easy to see why so many in the US could contemplate the joys of "payback," a sentiment that could only have been fortified by the fact that the occupant of the White House, Ulysses S. Grant, had led the Union army to the victory that Napoleon III had hoped would never occur. The French were stung by what they regarded as Grant's betrayal; he had not only abandoned them during the war but also insulted them following it, sending a congratulatory message to the emperor of the German Reich. Upon his death in 1885, Grant was routinely being vilified by French commentators for having been "one of the most unjust and deadliest enemies of France."[44]

The pro-Prussia sympathies of the government in Washington were echoed in elite opinion circles in the American Northeast.[45] Nor was it only gratitude for Prussian support during their own recent war that prompted these sympathies; there was also the view that among Europe's countries, it was Germany whose political model best represented the consummate civic virtue of good governance, with the country being seen as Europe's, and possibly the world's, exemplar of a "progressive constitutional state."[46] Paris, as it was said, may have been where good Americans went to die,[47] but Germany was where they went off to study, following the Civil War.[48]

Thus it only made sense to heap praise upon Prussia in its war against France. James Russell Lowell, writing to Charles Eliot Norton at the outbreak of hostilities in 1870, confessed that "as against the Gaul, I believe in the Teuton. And just now I wish to believe in him, for he represents civilization. Anything that knocks the nonsense out of Johnny Crapaud will be a blessing to the world." In a similar vein, Louisa May Alcott exclaimed, "I side with the Prussians, for they sympathized with us in our war. Hooray for old Pruss!"[49] This pro-German ardor would eventually cool, later in the nineteenth century, as a result of geopolitical disputes pitting Washington against Berlin over Samoa, China, and especially the Philippines.[50] But even though Americans' warm feelings toward Germany may have dissipated, that country continued to represent, for many, the most progressive, wholesome spot on the European map. To use Lowell's word, Germany *was* civilization.[51]

It might have been thought that when the geopolitical tides shifted as a result of those tensions in Asia, they would do so in France's favor. To an extent, of course, they did, and never more so than during the administration of Theodore Roosevelt, a president who, almost against all odds, turned out to be very popular with the French.[52] Roosevelt or not, however, French observers confronted a new worry: the possibility that American demography would make it highly unlikely for them to fully capitalize on the new, tenser stage in America's relations with Germany. In the realm of American public opinion, France would have to contend with the sheer size of the German presence in the US, and in light of demographic trends adumbrated earlier in this chapter, accompanied by even more distressing assumptions about France becoming "depopulated," there could be no question of its competing with Germany, even had it wished to do so, in this business of seeding "kinfolk" among the Americans—of giving them the schoolmates that Tardieu regretted they could never have. For many reasons, denizens of France preferred to stay much closer to home than did those of Germany. And the French who did venture farther afield, tended to travel to their country's ample colonial holdings rather than to America.[53]

At the beginning of the twentieth century, France had Europe's lowest natality rate, with a population growing at only a tenth the pace of Germany's. By the eve of the First World War, Germany was home to 64 million people, compared with France's 39 million.[54] Because Germany's population had been increasing so much faster than France's, it could tolerate, if not promote, large numbers of citizens quitting their homeland for a life abroad. That is how it was able to establish what many in France came to regard as those demographic beachheads in America. Nor were the French alone in thinking this; their German rivals also tended to have a greatly "exaggerated impression of the role of German Americans in the life of the nation."[55] The Germans abroad, it was assumed, could be counted upon to be of service to Germany, should the need arise.

That need arose in the first two decades of the twentieth century. England might well have been the hereditary foe of France that the Erbfeindschaft theorists and others imagined it to be, but by the twentieth century, especially with the formation of the Anglo-French *Entente Cordiale* of 1904, things appeared to the French in a much different light.[56] Now it was obvious that the French confronted a dangerous German problem of their own, much greater than that facing any other member of the international system.[57] In the altered threat environment of the early twentieth century, it was beginning to dawn upon French policymakers that perhaps American power might develop into a useful force multiplier for France, which could find applicability against Germany. This recognition began to set in during the administration of Theodore Roosevelt, with whom France's ambassador to Washington, Jean Jules Jusserand, developed an extremely close working and personal relationship.[58]

Tapping fully into this potential American asset, however, would require surmounting what was thought to be the huge challenge presented by the presence in the US of sizable numbers of evidently influential and increasingly politicized Germans, who as time went on were becoming more and more zealous in their defense of the reputation and interests of the Fatherland and of their own community.

If sheer numbers, on their own, constitute the objective basis of threat, then there certainly appeared to be a solid foundation for those French worries of more than a century ago. Germans, to say the least, were very thick on the American ground, and had been for a long time.[59] They had begun arriving during the late seventeenth century, and by the onset of the American Revolution in 1775 already accounted for nearly 10 percent of the total population of England's seaboard colonies, with an important presence in Pennsylvania (where they were mislabeled as Dutch).[60] Indeed, after the English themselves, the Germans usually constituted the largest European-origin ethnic group in America, though on a few occasions the Irish would nudge them from their second-ranking position.[61] By the latter half of the nineteenth century, when it started to matter to France, massive migration from Germany would make the US home to the third-largest number of German-speaking people in the world.[62] In fact, America's largest city and its cultural mecca, New York, was for a time the world's third-largest German-speaking city, after Berlin and Vienna, thanks to its nearly half million Germans.[63]

Consider that over the span of the century between the ending of the Napoleonic Wars and the beginning of the First World War, around 30 million Europeans quit their homelands for a life elsewhere; of this total, all but 3 million headed for the New World, mainly the United States.[64] Germans were conspicuous among this migratory flux, traveling in such numbers as to make the "*Völkerwanderung* of the Germanic tribes in the early Christian era sink ... to insignificance."[65] Successive waves of heavy immigration during the eight decades following 1830 brought roughly 6 million Germans to American shores, ensuring that German Americans would continue to rank second only to the English Americans among the European-descended ethnic groups in the country.[66]

The last federal census prior to the First World War, in 1910, revealed that out of a total American population of 92 million, some 2.5 million had been born in Germany, with another 5.8 million being second-generation

Germans (that is, American-born but with either one or both of the parents German-born, usually the latter). Combining first and second generations yielded a category known as the German "stock," said to comprise some 8 million people, a figure accounting for more than a quarter of America's total "foreign" (meaning neither English-descended nor African-descended) inhabitants.[67]

Yet even this understated the German presence in American demography, for to the first- and second-generation Germans had to be added those who had been in the country longer and who continued to identify themselves as German and to live, as much as possible, a German life in America. As one scholar notes, by the end of the nineteenth century every large city had a German district, wherein could be discerned a "pervasive 'foreignness' . . . reinforced by the sight of shops bearing signs in German, restaurants and public houses advertising their German fare, German bookshops and newspaper offices, German physicians, grocers and banking houses—all the elements of a rather complete and self-contained community."[68] Some were even arguing that there existed a German "element" in America (usually construed as meaning anyone with a significant admixture of German blood flowing through their veins) that made up more than a quarter of the country's *total* (not just its "foreign") population in the years just prior to the First World War.[69]

Little wonder, then, that before and during the war it could sometimes be asked whether America was more of a German country than an English one, or whether German Americans might even be in control of its foreign policy.[70] Numbers alone, though, do not tell the whole story. For diaspora members to be regarded as effective advocates on behalf of their kin state, they must also have attained a certain amount of stature within their host state, earned in part by their relative prosperity and in part by the host society's assessment of their accumulated "cultural capital." On both of these scores, German Americans would come, over time, to be adjudged by public opinion a very meritorious ethnic grouping, deemed "one of the most assimilable and reputable of immigrant groups."[71] This was a group that could aspire to receive—and until the outbreak of the First World War *did* receive—a considerable measure of deference from other, "old stock" Americans.[72]

German America, then, looked like an oncoming nightmare for French observers pari passu with the deterioration of Franco-German relations. The nightmare had only barely been glimpsed at the time of the Franco-Prussian

War, when the German Americans, though a large and increasingly respected diaspora, had yet to become politically mobilized around any particular foreign policy issue(s) that could be said to redound to France's detriment. It is true that the war, followed as it was by rapid German unification, triggered an upsurge in patriotic feeling on the part of a group that heretofore had been relatively unmoved by appeals to pride in the accomplishments of the kin state—in large measure because there had been no such single state around which to rally.[73] The Prussian victory at Sedan, followed by the triumphal entry into Paris and proclamation of the Reich, triggered great popular outbursts among America's German communities, with New York City playing host to a massive rally celebrating the war's ending, during which some 40,000 marched in what the New York *Tribune* labeled the "largest parade that New York had ever seen."[74]

But in the late nineteenth century there was not yet any noticeably relevant political organization crafted from within the German American diaspora capable of giving any appearance of threatening the security interests of France or any other country.[75] That would soon change, with the militancy of a newly formed German lobbying entity called the National German-American Alliance (NGAA), or as it was known in German, the Deutsch-Amerikanischer National-Bund der Vereinigten Staaten von Amerika. It was an outgrowth of a Pennsylvania German American organization founded in 1899 by Charles John Hexamer, the Deutsch-Amerikanischen Zentralbundes von Pennsylvanien.

At the outset of this group's "ethnic politicking," its energies were focused upon American domestic issues rather than on foreign policy. Specifically, it had launched a publicity campaign aimed at checking the spread of prohibitionist sentiment within the country—a sentiment seen to endanger German associative practices such as Sunday gatherings with family, food, and music in German America's numerous beer gardens. This antiprohibitionist, anti-Sabbatarian thrust was the first major activity of the organization and was in keeping with the group's stated desire to promote "everything that is good in German character and culture and that might be to the benefit and welfare of the whole American nation."[76]

The deteriorating geopolitical climate of the early 1900s shifted this diasporic entity's focus from domestic to foreign policy. The focus sharpened dramatically upon the outbreak of war in 1914, which had the effect of steering previously well-assimilated German Americans "back to a nationalistic, vulgarly patriotic group consciousness."[77] Kin state rallying functioned not only to advance the interests of the Fatherland; it also was intended to safeguard the social standing of German Americans, for whatever hurt Germany would hurt them.[78] By the time the war broke out in 1914, the NGAA claimed to have a membership in excess of 2 million, all presumably able and only too willing to rally to the kin country's side, doing what they could to frustrate not just an Anglo–American–French alliance but even a pro-Allied "neutrality" on the part of a Wilson administration, which many in the diaspora suspected strongly preferred a victory of the Entente Powers over the Fatherland, notwithstanding its preachments on the virtues of cognitive neutrality.

Keeping America neutral meant, in the first instance, that Washington should adopt legislation aimed at stanching the flow of war matériel and loans to either side (though in reality, given the control of the seas exercised by the Royal Navy, the consequence of the proposed munitions ban would be to favor the Central Powers).[79] Second, the diasporic lobbying was directed at guaranteeing the election of a president and Congress that were committed to strict neutrality, when the country next went to the polls in November 1916.[80] British and French publicists active in the battle for American opinion had little difficulty convincing themselves that the NGAA's agenda meant that it was little more than a puppet of German imperialism in the heart of America, and they applied themselves to convincing the American public to draw the same conclusion.[81]

As an experiment run in the laboratory of American history, the hypothesis of ethnic diaspora influence upon foreign policy was put to its sternest test during the months separating the outbreak of war in August 1914 and America's decision to enter in April 1917. If ever there has been a time when the diasporic tail wagged the dog of American foreign policy, it should have been during those months. This should have been all the more the case because the huge German American diaspora that so worried French analysts was aided and abetted in its campaign to keep America out of the war by the almost equally sized, and equally engaged, Irish diaspora in the US. The Irish too were committed to keeping America neutral, for dissimilar but compatible reasons—so that it could not come to the assistance of the despised British (with their erstwhile French friends becoming, for the Irish, regrettable collateral damage).[82]

Duroselle and Tardieu, then, surely were on to something in drawing our attention to the policy implications that would flow from the combination of Germany's extant diaspora and France's unfortunately nonexistent one. This state of affairs must have been an important "cultural" feature in the evolving Franco-American relationship. At least, the theory leads us to believe that it *should* have been such a feature. But what about the evidence?

Assessing the Duroselle-Tardieu Thesis

Claims about the importance, to France, of disparities in the size of the diasporas to which its formidable European rival could make useful appeal turn primarily upon events leading up to the American decision to intervene in the First World War. To a much lesser extent, these claims also need to be examined with two additional considerations in mind. The first concerns the presence of what so often seems to have altogether eluded French analysts of American foreign policy, which was France's *own* diaspora in the US during the era of the world wars. The second concerns the mooted role of ethnic diasporas in the American interwar debate over isolation. In this section, we cover these three aspects, with the lion's share of attention being fixed upon what was, by far, the most important of the three aspects: the debate over the American entry into the First World War.

If scholars of international relations, whether they be political scientists or historians, need any reminders about the wisdom of approaching with humility the always tricky notion of causality, they will find no better source of instruction than that provided by the voluminous historiography of the origins of the First World War.[83] More than a century after it ended, scholars continue to be divided over what, or who, started this war, with the major fault line separating those who insist that Germany was by far the principal cause of the conflict, more or less intentionally, from those who argue that no one really wanted the war and that in any event its outbreak had much more to do with tensions in the Balkans than it did with stresses in Germany's relations with France, Britain, Russia, or some combination of the three.[84] Regardless of what causal ax they choose to grind, however, few scholars who study international conflict would disagree with Jack Levy and John Vasquez's assertion that the First World War "remains *the* case to which nearly every IR conflict theorist is drawn" (emphasis in original).[85]

It is only slightly less challenging to explain why America entered the war. As with the broader question of the war's origins, the more limited inquiry over American entry also has sown discord. Among the welter of competing explanations we find a few dominant clusters, grouped under the rubrics of security (America was threatened and had to enter), honor (America's campaign on behalf of "neutral rights" obliged it to take up the challenge of German submarine warfare), economics (America's war trade, including loans, drew it into the fighting), propaganda (British and French public diplomacy campaigns suckered idealistic Americans into believing the war to be a noble crusade), and even presidential idiosyncrasy (Woodrow Wilson was deluded into thinking he had a divinely inspired obligation to make the world "right" by waging the war that would end all war).

Not completely lost among these various and conflicting explanatory encampments was another analytical cohort, comprising scholars who happened to believe that America's cultural pluralism *must* have had some influence upon the events leading up to April 1917, and that this did not bode well for French (or British) interests. After all, had not multiethnicity been the very reason for Wilson's bid to impose his version of "goodthink" on Americans, back in August 1914, so as to get them to entertain nothing but the purest neutral thoughts about the conflict? Indeed, a few historians and political scientists *have* highlighted ethnicity as somehow being causally implicated in the events taking place between August 1914 and April 1917—that is to say, in the intensely emotional debate over whether America should participate in the European fighting. Without exception, those few scholars who have looked at ethnicity emphasize the ability of the German Americans and Irish Americans to *delay* American entry into the war, and as a result to impose obvious and heavy costs upon France and its partners in the fighting.

If this really is the meaning of ethnic-diasporic militancy during the thirty-two-month period of American neutrality, then it would seem that Duroselle and Tardieu have a watertight case for claiming injury to France, and by extension to the bilateral relationship, stemming from America's demographic realities. Had the US entered alongside its future allies at the same time *they* went to war, how much less harm would France (and Britain) have suffered? And how much more smoothly would the postwar relationship between France and America have unfolded, stripped as it would have been, in this counterfactual past, of the unseemly squabbling over war debts? Finally, there is the question of the proper treatment of a German foe that had a hard time believing it had actually lost the war on the battlefield. An America more committed to combat from the outset, according to this counterfactual, would have meant a Germany more obviously defeated at the end.

Put this way, the ethnic lobbying mattered a great deal—even if the NGAA and its Irish American partners never could prevent American war matériel and other supplies from reaching France and Britain, along with the credits to fund their purchase, and notwithstanding the inability of the lobby (broadly construed) to prevent the reelection of Woodrow Wilson in November 1916. For although America entered the war eventually, it did so tardily, and therein, it is averred, lay the tragedy. From the French perspective, America's late entry could only be chalked up to the influence of the diasporas.

But what if this way of assessing the impact of ethnic lobbying has it all backwards? What if, instead of the German and Irish American militancy being construed as influential because of its ability to *block* early intervention, we were to construe the lobbying as working in favor of an eventual intervention made more, rather than less, likely because of this very militancy? After all, America had a long and hallowed tradition, handed down from George Washington and embellished by all successor administrations, of steering clear of involvement in the European balance of power. That tradition was presumably independent of the demographic realities of an ever more multiethnic America, for it traced its existence back to a time when America was not particularly multiethnic—or, better, was far from resembling the multiethnic country it would later become.

The Duroselle-Tardieu thesis makes much of France's supposedly missing diaspora in the United States, but it is silent on another dimly perceived diaspora, one to which a European belligerent could and did make appeal. This diaspora is generally overlooked, and not just by the two French scholars, yet it represented what was at the time the largest of the European-sourced ethnic entities in America, so large in fact that it constituted the majority of the American population. It was the English diaspora, and if any group outside its ancestral homeland deserves to be at the center of attention, it is this one. Nonetheless, it has received so little attention from scholars that it has justifiably earned for itself the label of the "hidden diaspora" of world politics.[86]

At the start of the twentieth century, the folk whom we might call "English-descended" Americans (Horace Kallen preferred the term "Brito-Americans")[87] represented some 60 percent of the country's population. Their roots were mainly in England, but also in Wales and Scotland, and indirectly, because of the latter, in Northern Ireland, whence originated the so-called Scotch Irish.[88] These roots were British at a time when it was hardly unusual to find the terms *British* and *English* employed synonymously, not just in the US but also in the UK. The conflation was especially widespread in America, where during the latter stages of the war it was common for the *Welshman* David Lloyd George to be referred to as the "English" prime minister. Americans were not alone in so conflating, for as one prominent British historian reminds us, "it was at least as usual to say England and English as Great Britain and British" during the era in which the war was fought.[89] Nor has this inclination toward conflation been limited, within Europe, to the British; one contemporary (and excitable) French public intellectual turned politician, Éric Zemmour, has fulminated against the post-1918 "betrayal" of Georges Clemenceau by those two dastardly allies, "the American Wilson and the Englishman Lloyd George."[90]

But it is not terminological punctiliousness—or at least, not it alone—that has tended to obscure the existence of the English diaspora in the US. Two more important reasons can be adduced for its obscurity, one being a definitional stipulation that we have already encountered and the other being an assumption that only "immigrants," and not "settlers," can be linked to diasporas. Let us take these in turn, starting with Rogers Brubaker's aforementioned insistence that one of the three necessary criteria for deeming a diaspora to be such is that its members must, in the host country, not be so assimilated as to fail to comprehend the sociological boundaries that keep them somewhat apart, ideationally, from the mainstream. In effect, it is claimed, if they cannot understand themselves to constitute a group apart, then they cannot shape and promote any political agenda noticeably prompted by ethnic sentiments and calculations.

Heeded literally, Brubaker's stricture would have us deny politically relevant ethnic sensibilities to any majority group in a society, simply because it happens to represent the demographic mainstream. This seems odd, both conceptually and empirically, because majorities can and do possess ethnic interests; the Han Chinese, to take just one case among many, exemplify this well.[91] No less odd is the second reason why America's English-descended population has for so long been regarded as unworthy of being deemed an ethnic diaspora. Like the Han Chinese today, this English-descended group was, a century ago, the demographic majority in its country (though it no longer retains this status). Unlike the Han Chinese, the American English *did* have an ancestral homeland other than the country in which they were living. Yet for some reason that defies easy comprehension, those English who departed their homeland for America and other new countries to live and raise families have tended to be styled by scholars as settlers rather than immigrants.[92] In reality, a more honest label for "settlers" might be "invaders."[93] Be that as it may, the settler/immigrant binary masks more than it reveals and might profitably be dispensed with altogether.

For starters, not all of the so-called European settlers in America hailed from England or other parts of Britain. From the earliest days of European colonization, a not inconsiderable minority of the country's European population consisted, as we have seen, of Germans, supplemented by a goodly number of Dutch and Irish.[94] To pursue this terminological muddle, we might even be on solid ground in considering much of America's Latino population, so uniformly labeled as immigrants, to be in their own right a settler group, since nearly all of today's Chicanos and Californios became Americans through the US absorption of territories where they had been long residing, that is, *settled*. It is with good reason that they claim they never crossed the border, the border crossed them.

Moreover, if not all settlers were English-descended Americans, not all English were settlers, either. Many English, Scottish, and Welsh entered America during the nineteenth century, along with vast streams of other immigrants.[95] It is sometimes forgotten that immigrants from Great Britain and Ulster (these latter being mainly non-Catholic Irish) constituted the third-largest cohort of European arrivals in America, after the Germans and Irish Catholics, in the dozen or so years prior to the Civil War, when some 500,000 migrants entered the US from England, Wales, Scotland, and Ulster. After the Civil War, though, things changed dramatically, with the British (including Ulster) share of new arrivals becoming halved, shrinking to about 12 percent by the 1880s.[96]

It helps to call these immigrants what they were, immigrants, because it enables us to understand that even though they might have had majoritarian status in the America of the early twentieth century, the English-descended Americans also could be susceptible to feeling the emotional tug of what

Woodrow Wilson called the "ancient affections," or what we would know today by the notion of kin country rallying. In sum, these English-descended Americans very much *were* a diaspora, if ever there has been such an entity in the United States. Moreover, and surprisingly, they would turn out to be the most important diaspora of them all, from the perspective of the Duroselle-Tardieu thesis, of far greater relevance than the large German diaspora that so worried the two French America watchers and many others.

Thus, to the extent France's interests were affected by America-based diasporas from other European lands, they were favorably rather than negatively affected, once Britain and France began, after 1904, to move closer to becoming allies. Duroselle and Tardieu may have been in the right church with their emphasis upon the stakes of diasporic politicking, but they were in the wrong pew. For if ethnic diasporas figured at all in the American decision for war in 1917, their impact was rather the reverse of what is so commonly believed. Instead of being blockers of intervention on the part of a country that had a long-standing tradition of nonintervention in the European balance of power, they became enablers of intervention. Although it would be unwise to overstate the impact of English American kin country rallying upon Wilson's decision to enter the war, at the very least the shift in American majoritarian sentiment from its traditional "anglophobic" orientation was to prove of critical significance to the short-term future of both Britain and France, as well as to the longer-term prospects of the Anglo-American bilateral relationship.

It also is sometimes forgotten these days that for much of America's history as an independent country, its majority English-descended population was so politically anti-British that the rote proclamation of an abiding hatred for England could be considered the litmus test for their own red-blooded Americanness.[97] It was precisely this rejection of English political practices that gave meaning to their identity as Americans. Given that they spoke the same language, professed mainly the same Protestant religion in its various denominations, and organized their economies along similar liberal lines as time went on in the nineteenth century, there would have been little point in having separated from the mother country in the first place were it not for the major cleavage over politics. From the perspective of what is sometimes referred to as ontological security,[98] Americans needed to feed their inner anglophobic beast so as to nourish their own sense of self-validation. Stephen

Tuffnell explains how anglophobia could play such a central role in shaping American identity by allowing Americans to "define themselves against Britain and British policy, in the process articulating a more positive vision of American nationality and branding those unsympathetic with their vision as unpatriotic. . . . A chimerical John Bull acted as a critical reference point for Americans' own national identity."[99]

But for all their differences, real or fantasized, from political England, Americans' civilizational wellsprings were, and remained, assuredly English insofar as the majority was concerned. Walter Russell Mead writes, "Even at the height of their war of independence, Americans did not believe that British civilization was an evil civilization; it was recognizably their own civilization and therefore obviously good."[100] This is what made the *Kulturkampf* conducted by the German Americans against England (and France) during the long months of American neutrality so ultimately counterproductive for Germany. In stressing repeatedly how "evil" Britain and British civilization were, and how only German and Irish Americans represented "real" Americanism, the two minority groups were striking at the heart of American self-awareness and stimulating what had hitherto seemed impossible to imagine: the promotion of kin country rallying on the part of majority American opinion.

Thus, to the extent that the large German diaspora in America possessed the kind of influence about which Duroselle and Tardieu wrote, it did so in a way that better served French and British interests than German ones.[101] That diaspora's attempts at influence, aided as they were by nationalist elements in the Irish American diaspora, backfired spectacularly, and in so doing they helped to fortify, rather than weaken, pro-Allied opinion in the United States. This does not mean that Woodrow Wilson took the country into war because he reacted to the sentiments of the majority, and that the latter had suddenly begun to clamor for war; the decision to go to war was Wilson's, not the public's. And while he valued public opinion, he did so more as an echo chamber than as a source of policy inspiration. He had no desire to follow the majority; he would *lead* them into a military conflict in the Old World. Depending on one's perspective, he would do this because he was left no choice, as a result of Germany's resumption of unrestricted submarine warfare, or so that he might earn for himself and his country a seat at the postwar peace table, where he would be able to reshape international politics by discarding the old system of balance of power and replacing it with the bright new vision of "collective security" enforced by a potent League of Nations.

Hence, German America's strident anti-Allied efforts not only helped France's position vis-à-vis the United States indirectly but also generated a kind of "slipstream" Francophilia on the part of a people, the Americans, who had gone a very long while without exhibiting any noticeable outpouring of love for their erstwhile oldest ally. If the British cause had become, by April 1917, America's cause, and if the French were Britain's core ally, then the French too must occupy an exalted place in American affections. And so they did, and would, for a short period of time during which American soldiers were engaged in combat on French soil against the German foe. Those were months during which France could even be said to have captured the "heart" of America, as one representative book put it at the time.[102] Indeed, according to France's ambassador to Washington, Jean Jules Jusserand, France was more popular than England among Americans in 1917 and 1918, such that had the question been put to them which of the two allies they liked the best, France would have come out on top by a "crushing majority."[103]

The Duroselle-Tardieu thesis can be criticized on another score. If it was blind to the advantages that the "missing" English diaspora in America could deliver to France during the First World War, it was no less unseeing when it came to France's own diaspora in America. For France actually *did* have a significant number of kinfolk residing in the United States a century or so ago. It turns out that those American youth about whom Tardieu had written actually had quite a few classmates with French names, especially in the very politically relevant northeastern states. These were mainly "indirect" immigrants, who had arrived not from France but from French Canada, and if their nationwide numbers never did come close to matching those of either the Germans or the Irish, they still constituted an impressive demographic presence in an important region of the United States. Over the course of the century spanning 1840 to 1940, a total of 2,825,000 Canadians would establish themselves in the US; of this figure, some 30 percent (825,000) were mainly French-speaking, mainly Catholic, Quebeckers. Most of the latter would settle in New England, where by 1900 French Canadians constituted, at 575,000, about 10 percent of the six-state region's total population.[104]

Jean Heffer has remarked of this French demographic presence that "they are the great absentees from our memory. It is not even correct to say we

French have forgotten about them, because we have never even known that they existed."[105] To this group must be added the older French communities that had become established in America out of political rather than economic necessity. Prominent among these were Huguenots, who had moved to America to escape religious persecution in France, and the Acadians, who were forcibly removed from New France to Louisiana, where, during the closing period of the intercolonial wars, they joined a previously established population of French inhabitants.[106]

But if France did in fact have a diaspora in the United States, it did not prove itself to be a very useful one from the perspective of Paris's foreign policy interests. Obviously, the Huguenots were not likely to shower much favor upon the kin state that had, under Louis XIV, made life so miserable for them at home as to force the lucky ones who managed to escape butchery to find exile abroad; they were to Paris what Cuban Americans have been to Havana since 1958. Nor were the Cajuns disbursed in the Louisianan hinterlands suitable candidates for militancy on behalf of a far-off foreign country about which they knew so little and cared even less.

The situation for Quebeckers in the United States was more complicated, for they were more than a bit like the Irish in America, in two senses. First, like the Irish Americans, Quebeckers had keen historical memories of grudges against the kin state government. Prior to the establishment of the Irish Free State in 1922, the government of Ireland had been based in London. Similarly, for the Quebeckers the government was and remained in Paris, and their grievance stemmed from a widespread belief, call it a myth, that France had "abandoned" them after the Conquest of New France (Canada), surrendering them gratuitously to the English enemy at the peace conference in 1763.[107] As such, they felt little desire, and even less need, to identify as their own the interests of the state that had rejected them and thus were not considered to be an easily mobilized folk from the point of view of promoting the interests of the French state. In this regard they were very much *unlike* the German Americans in the years 1914 to 1917, although in the context of a future war, Vichy France did attract a significant number of admirers among Franco-Americans, during the early 1940s.[108]

The second way in which Franco-Americans were similar to the Irish was in their Catholicism. Prior to the 1960s, French Canadians, whether in Quebec or in the US, tended to imbibe their religion in undiluted portions.

Anticlericalism in the ancestral homeland, beginning with the Revolution of 1789 and resuming spectacularly through the secularization initiatives of the Third Republic,[109] was not likely to inspire loyalty to the "heretical" French kin state at the best of times, although it did furnish a second reason for the level of support received by General Philippe Pétain's French government, from 1940 to 1942, for whom the secularization zeal of the republic had been an affront to national dignity.

The final point to make in this section concerns what happened to the German American diaspora after the bruising experience of the First World War. The manner in which the Duroselle-Tardieu thesis assessed diasporic "influence" in the war and its immediate aftermath has to be considered flawed, but the thesis also really did not have the significance that it is some-times thought to possess with regard to the *interwar* American experience with isolation. Certainly, there are scholars who argue that America's de-cision to absent itself so thoroughly from the European balance of power during the interwar period must have had a great deal to do with the coun-try's demographic composition, since the "ethnic vote" consistently went to candidates committed to staying out of European affairs.[110] Once again, however, as was the case in the First World War, when diasporas actually *were* important (albeit not for the reasons many thought them to be), the "usual suspects" were rounded up and made to stand alongside other cul-prits believed to be responsible for keeping America from doing its duty to the international community of the time. Those usual suspects were, of course, the German Americans and the Irish Americans—and after 1922, the Italian Americans.

There are a few problems with this geopolitical police lineup, which singly and together should make us realize how little diasporic lobbying in America ultimately mattered for France's foreign policy by the late 1930s. Importantly, it was hardly necessary to invoke any minorities at all when allocating blame for America's rejection of participation in the European balance of power in the interwar years. To nearly *all* Americans during the 1920s, and especially into the 1930s, the great lesson of intervention in 1917 was unmistakable: it had been a colossal blunder, one that quite apart from what it did to America, hardly made Europe any more secure than it would have been in the absence of that intervention (or so it was believed).[111] Ethnic minorities who were in-spired to militate against intervention, in an America fundamentally opposed to intervention, were pushing against a door that was more than wide open. Just about every American, no matter his or her ethnic roots, chose isolation from the European balance of power as their default option throughout the interwar period.[112]

Moreover, the Irish American militancy against Great Britain, which had worried French observers after 1904, simply disappeared upon the founding of the Irish Free State and the subsequent establishment of the Irish Republic in the following decade. There may have been, and still were, militants in the Emerald Isle willing to take the fight to the despised English, but the air had gone out of the Irish American diasporic balloon as a result of the interwar transformation of the political status of Ireland. Much more importantly, as far as French interests were concerned, the large German American diaspora simply ceased to play much of a political role, with the rise of Nazism in Germany after 1933, for the good reason that the vast majority of German Americans were neither sympathetic to nor capable of being mobilized on behalf of Hitler's Germany.[113]

To recapitulate, to the extent it mattered to France's security and defense interests at all, American ethnic-diasporic lobbying tended to work in favor of those interests rather than against them, irrespective of how many French schoolmates young Americans did or did not have. After the First World War, German American militancy on behalf of German interests, which had earlier been a dream of so many in the diaspora, simply ceased to be an option, save for a few committed Nazis, who would soon have alternative lodgments found for them by the Franklin D. Roosevelt administration, once the United States entered the Second World War in December 1941.[114] These German American Nazis numbered in the thousands, compared with the millions of German Americans who had strongly sympathized with the Fatherland the last time around.[115] To top it all off, the Second World War, in eliminating France's German "problem," made the earlier worries about America-based diasporas so irrelevant as to seem almost hallucinatory. However, this did not mean that American demography would suddenly disappear from the list of cultural items about America that troubled the French.

"Diasporas are dead, long live demographic variables in the United States!" might as well have become the rallying cry for new generations of French analysts, following the Second World War and down to the present. In the next chapter, we will see what this means. First, however, it remains to add a coda to the present chapter, to assist in the transition from one manner of comprehending culture, associated with diasporas, to another, associated with heterostereotyping.

France and the Enduring "Anglo-Saxon"

The introductory section of this chapter cited the opinion of France's President Macron that ideas stemming from America's multicultural demography were invading and even threatening the integrity of French society. In the process of highlighting what he took to be the subversive notions propagated by American social scientists, he invoked a long-standing cultural trope in discussions of Franco-American relations. "I'm thinking," Macron said, "of the Anglo-Saxon tradition, which has another history, and it is not ours."[116]

There are several reasons to dwell upon Macron's invocation of this trope—or better, tropism—in the special relationship between France and America. Some of these reasons might lead us to plump for relegating this category to the same conceptual scrap heap to which we earlier consigned the "oldest enemy" and "best friend" images. Indeed, the Anglo-Saxon construct seems so objectively flawed that we might wish to avoid it altogether as lacking all substance.

Yet spurning the trope would be a mistake. Anglo-Saxons, as an "ethnie,"[117] may be long gone from the face of the earth (assuming they ever existed at all), but some of their symbolic Doppelgängers have a way of loitering on the premises. This is actually fortunate, if for no other reason than that it helps us better comprehend why strategic culture might, as some scholars suggest, have much more to do with symbolic cognition than with ethnic context.[118] Indeed, the Anglo-Saxon construct is so useful that we might even say, paraphrasing Voltaire's comment about God, that if it did not exist, it would be necessary to invent it. Anglo-Saxons possess a marvelous, you might even think, preternatural ability to insert themselves into the enterprise of heterostereotyping, for which they are a ready-made prop in the construction of apparently important claims about how "identity" affects the quality of Franco-American strategic interaction. And heterostereotyping, as we will learn in chapter 5, has a lengthy pedigree in the Franco-American relationship, with consequences that to our own day continue to be taken seriously, perhaps with reason.

There remain a few items to clear up with regard to the category of Anglo-Saxons. As is plain from its intrusion into a very serious assertion made by a very serious politician, Emmanuel Macron, the Anglo-Saxon rubric enjoys enduring currency as a tool for policy analysis. This currency, admittedly, tends to be geographically circumscribed these days, and it typically is in greatest circulation in lands whose native tongue is not English. It is often employed in French-speaking parts of the world, not just France (though mainly there), where its invocation is taken to be code either for the United States alone or, when convenient, for the duo of the US and the United Kingdom.[119] The two together are often perceived to be a tandem bound and determined to frustrate the security and defense interests of France—save, that is, for those instances when France has been menaced by Germany, on which occasions Anglo-Saxons have managed to make themselves fairly useful.

Most of the time, though, Anglo-Saxons are not brought into policy discussions in France in a way that is intended to flatter the group; instead, they are routinely hypothesized as some kind of perturbing Other.[120] There are two problems with this hypothesizing. The first is the familiar definitional challenge. And that challenge leads, with a powerful twist of irony, to the second problem, conjured up when one (for instance, Macron) seeks to apply "Anglo-Saxonism" as a virtual synonym for "multiculturalism." Let's take the definitional aspect first.

Notwithstanding the relative absence of *Anglo-Saxon* from contemporary usage in English-speaking countries, there is a recent exception to the pattern, sufficiently instructive to call out for mention here. The American writer Thomas E. Hicks tells us more than he perhaps intends to about the putative ethnic (or "racial") content of *Anglo-Saxon*, in his review of James Holland's recent account of the Anglo-American invasion of Sicily in 1943.[121] In this review, Hicks provides valuable insight into what used to present such a genealogical conundrum to those who sought to invoke this contested ethnoracial construct, doing so through his lavishing of praise upon Holland for giving us "a history of Anglo-Saxon males slaughtering one another while Italians mainly try to get out of the way."[122]

His description of the battle for the island is apt enough on two counts. First, it is judicious in complimenting the Italians on their good sense in trying to stay out of harm's way. But what is primarily of interest to us here is how Hicks inadvertently puts his finger squarely upon the fundamental definitional dilemma that constantly used to frustrate scholars and others who, in an earlier age, sought to invest Anglo-Saxons with ethnoracial significance.[123] That challenge was how to define who actually made up this ostensibly formidable group, the Anglo-Saxons.

The best response to that challenge remains one proffered by Finley Peter Dunne's fictional character of more than a century ago, Mr. Dooley. Dunne was writing at the end of the nineteenth century, a historical juncture suddenly filled with much promise not only of Anglo-American rapprochement but also of what many—especially, but not only, in the UK—took to be the even more inspiring vision of geostrategic nirvana: the "universal peace" made possible through the "long-desired Anglo-Saxon 'alliance.'"[124] It was an era in which "patriotism of race" was sometimes extolled as being superior to mere national patriotism, as a patriotism that some saw as leading inexorably to a lasting peace predicated upon ethnicity.[125]

Expressive of this uplifting vision were remarks delivered at Harvard College in early March 1898 by former president Grover Cleveland's secretary of state, Richard Olney. The ex-diplomat told his audience that "there is a patriotism of race as well as of country—and the Anglo-American is as little likely to be indifferent to the one as the other. . . . Nothing less could be expected of the close community between them in origin, speech, thought, literature, institutions, ideals—in the kind and degree of civilization enjoyed by both. In that same community, and in that coöperation in good works that should result from it, lies, it is not too much to say, the best hope for the future not only for the two kindred peoples *but of the human race itself*" (emphasis added).[126]

With such a noble prospect in the offing, it was more than ever necessary to specify the alliance's membership, which in Olney's formulation of "Anglo-American" seemed to some to be missing an important piece, namely Germany.[127] It was precisely upon this question of who *were* the Anglo-Saxons that Mr. Dooley brought to bear his considerable ethnological insight, explaining to his companion, Hennessy, both the rationale for such an Anglo-Saxon alliance and the actual membership therein: "You an' me, Hinnissy, has got to bring on this here Anglo-Saxon 'lieance. An Anglo-Saxon, Hinnissy, is a German that's forgot who was his parents."[128] From the standpoint of ethnicity, Mr. Dooley's definition has stood the test of time, and it highlights the challenge posed to enthusiasts of the "peace through Anglo-Saxonism" vision—a challenge that was summed in one simple question: What to do about the Germans?

At the time when racial Anglo-Saxonism first became a policy notion taken with some degree of seriousness in Europe and North America, around the middle of the nineteenth century, it really did not matter much that this presumed ethnoracial category harbored in its midst, as logically it must, so many Germans. Logically, because how could a group labeled Anglo-Saxon *not* be heavily "Teutonic," given the geographic anchorage of both elements expressed in its very name? The Angles were a Germanic folk residing in northern Germany, close to the frontier with Denmark. As for the Saxons, a map of Germany tells us all we need to know about their ethnic roots, considering that three of the contemporary Federal Republic of Germany's sixteen *Länder* (states) bear the Saxon name, either in whole or in part: Saxony, Lower Saxony, and Saxony-Anhalt.

The problem was one of saving the construct in an era when it was every bit as embarrassing to be seen keeping geopolitical company with Germans as it has become, in our own day, for so many authoritarian politicians and pundits in Europe and America to be seen adulating the Russia of Vladimir Putin. How could this category be salvaged at a time, starting in the early twentieth century, when Germany was falling so far out of favor among the Americans and the British—the two countries that Macron and so many others today hold to be the very embodiment of Anglo-Saxondom? The short answer, which animated considerable intellectual gymnastics during the hyperracialized era of a century ago, was simply to eject the Germans altogether from membership in the family.[129]

One might have thought that the internecine squabbling within that self-same "family" would have revealed the definitional nakedness of the Anglo-Saxon concept and result in its disappearance from serious policy discussion. But this was not what happened. The name has been preserved, though its meaning has changed. As we will discover in chapter 5, its bowdlerization has been so thorough as to make of Macron's "ethnicization" thesis a veritable self-contradiction, because of the second, heavily ironic aspect associated with its contemporary invocation. To grasp the irony, we need to cast our minds back once again to early twentieth-century America, when policy debates raged regarding the meaning of ethnicity for America's very national identity. The cultural pluralists, associated intellectually with Horace Kallen and politically with the non- and even anti-English diasporic groups, never lost the opportunity to rail against the claims of America's "Anglo-Saxon" majority demographic, whom they ridiculed as unpatriotic Americans held to be utterly subservient to British interests.

Hence the sublime weirdness of America's multicultural demography being styled by Macron and so many others in his country as a challenge to France's identity, on the grounds that French ways are simply not compatible with Anglo-Saxon ones. Astonishingly, these Anglo-Saxon ways are now being taken as the very embodiment of multiculturalism! Of course, for the multiculturalists of Kallen's day (his "cultural pluralists"), the idea that somehow their ultimately victorious culture war against Anglo-Saxonism would end up being regarded as the *vindication* of Anglo-Saxonism would have come as nothing less than shocking, were the idea not so prima facie ridiculous.[130] One American analyst, reflecting upon this weirdness shortly after the Second World War, noted how the construct played its part in frustrating cooperation between the French and the Americans. Commented Arnold Rose, the United States "suffers in French minds by identification with England. . . . The French still speak of 'Anglo-Saxon' institutions with disdain. One thing that surprises most Americans is that their own country is also considered to be 'Anglo-Saxon.'"[131]

This "de-ethnicized" version is how Anglo-Saxonism lives on, even if no Anglo-Saxons can be found anywhere on the planet—and certainly not in the US—to endow the construct with its putative ethnoracial content of yore. In fact, it not only lives on but also does so with apparent policy muscularity, and Rose was not incorrect to note its place as an ideational buttress of heterostereotyping in the special Franco-American relationship, even if he may have been overstating England's place in this story. So let us now continue the quest to identify "cultural" variables thought to be responsible in some way for establishing the suboptimal tone of Franco-American cooperation, inter alia, by availing ourselves of the Anglo-Saxons as a sociological footbridge carrying us over the analytical chasm separating the realm of ethnicity from that of ideas.

5

Vive la différence?

Cognitive "Antinomies" of a Special Relationship

Perrin du Lac, Reversed

In chapter 2, we grappled with the manner in which scholars and policy-makers alike have employed the idea of strategic culture, and we saw that consensus is not the first word that comes to mind when we try to define and apply this confusing concept. In that chapter, I sought to simplify things by positing two sets of oppositional distinctions, guideposts serving to minimize our stumbles as we traverse the bumpy terrain of strategic culture. The first set concerned the purposes to which strategic culture could be put. I chose to regard those purposes as being active rather than passive, things that might be said to generate instead of merely to reflect policy outputs, and while I do not have enough faith in anyone's ability (my own included) to *certify* the attainment of reliable causality in foreign policy analysis, I did hint that strategic culture might be profitably construed as being more akin to cause than to effect. The second set of oppositional distinctions was a bit more artificial—or at least blurrier—than the first, with the analytical binaries of importance in this case being context and cognition. As we saw in chapter 2, these binaries were the battlefields upon which the two leading combatants in strategic culture's internecine warfare, the "contextualist" Colin Gray and the "cognitivist" Alastair Iain Johnston, waged their theoretical struggles.

So far in part 2 we have been following primarily the trail of context, in the hope that it would lead us to clues about the special, suboptimal pattern of Franco-American strategic interaction. The focus of chapters 3 and 4 was on the interplay between two specific and deeply interconnected varieties of context, namely historical and ethnic ones. In seeking to establish how culture might relate to strategic interaction, I relied in part upon the work of Robert

Kelley, a historian who took a selective approach to culture, embracing ideas and ethnicity and little else. I have dwelt at some length on the way(s) in which some scholars have thought that ethnicity played an important part in setting the tone of the Franco-American special relationship.

In particular, the inquiry into historical context in chapter 3 was in large measure intended to test one of Kelley's assumptions about the enduring legacy of historical enmities of an ethnic provenance, conveyed in his statement about "folk hostilities between ethnic and other culture groups [being] so firmly established that they drive these peoples into fixed political alignments that endure for generations. Fed by images of a communal enemy that assign hateful qualities to traditional adversaries, these hostilities summon up ancestral memories, many of them reaching back to distant mother countries."[1] This assumption, of course, lies at the base of the Erbfeindschaft thesis. In the end, we found that despite what has sometimes been claimed, ethnicity as it was presented in chapter 3 could not really get us too far toward understanding and explaining suboptimality in contemporary Franco-American security and defense relations.

Whatever else that bilateral relationship has tended to be over the course of the past century, it has not really been the kind of bitterly adversarial one associated with images of *hereditary* enmity, because neither the Americans nor the French nurture memories of those ancient "folk hostilities," and even if they did, it is doubtful that those memories could be mobilized in support of a contemporary policy agenda on either ally's part. Allies can and do feud about a lot of things, but they generally do not think of their ally as a mortal foe (Greece and Turkey being noteworthy exceptions to the rule). Nor has that *other* ethnic variable, addressed in the case study of the impact of diasporas in foreign policymaking (chapter 4), shown itself capable of carrying much, if any, of the explanatory burden for Franco-American suboptimality. As we saw, attempts at ethnic-diasporic influence, when they were being most exuberantly initiated during the 1914–1917 period of American neutrality, proved more likely to foster than to inhibit Franco-American cooperation in security and defense matters—if they did anything at all.

Now we switch gears, abandoning ethnicity and putting the focus on the cognitive variable of ideas, in hopes of finding more credible explanations for Franco-American suboptimality. In so doing, we will take our cues from the manner in which analysts have sought to extract value from strategic culture by considering it to be primarily an ideational concoction—that is, a cognitive dish that, at times, arrives highly seasoned with symbolism. Alastair Iain Johnston relied heavily on this understanding of culture in seeking to account for the sources of Chinese strategic thinking, or its "grand strategy."[2] Colin Dueck, like Johnston, also displays a Geertzian flourish in his operationalization of strategic culture (in his case, America's), with his central symbolic and ideational referent being liberalism.[3]

My own sense of what culture connotes builds upon the cognitive emphases of Johnston and Dueck and brings in the necessarily, indeed unavoidably, relational basis of cognition. Cognition is not simply a reflection of how decision-making elites "cognize" solely on the basis of their own state's preferences, arrived at, as it is sometimes said, "endogenously."[4] Instead, cognition, as an element in foreign policy decision-making, entails a process that incorporates and depends upon ideational interaction. It is subjective, of course, but more than that, it is *intersubjective,* and as a result, the discussion here will oblige us to revisit the notion of relational realism, which we encountered toward the end of chapter 3. Specifically, I will use the relational-realist lens to examine three ideational categories implicated in the generation of the "cognitive antinomies" of Franco-American relations. This somewhat arbitrarily demarcated trio consists of heterostereotyping, ideology, and structure, items that in this chapter take on the appearance of a kind of geo-cognitive matryoshka doll, in which the third item requires the second to complete its significance, with the second likewise needing the first.

What, in practice, do these three rubrics mean as applied to the Franco-American special relationship? *Heterostereotyping* primarily consists in the formation and use of images as a means of cognitive and normative differentiation between oneself and others who are ipso facto deemed problematic. Toward the end of chapter 4 I introduced the enduring "Anglo-Saxon" as a metaphoric bridge from that chapter's emphasis upon ethnicity to this chapter's focus on ideas. In particular, the idea upon which we will concentrate in the discussion of heterostereotyping is "anti-Americanism," which is in no small measure bound up with French myths about Anglo-Saxons. Anti-Americanism, we are going to see, is in France a controversial yet useful construct that can be taken as synonymous with an orientation that, in the words of one prominent student of the topic, reflects "critical discourse on the American other" and is characterized by "criticism of something important about America."[5]

The concept of *ideology* highlights the possibility that suboptimality in security and defense cooperation is driven by contrasting principles in the two countries' grand strategies, with the story line here concentrating upon how American (or "Anglo-Saxon") liberalism stands in contradistinction to French realism. According to this way of framing the matter, the two allies so often act as if they are in a continual state of oppositional animation precisely because they actually *are* animated by opposing ideologies, notwithstanding their supposedly being "sister republics."

Finally, *structure* places the emphasis upon the perceived ideational impact of symbolic attributes associated with the polarity of the international system upon the quality of bilateral cooperation. Of the three, this last rubric is sometimes considered to be the most important reason for the suboptimal quality of Franco-American cooperation.[6] In fact, though it is an analytically separable category, structure turns out to be as discursively inseparable from the other two constructs as any one doll in the matryoshka is physically inseparable from the other two; it is a feature of the nesting, from which it takes it significance. Absent that nesting, they are simply dolls, not matryoshka dolls.

But if structure clearly matters a lot, it should not be imagined as solely representing some kind of "material" aspect of international reality that sets it apart from those other ideational aspects, because the very manner in which structure is interpreted—what it symbolizes—can and does exert a powerful force upon how policymakers think about Franco-American strategic interaction. As we will discover in this chapter's final section, nothing symbolizes structure better than "multipolarity," an idea whose effect upon the quality of Franco-American cooperation is impossible to overstate.

We will begin with a discussion of concept and theory, to provide a framework for analyzing the potential impact of the trio of cognitive rubrics. The two clusters of concept and theory of greatest relevance to that analysis are ontological security and "status anxiety." Although it might be imagined that these two conceptual/theoretical clusters are of recent vintage, the burden of this chapter is to demonstrate otherwise. The attitudinal reflexes commented upon so long ago by Perrin du Lac remain as much alive today as they were in his time, and for more or less the same reasons, derivative of both ontological security and status anxiety.

But while the plotline may have stayed the same, the protagonists have switched roles. For most of the past century, the French have been the refractory partner, reacting with some degree of dudgeon to things done or not done by the Americans, much more frequently than the Americans react to *them*. Thus, while Perrin remains relevant, he does so with a difference. When he wrote, France was powerful and America was weak, and this obvious discrepancy in the capabilities of the two states guided his theorizing, which we can take to have represented relational realism avant la lettre. When Perrin expressed his disappointment in Americans' stubborn conviction "never to do anything as we do," he was reflecting an important truth about the bilateral relationship, representing a normative judgment born of asymmetries in power. To Perrin, French ways should self-evidently have been instructive for Americans, and the latter should have taken heed of the instruction. This, after all, is what great powers do when engaged in cooperative interaction with lesser powers: they lead the latter toward what they consider to be optimal outcomes, which in practice entails the furthering of their self-interest while at the same time trying to convince the others that their own interests are similarly being served. In our own day, this notion of leading is often bound up with another, more controversial notion: hegemony.[7]

Notwithstanding the manifold differences between Perrin's time and our own, this assumption that power conveys an entitlement to tutor remains alive. Great powers, and some not-so-great powers, tend to endow themselves with a belief in their own mission to show the rest of the world—or at least the rest of their own geostrategic cohort—the path of proper diplomatic comportment. All of them, irrespective of whether they admit it or disguise it, regard themselves as being in some important way(s) exceptional. Nor is just great powers that exalt themselves in this manner. Some so-called middle powers (for instance, Canada and Sweden) have not shied away from intermittently donning the mantle of an exceptionalism saturated with moral superiority.[8]

Two countries have stood out by the explicit manner by which they have announced their own exceptionalism: the United States and France.[9] Visions of exceptionalism have been dancing in both countries' heads for a very long time, and as Roger Cohen so nicely phrased it, "no other countries make such claims for the universality of their virtue."[10] Some will tell us that this virtue signaling results from each having had a revolution at roughly the same moment in the late eighteenth century, permitting if not compelling it to presume to speak on behalf of "universal" values associated with freedom and the "rights of man."[11]

Perrin's era coincided with the rise and demise of the first Franco-American alliance, yet for most of that alliance's existence, where France sought to lead, America preferred not to follow. It emphatically did not want to follow revolutionary France in its fight against Britain during the 1790s (hence America's acceptance of the divisive Jay Treaty). Once their first alliance expired, early in the following decade, this business of leadership and followership became a moot point, such that when France and the US became embroiled in military conflict against the same British enemy in the 1812–1814 period, they did so as cobelligerents rather than as allies, neither coordinating its military operations with the other.[12] Only in the twentieth century did they again become allies. During the nineteenth century, they may have ceased to be adversaries, but apart from those few instances of bilateral rancor discussed in chapter 3, their relationship remained mostly stuck in a holding pattern of mediocrity, with neither country mattering very much to the other. Things would change in the twentieth century, and ever since the "power transition" occurred in the Franco-American relationship, an increasingly robust United States has found it both puzzling and annoying that France should so consistently express reluctance to follow *its* lead.

Take this role reversal to heart and you might be left concluding that the structural realists are correct after all: power asymmetries should tell us most if not all we need to know about the special Franco-American relationship. France does not, today, choose to follow where America wishes it should go for the same reasons that America, in the 1780s and 1790s, did not choose to follow where France wished it to go: it senses that its identity and status both can be jeopardized by too close an alliance embrace. According to this way of presenting it, the "real" story of Franco-American relations is that there *is* no story. Their relationship represents nothing more or less than what should be expected by anyone conversant with a modicum of understanding of IR. It is a natural reaction of lesser partners in cooperative relations to wish to constrain the initiatives of their stronger partner, a response pattern virtually dictated by the nature of the international anarchic system and the desire of each member thereof to preserve the maximum degree of autonomy.

Of course, if this ur-structuralist reading of those realities were credible, there would be no point in a book asserting that the Franco-American relationship is special precisely because of the suboptimality in the two countries' habits of security cooperation. How *could* it be behaviorally special, if the structuralists are to be credited? All of America's security partners, being so much weaker than it, should manifest the same kind of behavioral tendencies as the French—tendencies that would ostensibly have the effect of rendering less optimal the quality of their own cooperation with their powerful ally. Because all would react the same way toward that ally, none could, by definition, be deemed to be acting in any behaviorally special manner. Yet the thrust of this book, as well as of countless other books and articles, is that France *is* different from the set of American allies, and the difference endows the bilateral relationship with its peculiar quality. As we know, this is what Kaspi meant in so succinctly—perfectly, even—encapsulating bilateral relations as *le différend franco-américain*.[13]

Within the context of the transatlantic alliance, France really *has* established a distinctive profile when it comes to dealing with America, resulting in the latter adopting a no less distinctive profile of its own in dealing with the former. To assert this is hardly to be provocative; it is merely to declare the obvious. Nor is asserting this a denial that structural features of the international system are relevant. But these features do not exist in a vacuum; they are very much dependent for their meaning on how the various states in that system interpret things. Structural "causes" can produce different "results" because of the differences in cultural attributes of the members of the set under examination. This is simply to remark that culture can affect the manner in which structure is said to work. Again, structure is it not entirely (or even chiefly) an objective datum, but it must be intersubjective as well as subjective. One good, if perhaps surprising, way to grasp the intersubjective wellsprings of the special Franco-American relationship would be to contextualize bilateral interaction with the aid of power transition theory (PTT).

It is an unexplored irony that international relations theorists, who put great intellectual stock in the phenomenon and dynamics of power transition in the international system, have given such short shrift to the Franco-American security and defense relationship, which might otherwise seem to be tailor-made for PTT enthusiasts. We met these enthusiasts in chapter 3, when the relevance of "historical context" was under discussion, to illustrate a point about one of the charges historians sometimes level against political scientists: that they adopt a "presentist" orientation to history, meaning that they put selective aspects of the past in the service of a very contemporary political agenda. Their doing so is often accompanied by a conviction that history imparts "lessons" of relevance not only for today but also, more importantly, for tomorrow, if we are but intelligent enough to seize them.

I invoke PTT again in this chapter, but not for the pedagogic purpose of soliciting lessons for future behavior. There may well be such lessons, but they are not of concern here. Rather, I employ PTT as a heuristic to assist in the comprehension of our cognitive matryoshka doll. Usually, when PTT enthusiasts bestir themselves to action, it is with policy advocacy uppermost in mind. They are guided by one core question: How and why do power transitions enhance the prospects of a war breaking out? Because of the obvious importance of the question, their choice of cases upon which to concentrate tends to be a relatively restricted one, delimited by the identification of countries that either have squared off against each other in a past "great power" war or give every appearance of being likely to do so in the future.

If they believe that events in the distant past possess as much contemporary relevance as those in the more recent past, they may, as we saw, seek to extract from the Peloponnesian War ongoing theoretical and policy significance. More often, though, it is the origins of the First World War that capture their attention. And when thoughts turn from past to present and future, it used to be the possibility of a Sino-American war that most fascinated and frightened them—until the outbreak of Putin's war on Ukraine, which for the moment has put on the back burner worries about a Sino-American showdown. But not all was worrisome on the PTT horizon, for there did remain that one transition story—the one involving the UK and the US—to demonstrate that power transition just might coincide with peace rather than war, Indeed, that particular PTT story can be and has been read as having laid the foundations for the transatlantic "zone of peace," otherwise known as the contemporary Western order.[14]

War and peace can be said to constitute the main business of the discipline of IR, which intends to sustain systematic inquiry into "the causes of war and the conditions of peace." But as important as this mission statement has been, power transition might have other consequences for foreign policy behavior, apart from shattering (or preserving) the peace. Surprisingly, for all the attention that PTT has been receiving as a result of the dual stimulus supplied by tales of China's "rise" and America's "decline," there has never been any explicit scholarly attempt to invoke power transition as a crucially important stage in the evolution of Franco-American relations.

This absence of scholarly curiosity no doubt is a function of what we can take to be the "purist" approach to power transition, predicated upon the insistence that the two countries in question must indisputably be adjudged as standing first and second in the international pecking order, construed in terms of the various (even if at times conflicting) metrics adopted for assessing power. According to the purists, the *only* countries about which it makes sense to worry in the context of PTT are the top dog and its leading challenger (or "peer competitor"), and the only real question is whether they are destined for the sort of armed showdown that is sometimes termed a "hegemonic war."[15] As to *why* they might be so destined, two answers are proffered.

The first focuses on the challenged state (the top dog) being confronted with the perhaps insurmountable temptation to avail itself of what remains of its dwindling supremacy and to smite its challenger while it can still be reasonably confident of victory, through the launching of a "preventive war."[16] The second answer directs attention to the challenger, held to be growing a little too big for its geopolitical britches and burning with a desire to attain from the top dog (and others) the deference that its enhanced capability convinces it must be forthcoming—or else. The "or else" in question entails starting a war of aggression.

With respect to the *Franco-American* relationship, it might appear that PTT is, at best, a very awkward fit. After all, there never has been a time, during the entire sweep of America's existence as an independent state, when it and France ranked as the top two powers in the system, so from the purist perspective, it might seem as if Franco-American relations are neither here nor there, the theory being simply inapplicable. But many PTT enthusiasts, Graham Allison first and foremost, are no purists in this business of seeking out the "lessons" of past power transitions. Allison's own historical data set consists of sixteen cases of power transition in history, and it is apparent that many if not most of these (I count at least ten) do not represent genuine instances of number one and number two being hypothetically or actually arrayed against each other. To illustrate the point, take just his most recent case, in which he posits post-1990 Germany, Britain, and France as the foci of a postulated power transition, even though none of these putative post–Cold War contestants could by any sensible reckoning have been regarded as even close to being number one or number two (or number three, for that matter) in the international hierarchy at the start of the 1990s.[17]

This is merely to observe that PTT is hardly an uncontroversial approach in IR. But for our purposes in trying to assess the cognitive antinomies of the Franco-American special relationship, it can prove to be a useful, even if not a perfect, analytical prop. Its many demerits aside, PTT in the Allisonian variant alerts us to the impact that changes in relative capability might have upon foreign policy conceptualizations, in our case, both in France and in the United States. In particular, PTT and the Allisonian "trap" metaphor direct us to two, related, bodies of IR theorizing regarding ontological security and status anxiety. In the next section, I will address these concepts and the theories built around them, as a prelude to their application in the three subsequent sections.

Concept and Theory:
Ontological Security and Status Anxiety in the Special Relationship

It is neither late-breaking news nor particularly surprising that international relations scholars have accorded so much attention to the First World War. Much of this scholarly fascination inheres in the desire to achieve greater insight into the causes of war, and for this task, one can hardly find a more useful laboratory in which to test various theories than the global conflict that broke out in August 1914.[18] But for the purposes of understanding suboptimality in France–American security cooperation, there is also good reason for us to cast our thoughts back to that war of more than a century ago, and to do so within a power-transition framework. Admittedly, that framework would need to appeal to the less "pure" variant of PTT, for by 1914 no one could sustain an argument predicated upon France and the United States, in any order, constituting the first- and second-ranking powers in the international system. They had never been such an ordered pair.

This said, the First World War has to be regarded as the grand climacteric in the Franco-American special relationship. It marked, as definitively as anything possibly could, the arrival of a new era in the two countries' security and defense interactions, one in which power could be unambiguously (and importantly) said to have "transited." America had already surpassed France in certain metrics of capability, especially those derivative of economic prowess, by the early post–Civil War years. It would soon do the same in respect of demographic strength. In 1870, America and France had roughly the same number of people, about 38 million; by 1914, France's population had barely grown, to 40 million, while America's had exploded, to 100 million.[19] Wide as this gap was, the economic spread between the two was even wider, with America's gross domestic product assessed in 1914 at almost $2 trillion (in today's dollars), while France's lagged far behind, at not quite $300 billion.

What these two underlying bases of material power (gross domestic product plus population)[20] had been signaling for decades was, with the war of 1914–1918, ratified by another power asset, once America's formidable military *potential* was translated into actual military capability by the exigencies of combat. Kaspi has rightly called this war, for France, the "time of the Americans." It has turned out to be a time without end, for reasons and with consequences that we will explore here.

For the United States, the war has usually been seen as marking a historic initial, if halting, evolution in its grand strategy, away from the venerated tradition of aloofness from the European balance of power and toward a recognition that there could be no exit from Europe, geopolitically. For France, the war similarly denoted the end of an era in which it could be maintained that a transatlantic alliance was a matter of strategic indifference to it. Henceforth, as Adam Tooze has commented, Paris would become more alive than at any time since the temporary alliance of 1778 to the idea that French security interests might need to be intertwined with American security interests in some cooperative, institutionalized fashion. The war fundamentally altered global power balances, "most obviously [in] the case in France, the most maligned of the 'old world powers.' After 1916, rather than remaining mired in ancient grudges, . . . Paris's overriding aim was to forge a novel, Western-orientated Atlantic alliance with Britain and the United States. . . . This search for an Atlantic alliance was the novel preoccupation of French policy that after 1917 unified individuals as far apart as Georges Clemenceau and Raymond Poincaré."[21] Initially, the search would be short-lived, persisting for a mere half dozen years after the war before being reluctantly abandoned by 1923, when it became obvious to France that America was going to revert to its traditional policy of absenting itself from the European balance and that Britain simply could not be counted on. In the case of both of the "Anglo-Saxon" countries, liberalism was said to have played a role in inhibiting their forming an alliance with France.[22]

The Goldilocks search for "just right," as I suggested in chapter 1, can be taken as a constant theme in French security and defense thinking about transatlantic alliance, and it has been so for most of the past century. For officials in Paris, getting the country's security and defense posture just right has entailed calibrating enough of an American presence to safeguard French physical security interests without incurring so much of an American presence that it endangers France's identity or threatens its status in the international system. This has never been an easy thing to do. For the United States, Goldilocks has been more of a bit player in transatlantic sagas, mainly because it has been a while since France could possibly have mattered as much to America as America has mattered to France.

An intriguing theoretical point of departure for a relational-realist inquiry into this asymmetrical Franco-American reality is ontological security. The conceptualizing and theorizing of ontological security, although a fairly recent innovation in the ranks of IR scholars,[23] actually builds upon a much older approach of relevance to strategic culture. That older scholarly approach, which we encountered in chapter 2, is associated with national character, suitably updated and upgraded to what some consider the more ethically palatable construct of national identity. For identity is the referent object of ontological security, in much the same way that territorial sovereignty serves as the referent object of physical security.

Identity and ontological security are tightly related, conceptually and theoretically, such that to understand the latter requires some attention being paid to the former. In chapter 2 we saw that during the 1990s, trends in both global politics and social science epistemology were converging in such a way as to put a *renewed* emphasis upon the importance of identity in foreign policy analysis. I stress "renewed" because, while they did not necessarily recognize or care to admit it, many scholars owed a debt to an earlier generation of analysts of national character. Yet for all the similarities between national character and national identity, there was one major difference between the two concepts that began to attract emphasis, as a result of the rise of constructivism to predominance among theoretical paradigms in IR. Henceforth, national identity was to be conceived more and more as a necessarily relational entity, something that was "constructed" as a result of sociological interaction rather than simply being a stable set of character traits passed along from one generation to another.

Only a very few students of national character (Kenneth Terhune, for one) had insisted that national character must be the result of such sociological interaction or it would be nothing at all; it had to be construed in a relational manner.[24] For the majority of national-character scholars, however, character was something immanent in discrete cultural entities, and while it could change, it could not do so rapidly or frequently; it had to be reasonably invariant or it would be meaningless.

Scholars of national identity, despite the otherwise easy correspondence between character and identity, have paid far greater attention to relational considerations. They have done so pari passu with their growing conviction that the psychologists' concept of identity could not make much sense unless its "bearer"—its referent object—was the group, not the individual. Starting in the 1960s and continuing to the present, identity has become a concept whose applicability increasingly was to be found at the group rather than the individual level, so much so that we usually employ it to mean "collective identity."[25]

A similar progression occurred with ontological security, a concept whose original analytical applicability likewise was encountered at the individual level. This is how R. D. Laing, the author who coined the term, intended ontological security to be applied.[26] As had happened with the concept of identity, however, so too did Laing's conceptual innovation become "sociologized." This was primarily the doing of the sociologist Anthony Giddens, who sought to use the concept to show how an individual's sense of existential (that is, ontological) security could best be captured by situating it in a group context transcending the individual level of analysis.[27]

Ultimately, some IR theorists would so scale up the concept that it could be pressed into service at the Waltzian third "image" (or level) of analysis, the systemic one, where it applied to states.[28] Foremost among those IR scholars has been Jennifer Mitzen, whose point of theoretical departure was the discipline's familiar concern with security, and in particular with its "security dilemma." This dilemma arises because of the well-nigh inexorable manner in which states can find themselves enmeshed in rivalry even if they do not intend to be, because they are "misperceiving" the defensive preparations of others as offensive preparations against themselves, requiring them to take countermeasures that have the effect of perpetuating the spiral.[29]

Mitzen agreed that this dilemma was a serious challenge to international peace and security, but she added a gloss that was even more troubling for international cooperation than competition over physical security. The name she gave to this additional systemic feature was the "ontological security dilemma," which she understood to result from states' need to protect their *identity* as well as, and sometimes even more than, their physical security. As a result, she claimed, state identity can itself be "embodied in . . . competitive routines and therefore become attached to the competition as an end in itself. . . . In short, where ontological needs are met by routinized competition, it is no longer accurate to say that states face a physical security dilemma, . . . On a deep level, they prefer conflict to cooperation, because only through conflict do they know who they are."[30]

If we needed a body of IR theorizing to instruct us on a fundamental reality of the France–US relationship in security and defense, then Mitzen has supplied just such a body, with one caveat. While she has been worried about an ontological security spiral that perpetuates *enmity,* the stakes in the Franco-American relationship are far less dire. What ontological security may stimulate in this bilateral relationship is not the cultivation or perpetuation of enemy images per se; rather, it is the reproduction of reactive sequences that generates patterns of suboptimal cooperation. In short, the argument would go, France and the US relate to each other less successfully *as allies* than they might otherwise do, because of concerns about ontological security. And for reasons embedded in structural asymmetries, these concerns are expressed much more by French than by American policymakers—so much more that it can be claimed that ontological security, within this particular relationship, has become a virtual monopoly of the French.

To understand this monopoly, and to complete our conceptual and theoretical stage-setting, we shift our gaze from ontological security to status anxiety, as status anxiety is filtered through yet another bit of theorizing known as social identity theory. This theory was developed by the Polish social psychologist Henri Tajfel,[31] and I invoke it because ontological security within the context of the special Franco-American relationship must be about national identity, if it is about anything at all. And national identity, like other collective identities, is unavoidably and indelibly *relational*; collectivities need to know who they are *not* in order to understand who they *are*.[32] Thus, contrast is essential to enable them to sift through the "whir and buzz" of their social environment.[33] If all that social identity theory did was to highlight locational boundaries, there would be little reason to bring it into this chapter's cataloging of cognitive antinomies.

But social identity theory suggests a second, more relevant distinction that betrays a strong tendency toward the sort of heterostereotyping that is on display in the phenomenon of French anti-Americanism. For to the locational function of social identity theory is added a normative one that enables members of the in-group to validate their identity by contrasting it (along with their "values") favorably against the identity of the out-group(s) of greatest significance to them. Doing this is said to make them feel better about themselves. As one scholar summed it up, the dual functions of categorization and comparison, subsumed in social identity theory, "account for group formation and group perception. But in addition, they also account for group behavior—or, differently put, for the behavior of individuals when acting in 'group mode.'"[34] This behavioral aspect is a function of the need to run down, or dispraise, that oppositional Other so as to build up, or praise, the worthiness of one's own group.[35] As two scholars of IR, Alexander Lanoszka and Michael A. Hunzeker, explained, "One way to gain self-esteem involves improving the status of the group in which the individual is a member. According to social identity theory, individuals bolster their self-image by praising the group in which they belong at the expense of others" (that is, by heterostereotyping).[36] This suggests that status anxiety might lie at or close to the center of any state's most important bilateral relationship, with its resolution being dependent upon, inter alia, the degree to which it senses it shares a "collective identity" with its more powerful ally.[37] As we will see, different American allies respond to the interaction between status anxiety and collective identity in different ways.

It would be difficult to account for the suboptimal course that bilateral relations have followed, including and especially at those times when France and the United States have been *allies,* without involving considerations of status discrepancy. Such considerations must be central to any contemplation of the antinomies of structure. The discrepant attribute of note is the anxiety that is said to accompany a state elite's belief that, like Rodney Dangerfield, it is getting no respect—or at least not as much as it is sure it deserves. The lack of respect can come from any number of countries, but for a state experiencing status anxiety, the obvious target of greatest upset must be its "significant oppositional Other," which in the context of an alliance often means the dominant security partner.

Again, not all the allies react in the same way; some buy in to the notion that there is a transnational (in our case, a transatlantic) collective identity within which they can psychologically and comfortably embed their own group identity. In that case, the zero-sum logic lying at the root of status anxiety can be, if not eliminated altogether, at least greatly attenuated, on the basis that a rising ontological tide must lift all boats. But other states may retain a far greater commitment to the national than to the transnational identity; for them, their standing in a systemic hierarchy is of utmost importance.

And status, whatever else it might mean, is very much a function of social hierarchies.[38] Of late, many IR scholars from a variety of paradigms have been evincing interest in the consequences that can result from the anxiety stemming from status discrepancy. For many scholars, those consequences include the ultimate policy failure, war.[39] They worry that status anxiety can motivate decisions to use force as a means of redressing the gap between the deference one thinks to be its due and the deference one is actually receiving. This is the logic undergirding the emotional aspect of Thucydides's Trap associated with the rising state's hubris.[40] But it is not just adherents of PTT who think this way; many other scholars also believe that status anxiety can lead to conflict, for reasons somewhat divorced from power transition. They are equally focused on the problem of great power war, even if they may not subscribe to PTT.[41]

The problem of great power war is important, but there also are other security consequences stemming from status anxiety, apart from its serving as a goad to armed conflict between heavyweights.[42] Status anxiety has played a key role in the Franco-American special relationship, even though no sentient observer would hold its effect to be so perniciously powerful as to instigate a war between the two. Still, status anxiety can tell us something important about the cultural roots of suboptimality in the Franco-American special relationship. The first of these roots is the kind of heterostereotyping associated with "anti-Americanism" in Franco-American relations.

L'Obsession anti-américaine

During France's last *rentrée* before the Iraq war—that is, the ending of the summer holiday season of 2002—two books appeared that raked anew those old emotional coals that forever resist banking, and which would again be glowing white hot with the beginning of the campaign to unseat Saddam Hussein, in just a few short months. The books were Jean-François Revel's *L'Obsession anti-américaine* and Philippe Roger's *L'Ennemi américain*. Their contemporaneous publication constituted the literary event of the season, triggering renewed debate about whether—and if so, why—the French seemed so different from other Western allies when it came to their attitudes toward America and its domestic and foreign policies.

Not surprisingly, the debate revealed some deep emotional fissures within France, where some thought to rebut Revel and Roger with the rejoinder that France was too fixated upon the US for anyone to construe it as being anti-American. This rejoinder was published by the director of *Le Nouvel Observateur* in response to charges not only of French anti-Americanism but also of anti-Semitism. Regarding the latter, he observed that his country had never been less anti-Semitic than it presently was (in late 2002), and as for its being anti-American, "I find the galloping Americanization of the French to be considerably more marked than their alleged anti-Americanism."[43]

By early 2003, though, it would become nearly impossible to pooh-pooh allegations of French anti-Americanism, such was the volume and the emotional pitch of the country's opposition to the invasion of Iraq. Illustrative of this opposition was a poll conducted by Ipsos–*Le Monde*–TF1 while the military campaign to unseat Saddam Hussein was under way, which found that nearly as many of the French were hoping for a victory of the Iraqi dictator (33 percent) as were prepared to admit they were "rather siding with France's allies, the US and the UK" (34 percent).[44] And while, as we saw in chapter 1, those crisis months of 2003 triggered spleen venting within the US as a counterpart to that occurring in France, the duration of that rare American flare-up of francophobia turned out to be brief and, in the scheme of transatlantic realities, basically inconsequential.

Few scholars say the same about French heterostereotyping of America. It is usually held (correctly) to be of long duration and (less correctly, perhaps) to possess considerable policy relevance, whereas in the United States extreme francophobia really did expire with the ending of the intercolonial wars. While it may have been going overboard to remark, as President William McKinley did in his own Woody Allen moment, in July 1897, that "there isn't an American who dislikes France," the reality is that American displeasure with France has, with some important exceptions, usually not accounted for very much geopolitically.[45] Even the satisfaction with which so many members of the American political and intellectual elite watched Prussia crush France in 1870 and 1871 proved to have no impact whatsoever on the course of the fighting.

The French debate over anti-Americanism has had a tendency to wax and wane during the past century. Its most intense eruptions, not surprisingly, have tended to be associated with wars and with the peace settlements ending those wars. This was particularly the case following the First and Second World Wars, but there have been other conflicts, often associated with decolonization or other controversies in the Global South, that have been linked to outbursts of heterostereotyping.

In all, there have been four periods during the past hundred years— that is, since the Franco-American power transition occurred—when anti-Americanism has been notably effervescent in France. The first, and probably the most significant, of these periods was during the interwar years. The second occurred after the Second World War and peaked during the middle of the 1950s. The third, of course, was during the first decade of the Fifth Republic, when Charles de Gaulle came to be seen, more rightly than wrongly, as the preeminent champion of opposition to American foreign policy in the entire transatlantic world.[46] The fourth was in the 1990s and early 2000s, during the short-lived era of "unipolarity" in the international system, when an America-inflected "globalization" appeared to be unstoppable.[47]

It needs to be said that there have been moments not only of relative emotional calm in the Franco-American relationship but also of interludes when French and American security and defense interests were so closely in step as to almost suggest that pro-Americanism had supplanted anti-Americanism as the default setting of bilateral relations. Some scholars, in fact, did make this latter claim, at a point during the 1980s when it looked as if a hardening French position toward the Soviet Union betokened a rapprochement between France and America that was likely to endure. Emblematic of this thaw in Franco-American relations was a *démarche* made by France's socialist president, François Mitterrand, who on January 20, 1983, ventured to the Bundestag in Bonn to lecture parliamentarians on their duty to approve the deployment, on German soil, of NATO's intermediate-range nuclear systems—American Pershing II and ground-launched cruise missiles—even though France itself had no intention of deploying these weapons on *its* territory.[48] Thus, to some, by the mid-1980s the time had come to publish the obituary notices for French anti-Americanism.[49]

Unfortunately, those death notices were similar to erroneous reports of Mark Twain's demise, many decades before, which the famous humorist called "an exaggeration."[50] Yet while the budding rapprochement of the 1980s proved to be short-lived, the fact that it existed at all reminds us that the story of heterostereotyping is a complicated one. Though anti-Americanism in France *is* a theme that regularly appears in discussions of transatlantic security and defense, it is not exactly clear how we should construe this dispensation. For starters, we might inquire into the definition (if one exists) of generic anti-Americanism. As usual, definitional consensus proves elusive in this matter. We have already glimpsed one such attempt, when Richard Kuisel succinctly referred to it as a negative discourse that orbited around "criticism of something important about America." But in what exactly does this criticism consist, and can we say there is a French species of this discursive genus? As well, how if at all does this discourse make itself felt in the strategic interaction of the two countries?

Let's begin by inquiring into the denotative qualities of the genus. It is true that one occasionally encounters the claim, in France as elsewhere, that the country cannot be considered to be anti-American in any meaningful sense, not because of any social-psychological traits of the French, or because they are simply too Americanized, but because the generic category of anti-Americanism is itself devoid of meaning. Therefore there *are* no denotative qualities worth bothering with. Anti-Americanism, according to this perspective, is simply a blanket term invoked primarily to express displeasure with and disdain for whoever happens to be opposing a particular American administration or policy path at a given time. In this critique, what some label anti-Americanism, in France or anywhere else, might better simply be considered as opposition to particular policies or presidents rather than aversion to a people and its culture. As a result, say some, we would be well-advised to discard the category altogether, even with respect to France, a country in which, according to Pascal Ory, so-called anti-Americanism has never been able to yield a coherent policy agenda and is only a vague, omnibus label obscuring far more than it reveals.[51]

Does the label, though, really obscure more than it reveals? There are two reasons, one general and the other specific, to doubt that it does. First, the concepts we employ in political analysis do not have to derive their meaning from their applicability; in fact, they usually do not do so. Not all conceptual analysis in IR has to yield policy recommendations. Some concepts may spawn political agendas of some coherence, but many others are intended to advance understanding rather than to shape policy. So even if it were accurate in the case of France to claim, as Ory does, that no *consistent* set of policies can be associated with the country's ostensive anti-American inclinations, it would not follow that the US is therefore bereft of characteristics calling out for emphasis. One certainly may dispute, in France as elsewhere, the policy implications of a term such as anti-Americanism, but to deny the term's analytical utility would surely be to defy the very promise of political discourse, given that "essentially contested concepts"[52] are the rule not the exception in IR (as in the other human sciences), and few would seriously maintain that the discipline could advance through the abolition of its core vocabulary.

This might seem to be a commonsensical observation, but it turns out, really as no surprise, that anti-Americanism is another one of those concepts with a meaning that is destined to be endlessly contested. In Kenneth Minogue's wise caution, analysts need to avoid succumbing to the fallacy of composition that holds the concept of anti-Americanism to represent a single thing, sort of "like aggression in tigers, merely awaiting a call to life."[53] Instead, it is a multifaceted thing, so much so that we might wish to extend Pascal Ory's criticism of the term as it applies to France and simply banish it from applicability to *any* country.

Succumbing to such an abolitionist temptation, however, would be a mistake, for the obvious reason that, like it or not, anti-Americanism has been, for some time now, an important conceptual touchstone in geopolitical analysis, perhaps nowhere more so than in the context of transatlantic relations.[54] It may be difficult to define the concept, but it is too important to be expurgated from our dictionaries, if only because it has attained the status of what two scholars call the "master narrative of our time," by which they mean "an international rhetoric of rejection that binds politics, economics, and ethics into a common story about how the world works and why it doesn't," with the principal target being the United States.[55]

There is a second reason for not jettisoning the concept, and it follows directly from the centrality of anti-Americanism to discussions about world order, with particular relevance to relations between transatlantic allies. As America's power continued to grow throughout the twentieth century and into the twenty-first century, a natural accompaniment was the increased frequency with which "critical discourse" (to use Kuisel's term) about America was encountered on the part of its most intimate partners in security and defense, basically the Western Europeans. To be sure, such discourse did not simply arise because of American power, for even when America was at its weakest, there had been no shortage of European commentators who were curious about the ultimate implications *for them* of the political experiment taking place across the ocean. This is what Antonello Gerbi had in mind when he so memorably referred to the "polemic" of the New World, a two-way transatlantic dialogue of the intermittently deaf in which both sides energetically appraised the promises and (more typically) the perils associated with growing interdependence.[56]

But as a result of the two world wars and the unstoppable expansion of both America's power and its European profile, interdependence started to seem an insipid term to describe the realities of transatlantic security and defense ties, which many of America's critics were arguing resembled nothing so much as *dependence*. Beginning in the 1990s and carrying on into the following decade, a new and particularly sharp tone in the transatlantic dispute became more apparent, once systemic bipolarity gave way to unipolarity. And while criticisms of what America was (or was not) doing could emanate from just about anywhere on earth, the ones that really caught Americans' attention stemmed from within the country's circle of traditional transatlantic allies.

Tellingly, Walter McDougall, a shrewd observer of America's foreign policy, chose early on in his magisterial 1997 study of the country's strategic culture to quote some lines from Randy Newman's satirical song "Political Science," highlighting the unerring ability of allies to, as McDougall put it, "get our goat" with their criticism of Washington's policies.[57] The quoted lines included these: "We give them money, but are they grateful? No, they're spiteful and they're hateful! They don't respect us, so let's surprise 'em! We'll drop the Big One and pulverize 'em. . . . *Boom* goes London! And *boom* Paree!" The last line suggests that it was not simply French anti-Americanism that irritated Americans; indeed, it could be maintained that British attitudes have sometimes bothered them even more.[58]

After the events of 9/11, it began to appear as if allies' criticisms that heretofore had simply been annoying for Americans suddenly became dangerous to them, and thus those criticisms were thought to be much more problematic than those critiques of America regularly voiced by countries that were far from being allies. For a time in the twenty-first century's first decade, there would appear a new political challenge confronting Washington and its allies, requiring them to address the damage that might be inflicted upon them all by what was now being styled as "friendly fire" or "lite" anti-Americanism.[59] It was becoming an article of widespread conviction that opposition to what America did, and even to what it stood for, had swelled to unprecedented proportions, with the obvious implication being that, unless these actions abated, the rising tide of transatlantic anti-Americanism was bound to have sinister implications for the United States, as well as, presumably, for the entire West, descending (as some thought it already was doing) into an "ideological civil war."[60]

Was it possible to detect within the broader category of "friendly fire anti-Americanism" a particular French variant? That is, did the French "contribution" to this genre distinguish itself in any notable way(s) from the broader category of anti-Americanism? That broader category has been said to manifest a set of attitudinal characteristics, springing from an eagerness and psychological need to construct negative images of an Other. As such, these characteristics do not necessarily bear any relation to a critique of American foreign or domestic policy behavior on more or less reasoned grounds.[61] Instead, these attitudinal characteristics represent, in Josef Joffe's words, "the obsessive stereotypization, denigration, and demonization of the country and the culture as a whole," in which images of a "Yahoo America" consistently find their counterpart in images of a "Superior Europe."[62]

Two American students of heterostereotyping have sought to provide four hallmarks of such attitudinal anti-Americanism. According to them, it is characterized by systematic antagonism toward an America held to incarnate evil; deliberate exaggeration of the country's shortcomings, coupled with a denial that it might possess any merits; sustained misrepresentation of America for the purposes of advancing a political agenda; and constant misperception and ridiculing of American society.[63] Some of these characteristics would not apply in the specific case of France. But some would.

It is obvious that at moments of crisis such as the one triggered by the Iraq war, demonization came more easily in France than elsewhere in Europe. One example of this is the impressive sales figures racked up by a particularly virulent diatribe insisting that the 9/11 attack (at least on the Pentagon) was a hoax perpetrated by the military-industrial complex, which was seeking a reason to invade the Middle East![64] But France does not exactly have a stranglehold on conspiracy theorizing and demonization of other people and states. As recent developments in America itself show only too well, it is far from difficult to gull large numbers of credulous people into swallowing the craziest of tales and the biggest of lies—even those concocted about their fellow citizens. For every Thierry Meyssan, it appears, there are two Alex Joneses. Yet even if France cannot be said quantitatively to dominate the transatlantic marketplace of crackpot ideas, there are some qualitative aspects of its anti-American heterostereotyping that really do deserve mention. There very much *is* a French specificity worth underscoring with respect to transatlantic anti-Americanism, and its roots can be traced back to theoretical substrata derivative of ontological security and status anxiety.

The French cannot be meaningfully "credited" with having been the inventors of anti-Americanism within the transatlantic world.[65] Nor are they the only Europeans to be associated with this attitudinal orientation. Still, France's numerous "*anti*-s" have cut quite a figure for themselves, such that Walter Russell Mead was not incorrect to claim, as he did in a review essay of the Roger and Revel books, that while France might not have been the place in which anti-Americanism originated, it is the one country in the entire transatlantic system where that dispensation has attained its "most sophisticated intellectual expression"—Meyssan to the contrary, notwithstanding.[66] For sure, the corpus of French anti-Americanism has included the usual assortment of criticisms of America that one frequently encounters elsewhere. Indeed, were France a restaurant instead of a country, no one who hungered for bad tidings about America could possibly push away from the table with appetite unsated; like Alice's Restaurant of Arlo Guthrie fame, France has long been the place where "you can get anything you want" in the way of dispraising America.

Among the staples on the menu of French critiques has been the civilizational one, holding that America's way of life is not only decadent but also dangerous, and in the imaginations of many, for many decades, it has been the thing most likely to menace European (and French) civilization. This critique began to gather steam with the inexorable rise of America to great power status in the late nineteenth century,[67] but it really only took off during the interwar period, which saw the appearance of Georges Duhamel's *pièce de résistance*. Writing a mere fifteen years after American and French soldiers died fighting side by side against the same German foe in what used to be styled a war for civilization,[68] Duhamel was convinced that he had seen the future and it did not work, at least insofar as European interests were concerned. That future was bleak, it was American, and "no one can be in any doubt that America's civilization is well along the road to vanquishing the Old Continent."[69] The theme would recur, with one of Duhamel's more memorable epigones being Jean Baudrillard, whose civilizational critique of the postwar period sought to replicate Duhamel's assessment of the interwar one.[70]

Again, French voices were hardly the only ones in Europe to sound off against American civilization, but to the extent that there has been, and continues to be, a particularly French variant of friendly fire anti-Americanism, it reveals itself in two traits. We encountered one of the traits in chapter 4. In discussing ethnicization and foreign policy, we saw that Anglo-Saxons were introduced as a convenient, not to say necessary, foil for those in France seeking political or other solace in heterostereotyping. In a way that sets French anti-Americanism apart from so much other transatlantic anti-Americanism, Anglo-Saxonism has been put into service as a handy ontological device for distinguishing what is good about French values—social and political ones, in our case—from what is not so good about American values. Anglo-Saxon tropes, as we will see, have inhibited the development of a transatlantic "collective identity" from attaining its fullest flowering, and this has been one of the important reasons why cooperation between the two "old allies" has been less optimal than it otherwise might have been.

Added to the symbol of Anglo-Saxonism is another referent that, once more, distinguishes French anti-Americanism from that of other European states. This second symbol inheres in near-mythical beliefs entertained about the structure of the international system and can be captured in one word, *multipolarity*. This symbol is definitely an ontological referent, but even more, it testifies to how status anxiety can contribute to the suboptimality of Franco-American security and defense cooperation. This will constitute the focus of this chapter's final section, but one more issue deserves brief mention before moving on from anti-Americanism: the potential consequences of heterostereotyping, not so much for the bilateral relationship as for France itself.

In chapter 6, I will once more allude to the issue of consequences and ask whether, had Franco-American cooperation been more "efficient" in the realm of security and defense, it would have generated different outcomes, such that a more coherent Franco-American tandem would have contributed to better foreign policy results for both countries and for that broader ensemble called the West. Many appear to believe this to be so, but demonstrating this is not so easy, as we will see. Perhaps it is less difficult to discern the consequences that France's anti-Americanism has had for *French* security and defense interests?

Some scholars believe there have been knowable, and important, consequences. Philippe Roger inclines toward this view, in his general indictment of French anti-Americanism as a largely self-inflicted ideological wound, manifesting itself in a defensive crouch that hurts France more than America. The tone was set during the interwar years and hardly varied throughout the remainder of the twentieth century, with France's anti-American discourse "having settled on its line—the Maginot Line."[71] For Roger, the interwar years, "that golden age of anti-Americanism," would establish the enduring pattern for what was to come, as the new anti-Americanism commencing in the early 1920s evolved into a "discourse that was at one and the same time reactive and resigned—a discourse of those who had already been defeated and colonized. The hatred of America took its nourishment from virulent self-contempt."[72] Jean-François Revel, despite his book's subtitle highlighting how "inconsequential" French anti-Americanism really is, nevertheless sees French (and other European) criticisms of America's enhanced power following the end of the first Cold War as having been responsible for that very aspect of Washington's foreign policy that most drew their ire, namely its tendency toward "unilateralism."[73]

To the extent that one can identify a clear and profound consequence of French anti-Americanism, it probably inheres less in those recent Franco-American upheavals about which Revel wrote and more in those of Roger's "golden age" of the interwar years. The argument, stripped to its basics, would go something like this: American isolationism proved to be a disaster for French security and defense interests, as became glaringly obvious with the defeat of 1940. French anti-Americanism was one factor contributing to American noninvolvement in the European balance of power; it prevented Americans from developing a sense of empathy for France. Had the Americans partaken of a "collective identity" with their sister republic, they would have been more inclined to assist France sooner. But they did not, and as William Keylor suggests, while there were many sources of American isolationism in the interwar period, one of the most noteworthy was the "mounting public disillusionment with and resentment of the country 'over there' that seemed to display a lack of gratitude for the American money spent and American lives lost in the Great War."[74]

Contributing to this public disillusionment was a swelling postwar volume of criticism of America mounted by French policy intellectuals.[75] Some of this critique was reasonable; some of it was not. Nothing so poignantly illustrated the unreasonable critique as a remarkable polemic that appeared in 1930, written by political journalist Isaac Kadmi-Cohen. He expressed the view that there exists a structural remedy for France's America "problem": the creation of a more "autonomous" Europe. Achieving this, Kadmi-Cohen was convinced, would require a tight bonding between the French and the Germans, for only an alliance between the two could endow the Old Continent with the means of warding off its transatlantic oppressor. "A United States of Europe!" exulted Kadmi-Cohen. "These words are on everyone's lips, they spring from the hearts, fire up the imagination, of all! The time has come to put an end to the intolerable American oppression!"[76] Kadmi-Cohen's touting of Franco-German reconciliation was not so much wrong as woefully and tragically premature. In July 1942, a dozen years after writing this stirring paean to "Carolingian" reunion, he was rounded up along with scores of thousands of other French Jews and sent to Auschwitz, where he was put to death in 1944.[77]

Apparently, not everyone's imagination had been as fired up by the vision of an autonomous Europe freed of American oppression; many Europeans continued to understand their fellow Europeans to be their oppressors—or their victims, which amounted to the same thing. By the end of the 1930s it was beginning to look to the French as if America might become a part of the solution to its security problem, rather than being the problem many thought it had been during anti-Americanism's golden age. For Kadmi-Cohen and countless others, this recognition came too late. French beliefs regarding Anglo-Saxons likely played a role in the delay.

That Anglo-Saxon "Cognitive Footbridge": From American Liberalism to French Realism?

In a thoughtful analysis of French anti-Americanism published not too long after the Iraq-inspired falling-out between the two countries, Princeton University's Sophie Meunier, herself a native of France, cautioned Americans not to overreact to its anti-Americanism. Not only was the French public, according to survey data she cited, similar to publics in other European allied countries when it came to their attitudes toward the US, but also what Americans overlooked was the propensity of the French to oppose *other* countries' policy initiatives as well. Indeed, she argues, to the extent one can divine anything meaningful from the category of national character, France demonstrates a strong inclination to be oppositional, featuring a zealous embrace of the role personified by the feisty comic book figure Astérix, that fictional warrior who fought the good fight against the Roman bully during the Gallic Wars of Julius Caesar.

This same point had been made earlier, minus the reference to comic book heroes, by a Spanish historian and diplomat who rooted French oppositional tendencies in a Cartesian mind-set emphasizing the analytical separation of object from subject, in contradistinction to an English (and American) tendency to blur the boundaries between the two.[78] For Meunier, it was not necessary to invoke René Descartes or any other philosopher, as the problem was rooted in the very culture of a people who have "a rebellious, grumpy character, and a high propensity for opposition. . . . They are very distrustful in general—of each other, of their government, of politicians, of America, and so on. The French just like to be 'anti,' especially when the disruption of French society created by the phenomenon in question is strong."[79]

But if, as Meunier suggests, the French are "equal opportunity" oppositionists, only too willing to express disagreement *tous azimuts,* there is one particular point of the compass that can be counted upon to excite their fancy, the one signaling the direction in which might be found lurking the "Anglo-Saxons." As I outlined in chapter 4, the Anglo-Saxon construct, no matter how absurd when taken to represent an ethnic (much less, a racial) grouping, provides yeoman service in an ideological context, where it serves as a sociological footbridge linking the two cultural realms of context and cognition, for if there has been one singularly noteworthy ideological aspect to French theorizing about the enduring Anglo-Saxon, it inheres in the notion that these so-called folk have an unsettling propensity toward "liberalism." In the view of many French political actors, liberalism is readily associated with a host of maladies, ranging from betrayal by allies in postwar settlements, through the destruction of France's republican social fabric, to the economic devastation presumably wrought by a globalization that has in France routinely served as a synonym for "Americanization."

Thus, there is a reason to invoke liberalism as one of the two key symbolic referents for Franco-American suboptimal cooperation in security and defense: it provides a cognitive boundary marker of great policy significance. The sister republics differ ideologically on few things more than they do on the foreign policy meaning and consequences of liberalism, and this has had an effect on how they deal with each other as allies. In addition to helping fuel the heterostereotyping associated with anti-Americanism, French views on liberalism have facilitated the development of other fissures in the bilateral relationship with the United States. These cognitive fissures show up in the different manner in which the same term, *liberalism,* gets construed by politically relevant actors in the two countries.

In France, much more than in America, liberalism is viewed with a jaundiced eye. We have already glimpsed this in the revelations of Emmanuel Macron's forebodings—whether heartfelt or merely opportunistic—that "Anglo-Saxon" (read: liberal) ways are not just incompatible with French ways but are in fact outright destructive of those ways. And Macron's is a mild case of allergy, compared to how liberalism gets received in other sectors of the French political class. As in America, where a current pastime of right-wing politicians and pundits is to play the game of "owning the libs" (that is, discrediting the left), so too in France can liberalism take on an unpleasant, sometimes even sulfurous, odor, betraying a whiff of the looming presence of Beelzebub himself and giving rise to such questions as "Is the devil liberal?"[80] The difference, of course, is that in the US, liberalism is caricatured by its enemies as an emphatically left-wing perversion, which they exuberantly conflate with socialism and communism, while to those Americans who embrace it, liberalism is usually regarded as synonymous with progressivism or even social democracy, only rarely with socialism, and never with communism.[81]

In reality, liberalism in America has been mostly a centrist—sometimes center-left, sometimes center-right—political phenomenon, with an economic content that can, to those critical of markets, admittedly make it look suspiciously right wing. So poorly understood is liberalism domestically that it has led classical liberals (Ronald Reagan, to take a conspicuous example) to advertise themselves as "conservative." Yet today's so-called conservative party in the US, the Republicans, used to be, until its takeover by Donald Trump's populism, a traditionally liberal party, as the French would understand the term.

Thus, liberalism is another one of those many essentially contested concepts that both plague and enliven political analysis. Yet as confused (and confusing) as have been the American discussions about the domestic meaning of liberalism,[82] when it comes to foreign policy, the confusion dissipates, and much more uniformity of thought reigns.

As an ideological lodestar for American foreign policymaking, liberalism elicits a surprising degree of definitional consensus. The experts will tell you that prior to the Trump interlude, liberalism had guided American grand strategy consistently since the advent of the first Cold War and the birth of the post-1945 liberal international order.[83] Whether presided over by Republican or Democratic administrations, from Franklin Roosevelt to Donald Trump, America has been said to be following a liberal grand strategy, one that sometimes gets adorned (even and especially by its supporters) with the label "liberal hegemony."[84]

To its American champions, liberalism has been an unalloyed strategic good, helping to spread peace and prosperity globally, and thus to safeguard liberty at home, by enabling America to set and enforce the rules of the game in both economic and security affairs—through free trade and investment as well as defense cooperation with "like-minded" allies.[85] To its critics, this has been a profoundly misguided strategic orientation, with consequences that have been felt both at home, through deepening inequalities and heightened partisan divisions, and abroad, first through a kind of "blowback" that has engendered anti-Americanism worldwide, and more recently by contributing to the undisputed rise of China as a peer competitor of the United States.[86]

By contrast, in France, a greater ecumenism characterizes the assault on liberalism, as befits a dispensation that attracts very few self-declared adherents. Domestically, it is an ideology that easily garners enemies from the right, the center, and the left of the political spectrum. If one wants to hurl an insult at a political foe in Paris, few epithets can top "liberal"—even better, "ultraliberal" or "neoliberal."[87] Especially audible has been the criticism of liberalism emanating from the French left, which sees it as a cloak for rapacious capitalism—and a cover for "Americanization," to boot. With some rare exceptions in France, liberalism is regarded as manifesting too much of a pro-business market orientation to hold out much appeal in a society that routinely genuflects before the altar of collective rights and "solidarity."[88] None of this is particularly new.[89]

It is not that France has been bereft of liberal political philosophers or of political parties promoting liberal principles.[90] It is just that, compared with the soi-disant Anglo-Saxon countries, liberalism's political hold in France has been a very tenuous one at the best of times. Save for the period of the July Monarchy (1830–1848), France's political system has never been deeply stamped with the liberal impress; to the contrary, liberalism has consistently been playing catch-up since 1848.[91] Nevertheless, the fact that the French political class, with some notable exceptions,[92] does not apply the label to itself should not stop us from asking whether other political figures in other lands might have found it possible to regard France as a liberal polity, and thus, presumably, as a liberal democratic one.

This matters, because if the United States had over time recognized France as being indisputably a sister liberal republic, some say, then the prospects of the two countries cooperating efficiently in security and defense policy would presumably have been greatly enhanced, because of the important role of sociopolitical "isomorphism" in fostering constructive bilateral relations. Many theorists of international relations assume that the felicific ending of the Anglo-American power transition story would have been impossible without the existence of pertinent political and even cultural commonalities shared by the two countries. Others, uncomfortable with the suggestion that close cooperation can only flourish as between countries sharing the cultural commonality of the English language, deemphasize this ethnolinguistic marker in favor of political–ideological conformity associated with liberal democracy.

Indeed, one of the most well-known theories in international relations is "democratic peace theory," and it has spun off a related theory with respect to the "democratic alliance." This derivative theory posits a strong causal connection between an alliance's ideological makeup and the quality of the cooperation among its members. As we saw in chapter 1, this is one of the reasons for the bout of pessimism regarding NATO's future that characterized the years prior to Putin's invasion of Ukraine, filled as those years had been by worries about the democratic "backsliding" of many member states, new as well as old.[93] The logic of this theoretical offshoot of democratic peace theory unfolds according to the following rough syllogism: liberal democracy is a reliable predictor of peaceful cooperation between like-minded states; such cooperation gives rise to liberal security communities, which can evolve into alliances; and these alliances between democracies are superior to other kinds of alliances, yielding a greater harvest of cooperative payoffs for their membership than do alliances that are not groupings of ideological soul mates.[94]

Thus, "democratic alliance" is far from being merely a redundant label to designate a security pact between liberal democracies. Instead, it is the kind of alliance whose members partake of a potent liberal collective identity, which renders otiose worries about ontological security and status. In the democratic alliance, empathy rather than analytical distinctiveness becomes the dominant geo-psychological mode. The members' fundamental liberalism leads them to recognize each other as ideological kith and kin, to such an extent that "it is a fair bet that the values engendered in Western cooperation in security affairs will be maintained in the years ahead, based on the assumption that these values have become internalized in the systems of Western alliance nations."[95]

Looked at it in this manner, NATO is more than a marriage of security convenience among partners possessed of interest-based reasons for cooperation; it is a community of shared liberal values, the foremost of which are human rights, the rule of law, and especially, democratic governance. In such a community, what room could there possibly be for self-regarding concerns derivative of ontological (in)security and status anxiety? Even better, perhaps, what need is there for an enemy to keep the allies cooperating optimally? Apropos of this latter, the leading theorist of the democratic alliance, Thomas Risse, writes, "If the Western Alliance is based primarily on shared values, norms, and a collective identity rather than on the perception of a common threat, one should expect the transatlantic security community to persist in one institutional form or another."[96] In sum, goes the thinking, democratic alliances are by their very nature stronger and more durable alliances than any other kind of security and defense organizations; their liberalism makes them so; and within them, bilateral cooperation becomes more efficient than it can ever possibly be among dyads whose members are not fortunate enough to be liberal democracies.

And here arises our fundamental dilemma: How can we account for *le différend franco-américain*, in ideological terms, if the two countries really are so tightly cosseted within the comforting folds of the democratic alliance? How can France be such an outlier within the alliance if it truly does share those liberal values that presumably made it possible for NATO to take shape and to endure? Maybe the simplest answer is the best answer. It is not just that the

French have no particularly well-advertised esteem for liberalism. We have already noticed that liberalism is not exactly a cherished political value, according to what the French themselves routinely say about it. More to the point, what if France's more liberal allies really do not regard the French as being on the same ideological page as them? In particular, what if Americans have fundamentally comprehended the French as being different from them, just as the French understand Americans to be different from *them*? Could this ideological divergence help us account for suboptimal cooperation, and if so, how?

There are two parts to the answer. The first has us asking whether there is something real about the divergence, rather than simply being a matter of rhetorical but false opposition. Has the apparent delectation the French derive from routinely denigrating liberalism manifested itself consistently in the real-world arena of French politics, such that France has traditionally been a polity that eschews liberal formulas for the good life? In other words, are the French both talking the talk and walking the walk?

The second part of the answer, which we will analyze in the final section of the chapter, turns our attention from the liberalism that really has been a feature of American grand strategy—whether consistently so or not—toward a *realism* that permeates France's strategic thought and conditions its strategic behavior.

First, however, we finish this section by looking at the issue of French liberalism in historical context, with special emphasis upon the years leading up to the formation of NATO. For if the alliance truly did evolve, as Risse tells us, from a preexisting liberal democratic security community consisting of the US, the UK, and France,[97] then it is fair to ask when was the period of time that we might call NATO's "deep origins"? Presumably, it must have been the decade or so leading up to the 1949 formation of the alliance. If so (and it is hard to see how NATO's temporal origins could be located any further back in time than a decade), can we make the argument that liberal democracy during this period was the most appropriate label for capturing the "essence" of French political culture?[98]

How would we actually go about gleaning that essence? Many argue that the place to begin is with "norms." These would come into play through their externalization,[99] which is another way of saying that if its fellow liberal democratic partners (in our case, its sister republic) understood France to have been a liberal democracy at the time of NATO's formation, then this really could give a leg up to the notion that the alliance did come into being as a "democratic" one in the sense the concept has been employed by some of the writers mentioned here.

France obviously was a founding member of the alliance, although it was not among the trio of countries that initially began to meet in 1948 to discuss the prospects of forging a permanent transatlantic security pact; that trio comprised the United States, the United Kingdom, and Canada. Initially, France was kept out the discussions because of the suspicion that communists were playing too large a role in French decision-making and thus it was feared that what was being said in secret would soon be known in Moscow.[100] That France was regarded as prone to communist subversion spoke volumes about the lack of confidence the ostensible Anglo-Saxons had in France's liberal democratic credentials following the Second World War, especially after 1947. Stable liberal democracies do not give the impression of being easily toppled by internal subversion.

But what about the manner in which French political culture was being assessed, especially in Washington, *prior* to the outbreak of the first Cold War and the rise in fears of communist subversion? How did France appear, on the scale of perceived liberal democracy, during, say, the decade preceding the onset of that Cold War, which we might date from 1948 and the Czech coup? This earlier decade leading up to NATO's birth, the years 1938 to 1948, could legitimately be regarded as the gestation period of the alliance, if the latter really *did*, as Risse tells us, evolve out of the wartime security community among the US, the UK, and France.

Here things become extremely murky, for we first need to ask what wartime images may have guided American (and British) decision-makers when thoughts turned to French political culture. The reason for the murkiness is that no one can say exactly what "France" represented during the war. Certainly, there was a rather free-floating, highly romanticized notion that wartime France must have continued to be the embodiment of liberal consciousness and Enlightenment values, and it was not uncommon during those war years to hear some referring to the country as nothing other than the guardian of Western culture.[101]

But free-floating France (the "France of tomorrow") was not the only version of wartime France, nor was it the dominant one. According to one French expatriate teaching in California during the war, four different labels could be affixed to the country: Vichy France, dedicated to isolation and reaction; Laval France, avid for collaboration with the Nazi "new order," under German tutelage; bourgeois-democratic France, incarnate in the Third Republic but bludgeoned into a stupor by the military catastrophe of the spring of 1940; and "European" France, existing as an aspiration for a post-war Europe purged of all national collective identities.[102]

Needless to say, France's future allies were somewhat perplexed about how they should take its political measure during the war years, and that perplexity revealed itself in spades through the often conflictual and sometimes pyrotechnic manner in which American and British leadership dealt with the one person, Charles de Gaulle, who *did* claim to embody the meaning of free-floating France.[103] The only sustainable conclusion about wartime France, then, would seem to be that of Christopher Coker, who argues that it simply disappeared as an element in whatever "Western" collective identity might be held to have existed while the fighting was raging,[104] so we had best look elsewhere than to wartime France to take the measure of its political "essence." The only other places to look, during the gestation period, are either the closing years of the Third Republic, before 1940, or the opening years of its successor Fourth Republic, after 1946. In other words, we would want to find liberal democratic France *somewhere* between 1938 and 1948, but not during the war years themselves.

The Third Republic was definitely a stable constitutional structure, in comparison with the regimes that had preceded it in the century following the French Revolution. Between the revolution and the founding of the Third Republic in 1870, France had not tended toward political tranquility, to put it mildly, though the contrast with America can be overdrawn, given that the "ordered liberty" of the US entailed waging a civil war that cost 600,000 lives, while France's closest comparable civic ordeal, the Paris Commune and its suppression in 1871, resulted in 50,000 deaths.[105]

But the Grim Reaper did manage to take a greater comparative toll on French constitutional orders. Prior to the establishment of the Third Republic, none of the country's dozen or so different constitutional regimes had lasted as long as two decades, with the Second Empire's eighteen years holding the record for longevity.[106] By contrast, the Third Republic endured for seventy years, albeit with some hundred different ministerial councils rising and falling over this period.[107] It was certainly a democratic republic, and throughout most of its seven-decade existence, France might even have looked to be as liberal as any other country in the transatlantic world, notwithstanding the astringent assessment of critics like Hubert Luethy, who regarded it as an "ossified, absolutist" creation, the "administrative state" par excellence.[108]

Others have been more charitably disposed toward the Third Republic. David Thomson renders a mixed verdict on the entirety of the Third Republic, noting that in some respects it could even be regarded as "hyper-democratic," though not thoroughly liberal democratic.[109] Another scholar, Michel Winock, has characterized the Third Republic as a fundamentally bourgeois enterprise held together by the cement of "republicanism," a political dispensation whose central tenets bore at least some resemblance to a few core political values of the Anglo-Saxon liberal democracies, particularly in the safeguarding of property rights and the belief in gradual social progress through the workings of a "meritocracy." But he did not consider it to be a full-fledged liberal democracy, either, because he insisted that its *idéologie de base* was corporatism rather than liberalism.[110]

What is more certain, however, is that the Third Republic did not age well, and the closer we get in time to the decade of NATO's deep origins, the less liberal it looks, including to observers in Washington. The great historian Marc Bloch certainly thought this to be so, and it is a sentiment echoed by Zeev Sternhell, who has argued that throughout that long republic, France possessed two political traditions that were constantly at war with each other. One derived from Enlightenment liberal values while the other was predicated upon a rejection of those same values and reflected the social crisis of industrialization of the late nineteenth century. The result, writes Sternhell, is that by the final decades of the Third Republic, the country's political culture was increasingly characterized by an infusion of nationalism and socialism that degraded its liberalism and laid the foundation for France's own home-grown fascism, which drew succor from both the right and the left.[111]

As for American images of the Fourth Republic, these, as we saw in chapter 1, reflected great anxiety about the country's political stability and its prospects for avoiding communist subversion. And while it is true that the Fourth Republic has often been unjustly trivialized and denigrated,[112] it is no less true that the creators of the postwar successor of the Third Republic intended, from its inception, that it would be almost everything the Third Republic was *not*—though in practice it did not take long for it to begin to look amazingly like its predecessor.[113] To the Fourth Republic's designers, it was going to represent a rejection of the decadent and dangerous "parliamentarianism" of the "bourgeois" Third Republic, which, as everyone conceded during the heady post-Liberation days in France, had been responsible for all of the country's recent calamities, even if no one could agree on what parliamentarianism actually meant. Everywhere among the new republic's leadership there reigned a view that a "break with capitalism" was long overdue, and even the most conservative of the three big parties, the Mouvement républicain populaire, participated eagerly in the nationalization vogue that began in late 1944 and lasted through 1946.[114] For the other two large parties that shared government with the Mouvement républicain populaire at the start of the new republic, the communists (Parti communiste français) and particularly the socialists (Section française de l'internationale ouvrière), the desire to part company with bourgeois, capitalist, and *liberal* ways burned even brighter.[115]

With the onset of the Cold War, France would join America's anticommunist front against the Soviet Union, and there was nothing surprising about its becoming one of the dozen charter members of the Atlantic alliance in 1949. But it did not adhere to the new grouping because it saw it as an ideal nest in which liberal democratic birds of a feather could snuggle down comfortably. Rather, it was seen as the kind of alliance that is quite familiar to those with an understanding of traditional IR realism—a defense pact intended to balance power and deter aggression. France, much more so than the United States, was precisely the kind of country for which realist precepts had a congenial ring.

French Realism and the Pursuit of Balance through "Multipolarity"

To conclude this chapter on cognitive antinomies, let's address the impact of the dichotomy between French realism and American liberalism upon the character of Franco-American cooperation in security and defense. To understand how this aversion to liberalism can factor into the quality of the bilateral relationship, we need to start with the obvious: France's security and defense policies, much more so than America's, have taken their cues from an IR theoretical paradigm loosely known as "realism."

There is a deep irony here, given that it is so often assumed that realism is and must be a quintessentially American strategic perspective, presumably because the more relative capability (that is, power) a state possesses, the greater the inclination of its defense and security policymakers, as well as its public intellectuals, to talk and act like realists. But of course the "reality" of realism's presence in the US suggests otherwise. Far from being a homegrown ideological product, it has been an import from Europe, and a fairly recent one at that, as these things go. So we might say not only that international relations is not really an "American" social science (pace Stanley Hoffmann), in terms of origin,[116] but also that realism has, for most of America's existence, been rather an "un-American" foreign policy perspective.[117]

Instead of America's grand strategy having been motivated by realist precepts, it has actually been liberalism that has been far more important as a source of foreign policy decision-making—not invariably so, but certainly during key turning points when American leaders have sought to rally global opinion, or at least assemble security partners, to enable the advancement of policy goals. As many have noted, and some have lamented, for much of the past century liberal internationalism (often known as Wilsonianism) has been a dominant idea in American foreign policy, maybe not consistently, but with greater staying power, ever since the Second World War, than any of the other foreign policy paradigms with which it has competed for influence.[118]

Others go even further and insist that liberalism has *always* been an important shaper of foreign policy. In fact, they tell us, liberalism and its inevitable dispositional sidekick, the commitment to "multilateralism," were present at the very creation of the new republic. Because of the need for compromise and conciliation imposed by America's federal ("Philadelphian") constitutional order, liberal ideology shaped the new country's identity, and its identity defined the country's "interests." Adherents to this view insist that, notwithstanding historical appearances to the contrary, America has had, and retains, a geopolitical soul marked by a strong preference for the multilateral norms and processes inherent in liberalism. It took some time, of course, for it to reclaim its true soul, only doing so consistently since the Second World War (at least, until the Trump era).[119] This, at any rate, has been the judgment of many who, prior to the Trump administration, saw fit to proclaim liberalism to be, in the words of one scholar, *the* "official ideology of the most powerful state in the world, the United States,"[120] and who sensed an unwavering fealty to this ideology through a succession of post–Second World War presidencies.

No one would make such a claim about liberalism's foreign policy appeal to France. For that country, realism has consistently had pride of conceptual and theoretical place in the shaping of foreign policy. So to the extent that any state can have an "official" foreign policy ideology, realism more than passes muster for France, where in recent decades it has sported the label of "Gaullism." Despite the relative newness of the label, realist precepts have guided France's foreign policy since long before Charles de Gaulle—or for that matter, George Washington—ever drew first breath.[121] It is an age-old foreign policy approach with affinities both to what is sometimes called human-nature realism and to more recent variants that focus on the structure of the international system.[122]

No French leader has been so wittily representative of this approach as Georges Clemenceau, the wartime leader whose human-nature realism always inclined him to adopt the qui vive when responding to the latest liberal visions for peace and security proffered by Woodrow Wilson. On hearing of Wilson's January 1917 appeal to France and the other belligerents for a "peace without victory," Clemenceau wryly lauded the president for having delivered "such a beautiful sermon on what humans would be capable of realizing, if only they were not humans." Later, he would ask, "How can I talk to a fellow who thinks himself the first man for two thousand years who has known anything about peace on earth?"[123]

But it is really the latter, structural version of realism that most concerns us here. Especially germane are its four most relevant assumptions: first, the anarchic international system obliges states, its central components, to elevate survival to the uppermost spot on their list of interests; second, security can best be assured through power balancing, which can and often does imply the need for alliances; third, there is a cyclical pattern to interstate relations, one that suggests "friendship" is at best a transient phenomenon, such that today's ally can be tomorrow's adversary and vice versa; and finally, competition for status can be nearly as important as—and sometimes more important than—the quest for physical security, which is a restatement of Mitzen's "ontological security dilemma."

The implications of France's inveterate realpolitik are clear: the world beyond its borders is a jungle, and France's safe transit through it can only be assured by the stubborn pursuit of a coolly calibrated national interest on the part of rational leaders forever vigilant against alluringly idealistic visions of lasting international comity among sovereign states. Commenting upon the country's grand strategy as it became subsumed under the rubric of Gaullism, Serge Berstein has asserted, accurately, that "we are incontestably in the presence of a conception of realpolitik that has made of Gaullism the natural heir of France's nationalist tradition."[124]

Anglo-Saxon schemes cloaked in the guise of liberal internationalism are especially to be avoided. The French have a tendency to suspect that America's sometimes lofty foreign policy pronouncements might be just a way to disguise and beautify what they regard to be rather homely and narrowly self-interested aims. More to the point, the French have a harder time than America's other Western allies in taking seriously the idea that states will act in a manner that is other than mainly and consistently self-serving. According to Stanley Hoffmann, Americans might think they possess a certain degree of freedom to shape policy in such a way that the interests of allies can be accommodated along with the promotion of their own preferences, whereas the French discount the impact of good intentions, even if they acknowledge that the intentions might be present in spirit. "The French were not denying America's good intentions: they were saying, in effect, that America's deepest drives were contradicting those intentions . . . and that what mattered was not the pure heart (occasionally betrayed by impure execution) but the behavior dictated by the drive."[125] Thus, assumptions about transatlantic collective identity that might have some appeal in, say, Berlin, London, Rome, or Ottawa will, in Paris, always be taken with a large grain of salt.[126] This skepticism translates easily into an oppositional stance against anything smacking of hegemony—including and especially when it is garbed in the ideology of liberalism.

"Hegemony" is another of those confusing concepts with which theorists of IR torment themselves. It has two relatively recognized significations, which tend to cancel each other out, or at least to serve as a warning about the possible contradictions waiting around the next bend in the definitional road. One meaning would have hegemony equate with "control over outcomes," or influence. This is the strong meaning of the word, and judging from how often it has been employed by scholars and other observers of American foreign policy since 1945, one would think that America veritably ruled the world and had been able to do so with even greater panache since the ending of the first Cold War—until, that is, troubles began to arrive in buckets, late in the new century's first decade.[127] In its strong definition, *hegemony* sometimes becomes a synonym for *imperialism,* and thus "liberal hegemony" can simply be another way of expressing the notion of American empire, both to its critics and its supporters alike.[128]

But even scholars like John Mearsheimer, who insist that global hegemony is, if not an oxymoron, at least an impossibility, will admit that regional hegemony is a useful concept and that America *is* such a hegemon—in fact, the only such in the world.[129] Nonetheless, regional hegemony, in the strong sense of the term, also remains objectively an illusion, for if America really did possess control over outcomes in its own neighborhood, then its Latin American "near abroad" would look decidedly less intractable than it has actually been over the years. Can anyone imagine that, were America truly capable of decreeing outcomes, it would desire today's Mexico—as opposed to a different Mexico—as its southern neighbor? Would it want today's Cuba ninety miles off the Florida coast? Would it be happy with Nicolás Maduro's Venezuela if it could simply will into existence another regime for the Bolivarian republic? As one expert on Sino-American relations noted, in response to Beijing's oft-trumpeted policy aim of resisting American hegemony, the US "does not have the option of imposing its will on China any more than it was able to do in Afghanistan, Iraq, Libya, Syria, or Venezuela. If the United States cannot bend Cuba to its will, then it is unrealistic to expect it will be able to do so with China."[130]

The inability of the strong definition of hegemony to withstand the assault of logic and evidence should remind us that if we are going to use the word, it is best to employ it weakly, as just another way of saying "leadership," which happens to be the definition that supporters of the concept's utility increasingly find themselves preferring, as we move further and further from the apogee of unipolarity.[131] Now it is the eternal fate of would-be leaders to keep on good terms with those whom they require as followers, for absent the followers, there can be no meaning in being a leader. And it is in this connection that France's well-publicized aversion to liberal hegemony attains whatever policy importance it possesses, for France rarely makes a secret of its belief that opposing American policies cannot, a priori, be a bad thing, should the need arise. This oppositional position would not stand out so much within the transatlantic alliance were it not for the fact that France, alone among the allies, gives the impression that "multipolarity" is the solution to whatever problems may be associated with American leadership.

Typically, the problem of leadership as perceived by other allies is that America too often strays from the path of multilateralism. Almost all of them would endorse the view that multilateralism—whatever *it* may mean[132]—is a good thing and that it is in the interest of all the allies that America understand this as well, because the ultimate alliance failure, in their eyes, would be a return to unilateralism on the part of Washington. They understand multilateralism to be fundamentally a liberal institutional dispensation, one that since 1945 has been unmistakably and energetically backstopped not just by American power but also by America's liberal values. This is why John Ruggie could write of that post-1945 dispensation that "it was less the fact of American *hegemony* that accounts for the explosion of multilateral arrangements than it was the fact of *American* hegemony" (emphasis in original).[133] The French, too, clearly prefer that America not adopt unilateral policies, but unlike the Germans, British, Canadians, Danes, and so many of the other allies, the French cannot bring themselves to see the solution to unilateralism as being found in anything that smacks of "benign" or "liberal" hegemony. France takes its foreign policy cues much more from realism than from liberalism.[134]

What this means in practice is that "fixing" the problem of American unilateralism requires, from the French perspective, some sort of structural solution, rather than a mere pledge of better behavior on Washington's part. Hence Paris's search for balancing options, even if only so-called soft ones, to remedy dissatisfaction with American leadership.[135] As we saw in chapter 1, even the putatively Atlanticist Emmanuel Macron has been consistent in emphasizing the need for European "autonomy" in security and defense, which represents nothing so much as continuity with a long-standing conviction predicated on optimistic assumptions about systemic multipolarity—assumptions that not even Russia's aggression against Ukraine has dethroned. While the impulse toward autonomy is nothing new, it did gain renewed attractiveness during the salad days of unipolarity shortly following the ending of the first Cold War—that dispensation's so-called moment[136]—at which time French leaders were making no secret of the fact that if they had any say in the matter, they would much prefer that the international system once again became a multipolar one.[137] Indeed, many believed this was going to happen, and that France's grand strategy should be fashioned in such a way as to help make it happen.[138]

That France's leaders have more or less consistently adhered to this aspiration must imply that they believe such a system to be the most congenial to France's global interests. And why not? *C'est logique,* and at first glance, the logic seems impeccable. Who would *not* want a multipolarity that is held to be tantamount to multilateralism, and who apart perhaps from some America-firsters, would want a unipolarity that was said to be synonymous with unilateralism?

But on second and third glances, two problems arise with the multipolarity remedy, as beneficial as it might otherwise seem. The first problem is more normative than anything else, and reflects the ironic—even sad—impact of multipolarity on French security and defense interests in the past. The second problem is an operational one, of trying to effect some means of actually bringing into existence a multipolar system.

Does it follow logically that multipolarity must correlate positively with multilateralism, or that multipolarity must therefore be a good in itself for France and its European partners? The historical record provides reason for caution, even skepticism. Take just the issue of multipolarity's postulated "goodness." To the extent that the record shows us anything at all, it leads to the unavoidable conclusion that France did not derive net—or at least, lasting—benefit from its centuries-long experience with multipolarity. A multipolar order is one in which there are at least three (and at times more) reasonably "equal" states contending for security, economic advantage, power, and status. The Westphalian era of multipolarity, which at moments featured as many as eight such equal states, is usually considered to have endured from the end of the Thirty Years' War, in 1648, to the ending of the Second World War, in 1945.

Early on, multipolarity certainly gave the impression of working in France's favor. In relatively short order after the Peace of Westphalia settlement, it managed to supplant Spain as the world's ranking power. As time went on during that long multipolar era, however, things went downhill for it, with the lasting specter of decline being glimpsed as early as 1692, when France suffered a significant naval defeat by British and Dutch vessels at La Hogue.[139] A series of four global contests in the eighteenth century would leave Britain as the dominant world power by 1763, though France did continue for a while to be the preeminent land power in Europe.

As bad as those eighteenth-century intercolonial wars were for France, though, worse lay in store for it during what the flaming anti-Semitic royalist, Léon Daudet, called the "stupid" nineteenth century.[140] Following a promising spike in its status in 1805, thanks to the genius of Napoleon, the rot again set in, symbolized early in the century by Waterloo[141] and later in the century by Sedan. Yet all this was as nothing compared with the curse multipolarity would lay upon France in the twentieth century, culminating in June 1940.[142] That secular experience was so depressing that by the midpoint of the twentieth century, a "rational" analyst could have been forgiven for drawing the conclusion that this country in particular should never wish to be so unfortunate as to live in a multipolar world again.

Not only was multipolarity not such a good structure when it came to the advancement of France's interests in security and defense, but also it turned out to be rather feckless as an inhibitor of American unilateralism. Over the past fifty years, many in Paris have dreamed of returning to the path of multi-polarity, but in their wanderlust they have lost sight of another empirical real-ity: multipolarity actually worked quite well for *American* interests, and (again, to the extent that we are allowed to vest causal powers in systemic structure) it enabled the US to evolve into the strongest power on earth. In addition, it was precisely during the closing decades of the multipolar era that American diplomacy became more "unilateral" than it ever had been before, with the heyday of this policy dispensation being the interwar period, when isola-tionists of all political stripes dominated America's foreign policy debate.[143]

So if multipolarity does not, in and of itself, imply good things for France and bad things for America, is there a "better" systemic structure on offer, from the point of view of French interests? Again, to the extent the historical record tells us anything, it might be that systemic bipolarity works best for those interests. This is generally not how the first Cold War era has been perceived in France, partly because of the hold on the imagination achieved by the "Yalta myth," in which a plucky and noble France was unjustly kept down by the superpowers, which basically, many believe, sought to cut it out of the design and management of the post-1945 world.[144] Yet in light of the dismal historical record preceding bipolarity, it would be hard to dismiss out of hand the counterintuitive conclusion reached by two commentators on the Franco-American relationship, who despite their lack of sympathy for Amer-ican leadership in Cold War Europe, nevertheless concede that bipolarity had been instrumental in facilitating France's return to prosperity, security, and *rang* (status) following 1945. "We forget," write Noël Mamère and Olivier Warin, "just how cozy the Cold War era was for France. . . . The superpower blocs butted up against each other, forming a roof under which France was able to shelter and prosper."[145]

Difficult as it may be to read the structural tea leaves in search of normative guidance, it is even harder to figure out a manner in which structural change could somehow be brought about as a result of France or some other state preferring it. In response to the well-advertised desire of French leaders for a multipolar world, Kenneth Waltz once remarked that "one cannot usefully will the end without willing the means."[146] On the twin (and dubious) assumptions that France's "America problem" had been exacerbated as a result of "unipolarity," and that unipolarity continues to be a helpful manner of describing the international systemic structure, it would seem there are three ways, and three ways only, by which a non-unipolar world might be brought into being.

The first way is the easiest, though perhaps not the most rewarding in the long term: do nothing and hope that America declines significantly enough on its own to close the gap between itself and the next most powerful member(s) of the system, so that the era of unipolarity can be pronounced well and truly dead. The second and third ways require some considerable effort on the part of France and whomever else it might seek to implicate in the balancing act. France could try to forge a more perfect and competent European Union, one in which that entity's political and military grasp is at last brought into harmony with its economic and monetary reach.

The problem here is that "Europe" is not an easy geostrategic edifice to build, mainly because its several major players do not see eye to eye on the architectural plans and do not all embrace the autonomy aspiration with the same gusto as the French. While it is obvious that the Russian war on Ukraine has triggered renewed interest in Europeans' beefing up their military capabilities, it has not resolved the older worries about greater autonomy being purchased at the price of alliance solidarity. Besides, Europe no longer carries the economic clout it once did, so even on the off chance it could achieve that "more perfect union," its loss of commercial and financial prowess vis-à-vis China would render balancing much more difficult than it currently is.

This leaves the third way, to foment an "antihegemonic" coalition, with most of those who had been dreaming this dream during the era of unipolarity concluding that the likely (indeed, the only) candidates for membership are France, Germany, and Russia.[147] This hardly seemed to be a promising option, or a realistic one, even when it was being bandied about by some in the first flush of unipolarity. Today, it seems a downright degenerate remedy, and hence the backtracking of such erstwhile Putin supporters in France as Marine Le Pen, Éric Zemmour, and Jean-Luc Mélenchon, all acting as if they had never heaped words of praise upon the Russian leader or otherwise been his fanboys and fangirl.

Thus, to the extent that Franco-American cooperation suffers from systemic peculiarities associated most recently with unipolarity, and that discrepant ideological visions lie at the heart of the Franco-American problem—and given how "culturally" conditioned and significant is the antinomy between American liberalism and French realism—it might seem as if there really is not much that can be done to improve the quality of bilateral cooperation. Or, conversely, it might seem that nothing much *need* be done, and that the remedy for the problem of systemic peculiarities is at hand, to be discerned in the "problem-solving" musings of a long-forgotten Chilean president, Ramón Barros Luco. When this early twentieth-century (1910 to 1915) leader was asked by a reporter whether it was a challenge to govern Chile, his response was blithely in the negative. Reflecting upon his own experience in politics, Barros Luco stated that there were really only two kinds of problems, "those that solve themselves, and those that have no solution."[148]

If—and this is a big *if*—systemic change holds out the prospect of an alteration in the quality of Franco-American security and defense cooperation, then it would seem that this prospect is at hand. The reason is China, about which Napoleon is famously supposed to have warned, "Let China sleep. For when she wakes, the world will tremble." The emperor almost certainly never expressed this caution in French, English, or any other tongue, but it is fitting that the words should so regularly be attributed to a French source.[149]

If unipolarity is not already dead and buried, it soon will be. But it is highly unlikely to cede its place to multipolarity, whatever the current delusions of Vladimir Putin may be. Russia can cause trouble because of its nuclear arsenal, in the absence of which NATO forces would have been operating in Ukraine early on in the war. But Russia lacks the economy to become a leading power, and what economy it has (roughly the size of Italy's or Canada's) has become smaller as a result of Putin's madcap venture. The reemergence of bipolarity is much more likely than the return of multipolarity, meaning that there are two relatively equally proportioned entities endowed with the requisite economic and military sinews to be the system's greatest powers: the United States and China.[150]

Whether this will bode well or ill for the Franco-American special relationship is not something anyone can know at this time. But what can be asked, certainly with the example of Napoleon (to say nothing of Putin) in mind, is whether the "agency" imputed to leaders might prove to have lasting causal bearing upon the quality of bilateral security and defense cooperation. This is a topic we address in chapter 6.

III

CULTURE AND INDIVIDUAL "AGENCY"

Do Leaders Matter?

Individuals and Their Relationship to Strategic Culture

The "Level-of-Analysis Problem" in Franco-American Relations

Elsewhere in these pages, reference was made to the familiar level-of-analysis problem in international relations theory and foreign policy analysis, highlighting the question of where we should shine the investigative spotlight in our search for "causal" clues. Is it the system to which our attention is primarily to be drawn? The units that make up the system? Or the leaders of those units?

There have been many attempts, over the years, to frame this problem of levels (or images), but by far the most parsimonious and elegant such construe has been that of Kenneth N. Waltz, in his first and in some ways most influential book, from the late 1950s, which was based on his Columbia University doctoral dissertation from earlier in the decade.[1] Twenty years after the publication of *Man, the State, and War,* Waltz produced another seminal work, giving impetus to the "structural-realist" school in IR theory—a work whose fame, or notoriety, was such that it came to eclipse in importance his earlier book among many of the discipline's professoriate. That 1979 contribution, *Theory of International Politics,*[2] partially replicated the level-of-analysis framework established in the earlier book, but unlike it, this later work saw Waltz enthusiastically hitching his argument to a powerful systemic engine, a "third-image" perspective in which primary explanatory prowess for relations between states was to be associated with the international system's structural attributes.

At times in the chapter 5, and especially in its final section, we caught glimpses of how third-image analysis might be brought to bear upon our inquiry into the cultural sources of Franco-American interaction in security and defense policy. We saw, for instance, a French systemic preference for a multipolarity that many seem to think must be beneficial to French interests. We also encountered the claim that asymmetries in power between the two countries had a lot to do with *le différend franco-américain*. Each of these structural aspects, however, only made sense because of the way in which it formed part of a postulated societal consciousness that influenced decision-makers' thinking. This was in keeping with the general approach taken in this book, which hews mainly to the Waltzian "second image." This is the level of analysis that focuses not on the system but instead on sociopolitical (and cultural) attributes of the *units* constituting the system.

In part 2, we dwelt at length upon three interrelated second-image, and therefore sociopolitical, "variables": collective historical memory (sometimes branded "memory transfer"), demographic composition, and ideological predispositions. These three categories were offered as being potentially the most revelatory sources of cultural insight into the puzzle lying at the heart of the special relationship between France and America, the chronic suboptimality of their cooperation in security and defense matters. In the end, I argued that among the three categories, ideational predispositions have done the most to keep the two countries' cooperation confined to a pattern of "bounded rationality," especially since they became permanent allies in 1949.

While the third image has at times been allowed to crash what has been a predominantly second-image analytical party in these pages, not much has yet been said about the Waltzian "first image." This level of analysis posits that the most important sources of foreign policy outputs are the actions and roles of individual leaders. I will seek to remedy that lack of discussion by grappling with the question of whether the suboptimal quality of bilateral cooperation in security and defense can most successfully be ascribed to things that central decision-makers have either done or failed to do.

Scholars of IR, with very few exceptions, have tended to be much more reluctant than historians to dwell upon the agency that individuals might possess in the shaping of their countries' foreign policies. The reasons for this disciplinary difference are partly anchored in the kinds of epistemological assumptions we discussed in chapter 3, where political scientists were said to be more inclined toward theorizing both explicitly and nomothetically, while historians were held to be too idiographically focused to permit them to indulge in sallies of deductive imagination capable of yielding causal connections between variables.

As with all caricatures, this one has some element of truth. The general-izing proclivities of political scientists *do* render them less than hospitable to the idea that explicative understanding of patterns in foreign policymaking can or should owe much to the desires and activities of individual leaders. This might seem to be an outrageously odd thing to state in a book focused on the special Franco-American relationship, in light of how often troubles between the countries have been traced back to single leaders, including—to cite just the most prominent examples—Franklin D. Roosevelt in the 1940s, Charles de Gaulle in the 1960s, George W. Bush in the early 2000s, or Don-ald Trump most recently. Somehow, the wistful thinking goes, if only some other leader had been at the helm, in the Élysée or the White House or both, how much differently things might have turned out in the two states' record of cooperation, leading them to behave more often as if they truly *were* the dependable old allies of legend.

Indeed, were this wish miraculously granted, there might seem to be no point at all in me or anyone else trying to invoke cultural (second-image) accounts of foreign policy behavior, since everything one needed to know could presumably be discovered by rigorous examination of the operational code that ostensibly guides the decision-making of the individual whose job it is to preside over the national interest. By "operational code" I mean a belief system that frames the manner in which decision-makers perceive and respond to reality. Historians tend to shun this political science construct, yet they have their own word for the same concept, borrowed from the Germans: they hold the leader's Weltanschauung to possess cognitive and behavioral impact.[3]

Regardless of whether we employ German or English terminology, the implications are the same when it comes to explicating Franco-American suboptimality. Find out what makes the leaders of the respective countries tick and you have found out why this bilateral relationship has been so behav-iorally special. Even better, say some, if you can figure out how to improve the quality of the leaders' ticking, you can enhance the effectiveness of their cooperation in security and defense.

There are good reasons for IR scholars who are political scientists to pay greater heed to individuals than they sometimes, to the chagrin of historians, are inclined to do. As Daniel Byman and Kenneth Pollack, two enthusiasts of first-image analysis who also specialize in security studies, remind us, it would be strange in the extreme for any "causal" analyst of, say, the origins of the Second World War to seek to account for that conflict without according prime importance to Adolf Hitler. And while the German Führer might be the most extraordinary case of an individual exercising agency in foreign policy-making, he is far from being the only such case—the current fighting between Russia and Ukraine is held by many to be solely the result of one demented leader's twisted operational code. Similar agency could be ascribed to Napoleon. Ergo, say these security experts, it is long past time for political scientists to shed their aversion to the first image and "to rescue men and women, as individuals, from the oblivion to which political scientists have consigned them."[4]

But before we forsake strategic-cultural analysis of the mainly second-image variety altogether for the first-image pleasures of biographical inquiry,[5] it is worth our while to ponder a bit of advice from Robert Jervis, who cautions against the seduction of according excessive causal significance to the exploits of even such consequential leaders as Woodrow Wilson, Winston Churchill, Josef Stalin, Franklin Roosevelt, or Mao Zedong, to name a few. Clearly, they mattered a great deal, but just as important—and likely more important—have been the "incentives and constraints posed by the environment, be it domestic or international"—meaning, regardless of whether the environment is a second- or a third-image one. "When Harold Macmillan was asked what caused him to alter his policies," Jervis continues, "he famously replied, 'Events, dear boy, events,' and Abraham Lincoln said, 'I claim not to have controlled events, but confess plainly that events have controlled me.'"[6]

Events are often assumed mainly to take the shape of third-image constraints standing between what a leader wishes to accomplish (sometimes called outputs) and what that same leader is actually able to accomplish (outcomes). This is what Macmillan was undoubtedly getting at. But not Lincoln. For him, it was second-image developments that did so much to strip him of control over outcomes and thus to minimize if not deny outright his agency, or so he averred. This is to point out the obvious: domestic determinants weigh heavily upon, and largely shape, the thinking of decision-makers. And if this is so, then cultural determinants must be important features of those domestic constraints.

It might not seem necessary to state this, as it should simply be common sense that leaders are influenced by the cultural milieu of the societies they lead, on matters related to both domestic and foreign policy. Yet sometimes the obvious is worth repeating. It is worth repeating in the case of the Franco-American special relationship, because if leaders are possessed of such agency as to bring about fundamental change, yet nothing ever fundamentally changes, a contradiction arises between that postulated agency and evident strategic–cultural continuity. Some might seek to resolve the contradiction by resorting to a deus ex machina and insist that the quality of the bilateral relationship actually *did* change as a result of the impact of Leader A (in America) or Leader F (in France), or both, at any given time, but that, unfortunately or otherwise, successors in one or both of the countries undid the changes, setting everything back to the status quo ante, through a process occasionally theoretically marketed as something called "redirecting counterfactuals."

Another, much simpler, way of resolving the contradiction would be to deny outright that there *is* any invariant pattern worth speaking of, such that all who profess to detect one, including myself, are plainly mistaken. Clearly, my own inclination *has* to be to firmly reject the denial-of-pattern school. This, then, leaves me no choice but to fall back, at least for the sake of the analysis in this chapter, on the deus ex machina argument. I will probe this in the following two sections, in which I concentrate upon two cases, each emphatically situated in the first image. Each case focuses on an American president who, for better or worse, was held to have been centrally responsible for the ongoing quality of Franco-American security and defense cooperation: the two presidents Roosevelt, Theodore and Franklin. We will glimpse them in a Dickensian light, echoing the famous "best/worst" temporal dichotomy upon which *A Tale of Two Cities* begins, save that in this instance it is Washington and Paris rather than London and Paris that capture our attention. We will want to see why, for some observers of the Franco-American special relationship, the two Roosevelts represent the best of times and the worst of times that the relationship has known over the past century or so.

Before starting out on our quest for first-image contingency through comparison, however, I need to make two observations about path dependency's conceptual helpmate, counterfactual reasoning. The first observation is that counterfactual reasoning has especial applicability to case studies, such as this entire book on the Franco-American special relationship. Many IR theorists regard counterfactual reasoning to be an appropriate, perhaps indispensable, method for establishing causality within case studies. A different (counterfactual) past, it is argued, might be expected to yield a different counterfactual present, all things being equal, and our challenge is to try to figure out why— or even whether—a counterfactual antecedent could be held to generate a counterfactual consequent. If it can, it is said to be causally significant. To advert to the example of Hitler, a counterfactual inquiry into the origins of the Second World War could be conducted on the basis of his nonexistence, which would allow crisper examination of other potentially causal considerations that may have led to war but that have been cast into the shadows by the glare of the klieg lights trained upon Hitler.[7]

In chapter 3, I put counterfactualism to the labor of helping us understand what might be considered to be cultural about this epistemology. I did this in a discussion of how strategic culture might itself be construed in a contextual manner, with context understood as either a historical or an "ethnic" instantiation of national character/identity. In the case of the historical, path-dependent logic plays an obvious part in the story by lending itself to the thought that the pattern of bilateral relations over time was itself a cultural datum, while in the case of ethnicity, relational (and thus path-dependent) dynamics were adduced to "complete" the meaning of a given state's national character/identity.

Where path-dependent dynamics are at work, counterfactuals are usually somewhere close at hand. They can tell us something important about the impress of culture upon Franco-American strategic interaction. This, in the end, was the point chapter 3 was trying to establish, and it in turn leads to the second observation worth making about counterfactual reasoning: for all its potential value, it is also fraught with difficulties. I called counterfactual reasoning a conceptual helpmate of path dependency, but if it is such a helpmate, it arrives on the explanatory battlefield with comrades of its own. The most relevant such help is the assistance supplied to counterfactual reasoning by the idea of "contingency." Contingency, however, is far from straightforward, in both meaning and applicability—or to put it more accurately, while its meaning might pose few difficulties, things are otherwise with its analytical *application*.

Let us start with its meaning. Contingency is often employed as a synonym for a critical turning point, or juncture, held to be that moment in time when there occurred an alteration in the future historical trajectory, thereby setting events yet to unfold on a path different from the anterior one. As we saw in chapter 3, contingency was invoked as a means of helping us grasp how the so-called initial conditions embedded in the Erbfeindschaft logic ceased to be able to shape the future, liberating the relationship from the path upon which it had been, and setting it upon a different one.

If the meaning of contingency might seem reasonably uncomplicated, things are anything but simple when we turn our attention to trying to identify the critical juncture that reoriented the future, for one analyst's application of the purported turning point often becomes someone else's historical fiction. This was the crux of my own contingency sleuthing in chapter 3, when I suggested that those who understood the contingent event of Franco-American strategic relations as having taken place in 1778, or even 1763, might not be looking far enough back into the history of the intercolonial wars. They should, or so I maintained, have been casting their thoughts back to 1745 and the events surrounding the capture and eventual return of the Fortress of Louisbourg. Whichever the year in which contingency became "applied," the consequence remained the same: exit Erbfeindschaft.

These difficulties illustrate why counterfactual reasoning, as a research methodology, can be so controversial, and why quite a few scholars can make no secret of their disdain for it as "make-believe history" serving no purpose other than titillation. Yet good defenses can be mounted on its behalf.[8] Among the best such defenses is that of Jack Levy, who as we recall from chapter 3, insists that counterfactual reasoning can serve as a valuable accompaniment to causal analysis. Pertinent here is his assertion regarding "necessary conditions," upon which many IR scholars rely heavily if not exclusively when trying to establish causation. Identify these conditions and you have gone a fairly long way toward demonstrating causation. A good way to make this identification, Levy says, is precisely by employing counterfactual reasoning, in the sense that if we can "retrofit" a historical account by removing something that *did* occur and replacing it with something that did *not* (something that is counterfactual), then we might be better able to grasp causality, by examining the consequence(s), if any, generated by the retrofitting. As Levy writes, "*necessary condition counterfactuals* take the form 'if $\sim x$, then $\sim y$' (if not x, then not y)" (emphasis in the original).[9]

I will try to determine whether "if not x, then not y" can be credibly inferred, by looking at claims regarding both presidents Roosevelt and their mooted impact upon Franco-American relations. Taking to heart Levy's instruction, I want to try to determine whether these leaders' preferences and actions were decisive in establishing something so important about the quality of the bilateral relationship as to have effectively constituted contingent "events," changing the course of history and setting the bilateral relationship on a new path. By the twentieth century, of course, Erbfeindschaft would have been so distant in the rearview mirror as to be out of sight, so the transformation that our counterfactual change agents would have been expected to effect would be to replace the stasis of suboptimality with something different—something better in the case of the first leader under examination, and something worse in the case of the second. In either case, if we can demonstrate a contingent and lasting impact of individual leaders, we might be able to answer in the affirmative the question posed by Robert Jervis.

It Was the Best of Times:
Theodore Roosevelt and Franco-American Relations

One might think, given the discussion of anti-Americanism in France in chapter 5, that the French have never cared very much for American political and military leaders, or even for the people they led. Whether this generalization happens to be sustainable or not, it is obvious that there have been some American political figures, though maybe not many, about whom the French (meaning informed elites or the broader public, or both) have cared a great deal, in an affectionate rather than a malevolent way. One French historian and biographer, Claude Fohlen, has lamented that though the number of certifiable "friends of France" in American leadership positions over the years may not have been large, the French still have managed to forget some of the most important members of this select group. Within the set of Francophile American political luminaries, Fohlen tells us, there have been two conspicuous absentees from France's collective memory. One of these is Thomas Jefferson, who served as America's representative to France during the years 1784 to 1789 and admittedly had a tough act to follow, since he immediately succeeded the hugely popular Benjamin Franklin.[10]

Jefferson would later go on to the White House, and while some Americans may recall that their third president gave every evidence of being a "friend of France" both before and during his presidency,[11] not so many French appear to realize this. Indeed, it took a successful popular movie of the mid-1990s, *Jefferson in Paris,* to remind Parisians that they should have been thinking more fondly of Jefferson all along. Somewhat ruefully (no pun intended), Fohlen noted that while one could walk down Paris streets bearing the names of a half dozen or so distinguished American political figures—Franklin, George Washington, Abraham Lincoln, Woodrow Wilson, Franklin D. Roosevelt, Dwight Eisenhower, and John F. Kennedy—one sought in vain to find any public thoroughfare or square named in honor of Jefferson. None of the aforementioned figures, said Fohlen, had done more than Jefferson on behalf of France. Only one other absentee from French collective memory had a comparable stature: the twenty-sixth president, Theodore Roosevelt, another true friend of France.[12]

Fohlen does well to draw our attention to Theodore Roosevelt, for he did turn out to be, somewhat surprisingly, a leader who at one time was extremely popular in France and was adjudged to be very beneficial for French interests. And while the presidency of this Roosevelt predated by a few years the onset of Kaspi's "time of the Americans," when France and the US once again became allies, I invoke the twenty-sixth president here because he makes such an interesting study from a first-image perspective. If leaders truly do matter, such that an individual *could* have effected a "reset" in the long-term pattern of Franco-American relations, he should have been that leader.

By contrast, a president whose name *does* adorn public space in Paris, Franklin D. Roosevelt, has had a much more mixed reputation among students of the Franco-American relationship. This is almost entirely a result of the ill will that was on such prominent display during the Second World War, between him and Charles de Gaulle, who led the Free French and who claimed to represent the "true" France—a claim routinely disregarded in Washington from June 1940 until the autumn of 1944. As we saw in chapter 2, many scholars are prepared to tell us that had Roosevelt gotten along more equably with the French leader than he evidently did, the quality of bilateral relations would have been fundamentally better than it has turned out to be since the 1940s. Ergo, Franklin Roosevelt was the personification of contingency in Franco-American relations, a change agent without whom bilateral ties would have developed in a more efficiently cooperative manner.

How could anyone possibly know this? One way to approach the question would be to employ Levy's formulation regarding necessary-condition counterfactuals and to assume that "if not *x*, then not *y*" translates into the assertion, If not for Franklin D. Roosevelt, Franco-American relations would not today be characterized by suboptimality in cooperation but rather by a "healthier" form of bilateral interaction. One is permitted to be skeptical regarding this counterfactual assertion; to test it, we would have to effectively "disappear" FDR from the Franco-American story and substitute for him a president ostensibly more well-disposed toward France.

The ground rules for counterfactuals, importantly, stipulate that when we "rewrite" history, we should do so in as minimal a manner as possible. Thus, we obviously cannot replace Franklin Roosevelt with, say, Joan of Arc or Louis XIV, each of whom could be counted upon to be charitably disposed toward French interests in the miraculous event that either had been transported through time and space and parachuted into the Oval Office of the early 1940s. But what if we were to rewrite the wartime history of Franco-American bad blood not by resorting to miracle counterfactuals such as these but by conjuring into the counterfactual American presidency during those crucial (or so it is assumed) years of 1940 to 1944 someone who not only was an American but also had been an American president, and who, to top it all off, even bore the name Roosevelt?

For the purpose of illustrating why it is not such a good idea to rely excessively on first-image explanations for the state of the Franco-American special relationship, let's make Theodore Roosevelt our counterfactual antecedent and then try to determine whether in fact we have good grounds for assuming there would have been a counterfactual consequent resulting from his occupying the White House from 1940 through 1944. To be clear, what we are trying to determine here is whether it would have made any lasting difference in the established pattern of Franco-American interaction to have Theodore rather than Franklin Roosevelt in power when Charles de Gaulle was posing such a challenge to American diplomacy.

There are many reasons to think it would not have made much difference, and nearly all of them relate, as Macmillan noted, to events, which so often cause even the best-laid plans of mice and leaders to go astray. In Theodore Roosevelt, we have, empirically speaking, the means at our disposal to aid our pondering of those long-term patterns of the Franco-American special relationship, because Fohlen was correct in his assessment of the twenty-sixth president, on two scores. First, Theodore Roosevelt *has* largely been forgotten by the French.[13] Second, he was certainly someone whom contemporaneous French observers regarded as their country's friend. So a brief look at the impression this Roosevelt made upon the French, and why it did not really have any effect upon secular trends in Franco-American relations, would be instructive. If even the most well-disposed and Francophile president imaginable can have had no lasting impact upon the *real* Franco-American past, what would be the basis of thinking such a leader could matter for the counterfactual past?

As I mentioned in chapter 1, to speak of a special relationship between France and the United States comes close, for many scholars, to speaking oxymoronically, if not blasphemously. In that chapter, I introduced the rubric of special relationships as connoting behavioral rather than normative qualities. I certainly am not claiming that France and the US have been the sort of friends that many scholars insist (maybe correctly) Britain and the US have been for the past half century, if not more. Yet there was a time when even the normative construe of "special relationship" would have been an apt description of Franco-American relations: during Theodore Roosevelt's second term in office. And even when he was out of office, he remained extremely popular in France, up until his death in 1919.[14]

Indeed, after his death in January of that year, Roosevelt became lionized in France, a country that had never cultivated a habit of gushing over American presidents, whether dead or alive. His popularity stemmed in part from policies undertaken while he was in office and in part from French appreciation of the efforts to which Roosevelt went, during the period of America's neutrality in the First World War, to rouse his country to "preparedness" for the time when military intervention in Europe might be needed.[15] Although Roosevelt had been among the overwhelming majority of Americans preferring nonintervention on the outbreak of the war in August 1914, he switched to a strident advocacy for intervention on Britain's and France's side, following the German sinking of the *Lusitania* in May 1915.[16]

He himself desperately aspired to serve on the Western front, even professing that it would be a fitting epitaph if it could be said of him that he died fighting for France, but his wish to lead a division into combat was never granted by his nemesis, and his country's commander in chief, Woodrow Wilson. Still, French observers could not fail to note and to be moved by the fact that all four of Roosevelt's sons went off to war, and that the youngest, the aviator Quentin, died in action in French skies in July 1918. Ted Jr. and Archie also saw combat (and were wounded) with the American Expeditionary Force in France, while Kermit served with the British army in the Middle East. Ted returned to the battlefield during the Second World War and died in France, two weeks after the Normandy landings, in which he had participated as a fifty-seven-year-old brigadier general, the oldest soldier to go ashore on June 6, 1944. He is buried in France, alongside Quentin.[17]

Thus, there was nothing unusual about the manner in which news of Theodore Roosevelt's death was received in postwar France, where he was fondly recalled as a great friend of France. Charles Lyon-Caen, the permanent secretary of l'Académie des Sciences morales et politiques, to which Roosevelt had been elected in 1909, spoke eloquently in this regard, in a eulogy delivered at l'Institut de France in late December 1921. Tribute, of course, was paid to the deceased president's admirable personal qualities, but above all, Lyon-Caen's words reflected gratitude for Roosevelt's unstinting efforts on behalf of France during the war. This president, said Lyon-Caen, would be remembered as someone who fought for liberty and the rule of law. "As well, he will be remembered for having been one of the greatest political and moral figures of the twentieth century."[18]

No less surprising than the fact of Roosevelt's being so *little* remembered today by the French is that they should have developed such affection for him in the first place. When he started to garner widespread acclaim in the United States, French images of America could hardly have been more negative, largely as a result of fear and loathing engendered by America's war against Spain in 1898.[19] This conflict was easy to link with Roosevelt, given the celebrity he and his fellow Rough Riders had achieved fighting in Cuba— celebrity that fueled Roosevelt's rapid electoral rise through the ranks of the Republican party, first to the governorship of New York, in 1898, and then, two years later, to the vice presidency under William McKinley. Following McKinley's assassination in September 1901 and Roosevelt's ascension to the presidency, some French observers of American politics grew even more worried about America than was customary.

The worry stemmed from the belief that the 1898 war represented a threat to *France*. The war against Spain was held to be contemptible in its own right, but it also was regarded, more ominously, as the first act in an unfolding geopolitical drama associated with America's "rise." Many in France felt that neither America's new grand strategy nor its new president foreshadowed anything good for French interests.[20] In words that could have passed muster among the legion of French critics of George W. Bush's foreign policy during the controversy over the Iraq war, Theodore Roosevelt was being excoriated for daring to confuse America's interests with the interests of the world. As one French observer summed things up, "In Mr. Roosevelt's opinion, anything that benefits America benefits all of humanity; anything that goes against the interests of America goes against those of all of civilization! . . . When we see him affirming in all sincerity that Cuba had to be freed from the Spanish yoke because justice and liberty demanded no less, we cannot help but worry what those same noble objectives might portend for us."[21]

Just as we have seen in recent years, many in the France of more than a century ago felt that American power needed balancing and that France was the natural candidate to lead the campaign to constrain Leviathan. The sobering lesson to be derived from the Spanish war was that weakness invites aggression. Given that America becoming a world power had so upset the global balance, it was imperative that equilibrium be rapidly restored. Only France could restore that lost balance. "France alone can inspire a coalition of willing European states to counterbalance the rising enemy across the Atlantic," thundered Joseph Ribet. This coalition, realistically, would have to be made up of Latin and Slavic states, given the likelihood that the Anglo-Saxons would themselves coalesce in a geopolitical bloc. But only within a multipolar world could safety for France be found, and happily, France "would constitute the center of gravity in the global balance."[22]

In reading these words of long ago, what strikes us is not just how much they resembled commentary of French observers who, beginning in the 1990s and culminating at the time of the Iraq war, were worrying aloud about the negative consequences for France of a *hyperpuissante* America swashbuckling its way through a "unipolar" world.[23] More than this, what impresses the contemporary reader is how ridiculous was this earlier perception of an American threat, given what we now know about what the subsequent decades of the twentieth century held in store for France. That country was not going to find salvation in multipolarity or any French-led balancing of America; rather, it was going to seek and find it in "bandwagoning" with America. Once they had made this discovery, French policy elites came to understand that Theodore Roosevelt's diplomacy would prove a boon to French interests.

Thus, in a very short span of time, and for reasons related directly even if not entirely to a changing assessment of what America and its president could do for France, the country's image of Theodore Roosevelt altered radically. Having initially been construed as representing a large part of France's problems, America and Roosevelt quickly came to be seen to embody an indispensable component of their needed solution, for by the start of Roosevelt's second and final term in office, France's security "problem" could be pretty well summarized in one word: Germany.

The recognition that America under Roosevelt might prove beneficial for French interests was powerfully stimulated by the president's involvement in diplomatic efforts to resolve a looming crisis over Morocco early during his first full term in office, which began in March 1905. Those efforts proved instrumental in getting the two disputants, France and Germany, to the Algeciras negotiating table, at which war would be avoided while French interests could be safeguarded. Even though Roosevelt's principal aim had been to avert a general European war rather than to promote French interests, the result was to enhance enormously his standing in France.[24] Indicative of French gratitude was André Tardieu's judgment that Roosevelt had provided France "a capital service," and that the Americans' intermediation during the crisis years of 1905 and 1906 had constituted something "precious" for Paris. "At Algeciras, we found them to be loyal friends."[25]

Roosevelt's image in France also owed something to changing views of his personality. The more the French learned about the young and energetic American president, the more they grew to like him. To say the least, he was cut from a decidedly different bolt of cloth than the succession of American presidents French observers had been witnessing during the years since Abraham Lincoln.[26] Indeed, to hear it told by more than a few of the country's America watchers, and not just those who were culturally and politically anti-American, he appeared to be the first president since Lincoln to possess much of a personality at all, or for that matter to have much of a brain. One sympathetic French biographer wrote of Roosevelt that he was the only president to establish himself as an intellectual (*un lettré*) prior to embarking on a political career. America, noted Albert Savine, as a rule so scantily endowed with political luminaries the likes of Lamartine, Thiers, Guizot, Disraeli, and Gladstone, finally had one of whom it could be proud, Roosevelt.[27]

The remarkable young leader was not only well-read and well-spoken but also had another personal attribute that set him in good stead with French opinion: he was a welcome departure from a long-established pattern of

America's chief executives betraying a uniform ethnic provenance. With the single exception of the Dutchman Martin Van Buren, all of America's presidents, from Washington to McKinley, had been a bit too "Anglo" for French taste. And though Roosevelt is often recalled as having been a true-blue enthusiast of Anglo-Saxonism, he himself rejected any such ancestry, insisting that "I am myself of Dutch descent (though mixed with Scotch, Irish, and French Huguenot)."[28] To his swooning French biographer Savine, Roosevelt's welcome ethnic mix conveyed positive political significance, and indeed, according to that writer, the president owed "his vivacity, his imagination, his daring" to his part-French ancestry. Nor did it hurt matters one bit that the president's wife, Edith, also seemed to be French-descended.[29]

So it transpired that Roosevelt was a real European—and a Frenchman, no less! Best of all was the growing recognition that among the foreign diplomats in the American capital whose company he kept and counsel he sought, no one stood closer to the president than France's own man in Washington, Jean Jules Jusserand. In a manner rarely if ever encountered in modern diplomatic circles, an American president was cultivating such close personal relations with certain foreign emissaries that he often relied upon them for policy advice. By far the favorite among Roosevelt's "tennis cabinet," many of whom were foreigners, was Jusserand, with whom he shared a variety of literary and athletic interests.[30]

Jusserand had taken up his ambassadorial duties in early 1903, and he served until 1925, the longest tenure ever of a French ambassador to Washington. One biographer of the president, commenting upon an overheard conversation between him and his French friend, writes, "Roosevelt made a point of consulting Jusserand as if he were an honorary Cabinet officer, and told a bewildered congressman, 'He has taken the oath as Secretary of State.'"[31] One consequence of the lofty esteem in which the president held Jusserand was that Roosevelt revised negative assessments he had once held of French national character. As one historian relates, in 1898 Roosevelt "had been writing that the French were incapable of self-government and that the day of the Latin races was over. But by 1905 the President had developed a real affection for France—and undoubtedly it was the France personified by the . . . learned little ambassador whom he had come to love."[32]

Therefore, it seems that if we were to seek a counterfactual stand-in for Franklin D. Roosevelt—and one, moreover, who could be guaranteed to alter the future trajectory of Franco-American relations in a positive direction—we could hardly do better than to retrofit into our account FDR's fifth cousin and predecessor. If one individual truly can make an enduring impact upon a bilateral relationship, then we need look no further than to Theodore Roosevelt. But here is the problem: that real Franco-American past *did* have Theodore Roosevelt in it, and the long-term pattern of Franco-American suboptimality nevertheless persisted, once Roosevelt was out of the picture.[33] Individual leaders come and individual leaders go, but *le différend franco-américain* continues on its course, more or less impervious to the desires and actions of those leaders, whether they are deemed beneficial or detrimental for the Franco-American special relationship.

It Was the Worst of Times?
Franklin Roosevelt and Franco-American Relations

To hear it said by some, if we had to find an American president who, in modern times, has done the most damage to the Franco-American relationship, we would be hard-pressed to come up with anyone who could outdo Franklin D. Roosevelt. While it would be inaccurate to claim that Franklin D. Roosevelt was somehow "anti-French," it certainly is a feature of the historiographical record that many scholars have, explicitly or implicitly, sought to use him to substantiate their claims regarding the powerful impact of first-image "variables." And this particular memory has lingered. Decades after the Second World War ended, it was still possible to encounter confident assertions that Roosevelt's wartime "incompatibility" with de Gaulle constituted the "roots of the American differences with France today."[34]

First-image explanations do not come more forcefully packaged than in this assertion by Milton Viorst. Yet there are two particularly obvious problems with the statement. First, as we know from previous chapters, difficult moments in the bilateral relationship were hardly unprecedented prior to the 1940–1944 experience; rather, they were the norm, so much so that what really stands out are those relatively rare interludes of uneventful and successful cooperation in the bilateral relationship. Thus, Viorst's causal statement, along with similar claims by other scholars who have zeroed in on the Roosevelt–de Gaulle friction as a contingent moment in the Franco-American record,[35] has to be seen as more than mildly anachronistic. Whatever else can be laid at Franklin D. Roosevelt's doorstep, it cannot be responsibility for having established a pattern of suboptimal cooperation with France. That pattern predated his administration, and it outlived it; he may not have changed it, but he certainly did not cause it.

The second problem with identifying Franklin Roosevelt as being, willingly or not, a source of continuing Franco-American difficulties is that it can often lead to the supposition that he was as anti-French as Theodore had been pro-French. While it is true that Theodore Roosevelt did evolve into a Francophile, it would be wildly off the mark somehow to conceive of FDR as hostile to France and the French, though at times he could give the impression of denigrating France's contribution to Western civilization.[36] And even if it is exaggerating things a bit to claim, as did Édouard Daladier, France's premier when the Second World War began, that "President [Franklin] Roosevelt was for France a very great and noble friend,"[37] it in no way follows that FDR felt any particular hostility toward France.

Instead of asking whether he was anti-French, let us inquire into what, if any, elements of his cognitive framework might have resulted in FDR being labeled as indifferent or even opposed to France, as many in that country have been wont to do. Two such elements stand out when it comes to his policy toward France. The first is his discovery (made belatedly during the interwar period, and even then only temporarily) that America had no business playing European power politics. The second is his conviction that liberal democracies were morally superior to any other form of government.

In neither of these convictions was Roosevelt particularly out of step with dominant trends in American society. Julian Hurstfield notes, correctly, that both presidents Roosevelt tended to run highly centralized foreign policy shops, in which the hub of activity always was the White House rather than other, and presumably relevant, executive branch departments such as State, War, or the Navy. But more than this, he tells us, Franklin Roosevelt's French policy also reflected "his overall vision, and to a large extent that of his fellow citizens." That presidential vision was predicated on three tenets: independence in policymaking, confidence in the superiority of American institutions, and a "moralistic suspicion" that European power politics led to war and imperialism.[38]

If Roosevelt seemed relatively indifferent to France until the tail end of his second term, it was thoroughly in keeping with the broader societal mood in the US, which favored seeking as little security and defense interdependence with European states as could be arranged. This is what the grand strategy of isolation meant, eschewing involvement in the European balance of power. This had been American tradition dating back to the administration of George Washington, and the recent departure from the tradition, in 1917 and 1918, appeared to most Americans during the 1920s and 1930s to have been a horrific mistake, the sort of blunder that was to be avoided at all cost in the future.

Importantly, especially since we are inquiring into the separability of leaders from those they lead, it is apparent that when he entered office, Roosevelt's outlook on foreign policy differed hardly at all from that of the vast majority of his fellow Americans, particularly when it came to the question of the wisdom of military involvement in the Old World. It is true that Franklin Roosevelt had supported the intervention in 1917, just as Theodore had, but by the time he won election to the presidency in 1932, Franklin Roosevelt had become as antimilitarist and anti-interventionist as most Americans. His views would, of course, change, as did theirs, with the passage of time and the growing perception of a German menace to American physical security interests. But until he and they abandoned their reluctance to see America again ensnared in European power politics, it could indeed appear to the French as if Roosevelt was callously indifferent to their interests. It was this very perception that Daladier later sought to dispel with his comment about FDR's friendliness toward France.

It may be surprising to learn that Franklin Roosevelt, whom posterity would remember as one of America's most internationalist presidents, steering his country through a world war and presiding over the gestation of the United Nations, should have for some long period of time conceptualized foreign policy within a framework that could be associated with the policy that has come to be known as isolationism. The surprise, or shock, is all the more pronounced because isolationism has so frequently been taken as a virtual synonym for blinkered thinking in matters related to foreign policy. As a result, it is regarded as something more to be abhorred than to be studied, and it is usually held to be a perspective that could only appeal to the benighted—those whom one historian dismissively terms the "graders."[39] As Walter Russell Mead insists, such was the revulsion felt by a generation of post–Second World War American policymakers and intellectuals that it became an article of faith among them that *nothing* in America's pre-1941 diplomatic tradition could possibly be worthy of emulating—or even remembering. It was as if the past had been airbrushed out of the picture of international relations being painted by the post-1945 generation of Americans.[40]

How should we square the conventional image of Franklin Roosevelt as a confirmed internationalist with the reality that until almost the end of his second complete term—for more than half of his total presidency—he followed a policy that bore all the hallmarks of isolationism, at least if we conceive of that policy orientation as signifying "nothing more nor less than the refusal to guarantee the post–World War I status quo in Europe and Asia against change by force of arms"?[41] Usually, that old devil of "expediency" is invoked to account for the president having looked, in practice, like someone who was not willing to use America's might to resolve problems stemming from the European balance of power. According to this view, he repeated a thousand times how much he hated war only because he wanted to hoodwink mossbacks in Congress into thinking that he was as one with them and their cause of keeping America safe from the entanglements of a morally degenerate Old World. Scholarship of the Roosevelt era, written by partisan and foe alike, often stresses how the president "during the paralyzing isolationism of the thirties . . . remained privately an internationalist willing only to work or toy with the isolationists."[42]

Yet this "internationalist" also took seriously the power of historical analogy to impart certain lessons that all Americans, including policymakers in Washington, ought to heed. Thus, FDR was as impressed as most Americans with the 1917 analogy, conveying its unmistakable "never-again" connotations. True, Roosevelt did not swallow the full draught of interwar revisionism—at least, he chose not to gulp down its more conspiratorial ingredients—but he nevertheless did come to regard America's participation in that conflict as having been a serious mistake.[43] He would later recant his newfound conviction that a war he had once applauded was now a blunder, insofar as America was concerned.[44] This does not erase the fact that during those long years of the 1930s, when FDR placed avoidance of war above the shoring up of the European balance of power, noninterventionism (or if one prefers, pacifism) constituted an essential element in his operational code, and that toward the end of the decade this was to clash with a French desire for an America more committed to the defense of French interests—at least among those French leaders who were prepared to stand up to Hitler (for France's own pacifists were inclined to cite the American president's foreign policy as one more reason for appeasing the Nazis).[45]

The other way in which Roosevelt's cognitive framework was related to second-image factors concerned his liberalism. Even if it was obvious that, starting during the later years of the 1920s and accelerating in the 1930s, Roosevelt had abandoned his earlier, Wilsonian outlook, he remained every bit a liberal, save that the foreign policy correlative of *his* kind of liberalism derived from what Mead terms the Jeffersonian tradition, of rejecting global activism and evincing a pronounced distrust of Europe qua Europe. This tradition is not to be confused with Fohlen's notion of Jefferson as friend of France. Instead, this tradition emphasized the need to build democracy at home rather than to attempt to export it to others.

If Jeffersonianism in its earliest instantiation during the late eighteenth and early nineteenth centuries had been supportive of France's revolutionary experiment, by the interwar period it had definitely shed those initial francophilic implications and instead stood for aloofness from European politics, France's included. As Mead suggestively puts it, "For the Jeffersonians on both the libertarian left and right, the struggle continues until civil liberties are protected everywhere at home; this is why Wilsonians could be styled the Trotskyites of America's revolution, meaning its sanctity at home demands its spread abroad, while the Jeffersonians are Stalinists who accept the concept of revolution in one country."[46] John Lamberton Harper captures this mind-set with the expression "Europhobic-hemispherism," the dominant tendency within the Roosevelt administration during most of the 1930s and consistent with the new president's public repudiation of the "so-called statesmen" and the "so-called peace" of 1919.[47]

It was not at all difficult, as we saw earlier, for French observers during the interwar years to find reasons aplenty to worry about American leaders, especially when those leaders came steeped in liberalism. This is because liberals of that era made little secret of their view that Weimar Germany had been shabbily treated by a vindictive France after 1918, with the corollary of this predication becoming obvious after 1933: if Weimar Germany had been more generously and "inclusively" handled, the world would have been a much safer place and Hitler would have remained an obscure plotter of beer hall fantasies. This was a staple of liberal outlooks on European security throughout the English-speaking precincts of the transatlantic world up through the mid-1930s, and FDR certainly shared in the ideological temper of the times, when "sympathy for the Germans was whole-hearted and generous, but there was less affection wasted on the French."[48]

FDR's liberalism could make it appear as if he was anti-French, but he was not. He was, however, very dubious about Charles de Gaulle's wartime insistence that de Gaulle represented France. Since, for those who regard him as having been hostile to France, Roosevelt's original sin was the way in which he treated the country that Charles de Gaulle insisted *he* personified, let us reflect upon how FDR's liberalism might be linked to that alleged transgression. That he detested de Gaulle did not imply that he detested France. To the contrary, some have argued that it was his *fondness* for France that inspired him to take the course he did with de Gaulle. More precisely, the claim is that the most important reason for Roosevelt's failure to recognize de Gaulle as provisional leader of France until the autumn of 1944 was his conviction that only the people of France had the right to determine who was to lead them, and that they would have to make such a decision, ideally in a fair and free election, once they had been liberated from the Nazi occupation.

There had been many salient steps in the deterioration of Franco-American relations during wartime, not of all which could be chalked up to Roosevelt's liberal ideological convictions. Some initiatives were undertaken, admittedly, for reasons of geopolitical necessity that even flew in the face of those convictions. The most important such initiatives included the decision to recognize the Vichy regime of Marshal Philippe Pétain as France's government from July 1940 until November 1942;[49] and the attempt the following year to promote General Henri Giraud as at least coequal with de Gaulle among Free French military leaders.[50] But the very late recognition of de Gaulle as legitimate leader of France, following the country's liberation, was not inconsistent with liberal values, since Roosevelt had a hard time convincing himself of the Free French leader's democratic credentials.[51]

Moreover, one further matter of discord between the two leaders was guaranteed to emerge, as a result of an ideological predisposition embedded in Rooseveltian liberalism. Unlike Theodore Roosevelt,[52] Franklin was fundamentally opposed to imperialism in general, and to European imperialism in particular. Like most liberals, Franklin Roosevelt was convinced that imperialism was a leading, perhaps *the* leading, cause of war—an interesting twist, considering how in an earlier generation, liberalism and imperialism were often seen to be self-reinforcing ideologies.[53] He was hardly well disposed to the empire of Great Britain, America's closest ally during the Second World War. But his attitude toward France's colonial holdings was harsher still. As William Roger Louis recounts, "With a sense of outrage, Roosevelt denounced the oppressive colonial rule by France, . . . about which he held stronger feelings than any of the other European colonial empires."[54] And if for purposes of encouraging French resistance against the Nazis he was inclined to mute his public opposition to France's empire, he had every intention of ensuring that after the war, French colonies would be turned over to an international trustee. De Gaulle, for his part, was fully aware of FDR's view on an empire that, as far as the leader of Free France was concerned, constituted an integral part of the French nation and could no more be severed from France than could Texas from the American union. Nor was de Gaulle a solitary figure in imagining that France's future greatness depended critically upon its retention of an empire and the furtherance of its *mission civilisatrice*.[55]

Some things are clear from this discussion of the impact of two presidents Roosevelt on France. At the very least, it can be said that Daladier misidentified his country's friend who bore the surname of Roosevelt, testimony to Fohlen's claim about just how little Theodore Roosevelt has been ensconced in France's collective memory. But with regard to the broader epistemological point being pursued in this chapter, we are left with one question. If the "real" Theodore Roosevelt, in the end, was unable to fundamentally alter the chronic pattern of Franco-American suboptimal cooperation, what is the case for thinking that the counterfactual Theodore Roosevelt of 1940 to 1944 would have achieved any lasting impact? And if he could not, what becomes of the claim of Viorst and so many others that Franklin Roosevelt left such lasting traces upon the bilateral relationship as to constitute an element of contingency?

Conclusion

Robert Jervis was surely on to something in reminding us how difficult it is to assess the degree of agency possessed by individuals in the shaping of any country's foreign policy. One of the major reasons for this difficulty concerns the connection, if any, between leaders and the cultural milieu of the countries they lead. The three chapters of part 2 sought to identify some aspects of both France's and America's cultural milieu that might be said to have "causal" bearing upon the quality of the two countries' cooperative dealings in matters related to security and defense, functioning in such a way as to constrain or otherwise guide the leaders' decision-making agency.

Some scholars will tell us that it is not simply difficult but well-nigh impossible to try to establish a connection between sociopolitical cultural constraints and leaders' decisions. Indeed, they would argue that leaders only *become* leaders because they are so different from their fellow citizens as to stand divorced from the cultural norms and practices shared by the latter. Thus, continues the argument, leaders cannot and should not be taken to personify or otherwise represent any national "character" or "identity."

Recall Bernard Hennessy's assertion, discussed in chapter 2, about the presumed link between a societal orientation toward a certain way of doing things and the actual decision-making by individuals at the top. Not for Hennessy was this business of rescuing men and women from political science oblivion. Just the opposite. He insisted that when all is said and done, it is events that determine state behavior—events subsumed under what Hennessy dared to label the "'hard' facts of geography, economics, historical traditions, and . . . more-or-less rationally calculated factors of power and prestige."[1] National character, he was confident, had basically no impact upon foreign policy behavior. How could it, if the leaders were by definition such a cut above the run-of-the-mill (or "modal") personality that is sometimes thought to endow national character with whatever meaning it might be said to possess? These leaders were cosmopolitans who had so little in common with the people whom they led as to render them impervious to being influenced by collective societal forces.

That is why Hennessy urged that cultural considerations be banished from the set of potentially important elements that go into shaping foreign policy, and that political scientists not poke their noses into places that clearly lie outside their field of expertise, which is restricted to government and governance. As far as he was concerned, all attempts to establish credible linkages between collectivities' attributes and leaders' decision-making would be fruitless. "There is," he insisted, "at this writing [1962], no empirical study relating aggregate personality or character traits . . . to actual policy. There is . . . speculation aplenty."[2]

Hennessy may be well within his rights to brand as "speculation" the efforts of scholars with whom he begs to differ. This happens all the time. But it is simply wrong—worse, it is sheer speculation—to pretend that leaders can and do remain so insulated from cultural trends in their societies and states as to be impervious to acting on such trends, or at least claiming not to be so acting. Speculation or not, many scholars insist that it is as fallacious as it is incredible to assume that policymaking can take place in a cognitive vacuum, with leaders' operational codes somehow miraculously formed with no reference whatsoever to important cultural debates and tendencies.

The issue is not so much whether these cultural attributes we call ideas "matter" in the crafting of foreign policy; it is more about trying to demonstrate *how* they matter. Is it public opinion that somehow holds the key to opening the repository of collective values, as some appear to believe?[3] Or must we canvass those "cultural products" that, as mentioned in chapter 2, would constitute an impressively expansionist set of potential cultural variables unless kept under tight control? In this book, I have sought to exercise such control by mainly focusing upon two varieties of cultural products, packaged respectively under the rubrics of ethnicity and ideology. In the end, I came down in favor of ideology as bearing the greater amount of causal weight. Ideas about the proper political order are what have contributed the most to the strategic culture of the Franco-American special relationship.

But if ideas about the proper political order are so important, and if it is *leaders'* ideas that determine the trajectory of interstate—in our case, Franco-American—relations, then how can it be maintained that this bilateral relationship could display such consistency as it apparently possesses, without also assuming that, in both countries, one leader must be more or less like any other leader? Yet if this assumption of the fundamental interchangeability of leaders holds, what becomes of the argument that leaders possess agency? So the problem is not that leaders stand apart from the hypothesized sociocultural consciousness; it is something else. It is the demonstrable empirical reality that one leader is *not* more or less like any other leader when it comes to Franco-American relations; they are hardly interchangeable parts of policymaking, no matter how the latter may be conceptualized.

Fungibility may be a concept that makes a lot of sense in the marketplace for, say, wheat, but it is a far less relevant concept in analyzing the marketplace for leadership. The quality of interactions between leaders of France and the US can and does fluctuate wildly in tone, and has done so from the time of George Washington and Louis XVI (and his revolutionary successors) down to the era of Joe Biden and Emmanuel Macron, soaring at times to the dazzling heights of ardent comradeship only to plummet into the dark depths of mutual antagonism, but usually landing somewhere in a middling spot neither paradisiacal nor infernal. And here arises the analytical dilemma: Why does suboptimality continue to be the default option in Franco-American cooperation in security and defense? Leaders come and leaders go, but *le différend* remains. As a result, the first-image focus on individuals must be handled with caution, for, as Jervis tells us, it poses questions that are as familiar as they are impossible fully to answer.

In chapter 2, I suggested that when historical context dons one of its hats, the one that has come to be known as path dependence, it offers a potential means by which strategic culturalists can try to account for the quality of suboptimal cooperation. Since the cultural turn in international relations has often been said to be a historical turn as well, it seems to me that culturalists could make some headway by invoking history, specifically through bringing into their analysis the "emplotment" that is part and parcel of accounts emphasizing the explicative prowess of narratives (sometimes termed "narrative positivism").

This suggestion can seem unorthodox—to some, possibly even daft—for it stretches beyond all recognition the sense of the meaning of culture. To such skeptics, culture can only apply to discrete societal collectivities, not to interaction patterns among those collectivities. However, as I have tried to demonstrate, the "essence" of a particular collectivity's character is only brought out fully when it is taken in relation to that of a significant Other. In other words, one needs the interaction to complete one's understanding of the culture. Hence my invocation of relational realism, which represents a third-image departure from an otherwise consistently second-image analytical trend.

Mainly, though, in telling the strategic-cultural story of the bilateral relationship, I chose to concentrate on second-image cultural referents associated with ethnicity and ideology rather than on third-image ones derivative of emplotment. And in so doing, I deliberately skirted first-image variables, saying as little as I could get away with saying—or better, *not* saying— about the actions of individual leaders as somehow being a root cause of Franco-American suboptimality in security and defense cooperation. One reason for my choice is the mind-boggling complexity involved in trying to demonstrate the bona fides of contingency, as we saw in chapter 6. This is so, even when contingency might be thought to result "merely" from the volition of an individual leader, as opposed to, for example, representing the consequence(s) of an unfolding set of larger and much more indecipherable historical forces.

But another, equally important, reason I have given such a wide berth to first-image contingency inheres in the self-canceling implications that contingency necessarily brings to first-image analysis, by introducing so many aleatory considerations as to almost make a mockery of any claim about enduring cultural patterns. For, to rephrase a point already made, if leaders really can and do personify contingency, while the overall pattern of Franco-American relations has remained so invariant over the past century (if not longer), then it would seem that we are facing a conundrum. How could such a formidable array of change agents interact in such a fashion that the ultimate product of their joint efforts has been the perpetuation of a status quo that is neither bad nor good but simply mediocre—one large, though admittedly fascinating, "nothing burger"?

There is a fundamental tension pitting the contention that leaders can and do bring about change against the wisdom contained in Alphonse Karr's well-known aphorism "Plus ça change, plus c'est la même chose." The more things change, the more they stay the same. This nineteenth-century French political journalist coined the phrase in early 1849 to betoken a certain repetitive feature of political life, and while his bon mot long predates the era in which France and the US became permanent security and defense partners, it can stand as testimony to the remarkable constancy of their suboptimal cooperation over the course of many, many decades.

As I write these concluding words, President Biden is meeting with President Macron and all other NATO leaders in Brussels to further develop the collective Western response to Russia's aggression against Ukraine. For the moment, and not for the first time in this disputatious alliance's lengthy history, the watchword is "solidarity." There is no reason to doubt the sincerity of the various leaders' desire to try to work seamlessly together to counteract the predations of the Russian dictator. But once the crisis ends, it would be as unreasonable as it might be desirable to expect to see a lasting change for the better in the quality of Franco-American security and defense cooperation. Instead, it may be assumed that the dominant trends in this special relationship that have generated *le différend franco-américain* in the past will continue to define the future of bilateral ties.

This should be cause for neither celebration nor lamentation. Despite the hopes of some and the fears of others, this relationship is not at risk of shattering. In fact, it is not a particularly bad bilateral relationship, compared with so many other dyadic relationships in world politics. Besides, it could be a lot worse—and indeed, as we saw in chapter 3, it *has* been worse in the past. For if the message of this book has been that the two countries are locked in a cultural cage that ensures bounded rationality will continue to characterize their interactions in security and defense matters, it still means that rationality more or less prevails, most of the time. This is not something that can be said to apply universally to interstate interactions outside the confines of the Atlantic alliance, where bilateral cooperation, even if suboptimal, would be regarded as almost a gift from the gods. The Franco-American special relationship is the transatlantic world's preeminent geopolitical example of "satisficing" in decision-making, in which acceptable even if never optimal degrees of cooperation constitute the norm. But so what?

In Quebec, folks might say "pas pire" to convey the meaning of what in English is connoted by "not bad." However, if the figurative translation of the expression suits the Franco-American special relationship, even more apt is the literal (if ungrammatical) rendering of it, as "not worse." That is about as good as it gets in this always fascinating bilateral relationship, and culture tells us why it is so.

Notes

Preface and Acknowledgments

1. See Gregory Mahler, ed., *Foreign Perceptions of the United States under Donald Trump* (New York: Lexington Books, 2021); and Jack Snyder, ed., *American Foreign Policy: Trump and After* (New York: Academy of Political Science, 2021).

2. "Biden's Debacle," *Economist*, 21–27 August 2021, 11. On the continuity thesis (of Biden's Afghan policy essentially being Trump's), see Kori Schake, "The Folly of Personal Diplomacy," *New York Times*, 29 August 2021, SR2.

3. Mark Landler, Katrin Bennhold, and Matina Stevis-Gridneff, "How the West Marshaled a Stunning Show of Unity Against Russia," *New York Times*, 5 March 2022, https://www.nytimes.com/2022/03/05/world/europe/russia-ukraine-invasion-sanctions.html.

4. Daniel W. Drezner, Ronald R. Krebs, and Randall Schweller, "The End of Grand Strategy: America Must Think Small," *Foreign Affairs* 99 (May/June 2020): 107–17. More generally, see Elizabeth Borgwardt, Christopher McKnight Nichols, and Andrew Preston, eds., *Rethinking American Grand Strategy* (Oxford: Oxford University Press, 2021).

5. Mira Rapp-Hooper, *Shields of the Republic: The Triumph and Peril of America's Alliances* (Cambridge, MA: Harvard University Press, 2020).

6. See Eugene Gholz, Darryl Press, and Harvey Sapolsky, "Come Home America: The Strategy of Restraint in the Face of Temptation," *International Security* 21 (Spring 1997): 5–48; Eric A. Nordlinger, *Isolationism Reconfigured: American Foreign Policy for a New Century* (Princeton, NJ: Princeton University Press, 1995); and A. Trevor Thrall and Benjamin H. Friedman, eds., *US Grand Strategy in the 21st Century: The Case for Restraint* (London: Routledge, 2018). On the lengthy background of this perspective, see Charles A. Kupchan, *Isolationism: A History of America's Efforts to Shield Itself from the World* (New York: Oxford University Press, 2020).

7. John J. Mearsheimer and Stephen M. Walt, "The Case for Offshore Balancing: A Superior US Grand Strategy," *Foreign Affairs* 95 (July/August 2016): 70–83.

8. See Joseph S. Nye Jr., "The Rise and Fall of American Hegemony: From Wilson to Trump," *International Affairs* 95 (January 2019): 63–80.

9. G. John Ikenberry, *A World Safe for Democracy: Liberal Internationalism and the Crises of Global Order* (New Haven, CT: Yale University Press, 2020), 200.

10. For the distinction between these two logics, see Joseph Grieco, Robert Powell, and Duncan Snidal, "The Relative-Gains Problem for International Cooperation," *American Political Science Review* 87 (September 1993): 727–43.

11. On this score, see Raymonde Carroll, *Cultural Misunderstandings: The French-American Experience*, trans. Carol Volk (Chicago: University of Chicago Press, 1988); Jean-Philippe Mathy, *French Resistance: The French-American Culture Wars* (Minneapolis:

University of Minnesota Press, 2000); and Beatrice Heuser, "Of Sibling Rivalry and Lovers Spurned: Franco-American Relations over Two Centuries," in *The France–US Leadership Race: Closely Watched Allies,* ed. David G. Haglund (Kingston: Queen's Quarterly, 2000), 43–61.

12. Paul Kennedy, *The Rise and Fall of the Great Powers: Economic Change and Military Conflict from 1500 to 2000* (New York: Random House, 1987). On the various phases of post–Second World War declinism, see Josef Joffe, *The Myth of America's Decline: Politics, Economics, and a Half Century of False Prophecies* (New York: Liveright, 2014).

13. David P. Calleo, *Beyond American Hegemony: The Future of the Western Alliance* (New York: Basic Books, 1987).

14. David G. Haglund, *Alliance within the Alliance? Franco-German Military Cooperation and the European Pillar of Defense* (Boulder, CO: Westview, 1991).

1. A Franco-American Special Relationship?

1. For a catalog of those insomnia-inducing anxieties, in an otherwise optimistic book, see Mark Webber, James Sperling, and Martin A. Smith, *What's Wrong with NATO and How to Fix It* (Cambridge: Polity Press, 2021).

2. See Hanns W. Maull, ed., *The Rise and Decline of the Post–Cold War Order* (Oxford: Oxford University Press, 2018).

3. For pessimism as a cognitive default option, see Richard Ned Lebow, "Pessimism in International Relations," in *Pessimism in International Relations: Provocations, Possibilities, Politics,* ed. Tim Stevens and Nicholas Michelsen (Cham: Palgrave Macmillan, 2019), 13–36.

4. Ikenberry, A *World Safe for Democracy,* 3–4.

5. See Michael Kimmage, *The Abandonment of the West: The History of an Idea in American Foreign Policy* (New York: Basic Books, 2020).

6. Constance Duncombe and Tim Dunne, "After Liberal World Order," *International Affairs* 94 (January 2018): 25–42.

7. Most memorably, see John Mueller, *Retreat from Doomsday: The Obsolescence of Major War* (New York: Basic Books, 1990).

8. Robert Kagan, *The Jungle Grows Back: America and Our Imperiled World* (New York: Alfred A. Knopf, 2018). See also Michael Mandelbaum, *The Rise and Fall of Peace on Earth* (New York: Oxford University Press, 2019).

9. The story of Western decline is a long-running one, the locus classicus of which might be taken to be Oswald Spengler, *The Decline of the West,* trans. Charles Francis Atkinson (London: Allen, 1926/28). Also see Barbara Ward, *The West at Bay* (New York: W. W. Norton, 1948); James Burnham, *Suicide of the West: An Essay on the Meaning and Destiny of Liberalism* (New York: John Day, 1964); Mary Kaldor, *The Disintegrating West* (New York: Hill and Wang, 1978); Owen Harries, "The Collapse of 'the West,'" *Foreign Affairs* 72 (September/October 1993): 41–53; Conor Cruise O'Brien, "The Future of 'the West,'" *National Interest* 30 (Winter 1992/93): 3–10; Christopher Coker, *Twilight of the West* (Boulder, CO: Westview, 1998); John O'Sullivan, "How the West Was Spun," *National Interest* 55 (Spring 1999): 87–96; Jacques Barzun, *From Dawn to Decadence: 1500 to the Present—500 Years of Western Cultural Life* (New York: HarperCollins, 2000); and

Charles A. Kupchan, *No One's World: The West, the Rising Rest, and the Coming Global Turn* (Oxford: Oxford University Press, 2012).

10. Stanley R. Sloan, *Defense of the West: Transatlantic Security from Truman to Trump*, 2nd ed. (Manchester: Manchester University Press, 2020), 4.

11. Mahler, *Foreign Perceptions of the United States under Donald Trump;* Snyder, *American Foreign Policy.*

12. James Kirchick, *The End of Europe: Dictators, Demagogues, and the Coming Dark Age* (New Haven, CT: Yale University Press, 2018). Also see Christopher Caldwell, *Reflections on the Revolution in Europe: Immigration, Islam, and the West* (New York: Doubleday, 2009).

13. For expressions of this concern, exacerbated by worry about an Obama "pivot to Asia" redounding negatively for European interests, see Arnaud Leparmentier and Corine Lesnes, "Les Européens ébranlés par l'indifférence d'Obama," *Le Monde*, 4 February 2010, 1, 6; Maud Quessard and Maya Kandel, eds., *Les États-Unis et la fin de la grande stratégie? Un bilan de la politique étrangère d'Obama* (Paris: Institut de Recherche Stratégique de l'École Militaire, 2017); and Maud Quessard, Frédéric Heurtebize, and Frédérick Gagnon, eds., *Alliances and Power Politics in the Trump Era: America in Retreat?* (New York: Palgrave Macmillan, 2020).

14. Maya Kandel, *Les États-Unis et le monde, de George Washington à Donald Trump* (Paris: Perrin, 2018), 174–75.

15. "A Continent in Peril," *Economist* 433 (9 November 2019): 9.

16. Peter Schmidt, "La conception allemande de la défense européenne," *Défense & Stratégie* 44 (Winter 2019): 1–18, at 17. On Franco-German differences over transatlantic and European security, see Hajnalka Vincze, "Germany's Transatlantic Ambiguities," Foreign Policy Research Institute, Center for the Study of America and the West, 5 March 2021, https://www.fpri.org/article/2021/03/germanys-transatlantic-ambiguities.

17. Steven Erlanger, "NATO Differences Stoke a Franco-German Feud," *New York Times*, 24 November 2019, 8.

18. Patrick Wintour and Dan Sabbagh, "Trump Blasts Macron over 'Brain Dead' NATO Remarks," *Guardian*, 3 December 2019, https://www.theguardian.com/world/2019/dec/03/trump-macron-brain-dead-nato-remarks.

19. Bill Grantham, "America the Menace: France's Feud with Hollywood," *World Policy Journal* 15 (Summer 1998): 58–65, at 58.

20. Michael W. Doyle, "Liberalism and World Politics," *American Political Science Review* 80 (December 1986): 1151–69.

21. For a thoughtful commentary on this tendency, see Felix Berenskoetter, "Friends, There Are No Friends? An Intimate Reframing of the International," *Millennium: Journal of International Studies* 35 (September 2007): 647–76. Also see Andrea Oelsner and Antoine Vion, eds., "Special Issue: Friendship in International Relations," *International Politics* 48 (January 2011): 1–9.

22. Among them, most preeminently, is Jean-Baptiste Duroselle, *France and the United States: From the Beginnings to the Present*, trans. Derek Coltman (Chicago: University of Chicago Press, 1978). More recently, see Alexandra de Hoop Scheffer and Martin Quencez, "The US–France Special Relationship: Testing the Macron Method," *GMF Policy Brief* 6 (Paris: German Marshall Fund of the United States, 2018).

23. See Alan P. Dobson and Steve Marsh, eds., *Churchill and the Anglo-American Special Relationship* (London: Routledge, 2017).

24. There are a few exceptions to this trend, an important one being Andrew J. Williams, *France, Britain and the United States in the Twentieth Century*, vol. 1, *1900–1940* (London: Palgrave Macmillan, 2014); and vol. 2, *1940–1961: A Reappraisal* (London: Palgrave Macmillan, 2020).

25. See Jean Guisnel, *Les Pires Amis du monde: les relations franco-américaines à la fin du XXe siècle* (Paris: Stock, 1999); and Catherine Durandin, *La France contre l'Amérique* (Paris: Presses Universitaires de France, 1994).

26. Even in southeast Asia; see Daniel Fineman, *A Special Relationship: The United States and the Military Government in Thailand, 1947–1958* (Honolulu: University of Hawai'i Press, 1966).

27. Klaus-Dieter Mensel, "The United States and the United Germany: Partners in Leadership?," in *Can America Remain Committed? US Security Horizons in the 1990s*, ed. David G. Haglund (Boulder, CO: Westview, 1992), 81–109.

28. To use the term employed by one scholar, who notes that alone among special relationships, the Anglo-American one is regularly signified through employment of the definite article, indicating it is *the* "special relationship ne plus ultra." Clive Webb, "Observing America: What Mass-Observation Reveals about British Views of the USA," *Journal of Transatlantic Studies* 18 (September 2020): 296–313, at 296.

29. Amazingly, the July 2020 edition of the "Transatlantic Scorecard," produced as part of a joint project of the Brookings Institution and Robert Bosch Stiftung, ranked America's bilateral relations with six transatlantic entities and found that they were poorest with Germany, even though two countries included in the set were Russia [!] and Turkey. The three other entities were the United Kingdom, France, and the European Union. Brookings Center on the United States and Europe, "Transatlantic Scorecard—July 2020," 24 July 2020, https://www.brookings.edu/research/trans-atlantic-scorecard-july-2020.

30. John Dumbrell and Axel R. Schäfer, eds., *America's "Special Relationships": Foreign and Domestic Aspects of the Politics of Alliance* (London: Routledge, 2009). Tellingly, although this volume features chapters on these countries—and even on Iran and Russia—there is no chapter on France.

31. George Orwell, *Animal Farm: A Fairy Story* (Harmondsworth: Penguin, 1951).

32. Steve Marsh, "Beyond Essential: Britons and the Anglo-American Special Relationship," *Journal of Transatlantic Studies* 18 (September 2020): 382–404, at 387.

33. Duroselle, *France and the United States*, 252–53. On this theme, also see Gabriel Louis Jaray, *Amitié américaine: raisons permanentes et crises passagères* (Paris: Sorlot, 1939).

34. On this tropism, which occasioned a great deal of scholarly interest in the first decade of the twenty-first century, see James W. Ceasar, "A Genealogy of Anti-Americanism," *Public Interest* 152 (Summer 2003): 3–18; Peter J. Katzenstein and Robert O. Keohane, eds., *Anti-Americanisms in World Politics* (Ithaca, NY: Cornell University Press, 2007); and Alan L. McPherson and Ivan Krastev, eds., *The Anti-American Century* (Budapest: Central European University Press, 2007). For biting critiques of the specific French variant, all penned by French authors, see Jean-François Revel, *L'Obsession anti-américaine: son*

fonctionnement, ses causes, ses inconséquences (Paris: Plon, 2002); Philippe Roger, *L'Ennemi américain: généalogie de l'antiaméricanisme français* (Paris: Seuil, 2002); Pierre Rigoulot, *L'Antiaméricanisme: critique d'un prêt-à-penser rétrograde et chauvin* (Paris: Robert Laffont, 2004); and Bernard-Henri Lévy, *American Vertigo: Traveling America in the Footsteps of Tocqueville,* trans. Charlotte Mandel (New York: Random House, 2006).

35. Marvin R. Zahniser, *Then Came Disaster: France and the United States, 1918–1940* (Westport, CT: Praeger, 2002), xv–xvi.

36. Arnold M. Rose, "Anti-Americanism in France," *Antioch Review* 13 (Autumn 1952): 468–84, at 484.

37. See Catarina Kinnvall and Jennifer Mitzen, "An Introduction to the Special Issue: Ontological Securities in World Politics," *Cooperation and Conflict* 52 (March 2017): 3–11; Jennifer Mitzen, "Ontological Security in World Politics: State Identity and the Security Dilemma," *European Journal of International Relations* 12 (September 2006): 341–70; and Jelena Subotić, "Narrative, Ontological Security, and Foreign Policy Change," *Foreign Policy Analysis* 12 (October 2016): 610–27.

38. André Kaspi, *Les États-Unis d'aujourd'hui: mal connus, mal aimés, mal compris* (Paris: Plon, 1999), 33.

39. See Steven Philip Kramer, "Les relations franco-américaines à l'épreuve de la crise au Kosovo," *Politique étrangère* 65 (Summer 2000): 359–74. Those bilateral tensions were not unique to the Kosovo war of 1999 but rather had been accumulating as a result of a series of Franco-American differences associated with the breakup of Yugoslavia earlier in the decade; see Ronald Hatto, *Les Relations franco-américaines à l'épreuve de la guerre en ex-Yougoslavie (1991–1995)* (Paris: Dalloz, 2006).

40. Hans-Georg Ehrhart, "Change by Rapprochement? Astérix's Quarrel with the New Roman Empire," in *The France–US Leadership Race: Closely Watched Allies,* ed. David G. Haglund (Kingston: Queen's Quarterly, 2000), 63–86, at 66.

41. Mark Hertsgaard, *The Eagle's Shadow: Why America Fascinates and Infuriates the World* (New York: Picador/Farrar, Straus and Giroux, 2003), 6.

42. Julia E. Sweig, *Friendly Fire: Losing Friends and Making Enemies in the Anti-American Century* (New York: Public Affairs, 2006); Moisés Naím, "The Perils of Lite Anti-Americanism," *Foreign Policy* 136 (May/June 2003): 95–96.

43. "Chirac dit non à la guerre américaine contre l'Irak," *Le Monde,* 12 March 2003, 1–2; John Vinocur, "Chirac's Casual 'No,'" *International Herald Tribune,* 12 March 2003, 1, 8.

44. See Frédéric Bozo, *A History of the Iraq Crisis: France, the United States, and Iraq, 1991–2003,* trans. Susan Emanuel (Washington, DC, and New York: Woodrow Wilson Center Press and Columbia University Press, 2017); and Philip H. Gordon and Jeremy Shapiro, *Allies at War: America, Europe, and the Crisis Over Iraq* (New York: McGraw-Hill, 2004).

45. Vyacheslav Nikonov, "Planet Earth: Russia and Transatlantic Relations," *International Journal* 59 (Winter 2003–2004): 87–104, at 91; Joseph Fitchett, "France Likely to Suffer Reprisals from America," *International Herald Tribune,* 15–16 March 2003, 3; Guillaume Parmentier, "France Will Have to Pay a Price," *International Herald Tribune,* 24 March 2003, 10.

46. See Anne C. Loveland, *Emblem of Liberty: Image of Lafayette in the American Mind* (Baton Rouge: Louisiana State University Press, 1971); Sarah J. Purcell, "Lafayette, Memory, and American Democracy," in *National Stereotypes in Perspective: Americans in France—Frenchmen in America*, ed. William L. Chew III (Amsterdam: Rodopi, 2001), 67–88; and Russell M. Jones, "The Flowering of a Legend: Lafayette and the Americans, 1825–1834," *French Historical Studies* 4 (Fall 1966): 384–410.

47. Michel Fortmann and Hélène Viau, "A Model Ally? France and the US During the Kosovo Crisis of 1998–99," in *The France–US Leadership Race: Closely Watched Allies*, ed. David G. Haglund (Kingston: Queen's Quarterly, 2000), 87–110, at 97. On the theme of sticking together when times get tough, also see Michel Tatu, "France-États-Unis: pour le meilleure et pour le pire," *Politique internationale* 75 (Spring 1997): 321–32; and Jean d'Ormesson, "Nos amis américains," *Revue des Deux Mondes* 145 (January 1974): 3–11.

48. For examples of the Francophobic mind-set prevalent from late 2002 into the middle of the decade, see John J. Miller and Mark Molesky, *Our Oldest Enemy: A History of America's Disastrous Relationship with France* (New York: Doubleday, 2004); and Kenneth R. Timmerman, *The French Betrayal of America* (New York: Crown Forum, 2004). For measured, but worried, summaries of the altered American mood during this period, see Simon Serfaty, *La France vue par les États-Unis: réflexions sur la francophobie à Washington* (Paris: Centre français sur les États-Unis/Institut français des relations internationales, November 2002); Justin Vaïsse, "American Francophobia Takes a New Turn," *French Politics, Culture and Society* 21 (Summer 2003): 33–49; Vaïsse, "Le nouvel âge postatlantique," *Commentaire* 103 (Autumn 2003): 541–48; and Barry Lando, "Brutale francophobie: une contre-enquête," *Le Monde*, 26 March 2003, 16.

49. Jean-Philippe Mathy, *Chronic Aftershock: How 9/11 Shaped Present-Day France* (Montreal and Kingston: McGill–Queen's University Press, 2021); and Timothy B. Smith, *France in Crisis: Welfare, Inequality and Globalization since 1980* (Cambridge: Cambridge University Press, 2004).

50. Jean-Louis Andreani, "Trente ans de blues français," *Le Monde*, 1 April 2008, 16–17.

51. Not surprisingly, Germany had often loomed large in Americans' contemplation of the hostile Other. See Ragnhild Fiebig-von Hase and Ursula Lehmkuhl, eds., *Enemy Images in American History* (Providence, RI: Berghahn, 1997).

52. Paul Koring, "Iran Seen as Worst Enemy of US, Poll Shows," *Globe and Mail* (Toronto), 24 February 2006, A17. Rounding out the list of Americans' self-declared top four foes were Iraq (22 percent), North Korea (15 percent), and China (10 percent).

53. Roger Cohen, "American Connection for a French Maverick," *International Herald Tribune*, 13 September 2006, 2.

54. William Wallace and Christopher Phillips, "Reassessing the Special Relationship," *International Affairs* 85 (March 2009): 263–84, at 283.

55. No fewer than twenty-five rounds of applause, ten of which were standing ovations, punctuated Nicolas Sarkozy's address to the House of Representatives on November 7. Natalie Nougayrède, "Sarkozy célèbre à Washington la réconciliation avec l'Amérique," *Le Monde*, 9 November 2007, 1, 4.

56. Marsh, "Beyond Essential," 384.

57. André Siegfried, *Les États-Unis d'aujourd'hui*, 14th ed. (1927; repr. Paris: Armand Colin, 1947), 313.

58. Thomas Meaney, "The Return of 'the West,'" *New York Times*, 13 March 2022, SR 2.

59. For a particularly thoughtful analysis, see Sophie Meunier, "Is France Still Relevant?," *French Politics, Culture and Society* 35 (Summer 2017): 59–75.

60. James N. Rosenau, *The Scientific Study of Foreign Policy*, rev. and enl. ed. (London: Frances Pinter, 1980), 25.

61. See Richard Wike et al., "Trump's International Ratings Remain Low, Especially Among Key Allies," Pew Research Center, 1 October 2018, https://www.pewresearch.org/global/2018/10/01/trumps-international-ratings-remain-low-especially-among-key-allies. Even in Canada, a country that normally is very favorably disposed toward its southern neighbor and, during the Obama years, sometimes gave the appearance of being well-nigh in love with it, opinion had soured on the US, in very large measure because of displeasure with President Trump. Such was the Trump effect north of the Canada–US border that survey data registered higher favorability scores for the UK (86 percent rating it "positively"), Germany (82 percent), France (77 percent), and even for Mexico (65 percent) than for the US itself (44 percent). Fortunately for what remained of the American image as a good neighbor, China at the time managed to rack up an even more dismal favorability score among Canadians, of only 23 percent. See Michelle Zilio, "Canadians More Positive about Ties with Europe than with the US, China: Poll," *Globe and Mail*, 3 May 2019, A6.

62. For one particularly enthusiastic endorsement, see Ronald Tiersky, "Macron's World: How the New President Is Remaking France," *Foreign Affairs* 97 (January/February 2018): 87–96. Also intriguingly taking the measure of the French president are William Drozdiak, *The Last President of Europe: Emmanuel Macron's Race to Revive France and Save the World* (New York: Public Affairs/Hachette, 2020); Joseph de Weck, *Emmanuel Macron: Der revolutionäre Präsident* (Düsseldorf: Lilienfeld Verlag, 2021); and Michel Duclos, *La France dans le bouleversement du monde* (Paris: Éd. de l'Observatoire, 2021).

63. André Kaspi, *Le Temps des Américains: le concours américain à la France en 1917–1918* (Paris: Publications de la Sorbonne, 1976). On the run-up to April 1917, see Yves-Henri Nouailhat, *France et États-Unis: Août 1914-Avril 1917* (Paris: Presses de la Sorbonne, 1979); and David Stevenson, "French War Aims and the American Challenge, 1914–1918," *Historical Journal* 22 (December 1979): 877–94.

64. On this supposition, see David G. Haglund and Maud Quessard, "How the West Was One: France, America, and the 'Huntingtonian Reversal,'" *Orbis* 62 (Fall 2018): 557–81.

65. See Robert B. Bruce, *A Fraternity of Arms: America and France in the Great War* (Lawrence: University Press of Kansas, 2003).

66. By 1880, America's gross domestic product surpassed that of not only France but also every other European country; by 1910, it was greater than the gross domestic products of Britain and Germany combined. See John M. Owen IV and Richard Rosecrance, *International Politics: How History Modifies Theory* (New York: Oxford University Press, 2019), 109; and Richard N. Cooper, "Economic Interdependence and War," in *The Next Great*

War? The Roots of World War I and the Risk of US–China Conflict, ed. Richard N. Rose-crance and Steven E. Miller (Cambridge, MA: MIT Press, 2014), 57–69.

67. See Gilles Delafon and Thomas Sancton, *Dear Jacques, Cher Bill: au cœur de l'Élysée et de la Maison Blanche, 1995–1999* (Paris: Plon, 1999), 351–52; and Richard Kuisel, "The Gallic Rooster Crows Again: The Paradox of French Anti-Americanism," *French Politics, Culture and Society* 19 (Fall 2001): 1–16. For examples of the America-as-problem thesis flourishing during the Clinton years, see Edward Behr, *Une Amérique qui fait peur* (Paris: Plon, 1995); Viviane Forrester, *L'Horreur économique* (Paris: Fayard, 1996); Michel Bugnon-Mordant, *L'Amérique totalitaire: les États-Unis et la maîtrise du monde* (Paris: Favre, 1998); and Patrick Gofman, *Le Cauchemar américain* (Lausanne: L'Age d'homme, 2000).

68. On this role, see Gérard Chaliand and Arnaud Blin, *America Is Back: les nouveaux Césars du Pentagone* (Paris: Bayard, 2003); and Richard Kuisel, "What Do the French Think of Us? The Deteriorating Image of the United States, 2000–2004," *French Politics, Culture and Society* 22 (Fall 2004): 91–119.

69. For instance, see Steven Philip Kramer, *Does France Still Count? The French Role in the New Europe* (Westport, CT: Praeger, 1994).

70. Tom Lansford, "The Question of France: French Security Choices at Century's End," *European Security* 5 (Spring 1996): 44–64, at 56.

71. Philip H. Gordon, *French Security Policy after the Cold War: Continuity, Change, and Implications for the United States* (Santa Monica: RAND, 1992), 1.

72. Albert Guérard, *France: A Short History* (London: George Allen and Unwin, 1947); Irwin M. Wall, *The United States and the Making of Postwar France, 1945–1954* (Cambridge: Cambridge University Press, 1991).

73. See Galen Jackson, "The Offshore Balancing Thesis Reconsidered: Realism, the Balance of Power in Europe, and America's Decision for War in 1917," *Security Studies* 21 (July 2012): 455–89.

74. Geir Lundestad, *"Empire" by Integration: The United States and European Integration, 1945–1997* (Oxford: Oxford University Press, 1997), 162.

75. Saul Padover, "France in Defeat: Causes and Consequences," *World Politics* 2 (April 1950): 305–37; Edgar S. Furniss Jr., *France, Troubled Ally* (New York: Praeger, 1960).

76. Arnold Wolfers, preface to Raymond Aron and August Heckscher, *Diversity of Worlds: France and the United States Look at Their Common Problems* (New York: Reynal, 1957), viii–ix.

77. David Schoenbrun, *As France Goes* (New York: Harper, 1957), 9, 15–16.

78. Jean-Pierre Rioux, *The Fourth Republic, 1944–1958,* trans. Godfrey Rogers (Cambridge: Cambridge University Press, 1987), 113.

79. Wall, *The United States and the Making of Postwar France,* 74–75.

80. See Frédéric Heurtebize, *Le Péril rouge: Washington face à l'eurocommunisme* (Paris: Presses Universitaires de France, 2014); Heurtebize, "Eurocommunism and the Contradictions of Superpower Détente," *Diplomatic History* 41 (September 2017): 747–71; Dominique Lejeune, *La Peur du "rouge" en France: des partageux aux gauchistes* (Paris: Belin, 2003); Alessandro Brogi, *Confronting America: The Cold War between the United States and the Commu-*

nists in France and Italy (Chapel Hill: University of North Carolina Press, 2011); and Irwin Wall, "Les États-Unis et l'eurocommunisme," *Relations internationales* 119 (2004): 363–80.

81. Jean-Philippe Mathy, *Melancholy Politics: Loss, Mourning, and Memory in Late Modern France* (University Park, PA: Penn State University Press, 2011), 3. Also see Éric Zemmour, *Le suicide français* (Paris: Albin Michel, 2014); Nicolas Baverez, *Les trente piteuses* (Paris: Flammarion, 1998); Baverez, *La France qui tombe* (Paris: Perrin, 2003); and Baverez, "L'étrange déclin: réponse à mes contradicteurs," *Commentaire* 105 (Spring 2004): 141–50. For a nuanced discussion, see Sophie Meunier, "Free-Falling France or Free-Trading France?," *French Politics, Culture and Society* 22 (Spring 2004): 98–107.

82. On the concept of soft balancing, see T. V. Paul, "Soft Balancing in the Age of US Primacy," *International Security* 30 (Summer 2005): 46–71; and Robert A. Pape, "Soft Balancing against the United States," *International Security* 30 (Summer 2005): 7–45. The rise and demise of European soft balancing against the United States is intelligently assessed in Lorenzo Cladi and Andrea Locatelli, eds., *International Relations Theory and European Security: We Thought We Knew* (London: Routledge, 2016).

83. Ronald Steel, *The End of Alliance: America and the Future of Europe* (New York: Viking Press, 1964).

84. Michael M. Harrison, *The Reluctant Ally: France and Atlantic Security* (Baltimore: Johns Hopkins University Press, 1981); Charles G. Cogan, *Oldest Allies, Guarded Friends: The United States and France Since 1940* (Westport, CT: Praeger, 1994); Frank Costigliola, *France and the United States: The Cold Alliance since World War II* (New York: Twayne, 1992).

85. As argued in Robert Kagan, *Of Paradise and Power: America and the New World Order* (New York: Alfred A. Knopf, 2003), 29–31.

86. Glenn H. Snyder, "The Security Dilemma in Alliance Politics," *World Politics* 36 (July 1984): 461–95, at 494–95. Implicit support for Snyder's claim about the Cold War's "cementing" impact is provided in Frédéric Bozo, "Les Etats-Unis, la France et la fin de la Guerre Froide," in *Conflit et coopération dans les relations franco-américaines: du Général de Gaulle à Nicolas Sarkozy*, ed. Renéo Lukic (Québec: Presses de l'Université Laval, 2009), 123–49.

87. "Nous sommes en guerre contre l'Amérique," quoted in Pierre Melandri and Justin Vaïsse, *L'Empire du milieu: les États-Unis et le monde depuis la fin de la Guerre Froide* (Paris: Éd. Odile Jacob, 2001), 455. On the tense period of bilateral relations post–Cold War, see Gilles Andréani, "La France et l'OTAN après la guerre froide," *Politique étrangère* 63 (Spring 1998): 77–92; and Frédéric Bozo, "Mitterrand's France, the End of the Cold War, and German Unification: A Reappraisal," *Cold War History* 7 (November 2007): 455–78.

88. James Baker to Roland Dumas, in Emil Bölte, "Zwischen Paris und Washington geht zur Zeit kaum etwas," *General-Anzeiger* (Bonn), 30 May 1992, 2.

89. Thierry de Montbrial, "La France est-elle 'l'ennemie numéro 1' des États-Unis?," *Le Figaro*, 16 June 1992, 3.

90. For an advocacy of just such a Europe, see Nicole Gnesotto, "Europe et États-Unis: visions du monde, visions de l'autre, " *Commentaire* 105 (Spring 2004): 17–27; and Gnesotto, *L'Europe et la puissance* (Paris: Presses de Sciences Po, 1998).

91. Timothy Garton Ash, *Free World: America, Europe, and the Surprising Future of the West* (New York: Random House, 2004), 59.

92. See Jolyon Howorth, "Britain, France and the European Defence Initiative," *Survival* 42 (Summer 2000): 33–55; and Jolyon Howorth and John T. S. Keeler, eds., *Defending Europe: The EU, NATO and the Quest for European Autonomy* (New York: Palgrave Macmillan, 2003).

93. For example, see Pierre Biarnès, *Le XXIe siècle ne sera pas américain* (Paris: Éd. du Rocher, 1998). Also see Jean-Marie Guéhenno, "Américanisation du monde ou mondialisation de l'Amérique?," *Politique étrangère* 64 (Spring 1999): 7–20.

94. See William Pfaff, "The Coming Clash of Europe with America," *World Policy Journal* 15 (Winter 1998/99): 1–9.

95. Samuel P. Huntington, *The Clash of Civilizations and the Remaking of World Order* (New York: Simon & Schuster, 1996), 308.

96. Seth Cropsey and Harry Halem, "Sam Was Partly Wrong," *American Interest* 14 (November/December 2018): 1–10.

97. Samuel P. Huntington, "The Lonely Superpower," *Foreign Affairs* 78 (March/April 1999): 35–49, at 48.

98. See Jacquelyn K. Davis, *Reluctant Allies and Competitive Partners: US–French Relations at the Breaking Point?* (Dulles, VA: Institute for Foreign Policy Analysis/Brassey's, 2003).

99. For one French analyst who believed this to be both possible and desirable, see Pascal Boniface, *La France est-elle encore une grande puissance?* (Paris: Presses de la Fondation Nationale des Sciences Politiques, 1998).

100. Charles A. Kupchan, "The End of the West," *Atlantic Monthly* 290 (November 2002): 42–44, at 44. This theme is echoed in André Glucksmann, *Ouest contre Ouest* (Paris: Plon, 2003); Jürgen Habermas, *The Divided West,* trans. Ciaran Cronin (Cambridge: Polity Press, 2006); and from an otherwise decidedly non-Habermasian perspective, Patrick Buchanan, *The Death of the West: How Dying Populations and Immigrant Invasions Imperil Our Country and Civilization* (New York: Thomas Dunne, 2002).

101. See Elizabeth Pond, *Friendly Fire: The Near-Death of the Transatlantic Alliance* (Washington, DC: Brookings Institution Press/European Union Studies Association, 2004). Similarly reflecting the alarmism of those years is Pierre Melandri, "L'unilatéralisme, stade suprême de l'exceptionnalisme?," *Le Débat* 127 (November–December 2003): 21–45.

102. Among those subscribing to this view was Charles A. Kupchan, *The End of the American Era: US Foreign Policy and the Geopolitics of the Twenty-First Century* (New York: Knopf, 2003).

103. For this roseate notion, see Lucile Eznack, "Crises as Signals of Strength: The Significance of Affect in Close Allies' Relationships," *Security Studies* 20 (April 2011): 238–65.

104. Charles Dickens, *A Christmas Carol* (London: Chapman and Hall, 1843).

105. For divergent perspectives on America's interest(s) in the dispute, highlighting, respectively, ideological versus material stakes, see Jennie A. Sloan, "Anglo-American Relations and the Venezuelan Boundary Dispute," *Hispanic American Historical Review* 4 (November 1938): 486–506; and Walter LaFeber, "The Background of Cleveland's Venezuelan Policy: A Reinterpretation," *American Historical Review* 66 (July 1961): 947–67.

106. See Marshall Bertram, *The Birth of Anglo-American Friendship: The Prime Facet of the Venezuelan Boundary Dispute—A Study of the Interrelation of Diplomacy and Public Opinion* (Lanham, MD: University Press of America, 1992); T. Boyle, "The Venezuela Crisis and the Liberal Opposition, 1895–96," *Journal of Modern History* 50 (September 1978, on-demand supplement): D1185–1212; and Bradford Perkins, *The Great Rapprochement: England and the United States, 1895–1914* (New York: Atheneum, 1968).

107. See Robert J. Young, *Marketing Marianne: French Propaganda in America, 1900–1940* (New Brunswick, NJ: Rutgers University Press, 2004); and Richard F. Kuisel, *Seducing the French: The Dilemma of Americanization* (Berkeley: University of California Press, 1993).

108. Richard Z. Chesnoff, *The Arrogance of the French: Why They Can't Stand Us—and Why the Feeling Is Mutual* (New York: Sentinel, 2005), 158.

109. "Woody Allen Promotes France in Video," *International Herald Tribune*, 16 June 2003, 2. Other celebrities appearing in the video were Robert De Niro, Wynton Marsalis, and George Plimpton.

110. See Frédéric Bozo, "France and NATO Under Sarkozy: End of the French Exception?," FIP Working Paper (Paris: Fondation pour l'Innovation Politique, March 2008). One analyst during the Obama years commented, "Critics of Obama like Dick Cheney and John Bolton really are criticizing him for following the path laid out by Bush in his last three years in office." Robert Jervis, "Do Leaders Matter and How Would We Know?," *Security Studies* 22 (April 2013): 153–79, at 178.

111. J. C. Casanova, "Le temps est venu pour l'Europe de s'émanciper des Etats-Unis," *Le Monde*, 17 November 2009, 21; Roger Cohen, "Obama in His Labyrinth," *International Herald Tribune*, 24 November 2009, 9.

112. David G. Haglund, "Happy Days Are Here Again? France's Reintegration into NATO and Its Impact on Relations with the United States," *European Security* 19 (March 2010): 123–42, at 132.

113. Mark Mazzetti and Michael R. Gordon, "Support Slipping, US Defends Plan for Syria Attack," *New York Times*, 31 August 2013, A1, A7; Steven Erlanger, "In Turnaround, It's France Backing Arms While Britain Sits on Syria Sidelines," *New York Times*, 31 August 2013, A6.

114. Maggie Haberman and Mark Landler, "In Paris, Trump Stands by His Son, and Praises Macron," *New York Times*, 14 July 2017, A15.

115. Kagan, *Of Paradise and Power*, 3–4.

116. Steven Erlanger, "The French Way of War," *New York Times*, 20 January 2013, SR 5. Also see, in this same vein, Roger Cohen, "French Muscle, American Cheese," *New York Times*, 15 November 2013, A25.

117. This term of derision was neither American in inspiration nor particularly recent in utterance; its origins date at least as far back as the Second World War. During the run-up to the June 2016 referendum on Brexit, one campaign ad sponsored by Leave.EU featured an interview with the founder of the Chelsea Pensioners, Arron Banks, who said that a veteran of the Second World War had made a donation of £30 to the cause, accompanied by a note reading, "I am an old soldier from the last war. I remember the French and the Belgians in 1940, what we called the surrender monkeys . . . who we saved. My father was an Old

Contemptible in France in 1914. He says you can't trust them and they proved him right. We were never thanked." Fintan O'Toole, *The Politics of Pain: Postwar England and the Rise of Nationalism* (New York: Liveright, 2019), 56.

118. Colin Dueck, *The Obama Doctrine: American Grand Strategy Today* (Oxford: Oxford University Press, 2015).

119. For a collection of interesting and balanced French assessments of the Obama foreign policy record, published shortly before the election of Donald Trump, see Frédéric Charillon and Célia Belin, eds., *Les États-Unis dans le monde* (Paris: CNRS Éditions, 2016).

120. See the op-ed written by the editorial director of *Le Monde,* Sylvie Kauffmann, "Can Biden Fix What Trump Broke?," *New York Times,* 16 September 2020, https://www.nytimes.com/2020/09/16/opinion/international-world/can-biden-fix-what-trump-broke.html.

2. The Role of "Strategic Culture" in Understanding Franco-American Relations

1. *Voyage dans les deux Louisianes et chez les régions sauvages du Missouri* (Paris: Capelle et Renand, 1805).

2. Roger, *Ennemi américain,* 64–69.

3. Alfred Grosser, *The Western Alliance* (New York: Continuum, 1980), xv; Michael J. Brenner and Guillaume Parmentier, *Reconcilable Differences: US–French Relations in the New Era* (Washington, DC: Brookings Institution Press, 2002), 2.

4. Jörg Nagler, "From Culture to *Kultur*: Changing American Perceptions of Imperial Germany, 1870–1914," in *Transatlantic Images and Perceptions: Germany and America Since 1776,* ed. David E. Barclay and Elisabeth Glaser-Schmidt (Cambridge: Cambridge University Press, 1997), 131–54; Michaela Hönicke, "'Know Your Enemy': American Wartime Images of Germany, 1942–1943," in *Enemy Images in American History,* ed. Ragnhild Fiebig-von Hase and Ursula Lehmkuhl (Providence, RI: Berghahn, 1997), 232–78.

5. Quoted in André Tardieu, *France and America: Some Experiences in Coöperation* (Boston: Houghton Mifflin, 1927), 64.

6. Tardieu, *France and America,* 50–51.

7. See Andrew A. G. Ross, "Coming in from the Cold: Constructivism and Emotions," *European Journal of International Relations* 12 (June 2006): 197–222. For examples spanning a diverse range of emotions, including status anxiety, fear, empathy, and anger, see Jonathan Renshon, *Fighting for Status: Hierarchy and Conflict in World Politics* (Princeton, NJ: Princeton University Press, 2017); Lilach Gilady, *The Price of Prestige: Conspicuous Consumption in International Relations* (Chicago: University of Chicago Press, 2018); Roland Bleiker and Emma Hutchison, "Fear No More: Emotions and World Politics," *Review of International Studies* 34 (January 2008): 115–35; Jonathan Mercer, "Emotional Beliefs," *International Organization* 64 (Winter 2010): 1–31; Renée Jeffery, *Reason and Emotion in International Ethics* (Cambridge: Cambridge University Press, 2014); and Todd H. Hall, *Emotional Diplomacy: Official Emotion on the International Stage* (Ithaca, NY: Cornell University Press, 2016).

8. William R. Taylor, *Cavalier and Yankee: The Old South and American National Character* (New York: George Braziller, 1961), 18–19.

9. For an interesting melding of grand strategy and strategic culture, see Colin Dueck, *Reluctant Crusaders: Power, Culture, and Change in American Grand Strategy* (Princeton, NJ: Princeton University Press, 2006).

10. Kaspi, *Temps des Américains*, 305; Simon Serfaty, "France-États-Unis: la querelle permanente," *Relations Internationales et Stratégiques* 25 (Spring 1997), 52–59.

11. Chesnoff, *Arrogance of the French*, xv.

12. Rudolph Binion, *Defeated Leaders: The Political Fate of Caillaux, Jouvenel, and Tardieu* (New York: Columbia University Press, 1960), 12–13.

13. Olivier Bernier, *Fireworks at Dusk: Paris in the Thirties* (Boston: Little, Brown, 1993), 61.

14. For Tardieu's earlier pro-Americanism, see André Tardieu, *Notes sur les États-Unis: la Société—la politique—la diplomatie* (Paris: Calmann-Lévy, 1908); and Donald Roy Allen, "French Views of America in the Nineteen-Thirties" (PhD diss., Boston University, 1970), 75, where Tardieu is described, correctly, as having been "usually very favorably disposed toward America."

15. Roger, *Ennemi américain*, 346.

16. Tardieu, *France and America*, 3–4.

17. For valuable overviews of the bilateral relationship, see Henry Blumenthal, *France and the United States: Their Diplomatic Relations, 1789–1914* (Chapel Hill: University of North Carolina Press, 1970); Blumenthal, *A Reappraisal of Franco-American Relations, 1830–1871* (Chapel Hill: University of North Carolina Press, 1959); Marvin R. Zahniser, *Uncertain Friendship: American-French Diplomatic Relations through the Cold War* (New York: John Wiley & Sons, 1975); and Donald C. McKay, *The United States and France* (Cambridge, MA: Harvard University Press, 1951).

18. Crane Brinton, *The Americans and the French* (Cambridge, MA: Harvard University Press, 1968), 51–52.

19. Walter Russell Mead, *Special Providence: American Foreign Policy and How It Changed the World* (New York: Alfred A. Knopf, 2001), 7–8.

20. Walter A. McDougall, *Promised Land, Crusader State: The American Encounter with the World Since 1776* (Boston: Houghton Mifflin, 1997), 25. For the peace deliberations, see Robert D. Sayre, *Britain and France at the Birth of America: The European Powers and the Peace Negotiations of 1782–1783* (Exeter: University of Exeter Press, 2001); and Ronald Hoffman and Peter J. Albert, eds., *Peace and Peacemakers: The Treaty of 1783* (Charlottesville: University of Virginia Press, 1986).

21. Richard W. Van Alstyne, *The Rising American Empire* (New York: Oxford University Press, 1960), 70–76. Also see Charles Marion Thomas, *American Neutrality in 1793: A Study in Cabinet Government* (New York: Columbia University Press, 1931); Todd Estes, *The Jay Treaty Debate, Public Opinion, and the Evolution of Early American Political Culture* (Amherst: University of Massachusetts Press, 2006); Albert H. Bowman, *The Struggle for Neutrality: Franco-American Diplomacy During the Federalist Era* (Knoxville: University of Tennessee Press, 1974); and Bradford Perkins, *The First Rapprochement: England and the United States, 1795–1805* (Berkeley: University of California Press, 1967).

22. On Franco-British enmity, see Robert Tombs and Isabelle Tombs, *That Sweet Enemy: The French and the British from the Sun King to the Present* (London: William Heine-

mann, 2006); and Alexander Mikaberidze, *The Napoleonic Wars: A Global History* (Oxford: Oxford University Press, 2020).

23. See Gardner W. Allen, *Our Naval War with France* (Boston: Houghton Mifflin, 1909); Alexander DeConde, *The Quasi-War: The Politics and Diplomacy of the Undeclared War with France, 1797–1801* (New York: Scribner, 1966); Howard P. Nash, *The Forgotten Wars: The Role of the US Navy in the Quasi-War with France and the Barbary Wars, 1798–1805* (South Brunswick, NJ: A. S. Barnes, 1968); Michael A. Palmer, *Stoddert's War: Naval Operations during the Quasi-War with France, 1798–1801* (Columbia: University of South Carolina Press, 1987); Peter P. Hill, *William Vans Murray, Federalist Diplomat: The Shaping of Peace with France, 1797–1801* (Syracuse, NY: Syracuse University Press, 1971); and Georges-Nestler Tricoche, "Une page peu connue de l'histoire de France: la guerre franco-américaine, 1798–1801," *La Revue Historique* 85 (May–August 1904): 288–99.

24. On the distinction between cobelligerent and ally during those years, see Lawrence S. Kaplan, "France and Madison's Decision for War, 1812," *Mississippi Valley Historical Review* 50 (March 1964): 652–71.

25. Although President Wilson insisted that America had entered the war in 1917 as an "associated" rather than an allied power, the reality is otherwise; for a short time, the US *was* a de facto but very real ally of France and Britain. On the rise and demise of that alliance, see David F. Trask, *The AEF and Coalition Warmaking, 1917–1918* (Lawrence: University Press of Kansas, 1993); Bruce, *Fraternity of Arms;* and Keith L. Nelson, *Victors Divided: America and the Allies in Germany, 1918–1923* (Berkeley: University of California Press, 1975).

26. See in particular Georges Duhamel, *Scènes de la vie future* (Paris: Mercure de France, 1930), a runaway bestseller that would be published in English a year later under the title *America the Menace: Scenes from the Life of the Future* (Boston: Houghton Mifflin, 1931); and Jean-Philippe Mathy, *Extrême-Occident: French Intellectuals and America* (Chicago: University of Chicago Press, 1993), 48–59.

27. See Brooke L. Blower, *Becoming Americans in Paris: Transatlantic Politics and Culture between the World Wars* (New York: Oxford University Press, 2011).

28. Typical of this line of criticism was Frederick Bausman, *Let France Explain* (London: George Allen and Unwin, 1922). Despite the book's city of publication, Bausman was an American, and a judge no less, having served on the bench of Washington state's supreme court. For an effective critique of Bausman and those (many) who thought like him, see Denna Frank Fleming, "Our Entry into the World War in 1917: The Revised Version," *Journal of Politics* 2 (February 1940): 75–86. For another sharp retort to the "blame France" thesis that was gaining such a head of steam in the US and UK early in the 1920s, see André Tardieu, "The Policy of France," *Foreign Affairs* 1 (September 1922): 11–28.

29. See Elizabeth Brett White, *American Opinion of France: From Lafayette to Poincaré* (New York: Alfred A. Knopf, 1927). For comparative assessments of American attitudes at the time toward both Germany and France, see Hans W. Gatzke, *Germany and the United States: A "Special Relationship"?* (Cambridge, MA: Harvard University Press, 1980), 81–96; Peter Krüger, "Germany and the United States, 1914–1933: The Mutual Perception of Their Political System," in *Transatlantic Images and Perceptions: Germany and America Since 1776,* ed. David E. Barclay and Elisabeth Glaser-Schmidt (Cambridge: Cambridge

University Press, 1997), 171–90; Peter Berg, *Deutschland und Amerika, 1918–1929: Über das deutsche Amerikabild der zwanziger Jahre* (Lübeck: Matthiesen, 1963); and Jennifer D. Keene, *Doughboys, the Great War, and the Remaking of America* (Baltimore: Johns Hopkins University Press, 2001), especially chapter 5, "Forging Their Own Alliances: American Soldiers' Relations with the French and the Germans."

30. On the significance of the war debt wrangling for bilateral relations, see Denise Artaud, *La France et le problème des dettes de guerre, 1917–1929* (Lille: Atelier Reproduction des Thèses, 1978); and Ellen Schrecker, *The Hired Money: The French Debt to the United States, 1917–1929* (New York: Arno, 1979). For the tone of French criticism of America during the interwar period, see Octave Homberg, *La Grande Injustice: la question des dettes interalliés* (Paris: Grasset, 1926); Robert Aron and Arnaud Dandieu, *Le Cancer américain* (Paris: Rieder, 1931); J.-L. Chastanet, *L'Oncle Shylock: ou l'impérialisme américain à la conquête du monde* (Paris: Flammarion, 1927); Lucien Romier, *Who Will Be Master: Europe or America?*, trans. Matthew Josephson (New York: Macaulay, 1928); and, especially, Isaac Kadmi-Cohen, *L'Abomination américaine: essai politique* (Paris: Flammarion, 1930). For an assessment of this French criticism, see Benjamin D. Rhodes, "Reassessing 'Uncle Shylock': The United States and the French War Debt, 1917–1929," *Journal of American History* 55 (March 1969): 787–803.

31. Janet Flanner, *Paris Was Yesterday, 1925–1939* (London: Angus and Robertson, 1973), 62. Flanner had been Paris correspondent of the *New Yorker* during the 1920s and 1930s, and again following the liberation of Paris; she wrote under the pseudonym "Genêt." See Brenda Wineapple, *Genêt: A Biography of Janet Flanner* (Lincoln: University of Nebraska Press, 1989).

32. Michael Jabara Carley, *1939: The Alliance that Never Was and the Coming of World War II* (Chicago: Ivan R. Dee, 1999).

33. See Williams, *France, Britain and the United States*, vol. 1.

34. For the claim that Roosevelt had scant regard for both de Gaulle, whom he called "that nut," and France, see Costigliola, *France and the United States*, 30–31.

35. Walter M. Hudson, "A Certain Idea of Charles de Gaulle," *American Interest* 15 (March/April 2020): 36–38, at 37.

36. See André Béziat, *Franklin Roosevelt et la France (1939–1945): la diplomatie de l'entêtement* (Paris: L' Harmattan, 1997); Béziat, "Le Réalisme diplomatique à rude épreuve: Washington et Vichy (juillet 1940-novembre 1942)," in *Les Relations franco-américains au XXe siècle*, ed. Pierre Melandri and Serge Ricard (Paris: L'Harmattan, 2003), 85–100; Raoul Aglion, *Roosevelt and de Gaulle: Allies in Conflict, a Personal Memoir* (New York: Free Press, 1988); John Newhouse, *De Gaulle and the Anglo-Saxons* (New York: Viking, 1970); Mario Rossi, *Roosevelt and the French* (Westport, CT: Praeger, 1993); Milton Viorst, *Hostile Allies: FDR and Charles de Gaulle* (New York: Macmillan, 1965); Dorothy Shipley White, *Seeds of Discord: De Gaulle, Free France and the Allies* (Syracuse, NY: Syracuse University Press, 1964); and Sebastian Reyn, *American Power and the Cloak of Idealism: The "Great Quarrel" between Charles de Gaulle and Uncle Sam* (Den Haag: Atlantische Commissie, 2021).

37. See David G. Haglund, "Theodore Roosevelt and the 'Special Relationship' with France," in *A Companion to Theodore Roosevelt*, ed. Serge Ricard (Oxford: Wiley-Blackwell, 2011), 329–49.

38. See John H. Finley, *The French in the Heart of America* (New York: Charles Scribner's Sons, 1918); and David G. Haglund and Justin Massie, "The French in the Heart of North America? 'Civilization Rallying,' National Unity, and the Geopolitical Significance of 1917," *Journal of Transatlantic Studies* 16 (June 2018): 117–36.

39. See Robert O. Paxton, *Vichy France: Old Guard and New Order, 1940–1944* (New York: Columbia University Press, 1992), 305–6; and Kenneth W. Pendar, *Adventure in Diplomacy: Our French Dilemma* (New York: Dodd, Mead, 1945), 110.

40. There is a voluminous scholarly corpus on Anglo-American friction, so often triggered by British opposition to American territorial expansion in North America and elsewhere in the western hemisphere. See, for instance, Kenneth Bourne, *Britain and the Balance of Power in North America, 1815–1908* (Berkeley: University of California Press, 1967); James E. Lewis, *The American Union and the Problem of Neighborhood, 1783–1829* (Chapel Hill: University of North Carolina Press, 1998); J. Fred Rippy, *Rivalry of the United States and Great Britain over Latin America, 1808–1830* (Baltimore: Johns Hopkins Press, 1929); and Wilbur Devereux Jones, *The American Problem in British Diplomacy, 1841–1861* (London: Macmillan, 1974). For specific expansion-engendered diplomatic clashes prior to the Civil War, see Bradford Perkins, *Castlereagh and Adams: England and the United States, 1812–1823* (Berkeley: University of California Press, 1965); Howard Jones, "Anglophobia and the Aroostook War," *New England Quarterly* 48 (December 1975): 519–39; Jones, *To the Webster–Ashburton Treaty: A Study in Anglo-American Relations, 1783–1843* (Chapel Hill: University of North Carolina Press, 1977); Frederick Merk, "British Government Propaganda and the Oregon Treaty," *American Historical Review* 40 (October 1934): 38–62; Merk, *The Oregon Question* (Cambridge, MA: Belknap Press of Harvard University Press, 1967); Sam W. Haynes, "Anglophobia and the Annexation of Texas: The Quest for National Security," in *Manifest Destiny and Empire: American Antebellum Expansion*, ed. Haynes and Christopher Morris (Arlington: Texas A&M University Press, 1997), 115–46; Ephraim Douglas Adams, *British Interests and Activities in Texas, 1838–1846* (Baltimore: Johns Hopkins Press, 1910); Adams, "English Interest in the Annexation of California," *American Historical Review* 14 (July 1909): 744–63; Robert A. Naylor, "The British Role in Central America Prior to the Clayton-Bulwer Treaty of 1850," *Hispanic American Historical Review* 40 (August 1960): 361–82; Richard W. Van Alstyne, "Anglo-American Relations, 1853–1857: British Statesmen on the Clayton-Bulwer Treaty and American Expansion," *American Historical Review* 42 (April 1937): 491–500; Martin Crawford, *The Anglo-American Crisis of the Mid-Nineteenth Century: The Times and America, 1850–1862* (Athens: University of Georgia Press, 1987); and Kenneth Bourne, "The Clayton-Bulwer Treaty and the Decline of British Opposition to the Territorial Expansion of the United States, 1857–1860," *Journal of Modern History* 33 (September 1961): 287–91.

41. Charles S. Campbell Jr., *The Transformation of American Foreign Relations, 1865–1900* (New York: Harper & Row, 1976).

42. Thierry Maulnier, "L'Antiaméricanisme et les Américains," *Revue des Deux Mondes* 145 (March 1975): 522–26.

43. Although dated in many respects, still valuable is the book by the renowned political scientist, Edward S. Corwin, *French Policy and the American Alliance of 1778* (Princeton, NJ: Princeton University Press, 1916).

44. James March, "Bounded Rationality, Ambiguity and Engineering of Choice," *Bell Journal of Economics* 9 (Autumn 1978): 587–608, at 592. Also see Robert Nozick, *The Nature of Rationality* (Princeton, NJ: Princeton University Press, 1993); Jon Elster, *Solomonic Judgments: Studies in the Limitation of Rationality* (New York: Cambridge University Press, 1989); and Karen S. Cook and Margaret Levi, eds., *The Limits of Rationality* (Chicago: University of Chicago Press, 1990).

45. Donald A. Green and Ian Shapiro, *Pathologies of Rational Choice Theory: A Critique of Applications in Political Science* (New Haven, CT: Yale University Press, 1994), 13–17.

46. See Robert Axelrod, *The Evolution of Cooperation* (New York: Basic Books, 1984).

47. I stress *apparently,* for reasons that will become clear in chapter 5.

48. Ikenberry, A *World Safe for Democracy,* 200.

49. Aron and Heckscher, *Diversity of Worlds,* 6. The book's coauthors wrote separate sections; Aron's section is pages 3–72. Making the same point about familiarity breeding contempt was the contemporaneous treatise by Cyrille Arnavon, *L'Américanisme et nous: essai* (Paris: Del Duca, 1958).

50. On the general proposition that liberal democratic allies, precisely because they *are* liberal democracies, manifest reliably optimal levels of cooperation, see Thomas Risse-Kappen, *Cooperation among Democracies: The European Influence on US Foreign Policy* (Princeton, NJ: Princeton University Press, 1995).

51. There is a lively debate about whether the realm of international relations actually can or should be amenable to being studied systematically from the perspective(s) of rational action. See in particular Michael C. Desch, *Cult of the Irrelevant: The Waning Influence of Social Science on National Security* (Princeton, NJ: Princeton University Press, 2019); Stephen M. Walt, "Rigor or Rigor Mortis? Rational Choice and Security Studies," *International Security* 23 (Spring 1999): 5–48; and Miles Kahler, "Rationality in International Relations," *International Organization* 52 (Autumn 1998): 919–41. This debate echoes more general discussions about the utility of rational action assumptions in the discipline of political science. For some instances of that broader debate, Jeffery Friedman, ed., *The Rational Choice Controversy: Economic Models of Politics Reconsidered* (New Haven, CT: Yale University Press, 1996); Kristen Monroe, ed., *The Economic Approach to Politics: A Critical Reassessment of the Theory of Rational Action* (New York: HarperCollins, 1991); and Gerardo L. Munck, "Game Theory and Comparative Politics: New Perspectives and Old Concerns," *World Politics* 53 (January 2001): 173–204.

52. Michael Kammen, "Review Essay," *History and Theory* 34 (October 1995): 245–61, at 253. Also see Jeffrey W. Legro, "Culture and Preferences in the International Cooperation Two-Step," *American Political Science Review* 90 (March 1996): 118–37.

53. Robert H. Bates, Rui J. P. de Figueiredo, and Barry R. Weingast, "The Politics of Interpretation: Rationality, Culture and Transition," *Politics and Society* 26 (December 1998): 603–42, at 603.

54. For a helpful critique of the claim that interests can themselves take shape independently of cultural considerations, see Aaron Wildavsky, "Choosing Preferences by Constructing Institutions: A Cultural Theory of Preference Formation," *American Political Science Review* 81 (March 1987): 3–21.

55. Herbert A. Simon, *Models of Man—Social and Rational: Mathematical Essays on Rational Human Behavior* (New York: John Wiley and Sons, 1957).

56. Macron's New Year's Eve remarks quoted in Arthur Berdah, "Ce qu'il faut retenir des premier vœux aux Français d'Emmanuel Macron," *Le Figaro,* 1 January 2018, http://www.lefigaro.fr/politique/le-scan/2017/12/31/25001-20171231ARTFIG00096-ce qu-il-faut-retenir-des-premiers-voeux-aux-francais-d-emmanuel-macron.php. For the Sorbonne address, see Mélissa Kalaydjian and Peter Esser, "Le discours de Macron sur l'Europe divise la presse européenne," *Libération,* 27 September 2017, http://www.liberation.fr/planete/2017/09/27/le-discours-de-macron-sur-l-europe-divise-la-presse europeenne_1599294.

57. A tension detected and dissected in Philip H. Gordon, *A Certain Idea of France: French Security Policy and the Gaullist Legacy* (Princeton, NJ: Princeton University Press, 1993).

58. Among them, Sten Rynning, "The European Union: Towards a Strategic Culture?," *Security Dialogue* 34 (December 2003): 479–96; Christoph O. Meyer, "Convergence Towards a European Strategic Culture? A Constructivist Framework for Explaining Changing Norms," *European Journal of International Relations* 11 (December 2005): 523–49; Per M. Norheim-Martinsen, "EU Strategic Culture: When the Means Becomes the End," *Contemporary Security Policy* 32 (December 2011): 517–34; Paul Cornish and Geoffrey Edwards, "The Strategic Culture of the European Union: A Progress Report," *International Affairs* 81 (July 2005): 801–20; and Janne Haaland Matlary, "When Soft Power Turns Hard: Is an EU Strategic Culture Possible?," *Security Dialogue* 37 (March 2006): 105–21.

59. Jon Elster, *Explaining Social Behavior: More Nuts and Bolts for the Social Sciences* (Cambridge: Cambridge University Press, 2007), 1.

60. Kagan, *Of Paradise and Power,* 27–28.

61. See Philip H. Gordon, "Europe's Uncommon Foreign Policy," *International Security* 22 (Winter 1997/98): 74–100; Howorth, "Britain, France and the European Defence Initiative," 33–55; Stephanie C. Hofmann, "Overlapping Institutions in the Realm of International Security: The Case of NATO and ESDP," *Perspectives on Politics* 7 (March 2009): 45–52; Asle Toje, *America, the EU, and Strategic Culture: Renegotiating the Transatlantic Bargain* (New York: Routledge, 2008); and David G. Haglund and Frédéric Mérand, "Transatlantic Relations in the New Strategic Landscape: Implications for Canada," *International Journal* 66 (Winter 2010–11): 23–38.

62. Craig B. Greathouse, "Examining the Role and Methodology of Strategic Culture," *Risk, Hazards & Crisis in Public Policy* 1 (2010): 57–85, at 81.

63. Oscar Wilde, *A Woman of No Importance* (London: John Lane, 1894), 16.

64. For the results of that project, see Jeannie L. Johnson, Kerry M. Kartchner, and Jeffrey A. Larsen, eds., *Strategic Culture and Weapons of Mass Destruction: Culturally Based Insights into Comparative National Security Policymaking* (New York: Palgrave Macmillan, 2009).

65. Jeffrey S. Lantis, "Strategic Culture: From Clausewitz to Constructivism," a paper prepared for the Advanced Systems and Concepts Office, Defense Threat Reduction Agency, Washington, DC, 31 October 2006, 13.

66. Colin S. Gray, "Out of the Wilderness: Prime Time for Strategic Culture," *Comparative Strategy* 26 (January–March 2007): 1–20, at 1.

67. On the necessity for structural realists to conceive of power as "aggregate capability," see John J. Mearsheimer, *The Tragedy of Great Power Politics* (New York: W. W. Norton, 2001), 60. But for pitfalls associated with the actual measurement of this capability, see Michael Beckley, "The Power of Nations: Measuring What Matters," *International Security* 43 (Fall 2018): 7–44; Stephen G. Brooks and William C. Wohlforth, "The Rise and Fall of the Great Powers in the Twenty-First Century: China's Rise and the Fate of America's Global Position," *International Security* 40 (Winter 2015/16): 7–53; and Carsten Rauch, "Challenging the Power Consensus: GDP, CINC, and Power Transition Theory," *Security Studies* 26 (October 2017): 642–64.

68. For valuable, nuanced, conceptual analyses, see David A. Baldwin, *Paradoxes of Power* (Oxford: Basil Blackwell, 1989), especially chapter 4: "Power Analysis and World Politics: New Trends versus Old Tendencies"; as well as Baldwin, *Power and International Relations: A Conceptual Approach* (Princeton, NJ: Princeton University Press, 2016).

69. Some would object and insist instead that unless we can come to agreed-upon working definitions, we can never assign a value to our terms and thus cannot hope to measure them "scientifically." This insistence strikes me as being, in its own way, unscientific, if by the term *science* we simply mean the systematic organization and use of knowledge in a given area of inquiry. For a refreshingly catholic view of such a way to organize thinking about foreign policy, see Rosenau, *Scientific Study of Foreign Policy.*

70. Stanley Hoffmann, "An American Social Science: International Relations," *Daedalus* 106 (Summer 1977): 41–60, at 45.

71. Jack Snyder is often credited with being the first writer to employ the rubric explicitly, in his *The Soviet Strategic Culture: Implications for Nuclear Options* (Santa Monica: RAND Corporation, 1977).

72. For a cautionary reminder, see Giovanni Sartori, "Concept Misformation in Comparative Politics," *American Political Science Review* 64 (December 1970): 1033–53. But for a tacit recognition that the problem may have no resolution, see David Collier and James E. Mahon, "'Conceptual Stretching' Revisited: Adapting Categories in Comparative Analysis," *American Political Science Review* 87 (December 1999): 845–55.

73. Raymond Williams, cited by William H. Sewell Jr., "The Concept(s) of Culture," in *Beyond the Cultural Turn: New Directions in the Study of Society and Culture,* ed. Victoria E. Bonnell and Lynn Hunt (Berkeley: University of California Press, 1999), 35–61. For an extensive catalog of *culture*'s many, and at times contradictory, meanings, see A. L. Kroeber and Clyde Kluckhohn, *Culture: A Critical Review of Concepts and Definitions* (New York: Vintage Books, 1963).

74. Alastair Iain Johnston, *Cultural Realism: Strategic Culture and Grand Strategy in Chinese History* (Princeton, NJ: Princeton University Press, 1995), 1.

75. For such a confined understanding of strategic culture, see Yitzhak Klein, "A Theory of Strategic Culture," *Comparative Strategy* 10 (January–March 1991): 3–23. Sometimes an even more limiting modifier than *strategic* is chosen, as in the case of the debate over France's and other states' *military* culture. For that debate see Elizabeth Kier, "Culture and Military Doctrine: France between the Wars," *International Security* 19 (Spring 1995): 65–93; Kier, *Imagining War: French Military Doctrine between the Wars* (Princeton, NJ: Princeton

University Press, 1997); Douglas Porch, "Military 'Culture' and the Fall of France in 1940: A Review Essay," *International Security* 24 (Spring 2000): 157–80; Isabel V. Hull, *Absolute Destruction: Military Culture and the Practices of War in Imperial Germany* (Ithaca, NY: Cornell University Press, 2006); Carnes Lord, "American Strategic Culture," *Comparative Strategy* 5 (January 1985): 269–94; and H. Christian Breede, ed., *Culture and the Soldier: Identities, Values, and Norms in Military Engagement* (Vancouver: UBC Press, 2019).

76. John Lewis Gaddis, *Strategies of Containment: A Critical Appraisal of Postwar American National Security Policy* (Oxford: Oxford University Press, 1982), viii.

77. Ronald Jepperson and Ann Swidler, "What Properties of Culture Should We Measure?," *Poetics* 22 (1994): 359–71, at 359–60.

78. Donald R. Kelley, "The Old Cultural History," *History of the Human Sciences* 9 (August 1996): 101–26, at 101.

79. The term appears in the first volume of his magnum opus. Giovanni Andres, *Dell'origine, progressi e stato attuale d'ogni letteratura*, 7 vols. (Parma: Stamperia reale, 1782–99).

80. Kelley, "Old Cultural History," 109. Edward B. Tylor's book, originally published in 1865, was *Researches into the Early History of Mankind and the Development of Civilization*, 2nd ed. (London: Murray, 1870).

81. Kelley, "Old Cultural History," 114–16.

82. See David Brion Davis, "Some Recent Directions in American Cultural History," *American Historical Review* 73 (February 1968): 696–707.

83. Dueck, *Reluctant Crusaders*, 14–15. On the ideas–culture nexus, see Michael H. Hunt, *Ideology and U.S Foreign Policy* (New Haven, CT: Yale University Press, 1988); Akira Iriye, "Culture," *Journal of American History* 77 (June 1990): 99–107; Jerel Rosati, "The Power of Human Cognition in the Study of World Politics," *International Studies Review* 2 (Autumn 2000): 45–75; Albert S. Yee, "The Causal Effects of Ideas on Politics," *International Organization* 50 (Winter 1996): 69–108; and Sheri Berman, "Ideas, Norms, and Culture in Political Analysis," *Comparative Politics* 33 (January 2001): 231–50.

84. Robert Kelley, *The Cultural Pattern in American Politics: The First Century* (New York: Alfred A. Knopf, 1979), 6–9. For an early attempt to associate culture with ethnonationalism, through the concept of national "genius" (or as it would alternatively be rendered, "national character"), see Edward Sapir, "Culture, Genuine and Spurious," *American Journal of Sociology* 29 (January 1924): 401–29.

85. Clifford Geertz, *The Interpretation of Cultures* (New York: Basic Books, 1973).

86. Victoria E. Bonnell and Lynn Hunt, eds., "Introduction," in *Beyond the Cultural Turn: New Directions in the Study of Society and Culture* (Berkeley: University of California Press, 1999), 1–32, at 3.

87. Quoted in Kelley, *Cultural Pattern in American Politics*, 12.

88. Sewell, "Concept(s) of Culture," 48.

89. Johnston, *Cultural Realism*, 36–37. Also see Alastair Iain Johnston, "Thinking about Strategic Culture," *International Security* 19 (Spring 1995): 32–64.

90. On culture conceived as symbolism, see Ann Swidler, "Culture in Actions: Symbols and Strategies," *American Sociological Review* 51 (April 1986): 273–86.

91. Examples of what Johnston interprets as first- and second-generation strategic culturalists are, respectively, Colin S. Gray, "Strategic Culture as Context: The First Generation of Theory Strikes Back," *Review of International Studies* 25 (January 1999): 49–69; and Bradley Klein, "Hegemony and Strategic Culture: American Power Projection and Alliance Defence Politics," *Review of International Studies* 14 (April 1988): 133–48. For a somewhat rare endorsement of the "second" generation, see Edward Lock, "Refining Strategic Culture: Return of the Second Generation," *Review of International Studies* 36 (July 2010): 685–708.

92. Some of those developments had their origins in internal disciplinary schisms; see Morten Valbjørn, "Before, During and After the Cultural Turn: A 'Baedeker' to IR's Cultural Journey," *International Review of Sociology* 18 (March 2008): 55–82; Terrence J. McDonald, ed., *The Historic Turn in the Human Sciences* (Ann Arbor: University of Michigan Press, 1996). Also see Mark M. Blyth, "'Any More Bright Ideas?' The Ideational Turn of Comparative Political Economy," *Comparative Politics* 29 (January 1997): 229–50; David Chaney, *The Cultural Turn: Scene-Setting Essays on Contemporary Cultural History* (London: Routledge, 1994); and Pedro Aires Oliviera, Bruno Cardoso Reis, and Patrick Finney, "The Cultural Turn and Beyond in International History," *International History Review* 40 (June 2018): 573–75.

93. Prominent among these was Robert Gilpin, who worried that bipolarity might be unstable and very dangerous. Gilpin, *War and Change in World Politics* (Cambridge: Cambridge University Press, 1981). On splits within realist ranks, see Stephen G. Brooks, "Dueling Realisms," *International Organization* 51 (Summer 1997): 445–77; and William C. Wohlforth, "Gilpinian Realism and International Relations," *International Relations* 25 (December 2011): 499–511.

94. "So-called" because realism had been losing persuasiveness for some time and has continued to slide as a preferred international relations paradigm among the professoriate. Data periodically assembled by the Teaching, Research, and International Policy survey testify to the nondominance of what, not so long ago, was believed by some to be a hegemonic if not totemic fixture on the international epistemological scene. See Daniel Maliniak et al., "Is International Relations a Global Discipline? Hegemony, Insularity, and Diversity in the Field," *Security Studies* 27 (July 2018): 448–84.

95. See Stephen M. Walt, "International Relations: One World, Many Theories," *Foreign Policy* 110 (Spring 1998): 29–46.

96. As is claimed, for instance, in Adrian Hyde-Price, "Reflections on Security and Identity in Europe," in *Security and Identity in Europe*, ed. Lisbeth Aggestam and Hyde-Price (New York: St. Martin's, 2000), 22–48, at 23–24.

97. For a thoughtful and highly nuanced assessment of this question, see John Glenn, "Realism versus Strategic Culture: Competition and Collaboration?," *International Studies Review* 11 (September 2009): 523–51.

98. Gray, "Strategic Culture as Context," 58. In this regard, Gray's understanding of strategic culture is similar to the way in which Francis Fukuyama defines culture, as "inherited ethical habit." See Fukuyama, *Trust: The Social Virtues and the Creation of Prosperity* (New York: Free Press, 1995), 34.

99. The claim that strategic culture should be invested with such prowess is made in Christopher P. Twomey, "Lacunae in the Study of Culture in International Security," *Contemporary Security Policy* 29 (August 2008): 338–57.

100. See Adrian Kuzminski, "The Paradox of Historical Knowledge," *History and Theory* 12 (1973): 269–80, at 271–72.

101. Georg Henrik von Wright, *Explanation and Understanding* (Ithaca, NY: Cornell University Press, 1971), 4–6.

102. For one claim that historical explanation is possible but requires taking the "inside view"—that is, getting into the heads of sentient decision-makers so as to comprehend how *they* understood reality—see Isaiah Berlin, "History and Theory: The Concept of Scientific History," *History and Theory* 1 (1961): 1–31.

103. Von Wright, *Explanation and Understanding*, 134–35. Also see Richard Biernacki, "Method and Metaphor after the New Cultural History," in *Beyond the Cultural Turn: New Directions in the Study of Society and Culture*, ed. Victoria E. Bonnell and Lynn Hunt (Berkeley: University of California Press, 1999), 62–92; Patrick L. Gardiner, *The Nature of Historical Explanation* (Oxford: Oxford University Press, 1952); and Marc Trachtenberg, *The Craft of International History: A Guide to Method* (Princeton, NJ: Princeton University Press, 2006).

104. Michael C. Desch, "Culture Clash: Assessing the Importance of Ideas in Security Studies," *International Security* 23 (Summer 1998): 141–70.

105. Ruth Benedict, *The Chrysanthemum and the Sword: Patterns of Japanese Culture* (Boston: Houghton Mifflin, 1946). On the prominence of Benedict and other anthropologists among this pioneering generation of strategic culturalists, see E. Adamson Hoebel, "Anthropological Perspectives on National Character," *Annals of the American Academy of Political and Social Science* 370 (March 1967): 1–7.

106. David Rodnick, *Postwar Germans: An Anthropologist's Account* (New Haven, CT: Yale University Press, 1948), x.

107. Victor T. Le Vine, "Conceptualizing 'Ethnicity' and 'Ethnic Conflict': A Controversy Revisited," *Studies in Comparative International Development* 32 (Summer 1997): 47–75, at 49.

108. See Peter J. Katzenstein, ed., *The Culture of National Security: Norms and Identity in World Politics* (New York: Columbia University Press, 1996).

109. For an intriguing argument that nationalism did not so much cause the First World War as become exacerbated by that conflict's brutality, see Michael S. Neiberg, *Dance of the Furies: Europe and the Outbreak of World War I* (Cambridge, MA: Harvard University Press, 2011).

110. Hamilton Fyfe, *The Illusion of National Character* (London: Watts, 1940).

111. Dean Peabody, *National Characteristics* (Cambridge: Cambridge University Press, 1985), 10.

112. See Alex Inkeles and Daniel J. Levinson, "National Character: The Study of Modal Personality and Sociocultural Systems," in *The Handbook of Social Psychology* (2nd ed.), vol. 4, *Group Psychology and Phenomena of Interaction*, ed. Gardner Lindzey and Elliot Aronson (Reading, MA: Addison-Wesley, 1969), 418–506, at 424–25.

113. Morris Ginsberg, "National Character," *British Journal of Psychology* 32 (January 1942): 183–205, at 187–88.

114. Bernard C. Hennessy, "Psycho-Cultural Studies of National Character: Relevances for International Relations," *Background* 6 (Autumn 1962): 27–49, at 43–45, 47.

115. See Akira Iriye, "Culture and Power: International Relations as Intercultural Relations," *Diplomatic History* 3 (April 1979): 115–28.

116. In addition to Renshon, *Fighting for Status,* see William C. Wohlforth, "Unipolarity, Status Competition, and Great Power War," *World Politics* 61 (January 2009): 28–57; Reinhard Wolf, "Respect and Disrespect in International Politics: The Significance of Status Recognition," *International Theory* 3 (February 2011): 105–42; and T. V. Paul, Deborah Welch Larson, and William C. Wohlforth, eds., *Status in World Politics* (New York: Cambridge University Press, 2014).

117. See, in particular, Amy Chua, "Tribal World: Group Identity Is All," *Foreign Affairs* 97 (July/August 2018): 25–33; and Jonathan Mercer, "Anarchy and Identity," *International Organization* 49 (Spring 1995): 229–52.

118. Desch, "Culture Clash," 166–69. This article sparked a rebuttal from analysts more inclined toward constructivism; see in particular the separate contributions in John S. Duffield, Theo Farrell, and Richard Price, "Isms and Schisms: Culturalism versus Realism in Security Studies," *International Security* 24 (Summer 1999): 156–72.

119. See Christina Rowley and Jutta Weldes, "Identities and US Foreign Policy," in *US Foreign Policy,* ed. Michael Cox and Doug Stokes (Oxford: Oxford University Press, 2008), 183–209.

120. Samuel P. Huntington, *Who Are We? The Challenges to America's National Identity* (New York: Simon & Schuster, 2004), 9–10. Also see Carson Holloway, "*Who Are We?* Samuel Huntington and the Problem of American Identity," *Perspectives on Political Science* 40 (April 2011): 106–14.

121. The label "neoclassical realist" apparently originated in Gideon Rose, "Neoclassical Realism and Theories of Foreign Policy," *World Politics* 51 (October 1998): 144–72. More generally, see Gustav Meibauer et al., "Forum: Rethinking Neoclassical Realism at Theory's End," *International Studies Review* 23 (March 2021): 268–95. Scholars of a neoclassical realist persuasion cannot seem to decide whether their variant of realism borrows more from structural realism or from its classical forebear. For claims of structural versus classical pedigree, see, respectively, Brian Rathbun, "A Rose by Any Other Name: Neoclassical Realism as the Logical and Necessary Extension of Structural Realism," *Security Studies* 17 (May 2008): 294–321; and Tudor Onea, "Putting the 'Classical' in Neoclassical Realism: Neoclassical Realist Theories and US Expansion in the Post–Cold War," *International Relations* 26 (June 2012): 139–64. Some classical realists agree that neoclassical realism is neither structural fish nor classical fowl; on this point, see Jonathan Kirshner, "The Tragedy of Offensive Realism: Classical Realism and the Rise of China, " *European Journal of International Relations* 18 (March 2012): 53–75.

122. For two particularly useful inquiries in the American context, see Peter Trubowitz, *Defining the National Interest: Conflict and Change in American Foreign Policy* (Chicago: University of Chicago Press, 1998); and Stephen D. Krasner, *Defending the National Interest: Raw Materials Investments and US Foreign Policy* (Princeton, NJ: Princeton University Press, 1978).

123. Just *how* ambiguous this concept can be is explicated wonderfully in Philip Gleason, "Identifying Identity: A Semantic History," *Journal of American History* 69 (March 1983): 910–31; Rogers Brubaker and Frederick Cooper, "Beyond 'Identity,'" *Theory and Society* 29 (February 2000): 1–47; and Peter Mandler, "What Is 'National Identity'? Definitions and Applications in Modern British Historiography," *Modern Intellectual History* 3 (August 2006): 271–97. Also see Sheldon Stryker and Peter J. Burke, "The Past, Present, and Future of an Identity Theory," *Social Psychology Quarterly* 63 (December 2000): 284–97; and Rawi Abdelal et al., "Identity as a Variable," *Perspectives on Politics* 4 (December 2006): 695–711.

124. William M. Reisinger, "The Renaissance of a Rubric: Political Culture as Concept and Theory," *International Journal of Public Opinion Research* 7 (Winter 1995): 328–52.

125. Lucian Pye, "Political Culture Revisited," *Political Psychology* 12 (September 1991): 487–508.

126. Ronald Inglehart, "The Renaissance of Political Culture," *American Political Science Review* 82 (December 1988): 1203–30.

127. Reisinger, "Renaissance of a Rubric," 331. Also see Richard Wilson, "The Many Voices of Political Culture," *World Politics* 52 (January 2000): 246–73.

128. On the level-of-analysis problem, see David J. Elkins and Richard E. B. Simeon, "A Cause in Search of Its Effect, or What Does Political Culture Explain?," *Comparative Politics* 11 (July 1979): 127–45; and Ruth Lane, "Political Culture: Residual Category or General Theory?," *Comparative Political Studies* 25 (October 1992): 362–87.

129. Lowell Dittmer, "Political Culture and Political Symbolism," *World Politics* 29 (July 1977): 552–83.

130. Michael Walzer, "On the Role of Symbolism in Political Thought," *Political Science Quarterly* 82 (June 1967): 191–204, at 196.

131. As argued by Edward W. Lehman, "On the Concept of Political Culture: A Theoretical Reassessment," *Social Forces* 50 (March 1972): 361–70.

132. The case for exploring myth as a method of "pattern recognition" is made in William H. McNeill, "Mythistory, or Truth, Myth, History, and Historians," *American Historical Review* 91 (February 1986): 1–10; and Cyril Buffet and Beatrice Heuser, eds., *Haunted by History: Myths in International Relations* (Providence, RI: Berghahn, 1998).

133. For instance, see Yaacov Y. I. Vertzberger, *The World in Their Minds: Information Processing, Cognition, and Perception in Foreign Policy Decisionmaking* (Stanford, CA: Stanford University Press, 1990), 270–73, where a country's strategic culture is held to be a function of both context (that is, its historical experience and geopolitical setting) and cognition, with the latter directing our attention to the manner in which decision makers utilize myth, metaphor, analogy, and extrapolation in order to comprehend reality.

134. On the rise, decline, and reemergence of historical sociology, see Harry Elmer Barnes, *Historical Sociology: Its Origins and Development* (New York: Philosophical Library, 1948); and Dennis Smith, *The Rise of Historical Sociology* (Cambridge: Polity Press, 1991).

135. On the arrival of identity as an element of conceptual high fashion, see Glenn Chafetz, Michael Spirtas, and Benjamin Frankel, "Introduction: Tracing the Influence of Identity on Foreign Policy," *Security Studies* 8 (Winter 1998/99–Spring 1999): vii–xxii.

Also see Bill McSweeney, *Security, Identity, and Interests: A Sociology of International Relations* (Cambridge: Cambridge University Press, 1999).

136. Stuart Poore, "What Is the Context? A Reply to the Gray–Johnston Debate on Strategic Culture," *Review of International Studies* 29 (April 2003): 279–84, at 284.

137. Paul Pierson, *Politics in Time: History, Institutions, and Social Analysis* (Princeton, NJ: Princeton University Press, 2004), 167–69.

138. Paul Pierson, "Increasing Returns, Path Dependence, and the Study of Politics," *American Political Science Review* 94 (June 2000): 251–68, at 252.

139. Andrew Abbott, "From Causes to Events: Notes on Narrative Positivism," *Sociological Methods and Research* 20 (May 1992): 428–55; George Lawson, "The Eternal Divide? History and International Relations," *European Journal of International Relations* 18 (June 2012): 203–26. Also relevant here are Kevin Fox Gotham and William G. Staples, "Narrative Analysis and the New Historical Sociology," *Sociological Quarterly* 37 (Summer 1996): 481–501; John Gerard Ruggie, "Peace in Our Time? Causality, Social Facts and Narrative Knowing," *American Society of International Law: Proceedings 89th Annual Meeting* (1995): 93–100; and Lawrence Stone, "The Revival of the Narrative: Reflections on a New Old History," *Past and Present* 85 (November 1979): 3–24.

140. See Theda Skocpol, ed., "Sociology's Historical Imagination," in *Vision and Method in Historical Sociology* (Cambridge: Cambridge University Press, 1984), 1–21.

141. See Jack A. Goldstone, "Initial Conditions, General Laws, Path Dependence, and Explanation in Historical Sociology," *American Journal of Sociology* 104 (November 1998): 829–45.

142. James Mahoney, "Path Dependence in Historical Sociology," *Theory and Society* 29 (August 2000): 507–48. For an illuminating application of path dependency to a country's strategic culture, see Thomas F. Banchoff, *The German Problem Transformed: Institutions, Politics, and Foreign Policy* (Ann Arbor: University of Michigan Press, 1999).

3. Historical Context

1. The case for interdisciplinary reconciliation has been made by Dennis Kavanagh, "Why Political Science Needs History," *Political Studies* 39 (September 1991): 479–95; and Colin Elman and Miriam Fendius Elman, eds., *Bridges and Boundaries: Historians, Political Scientists, and the Study of International Relations* (Cambridge, MA: MIT Press, 2001). Also see Ian Clark, "International Relations: Divided by a Common Language?," *Government and Opposition* 37 (April 2002): 271–79.

2. For one delightfully witty example, see John Lewis Gaddis, "History, Theory, and Common Ground," *International Security* 22 (Summer 1997): 75–85.

3. See Ernst Mayr, "When Is Historiography Whiggish?," *Journal of the History of Ideas* 51 (April–June 1990): 301–9.

4. Cameron G. Thies, "A Pragmatic Guide to Qualitative Historical Analysis in the Study of International Relations," *International Studies Perspectives* 3 (2002): 351–72, at 360.

5. Goldstone, "Initial Conditions."

6. Joseph S. Nye Jr., *Do Morals Matter? Presidents and Foreign Policy from FDR to Trump* (New York: Oxford University Press, 2020), 1–2. Also see Berman, "Ideas, Norms, and Culture in Political Analysis"; Yee, "Causal Effects of Ideas on Policies"; and Hunt, *Ideology and US Foreign Policy.*

7. Kelley, *Cultural Pattern in American Politics,* 6–9. Also see Robert Kelley, "Ideology and Political Culture from Jefferson to Nixon," *American Historical Review* 82 (June 1977): 531–62.

8. Burl Noggle, *Into the Twenties: The United States from Armistice to Normalcy* (Urbana: University of Illinois Press, 1974), 116–17.

9. Nell Irvin Painter, *The History of White People* (New York: W. W. Norton, 2010), 356–57.

10. For this argument, see Carl F. Wittke, *We Who Built America: The Saga of an Immigrant,* rev. ed. (New York: Prentice-Hall, 1939).

11. Horace M. Kallen. *Culture and Democracy in the United States: Studies in the Group Psychology of the American Peoples* (1924; repr. New York: Arno Press, 1970), 122–23.

12. For instance, Émile Boutmy, *Éléments d'une psychologie politique du peuple américain* (Paris: Armand Colin, 1911).

13. Denis Lacorne, *La Crise de l'identité américaine: du melting-pot au multiculturalisme* (Paris: Fayard, 1997), 20; Nathan Glazer, *We Are All Multiculturalists Now* (Cambridge, MA: Harvard University Press, 1997), 8.

14. See Amy Chua, *Political Tribes: Group Instinct and the Fate of Nations* (New York: Penguin Press, 2018).

15. Duroselle, *France and the United States,* 252–53.

16. Timmerman, *French Betrayal of America,* 4.

17. Sarah Vowell, *Lafayette in the Somewhat United States* (New York: Riverhead, 2015). Also see Loveland, *Emblem of Liberty;* and David A. Clary, *Adopted Son: Washington, Lafayette, and the Friendship That Saved the Revolution* (New York: Bantam, 2007).

18. William Faulkner, *Requiem for a Nun* (New York: Random House, 1951), 92.

19. For an interesting effort to approach this Faulknerian perspective through a variety of country-specific case studies, see "The Undead Past: How Nations Confront the Evils of History," *Foreign Affairs* 97 (January/February 2018): 2–41.

20. On this retrofitting from the perspective of ethnic conflict, see Badredine Arfi, "Ethnic Fear: The Social Construction of Insecurity," *Security Studies* 8 (Autumn 1998): 151–203.

21. Jonathan Friedman, "The Past in the Future: History and the Politics of Identity," *American Anthropologist* 94 (December 1992): 837–59, at 837.

22. On the unavoidable reliance upon myth in historical reconstructions, see McNeill, "Mythistory"; and Buffet and Heuser, *Haunted by History.*

23. For a thoughtful collection on how history informs policymaking, see Hal Brands and Jeremi Suri, eds., *The Power of the Past: History and Statecraft* (Washington, DC: Brookings Institution Press, 2016).

24. Richard E. Neustadt and Ernest R. May, *Thinking in Time: The Uses of History for Decision Makers* (New York: Free Press, 1986). For insight as to *how* such meaning might be

obtained, see Jeffrey Haydu, "Making Use of the Past: Time Periods as Cases to Compare and as Sequences of Problem Solving," *American Journal of Sociology* 104 (September 1998): 339–71.

25. White, *American Opinion of France*, xi–xii.

26. Lawson, "Eternal Divide?"; Jack S. Levy, "Too Important to Leave to the Other: History and Political Science in the Study of International Relations," *International Security* 22 (Summer 1997): 22–33.

27. Thucydides, *History of the Peloponnesian War* (London: J. M. Dent & Sons, 1910).

28. Graham Allison, *Destined for War: Can America and China Escape Thucydides's Trap?* (Boston: Houghton Mifflin Harcourt, 2017); Allison, "China vs. America: Managing the Next Clash of Civilizations," *Foreign Affairs* 96 (September/October 2017): 80–89.

29. See especially Jonathan Kirshner, "Handle Him with Care: The Importance of Getting Thucydides Right," *Security Studies* 28 (January 2019): 1–24.

30. See David A Welch, "Why International Relations Theorists Should Stop Reading Thucydides," *Review of International Studies* 29 (July 2003): 301–19.

31. Examples include Ja Ian Chong and Todd H. Hall, "The Lessons of 1914 for East Asia Today: Missing the Trees for the Forest," *International Security* 39 (Summer 2014): 7–43; Reinhard Wolf, "Rising Powers, Status Ambitions, and the Need to Reassure: What China Could Learn from Imperial Germany's Failures," *Chinese Journal of International Politics* 7 (Summer 2014): 185–219; and David Stevenson, "Learning from the Past: The Relevance of International History," *International Affairs* 90 (January 2014): 5–22.

32. Miller and Molesky, *Our Oldest Enemy*, 6.

33. Miller and Molesky, *Our Oldest Enemy*, 7.

34. On that history, see Francis Russell, *The French and Indian Wars* (New York: Harper & Row, 1962).

35. Jeremy Ravinsky, "12 Gore Vidal Foreign Policy Quotes," *GlobalPost*, 1 August 2012, https://www.pri.org/stories/2012-08-01/12-gore-vidal-foreign-policy-quotes.

36. Anne D. Neal, Jerry L. Martin, and Mashad Mose, *Losing America's Memory: Historical Illiteracy in the 21st Century* (Washington, DC: American Council of Trustees and Alumni, 2000), 2–3.

37. Shoshana Zuboff, "The Knowledge Coup," *New York Times*, 31 January 2021, SR4–5. Also see the sobering critique of social media's negative impact upon civic consciousness, in Philip N. Howard, *Lie Machines* (New Haven, CT: Yale University Press, 2020).

38. On the fiftieth anniversary of the outbreak of the First World War, one Serbian analyst noted that "among the rural South Slavs the belief flourished that to kill a foreign tyrant was the noblest goal in life, and this was expressed in the Kosovo cycle of the folklore epics. This saga grew up after the Battle of Kosovo, on June 28, 1389, when the Turks destroyed the independent, mediaeval state of Serbia." Vladimir Dedijer, "Sarajevo Fifty Years Later," *Foreign Affairs* 42 (July 1964): 569–84, at 576.

39. Margaret MacMillan, "Putin's War on Ukraine Has Brought the Past to the Present, and Made the Future Uncertain," *Globe and Mail*, 25 February 2022, A12. On that evocative battle, see Serhii Plokhy, "Poltava: The Battle That Never Ends," *Harvard Ukrainian Studies* 31 (2009–2010), xiii–xxv.

40. On this claim that humans, both individually and as members of a collectivity, have a psychological requirement for an enemy so as to better shape their self-conceptions, see Vamik D. Volkan, *The Need to Have Enemies and Allies: From Clinical Practice to International Relations* (Northvale, NJ: Jason Aronson, 1994), 4–5, 94–95. Also see Noel Kaplowitz, "National Self-Images, Perception of Enemies, and Conflict Strategies: Psychological Dimensions of International Relations," *Political Psychology* 11 (March 1990): 39–82; and Frederick Hartmann, *The Conservation of Enemies: A Study in Enmity* (Westport, CT: Greenwood Press, 1982).

41. A critique made by, among others, Mead, *Special Providence*.

42. For differentiations between these variants of nationalism, see Hans Kohn, *The Idea of Nationalism: A Study in Its Origin and Development* (New York: Macmillan, 1951); John A. Hall, "Nationalisms: Classified and Explained," *Daedalus* 122 (Summer 1993): 1–28; Anthony D. Smith, "The Ethnic Sources of Nationalism," *Survival* 35 (Spring 1993): 48–62; Walker Connor, *Ethnonationalism: The Quest for Understanding* (Princeton, NJ: Princeton University Press, 1994); and Vanessa May et al., "Introduction: Nationalism's Futures," *Sociology* 54 (December 2020): 1055–71.

43. Hans Kohn, *The Age of Nationalism: The First Era of Global History* (New York: Harper Torchbooks, 1962), 31. For discussions of the "civic nation," see Yael Tamir, *Liberal Nationalism* (Princeton, NJ: Princeton University Press, 1993); Ken H. Wolf, "Hans Kohn's Liberal Nationalism: The Historian as Prophet," *Journal of the History of Ideas* 37 (October–December 1976): 651–72; and Lowell W. Barrington, "'Nation' and 'Nationalism': The Misuse of Key Concepts in Political Science," *PS* 30 (December 1997): 712–16. But for challenges to this position, see Taras Kuzio, "The Myth of the Civic State: A Critical Survey of Hans Kohn's Framework for Understanding Nationalism," *Ethnic and Racial Studies* 25 (January 2002): 20–39; Bernard Yack, "The Myth of the Civic Nation," *Critical Review* 10 (Spring 1996): 193–211; and Nicholas Xenos, "Civic Nationalism: Oxymoron?," *Critical Review* 10 (Spring 1996): 213–31.

44. For conceptual analyses of republicanism, see Philip Pettit, *On the People's Terms: A Republican Theory and Model of Democracy* (Cambridge: Cambridge University Press, 2012); Joyce Appleby, *Liberalism and Republicanism in the Historical Imagination* (Cambridge, MA: Harvard University Press, 1992); Nicholas Onuf, *The Republican Legacy in International Thought* (Cambridge: Cambridge University Press, 1997); Claude Nicolet, *L'Idée républicaine* (Paris: Gallimard, 1982); and Daniel T. Rodgers, "Republicanism: The Career of a Concept," *Journal of American History* 79 (June 1992): 11–36.

45. Patrice Higonnet, *Sister Republics: The Origins of French and American Republicanism* (Cambridge, MA: Harvard University Press, 1988). Also see Albert Guérard, *Beyond Hatred: The Democratic Ideal in France and America* (New York: Scribner's, 1925); Sudhir Hazareesingh, *Intellectual Founders of the Republic: Five Studies in Nineteenth-Century French Republican Political Thought* (Oxford: Oxford University Press, 2001); J. G. A. Pocock, "Between Gog and Magog: The Republican Thesis and the *Ideologia Americana*," *Journal of the History of Ideas* 48 (April 1987): 325–46; Robert E. Shallope, "Toward a Republican Synthesis: The Emergence of an Understanding of Republicanism in American Historiography," *William and Mary Quarterly* 29 (January 1972): 49–80; and Walter A. McDougall,

"America's Machiavellian Moment: Origins of the Atlantic Republican Tradition," *Orbis* 62 (Fall 2018): 505–17.

46. On the dichotomous relationship between primordialists and optionalists, see Gleason, "Identifying Identity."

47. Henry Hale, "Explaining Ethnicity," *Comparative Political Studies* 37 (May 2004): 458–85, at 461–62.

48. Peter L. Berger and Thomas Luckmann, *The Social Construction of Reality: A Treatise in the Sociology of Knowledge* (Garden City, NY: Doubleday, 1966).

49. Robert Gildea, *The Past in French History* (New Haven, CT: Yale University Press, 1994), 3–4.

50. Perry Miller, *Errand into the Wilderness* (New York: Harcourt and Row, 1956), 169; quoting from Locke's *An Essay Concerning Human Understanding,* first published in 1690.

51. As is cogently argued in Francisco Gil-White, "How Thick Is Blood? The Plot Thickens . . . : If Ethnic Actors Are Primordialists, What Remains of the Circumstantialist/Primordialist Controversy?," *Ethnic and Racial Studies* 22 (September 1999): 789–820. On the difficulties constructivists run into when they try to untangle themselves from primordialist categories, see James D. Fearon and David D. Laitin, "Violence and the Social Construction of Ethnic Identity," *International Organization* 54 (Autumn 2000): 845–77.

52. Martin Bulmer and John Solomos, "Introduction: Re-thinking Ethnic and Racial Studies," *Ethnic and Racial Studies* 21 (September 1998): 819–37.

53. For a reminder of the ongoing capacity of ethnonationalism to foment violence, see Jerry Z. Muller, "Us and Them: The Enduring Power of Ethnic Nationalism," *Foreign Affairs* 87 (March/April 2008): 18–35; and Robert Sapolsky, "This Is Your Brain on Nationalism: The Biology of Us and Them," *Foreign Affairs* 98 (March/April 2019): 42–47.

54. John Mueller, "The Banality of 'Ethnic War,'" *International Security* 25 (Summer 2000): 42–70, at 42, 53.

55. Bruce Gilley, "Against the Concept of Ethnic Conflict," *Third World Quarterly* 25 (September 2004): 1155–66, at 1160.

56. Charles King, "The Myth of Ethnic Warfare," *Foreign Affairs* 80 (November/December 2001): 165–70.

57. See Robert A. Levine and Donald T. Campbell, *Ethnocentrism: Theories of Conflict, Ethnic Attitudes, and Group Behavior* (New York: John Wiley & Sons, 1972), 29.

58. Fred Anderson and Andrew Cayton, *The Dominion of War: Empire and Liberty in North America, 1500–2000* (New York: Viking, 2005).

59. Tombs and Tombs, *That Sweet Enemy.*

60. See David A. Bell, "Recent Works on Early Modern French National Identity," *Journal of Modern History* 68 (March 1996): 84–113.

61. For one heated interrogation of this core, see Éric Zemmour, *Mélancolie française* (Paris: Fayard/Denoël, 2010).

62. On the consolidation of the French state, see Pierre Goubert, *The Course of French History,* trans. Maarten Ultee (London: Routledge, 1991), 51; and Marc Ferro, *Histoire de France* (Paris: Éditions Odile Jacob, 2001), 119–20. On the ethnic makeup of the French nation, see Fernand Braudel, *The Identity of France,* vol. 1, *History and Environment* (London:

Collins, 1988), 318–19; Jacques Barzun, *The French Race: Theories of Its Origins and Their Social and Political Implications Prior to the Revolution* (1932; repr. Port Washington, NY: Kennikat Press, 1966), 41, 251–59; and William Bloom, *Personal Identity, National Identity and International Relations* (Cambridge: Cambridge University Press, 1990), 63. On the Anglo-Saxon element in French identity construction, see Jack Hayward, *Fragmented France: Two Centuries of Disputed Identity* (Oxford: Oxford University Press, 2007).

63. Anna Triandafyllidou, "National Identity and the 'Other,'" *Ethnic and Racial Studies* 21 (July 1998): 593–612, at 600. Also see Iver B. Neumann, "Self and Other in International Relations," *European Journal of International Relations* 2 (June 1996): 139–74.

64. See, for instance, James Banner, "France and the Origins of American Political Culture," *Virginia Quarterly Review* 64 (Autumn 1988): 651–70; Ralph L. Ketcham, "France and American Politics, 1763–1793," *Political Science Quarterly* 78 (June 1963): 198–223; Clyde Augustus Duniway, "French Influence on the Adoption of the Federal Constitution," *American Historical Review* 9 (January 1904): 304–9; and Morton Borden, *Parties and Politics in the Early Republic, 1789–1815* (New York: Thomas Y. Crowell, 1967).

65. Hugh Donald Forbes, "Toward a Science of Ethnic Conflict?," *Journal of Democracy* 14 (October 2003): 172–77, at 175.

66. No one covered this terrain more thoroughly, or with more literary skill, than the great nineteenth-century historian Francis Parkman. A useful capsule summary of his voluminous output is Parkman, *A Half-Century of Conflict* (Boston: Little, Brown, 1907). For assessments of his work, see Laurence Cros, "Histoire, lyrisme et mythe: la Nouvelle-France et la Nouvelle-Angleterre dans l'œuvre de Francis Parkman," *Écrire l'histoire* 2 (Autumn 2008): 131–140; Francis Jennings, "Francis Parkman: A Brahmin among Untouchables," *William and Mary Quarterly* 42 (July 1985): 305–28; Simon Schama, *Dead Certainties: Unwarranted Speculations* (New York: Alfred A. Knopf, 1991); David Levin, *History as Romantic Art* (Stanford, CA: Stanford University Press, 1959); Mason Wade, *Francis Parkman: Heroic Historian* (New York: Viking, 1942); and Wilbur R. Jacobs, *Francis Parkman: Historian as Hero* (Austin: University of Texas Press, 1991).

67. Jean Pellerin, *La Nouvelle-France démaquillée* (Montréal: Éditions Varia, 2001), 66–67; Douglas Edward Leach, *Arms for Empire: A Military History of the British Colonies in North America, 1607–1763* (New York: Macmillan, 1973); Van Alstyne, *Rising American Empire*, 9–11.

68. George T. Hunt, *The Wars of the Iroquois: A Study in Intertribal Trade Relations*, 2nd ed. (Madison: University of Wisconsin Press, 1960). Also see Richard White, *The Middle Ground: Indians, Empires and Republics in the Great Lakes Region, 1650–1815* (Cambridge: Cambridge University Press, 1991); and Neta C. Crawford, "A Security Regime among Democracies: Cooperation among Iroquois Nations," *International Organization* 48 (Summer 1994): 345–85.

69. Alden Vaughan, *New England Frontier: Puritans and Indians, 1620–1675* (Boston: Little, Brown, 1965).

70. Jill Lepore, *The Name of War: King Philip's War and the Origins of American Identity* (New York: Knopf, 1998), xi–xiii; Alvin M. Josephy Jr., "The Betrayal of King Philip," in *The Patriot Chiefs: A Chronicle of American Indian Resistance* (New York: Viking Press, 1969), chapter 2.

71. Douglas Edward Leach, *Flintlock and Tomahawk: New England in King Philip's War* (New York: Macmillan, 1958), 243. Also see James D. Drake, *King Philip's War: Civil War in New England, 1675–1676* (Amherst: University of Massachusetts Press, 1999).

72. Stephen Saunders Webb, *1676: The End of American Independence* (New York: Alfred A. Knopf, 1984), xxv–xxvi.

73. James A. Morone, *Hellfire Nation: The Politics of Sin in American History* (New Haven, CT: Yale University Press, 2003), 80–81.

74. Stella H. Sutherland, *Population Distribution in Colonial America* (New York: Columbia University Press, 1936); Evarts B. Greene and Virginia D. Harrington, *American Population before the Federal Census of 1790* (New York: Columbia University Press, 1931); Pierre Goubert, *Louis XIV and Twenty Million Frenchmen*, trans. Anne Carter (New York: Pantheon, 1970).

75. Richard Aguila, *The Iroquois Restoration: Iroquois Diplomacy on the Canadian Frontier, 1701–1754* (Detroit, MI: Wayne State University Press, 1983); and Gilles Havard, *The Great Peace of Montreal of 1701: French-Native Diplomacy in the Seventeenth Century*, trans. Phyllis Arnoff and Howard Scott (Montreal and Kingston: McGill–Queen's University Press, 2001).

76. Leach, *Flintlock and Tomahawk*, 250.

77. Andrew J. Bacevich, *The Age of Illusions: How America Squandered Its Cold War Victory* (New York: Metropolitan Books, 2020), 209, note 15.

78. Kandel, *Les États-Unis et le monde*, 56. Also see John Grenier, *The First Way of War: American War Making on the Frontier, 1607–1814* (New York: Cambridge University Press, 2005).

79. David G. Haglund and Stéphane Roussel, "From Parkman to Pearson: Historical Context and the Transformation of Quebec's Strategic Culture," *International Journal* 75 (December 2020): 563–75.

80. Thomas Hobbes, *Leviathan*, ed. Michael Oakeshott (Oxford: Blackwell, 1946), 82.

81. Samuel A. Drake, *The Border Wars of New England: Commonly Called King William's and Queen Anne's Wars* (New York: Charles Scribner's Sons, 1897), 1–2.

82. Thomas E. Burke Jr., *Mohawk Frontier: The Dutch Community of Schenectady, New York, 1661–1710* (Ithaca, NY: Cornell University Press, 1991).

83. Marion L. Starkey, *The Devil in Massachusetts: A Modern Inquiry into the Salem Witch Trials* (1949; repr. New York: Time, 1963), 11. Also see Chadwick Hansen, *Witchcraft at Salem* (New York: George Braziller, 1969).

84. Howard H. Peckham, *The Colonial Wars, 1689–1762* (Chicago: University of Chicago Press, 1964), 54–55. Also see Allen W. Trelease, *Indian Affairs in Colonial New York: The Seventeenth Century* (Ithaca, NY: Cornell University Press, 1960); and Robert Leckie, *"A Few Acres of Snow": The Saga of the French and Indian Wars* (New York: John Wiley, 1999).

85. Richard I. Melvoin, *New England Outpost: War and Society in Colonial Deerfield* (New York: W. W. Norton, 1989), 93–96.

86. Ian Kenneth Steele, *Guerillas and Grenadiers: The Struggle for Canada, 1689–1760* (Toronto: Ryerson Press, 1969), at 5.

87. On the raid and its sequel, see Evan Haefeli and Kevin Sweeney, *Captors and Captures: The 1704 French and Indian Raid on Deerfield* (Amherst: University of Massachusetts Press, 2003); and John Demos, *The Unredeemed Captive: A Family Story from Early America* (New York: Alfred A. Knopf, 1994).

88. Lois Kimball Mathews, *The Expansion of New England: The Spread of New England Settlement and Institutions to the Mississippi River, 1620–1865* (Boston: Houghton Mifflin, 1909), 86–102.

89. To use the delightful label in the equally delightful book by Roger, *L'Ennemi américain.*

90. Kaspi, *Temps des Américains,* 305.

91. Edgar Kiser and Michael Hechter, "The Debate on Historical Sociology: Rational Choice Theory and Its Critics," *American Journal of Sociology* 104 (November 1998): 785–816.

92. Margaret R. Somers, "'We're No Angels': Realism, Rational Choice, and Relationality in Social Science," *American Journal of Sociology* 104 (November 1998): 722–84.

93. Interpreted by her as implying that "belief in an explanation depends on belief in the a priori theory from which it is imputed." Somers, "We're No Angels," 727.

94. Somers, "We're No Angels," 767–68.

95. Quoted in Tardieu, *France and America,* 64.

96. Kramer, *Does France Still Count?,* 89.

97. Kenneth W. Terhune, "From National Character to National Behavior: A Reformulation," *Journal of Conflict Resolution* 14 (June 1970): 203–63, at 256.

98. Jan B. Heide and Anne S. Miner, "The Shadow of the Future: Effects of Anticipated Interaction and Frequency of Contact on Buyer–Seller Cooperation," *Academy of Management Journal* 35 (June 1992): 265–91.

99. Mahoney, "Path Dependence in Historical Sociology."

100. Giovanni Capoccia and R. Daniel Kelemen, "The Study of Critical Junctures: Theory, Narrative and Counterfactuals in Historical Institutionalism," *World Politics* 59 (April 2007): 341–69, at 369.

101. Jack S. Levy, "Counterfactuals, Causal Inference, and Historical Analysis," *Security Studies* 24 (July–September 2015): 378–402, at 384–85, 401–2. Also see James D. Fearon, "Counterfactuals and Hypothesis Testing in Political Science," *World Politics* 43 (January 1991): 169–95.

102. Corwin, *French Policy and the American Alliance of 1778*; Frank W. Brecher, *Securing American Independence: John Jay and the French Alliance* (Westport, CT: Praeger, 2003); William C. Stinchcombe, *The American Revolution and the French Alliance* (Syracuse, NY: Syracuse University Press, 1969); André Kaspi, *L'Indépendance américaine, 1763–1789* (Paris: Gallimard, 1976); René de Castries, *La France et l'Indépendance américaine: le livre du bicentenaire de l'Indépendance* (Paris: Perrin, 1975); and Claude H. Van Tyne, "Influences which Determined the French Government to Make the Treaty with America, 1778," *American Historical Review* 21 (April 1916): 528–41.

103. See Fred Anderson, *Crucible of War: The Seven Years' War and the Fate of Empire in British North America, 1754–1766* (New York: Alfred A. Knopf, 2000).

104. James Truslow Adams, *The Founding of New England* (Boston: Atlantic Monthly Press, 1921), 195. Others stress not so much the geographic *region* as they do the Puritan *ideology* as being at the core of American identity; see Sacvan Bercovitch, *The Puritan Origins of the American Self* (New Haven, CT: Yale University Press, 1975); and Ralph Barton Perry, *Puritanism and Democracy* (1944; repr. New York: Harper and Row, 1964). But for a rebuttal in which Puritanism is but one of four chief sources of early American identity, see David Hackett Fischer, *Albion's Seed: Four British Folkways in America* (New York: Oxford University Press, 1989).

105. Frankly critical of this version are Ian McKay and Jamie Swift, *The Vimy Trap: Or, How We Learned to Stop Worrying and Love the Great War* (Toronto: Between the Lines, 2016). For a pair of concise summaries of the dispute, see Robert Everett-Green, "Vimy: Birthplace of a Nation—or a Myth?," *Globe and Mail,* 1 April 2017, F3; and Amy Shaw, "Battle Wary," *Literary Review of Canada* 25 (April 2017): 14–15.

106. In French Canada, whatever enthusiasm might have been felt regarding Vimy Ridge was more than eclipsed by a growing dread that the Canadian government was likely to impose conscription to maintain the war effort. See Elizabeth H. Armstrong, *The Crisis of Quebec, 1914–1918* (New York: Columbia University Press, 1937).

107. On the significance of this battle, fought from April 9 to April 12, 1917, see Geoffrey Hayes, Andrew Iarocci, and Michael Bechtold, eds., *Vimy Ridge: A Canadian Reassessment* (Waterloo: Wilfrid Laurier University Press, 2007); and Tim Cook, *Vimy: The Battle and the Legend* (Toronto: Penguin Canada, 2018).

108. Webb, *1676: The End of American Independence.*

109. Richard R. Johnson, *Adjustment to Empire: The New England Colonies, 1675–1715* (New Brunswick, NJ: Rutgers University Press, 1981).

110. Harry S. Stout, *The New England Soul: Preaching and Religious Culture in Colonial New England* (New York: Oxford University Press, 1986), 185.

111. Stout, *New England Soul,* 236–37.

112. A claim made, inter alios, by Nathan O. Hatch, "The Origins of Civil Millennialism in America: New England Clergymen, War with France, and the Revolution," *William and Mary Quarterly* 31 (April 1974): 407–30.

113. Reuben Gold Thwaites, *France in America, 1497–1763* (New York: Harper & Bros., 1905), 122–23. On the reasons for the return of Louisbourg, see Jack M. Sosin, "Louisburg and the Peace of Aix-la-Chapelle, 1748," *William and Mary Quarterly* 14 (October 1957): 516–35.

114. Stout, *New England Soul,* 238.

115. Blumenthal, *France and the United States;* Clifford Egan, *Neither Peace nor War: Franco-American Relations, 1803–1812* (Baton Rouge: Louisiana State University Press, 1983). French views of America in the first half of the century are the subject of René Rémond, *Les États-Unis devant l'opinion française, 1815–1852,* 2 vols. (Paris: Armand Colin, 1962).

116. Richard A. McLemore, *Franco-American Diplomatic Relations, 1816–1836* (Baton Rouge: Louisiana State University Press, 1941); Charles K. Webster, "British Mediation between France and the United States in 1834–1836," *English Historical Review* 42 (January 1927): 58–78; Rufus K. Wyllys, "French Imperialists in California," *California Historical So-*

ciety Quarterly 8 (June 1929): 116–29; Lynn Marshall Case, ed., *French Opinion on the United States and Mexico, 1860–1867* (Hamden, CT: Archon Books, 1969); Lynn Marshall Case and Warren F. Spencer, *The United States and France: Civil War Diplomacy* (Philadelphia: University of Pennsylvania Press, 1970); Nancy Nichols Barker, "France, Austria, and the Mexican Venture, 1861–1864," *French Historical Studies* 3 (Spring 1963): 224–45.

4. "Ethnicization" and Foreign Policy

1. See David G. Haglund, "France and the Issue of a 'Usable' Diaspora in (North) America: The Duroselle-Tardieu Thesis Reconsidered," *International History Review* 34 (March 2012): 71–88. The sequence of names is in keeping with alphabetical order, though it violates chronological order.

2. Gilbert Chinard, "Foreword," in Durand Echeverria, *Mirage in the West: A History of the French Image of American Society to 1815* (Princeton, NJ: Princeton University Press, 1957), xiii.

3. Duhamel, *America the Menace.*

4. Norimitsu Onishi, "Will American Ideas Tear France Apart? Some of Its Leaders Think So," *New York Times,* 9 February 2021, https://www.nytimes.com/2021/02/09/world/europe/france-threat-american-universities.html. Also see Zineb Dryef, "Genre, identités, cancel culture . . . Le fantasme du péril américain," *Le Monde,* 22 December 2020, https://www.lemonde.fr/m-le-mag/article/2020/12/21/genre-identites-cancel-culture le-fantasme-du-peril-americain_6064150_4500055.html.

5. See, for instance, George M. Fredrickson, "Diverse Republics: French and American Responses to Racial Pluralism," *Daedalus* 134 (Winter 2005): 88–101.

6. Duroselle, *France and the United States,* 46–48. Also see Duroselle's preface in Nouailhat, *France et États-Unis,* 1–3. One American scholar has endorsed this thesis, and even extended its chronological ambit into the early post–Second World War years, when a "further disadvantage plagued the French in their dealings with the United States: Alone among the European nations, they lacked a constituency in America." Wall, *The United States and the Making of Postwar France,* 12.

7. Keene, *Doughboys,* 121. On tensions between Americans and French in the early post-war years, see Henry T. Allen, *The Rhineland Occupation* (Indianapolis, IN: Bobbs-Merrill, 1927); Peter Jackson, *Beyond the Balance of Power: France and the Politics of National Security in the Era of the First World War* (Cambridge: Cambridge University Press, 2013); Nelson, *Victors Divided*; Benjamin F. Martin, *France and the Après Guerre, 1918–1924: Illusions and Disillusionment* (Baton Rouge: Louisiana State University Press, 1999); Selig Adler, "The War-Guilt Question and American Disillusionment, 1918–1928," *Journal of Modern History* 23 (March 1951): 1–28; and William R. Keylor, "'How They Advertised France': The French Propaganda Campaign in the United States during the Breakup of the Franco-American Entente, 1918–1923," *Diplomatic History* 17 (Summer 1993): 351–73.

8. John B. Duff, "German-Americans and the Peace, 1918–1920," *Jewish Historical Quarterly* 59 (June 1970): 424–44.

9. Tardieu, *France and America,* 302–3. For varying expressions of French fascination with American demography in Tardieu's era, see Urbain Gohier, *Le Peuple du vingtième*

siècle: cinq mois aux États-Unis (Paris: E. Fasquelle, 1903); Félix Klein, *L'Amérique de demain* (Paris: Plon, 1910); Boutmy, *Éléments d'une psychologie politique du peuple américain;* Firmin Roz, *L'Énergie américaine* (Paris: Flammarion, 1914); André Siegfried, *Deux mois en Amérique du Nord à la veille de la guerre* (Paris: Armand Colin, 1916); and Régis Michaud, *Ce qu'il faut connaître de l'âme américaine* (Paris: Boivin, 1929); and for a useful summary of those expressions, Charles W. Brooks, *America in France's Hopes and Fears, 1890–1920* (New York: Garland, 1987).

10. Ernst Weisenfeld, *Quelle Allemagne pour la France? la politique étrangère française et l'unité allemande depuis 1944* (Paris: Armand Colin, 1989); and David G. Haglund, "Has France Finally Said *auf Wiedersehen* to Its German Problem?," *Orbis* 48 (Summer 2004): 381–95.

11. Alfred Grosser, "France-Allemagne: 1936–1986," *Politique étrangère* 51 (Spring 1986): 247–55, at 252–53. Also see George P. Gooch, "Franco-German Coexistence at Last?," *Foreign Affairs* 37 (April 1959): 432–42; and Michael Creswell and Marc Trachtenberg, "France and the German Question, 1945–55," *Journal of Cold War Studies* 5 (Summer 2003): 5–28.

12. André François-Poncet, *De Versailles à Potsdam: la France et le problème allemand contemporain, 1919–1945* (Paris: Flammarion, 1948). Also see the lament penned by France's wartime leader, Georges Clemenceau, *Grandeurs et misères d'une victoire* (Paris: Plon, 1930).

13. See Koenraad W. Swart, *The Sense of Decadence in Nineteenth-Century France* (The Hague: Martinus Nijhoff, 1964); Michel Winock, *La Belle Époque: la France de 1900 à 1914* (Paris: Perrin, 2002), 34–41; Gustave Cauderlier, *Les Causes de la dépopulation de la France* (Paris: Librairie Guillaumin, 1901); Robert Aron and Arnaud Dandieu, *Décadence de la nation française* (Paris: Rieder, 1931); Joseph J. Spengler, *France Faces Depopulation: Postlude Edition, 1936–1976* (Durham, NC: Duke University Press, 1979) ; and Jean Cau, *Discours de la décadence* (Paris: Copernic, 1978).

14. Ernest R. May, ed., *The Coming of War, 1917* (Chicago: Rand-McNally, 1963), 1.

15. Ernest R. May, *The World War and American Isolation, 1914–1917* (Cambridge, MA: Harvard University Press, 1959), 34. More generally on this question, see Joseph P. O'Grady, ed., *The Immigrants' Influence on Wilson's Peace Politics* (Lexington: University of Kentucky Press, 1967).

16. For some examples of this interest triggered during the era of unipolarity, see Myron Weiner, ed., *International Migration and Security* (Boulder, CO: Westview, 1993); Robin Cohen, "Diasporas and the Nation-State: From Victims to Challengers," *International Affairs* 72 (July 1996): 507–20; Stephen M. Saideman, *The Ties That Divide: Ethnic Politics, Foreign Policy, and International Politics* (New York: Columbia University Press, 2001); Will H. Moore, "Ethnic Minorities and Foreign Policy," *SAIS Review* 22 (Summer–Fall 2002): 77–91; Hazel Smith and Paul Stares, eds. *Diasporas in Conflict: Peace-Makers or Peace-Wreckers?* (Tokyo: United Nations Press, 2007); and Milton J. Esman, *Diasporas in the Contemporary World* (Cambridge: Polity Press, 2009).

17. There is a lengthy list of titles on the practice, including Karl Schriftgiesser, *Lobbyists: The Art and Business of Influencing Lawmakers* (Boston: Little, Brown, 1951); James Deakin, *The Lobbyists* (Washington, DC: Public Affairs Press, 1966); Jeffrey M. Berry,

Lobbying for the People: The Political Behavior of Public Interest Groups (Princeton, NJ: Princeton University Press, 1977); Russell Warren Howe and Sarah Hays Trott, *The Power Peddlers: How Lobbyists Mold America's Foreign Policy* (Garden City, NY: Doubleday, 1977); and Frank R. Baumgartner et al., *Lobbying and Policy Change: Who Wins, Who Loses, and Why* (Chicago: University of Chicago Press, 2009).

18. For that older tradition, see Tony Smith, *Foreign Attachments: The Power of Ethnic Groups in the Making of American Foreign Policy* (Cambridge, MA: Harvard University Press, 2000); Alexander DeConde, *Ethnicity, Race, and American Foreign Policy: A History* (Boston: Northeastern University Press, 1992); and David G. Haglund and Elizabeth Stein, "Ethnic Diasporas and US Foreign Policy," in *Oxford Bibliographies in Political Science*, ed. Sandy Maisel (New York: Oxford University Press, 2020).

19. And in this respect, Rogers Brubaker pays heed to the cautionary advice tendered to those who might wish to loosen the denotative qualities of a concept, best expressed in Sartori, "Concept Misformation in Comparative Politics."

20. Rogers Brubaker, "The 'Diaspora' Diaspora," *Ethnic and Racial Studies* 28 (January 2005): 1–19, at 3–4.

21. Brubaker, "'Diaspora' Diaspora," 11–13.

22. Laurence Halley, *Ancient Affections: Ethnic Groups and Foreign Policy* (New York: Praeger, 1985).

23. Michael Lind, *The Next American Nation: The New Nationalism and the Fourth American Revolution* (New York: Free Press, 1995), 286–87.

24. See especially Samuel P. Huntington, "The Erosion of American National Interests," *Foreign Affairs* 76 (September/October 1997): 28–49; and James R. Schlesinger "Fragmentation and Hubris: A Shaky Basis for American Leadership," *National Interest* 94 (Fall 1997): 3–9.

25. Yossi Shain, *Marketing the American Creed Abroad: Diasporas in the US and Their Homelands* (Cambridge: Cambridge University Press, 1999), as well as Shain, "Ethnic Diasporas and US Foreign Policy," *Political Science Quarterly* 109 (Winter 1994–95): 811–42.

26. See Diane E. Davis, "Non-State Armed Actors, New Imagined Communities, and Shifting Patterns of Sovereignty and Insecurity in the Modern World," *Contemporary Security Policy* 30 (August 2009): 221–45.

27. Indirectly, it also comes from the Dutch word for "freebooter," or mercenary, *vrijbuiter;* see "Motion to Dismiss," *Economist*, 13 March 2021, 19.

28. See, for instance, Mark R. Levy and Michael S. Kramer, *The Ethnic Factor: How America's Minorities Decide Elections* (New York: Simon and Schuster, 1972); and Samuel Lubell, *The Future of American Politics* (New York: Harper, 1952).

29. Melvin Small, *Democracy and Diplomacy: The Impact of Domestic Politics on US Foreign Policy* (Baltimore: Johns Hopkins University Press, 1996), xvi.

30. Trevor Rubenzer, "Ethnic Minority Interest Group Attributes and US Foreign Policy Influence: A Qualitative Comparative Analysis," *Foreign Policy Analysis* 4 (April 2008): 169–85. Also urging caution on this matter is James M. Lindsay, "Getting Uncle Sam's Ear: Will Ethnic Lobbies Cramp America's Foreign Policy Style?," in *Diversity and US Foreign Policy: A Reader*, ed. Ernest J. Wilson III (New York: Routledge, 2004), 143–47; Moham-

med E. Ahrari, ed., *Ethnic Groups and US Foreign Policy* (Westport, CT: Greenwood, 1987); and David M. Paul and Rachel Anderson Paul, *Ethnic Lobbies and US Foreign Policy* (Boulder, CO: Lynne Rienner, 2009).

31. See Thomas N. Brown, *Irish-American Nationalism, 1870–1890* (Philadelphia: J. B. Lippincott, 1966); and Brown, "The Origins and Character of Irish-American Nationalism," *Review of Politics* 18 (July 1956): 327–58.

32. Stephen Lucius Gwynn, *Dublin Old and New* (Dublin: Browne and Nolan, 1937), 105. On the frequency of political upheaval in Ireland, see Brian Jenkins, *Irish Nationalism and the British State: From Repeal to Revolutionary Nationalism* (Montreal and Kingston: McGill–Queen's University Press, 2006); D. George Boyce, *Nationalism in Ireland*, 2nd ed. (London: Routledge, 1991); and Richard English, *Irish Freedom: The History of Nationalism in Ireland* (London: Macmillan, 2006).

33. On the agrarian unrest, see T. W. Moody, *Davitt and the Irish Revolution, 1846–82* (Oxford: Clarendon Press, 1981); and Anne Kane, "Narratives of Nationalism: Constructing Irish National Identity during the Land War, 1879–82," *National Identities* 2 (November 2000): 245–64. On the urban bombings, see Kenneth R. M. Short, *The Dynamite War: Irish American Bombers in Victorian Britain* (Atlantic Highlands, NJ: Humanities Press, 1979); and Niall Whelehan, *The Dynamiters: Irish Nationalism and Political Violence in the Wider World, 1867–1900* (Cambridge: Cambridge University Press, 2012).

34. Christy Campbell, *Fenian Fire: The British Government Plot to Assassinate Queen Victoria* (London: HarperCollins, 2002), 7.

35. Philip H. Bagenal, *The American Irish and Their Influence on Irish Politics* (London: Kegan Paul, Trench, 1882), 151, 244–45.

36. On those "two king-sized minority groups," see Lawrence H. Fuchs, "Minority Groups and Foreign Policy," *Political Science Quarterly* 74 (June 1959): 161–75, at 162.

37. See Kathleen Neils Conzen, "German-Americans and the Invention of Ethnicity," in *America and the Germans: An Assessment of a Three-Hundred-Year History,* ed. Frank Trommler and Joseph McVeigh, 2 vols. (Philadelphia: University of Pennsylvania Press, 1985), 1:131–47.

38. Warren Reed West, *Contemporary French Opinion on the American Civil War* (Baltimore: Johns Hopkins Press, 1924); Belle Becker Sideman and Lillian Friedman, eds., *Europe Looks at the Civil War: An Anthology* (New York: Orion, 1960); and Dean Mahin, *One War at a Time: The International Dimensions of the American Civil War* (Washington, DC: Brassey's, 1999).

39. Roger, *Ennemi américain,* 131–33. Also see Egon Caesar Corti, *Maximilian and Charlotte of Mexico,* trans. Catherine Alison Phillips (New York: Alfred A. Knopf, 1928); Michele Cunningham, "Mexico and the Foreign Policy of Napoleon III" (PhD diss., University of Adelaide, 1996); and Richard Blaine McCormack, "James Watson Webb and French Withdrawal from Mexico," *Hispanic American Historical Review* 31 (May 1951): 274–86.

40. Michael Howard, *The Franco-Prussian War: The German Invasion of France, 1870–1871* (London: Routledge, 1991); David Wetzel, *A Duel of Giants: Bismarck, Napoleon III, and the Origins of the Franco–Prussian War* (Madison: University of Wisconsin Press, 2001).

41. Otto Pflanze, *Bismarck and the Development of Germany,* vol. 1, *The Period of Unification, 1815–1871* (Princeton, NJ: Princeton University Press, 1990); Daniel Silverman, *Reluctant Union: Alsace-Lorraine and Imperial Germany, 1871–1918* (University Park, PA: Penn State University Press, 1972).

42. See Adolf Hepner, *America's Aid to Germany in 1870–1871* (St. Louis, MO: F. Leypoldt, 1904).

43. See Ralph Lutz, *Die Beziehungen zwischen Deutschland und den Vereingten Staaten während des Sezessionskrieges* (Heidelberg: C. Winter, 1911); and Henry Mason Adams, *Prussian-American Relations, 1775–1871* (Cleveland, OH: Press of Western Reserve University, 1960).

44. Blumenthal, *Reappraisal of Franco-American Relations,* 205–6. On the French perception of Grant, see Jacques Portes, *Fascination and Misgivings: The United States in French Opinion, 1870–1914,* trans. Ellborg Forster (Cambridge: Cambridge University Press, 2000), 207–10.

45. See Otto Graf zu Stolberg-Wernigerode, "Bismarck and His American Friends," *Virginia Quarterly Review* 5 (July 1929): 394–410; and Henry Blumenthal, "George Bancroft in Berlin, 1867–1874," *New England Quarterly* 37 (June 1964): 224–41.

46. Ido Oren, *Our Enemies and US: America's Rivalries and the Making of Political Science* (Ithaca, NY: Cornell University Press, 2003), 8–9.

47. Thomas Gold Appleton is said to have uttered the bon mot, "When good Americans die they go to Paris"; see David McCullough, *The Greater Journey: Americans in Paris* (New York: Simon & Schuster, 2011), 229.

48. See Carl Diehl, *Americans and German Scholarship, 1770–1870* (New Haven, CT: Yale University Press, 1978); Thomas Neville Bonner, *American Doctors and German Universities: A Chapter in International Intellectual Relations, 1870–1914* (Lincoln: University of Nebraska Press, 1963); and Charles F. Thwing, *The American and German University: One Hundred Years of History* (New York: Macmillan, 1928). More generally, see Henry A. Pochmann, *German Culture in America: Philosophical and Literary Influences, 1600–1900* (Madison: University of Wisconsin Press, 1957).

49. White, *American Opinion of France,* 178–79.

50. See Paul M. Kennedy, "Bismarck's Imperialism: The Case of Samoa, 1880–1890," *Historical Journal* 15 (June 1972): 261–83; Thomas A. Bailey, "Dewey and the Germans at Manila Bay," *American Historical Review* 45 (October 1939): 59–81; Lester Burrell Shippee, "Germany and the Spanish–American War," *American Historical Review* 30 (July 1925): 754–77; and William R. Braisted, *The United States Navy in the Pacific, 1897–1909* (Austin: University of Texas Press, 1958).

51. On the rise and decline of the German image in America, see Daniel T. Rodgers, *Atlantic Crossings: Social Politics in a Progressive Age* (Cambridge, MA: Harvard University Press, 1998); Clara Eve Schieber, *The Transformation of American Sentiment Toward Germany, 1870–1914* (New York: Russell and Russell, 1923); and Manfred Jonas, *The United States and Germany: A Diplomatic History* (Ithaca, NY: Cornell University Press, 1984).

52. See David G. Haglund, "Roosevelt as 'Friend of France'—but Which One?," *Diplomatic History* 31 (November 2007): 883–907.

53. See especially Christopher M. Andrew and Anya S. Kanya-Forster, *France Overseas: The Great War and the Climax of French Imperial Expansion* (London: Thames and Hudson, 1981); and Alice L. Conklin, *A Mission to Civilize: The Republican Idea of Empire in France and West Africa, 1895–1930* (Stanford, CA: Stanford University Press, 1997).

54. Shelby Cullom Davis, *The French War Machine* (London: Allen and Unwin, 1937), 29–30.

55. Earl R. Beck, *Germany Rediscovers America* (Tallahassee: Florida State University Press, 1968), 2.

56. Christopher M. Andrew, *Théophile Delcassé and the Making of the Entente Cordiale* (New York: St. Martin's Press, 1968); Paul Jacques Victor Rolo, *Entente Cordiale: The Origins and Negotiation of the Anglo-French Agreements of 8 April 1904* (London: Macmillan, 1969).

57. Michel Korinman, *Quand l'Allemagne pensait le monde: grandeur et décadence d'une géopolitique* (Paris: Fayard, 1990); Michael E. Nolan, *The Inverted Mirror: Mythologizing the Enemy in France and Germany, 1898–1914* (New York: Berghahn, 2005); Claude Digeon, *La Crise allemande de la pensée française, 1870–1914* (Paris: Presses Universitaires de France, 1992); Pierre Viénot, *Incertitudes allemandes: la crise de la civilisation bourgeoise en Allemagne* (Paris: Librairie Valois, 1931).

58. For the diplomatic legacy of this long-serving French ambassador (1903 to 1925), see Robert J. Young, *An American by Degrees: The Extraordinary Lives of French Ambassador Jules Jusserand* (Montreal and Kingston: McGill–Queen's University Press, 2009).

59. Wolfgang Köllmann and Peter Marschalk, "German Emigration to the United States," *Perspectives in American History* 7 (1973): 499–554; Frederick C. Luebke, *Germans in the New World: Essays on the History of Immigration* (Urbana: University of Illinois Press, 1990).

60. Aaron Spencer Fogleman, *Hopeful Journeys: German Immigration, Settlement, and Political Culture in Colonial America, 1717–1775* (Philadelphia: University of Pennsylvania Press, 1989); Lucy F. Bittinger, *The Germans in Colonial Times* (New York: Russell & Russell, 1901); and Fredric Klees, *The Pennsylvania Dutch* (New York: Macmillan, 1961).

61. Alexander Emmerich, *Die Geschichte der Deutschen in Amerika: Von 1680 bis zur Gegenwart* (Köln: Fackelträger, 2010); Kevin Kenny, *The American Irish: A History* (London: Longman, 2000).

62. La Vern J. Rippley, *The German-Americans* (Boston: Twayne, 1976); Richard O'Connor, *The German-Americans: An Informal History* (Boston: Little, Brown, 1968); and Victor Wolfgang von Hagen, *The Germanic People in America* (Norman: University of Oklahoma Press, 1976).

63. Stanley Nadel, *Little Germany: Ethnicity, Religion, and Class in New York City, 1845–80* (Urbana: University of Illinois Press, 1990), 41. Also see Tom Goyens, *Beer and Revolution: The German Anarchist Movement in New York City, 1880–1914* (Urbana: University of Illinois Press, 2007).

64. Leonard Dinnerstein and David M. Reimers, *Ethnic Americans: A History of Immigration*, 4th ed. (New York: Columbia University Press, 1999); Walter T. K. Nugent, *Crossings: The Great Transatlantic Migrations, 1870–1914* (Bloomington: Indiana University Press, 1992).

65. John A. Hawgood, *The Tragedy of German-America: The Germans in the United States of America during the Nineteenth Century—and After* (New York: G. P. Putnam's Sons, 1940), xi–xii.

66. Mack Walker, *Germany and the Emigration, 1816–1885* (Cambridge, MA: Harvard University Press, 1964); Klaus J. Bade and Myron Wiener, eds., *Migration Past, Migration Future: Germany and the United States* (Providence, RI: Berghahn, 1997).

67. Frederick C. Luebke, *Bonds of Loyalty: German-Americans and World War I* (De Kalb: Northern Illinois University Press, 1974), 29–30, 34.

68. James M. Berquist, "German Communities in American Cities: An Interpretation of the Nineteenth-Century Experience," *Journal of American Ethnic History* 4 (Fall 1984): 9–30, at 9.

69. Hawgood, *Tragedy of German-America,* 59–60; Gatzke, *Germany and the United States,* 28–31.

70. James Middleton, "Are Americans More German than English?," *World's Work* 31 (December 1915): 141–47; William Weber, "Do the German-Americans Dictate Our Foreign Policy?," *American Review of Reviews* 41 (March 1910): 349–50.

71. John Higham, *Strangers in the Land: Patterns of American Nativism, 1860–1925* (New York: Atheneum, 1971), 196. One Boston-based sociologist, in 1903, even adjudged Germans the very best of all the city's immigrants. Frederick A. Bushee, *Ethnic Factors in the Population of Boston* (New York: Macmillan/American Economic Association, 1903). Another writer from this era found the easily assimilated German American to be a definite upgrade on the European original; see Josiah Flynt, "The German and the German-American," *Atlantic Monthly* 78 (November 1896): 655–65.

72. See Phyllis Keller, *States of Belonging: German-American Intellectuals and the First World War* (Cambridge, MA: Harvard University Press, 1979); Russell A. Kazal, "Revisiting Assimilation: The Rise, Fall, and Reappraisal of a Concept in American Ethnic History," *American Historical Review* 100 (April 1995): 437–71; and Kazal, *Becoming Old Stock: The Paradox of German-American Identity* (Princeton, NJ: Princeton University Press, 2004).

73. Abigail Green, *Fatherlands: State-Building and Nationhood in Nineteenth-Century Germany* (Cambridge: Cambridge University Press, 2001).

74. John G. Gazley, *American Opinion of German Unification, 1848–1871* (New York: Columbia University Press, 1926), 486–87.

75. Guido A. Dobbert, "German-Americans between New and Old Fatherland, 1870–1914," *American Quarterly* 19 (Winter 1967): 663–80; Heinrich H. Maurer, "The Earlier German Nationalism in America," *American Journal of Sociology* 22 (January 1917): 519–43.

76. Don Heinrich Tolzmann, ed., *German Achievements in America: Rudolf Cronau's Survey History* (Bowie, MD: Heritage Books, 1995), 218–19.

77. Reinhard R. Doerries, *Imperial Challenge: Ambassador Count Bernstorff and German-American Relations, 1908–1917* (Chapel Hill: University of North Carolina Press, 1989), 72–73.

78. Julius Goebel, *Der Kampf um deutsche Kultur in Amerika* (Leipzig: Verlag der Durr'schen Buchhandlung, 1914).

79. Clifton James Child, *The German-Americans in Politics, 1914–1917* (Madison: University of Wisconsin Press, 1939); and Child, "German-American Attempts to Prevent Exportation of Munitions of War, 1914–1915," *Mississippi Valley Historical Review* 25 (December 1938): 351–68.

80. See Thomas J. Kerr IV, "German-Americans and Neutrality in the 1916 Election," *Mid-America* 43 (April 1961): 95–105.

81. See Charles Thomas Johnson, *Culture at Twilight: The National German-American Alliance, 1901–1918* (New York: Peter Lang, 1999). For attempts to portray the National German-American Alliance as the Kaiser's minion, see Frederic William Wile, *The German-American Plot* (London: Pearson, 1915); William H. Skaggs, *German Conspiracies in America* (London: T. Fisher Unwin, 1915); and André Chéradame, *The United States and Pan-Germania* (New York: Scribner's, 1918).

82. Prior to the Franco-British *Entente Cordiale* of 1904, France used to enjoy a favorable image among Irish nationalists bent on separating from the United Kingdom, and counting on French help to do so. See Pierre Ranger, *La France vue d'Irlande: l'histoire du mythe français de Parnell à l'État Libre* (Rennes: Presses Universitaires de Rennes, 2011); and Jérôme Aan De Wiel, "Austria-Hungary, France, Germany and the Irish Crisis from 1899 to the Outbreak of the First World War," *Intelligence & National Security* 21 (April 2006): 237–57.

83. On this extensive historiography, see John W. Langdon, *July 1914: The Long Debate, 1918–1990* (Oxford: Berg, 1991); and Hew Strachan, *The Outbreak of the First World War* (Oxford: Oxford University Press, 2004).

84. For the "German paradigm," the seminal works are Fritz Fischer, *Germany's Aims in the First World War* (London: Chatto and Windus, 1967); and Fischer, *War of Illusions: German Policies from 1911 to 1914*, trans. Marian Jackson (New York: Norton, 1975). In general agreement with the Fischer thesis are Michael R. Gordon, "Domestic Conflict and the Origins of the First World War: The British and German Cases," *Journal of Modern History* 26 (June 1974): 191–226; Fritz Stern, *The Failure of Illiberalism: Essays on the Political Culture of Modern Germany* (New York: Alfred A. Knopf, 1972); James Joll, "The 1914 Debate Continues: Fritz Fischer and His Critics," *Past & Present* 34 (July 1966): 100–13; and John C. G. Röhl, "Goodbye to All That (Again)? The Fischer Thesis, the New Revisionism and the Meaning of the First World War," *International Affairs* 91 (January 2015): 153–66. But for the contrasting, "Balkans inception" thesis, see Samuel R. Williamson Jr., "The Origins of World War I," *Journal of Interdisciplinary History* 18 (Spring 1988): 795–818; Christopher Clark, *The Sleepwalkers: How Europe Went to War in 1914* (New York: Harper, 2013); and Alan Kramer, *Dynamic of Destruction: Culture and Mass Killing in the First World War* (Oxford: Oxford University Press, 2007).

85. Jack S. Levy and John A. Vasquez, eds., "Introduction: Historians, Political Scientists, and the Causes of the First World War," in *The Outbreak of the First World War: Structure, Politics, and Decision-Making* (Cambridge: Cambridge University Press, 2014), 3–29, at 4. Also see Richard Ned Lebow, "What Can International Relations Theory Learn from the Origins of World War I?," *International Relations* 28 (December 2014): 387–410; and Keir A. Lieber, "The New History of World War I and What It Means for International Relations Theory," *International Security* 32 (Fall 2007): 155–91.

86. In particular, see Tanja Bueltmann, David T. Gleeson, and Donald M. MacRaild, "Invisible Diaspora? English Ethnicity in the United States before 1920," *Journal of American Ethnic History* 33 (Summer 2014): 5–30; Tanja Bueltmann and Donald M. MacRaild, "Globalizing St George: English Associations in the Anglo-World to the 1930s," *Journal of Global History* 7 (2012): 79–105; David T. Gleeson, ed., *English Ethnicity and Culture in North America* (Columbia: University of South Carolina Press, 2017); and Stephen Bowman, *The Pilgrims Society and Public Diplomacy, 1895–1945* (Edinburgh: Edinburgh University Press, 2018).

87. Kallen, *Culture and Democracy in the United States*, 99.

88. Also known in North America as Scots Irish and in the north of Ireland as Ulster Scots. See Patrick Griffin, *The People with No Name: Ireland's Ulster Scots, America's Scots Irish, and the Creation of a British Atlantic World, 1689–1764* (Princeton, NJ: Princeton University Press, 2001); and Leroy V. Eid, "Irish, Scotch and Scotch-Irish: A Reconsideration," *American Presbyterians* 64 (Winter 1986): 211–25.

89. James Joll, *The Origins of the First World War*, 2nd ed. (London: Longman, 1992), xi.

90. Éric Zemmour, *Destin français* (Paris: Albin Michel, 2018), 468.

91. On this point, see Ge Zhaoguang, *What Is China? Territory, Ethnicity, Culture, and History*, trans. Michael Gibbs Hill (Cambridge, MA: Belknap Press, 2018).

92. Among others insistent upon this distinction, are James Belich, *Replenishing the Earth: The Settler Revolution and the Rise of the Anglo-World, 1783–1939* (Oxford: Oxford University Press, 2009); Christopher Hitchens, *Blood, Class, and Empire: The Enduring Anglo-American Relationship* (New York: Nation Books, 2004); and Samuel P. Huntington, "The Hispanic Challenge," *Foreign Policy* 141 (March/April 2004): 30–45.

93. For that perhaps more honest appellation, see Francis Jennings, *The Invasion of America: Indians, Colonialism, and the Cant of Conquest* (Chapel Hill: University of North Carolina Press, 2010).

94. Sometimes the second of these, the Dutch, can be overlooked altogether, due to their relatively small impress upon American demography, compared with that of the larger German and Irish diasporas, but for an intriguing corrective, see Russell Shorto, *The Island at the Center of the World: The Epic Story of Dutch Manhattan and the Forgotten Colony That Shaped America* (New York: Vintage, 2005).

95. See Donald M. MacRaild, "Ethnic Conflict and English Associational Culture in America: The Benevolent Order of the Society of St. George," in *English Ethnicity and Culture in North America*, ed. David T. Gleeson (Columbia: University of South Carolina Press, 2017), 37–63; and Rowland Tappan Berthoff, *British Immigrants in Industrial America, 1790–1950* (Cambridge, MA: Harvard University Press, 1953).

96. Kevin P. Phillips, *The Cousins' Wars: Religion, Politics, and the Triumph of Anglo-America* (New York: Basic Books, 1999), 498.

97. See George Herbert Adams, *Why Americans Dislike England* (Philadelphia: Henry Altemus, 1896); and Goldwin Smith, "The Hatred of England," *North American Review* 150 (May 1890): 547–62. Also see Elizabeth Wallace, "Goldwin Smith on England and America," *American Historical Review* 59 (July 1954): 884–94; and William C. Reuter, "The Anatomy of Political Anglophobia in the United States, 1865–1900," *Mid-America* 61 (April–July 1979): 117–32.

98. On this concept, see Chris Rossdale, "Enclosing Critique: The Limits of Ontological Security," *International Political Sociology* 9 (December 2015): 369–86; Mitzen, "Ontological Security in World Politics"; and Brent J. Steele, *Ontological Security in International Relations: Self-Identity and the IR State* (London: Routledge, 2008).

99. Stephen Tuffnell, "'Uncle Sam Is to Be Sacrificed': Anglophobia in Late Nineteenth-Century Politics and Culture," *American Nineteenth Century History* 12 (March 2011): 77–99, at 79. Also see Goldwin Smith, "American Anglophobia," *Saturday Review* 81 (22 February 1896): 190–92.

100. Walter Russell Mead, *God and Gold: Britain, America, and the Making of the Modern World* (New York: Alfred A. Knopf, 2008), 34–35.

101. See Felice A. Bonadio, "The Failure of German Propaganda in the United States, 1914–1917," *Mid-America* 41 (January 1959): 40–57; and Reinhold Niebuhr, "The Failure of German-Americanism," in *World War I at Home: Readings on American Life, 1914–1920,* ed. David F. Trask (New York: John Wiley & Sons, 1970), 145–49.

102. Finley, *French in the Heart of America.* The feeling was reciprocated, French pro-Americanism being exemplified in Jean Giraudoux, *Amica America,* rev. ed. (Paris: Grasset, 1938), which originally appeared in 1918, the same year as Finley's book. Donald Allen calls *Amica America* "one of the most popular books ever written in France on America." Allen, "French Views of America," 162.

103. Jean Jules Jusserand, *Le Sentiment américain pendant la guerre* (Paris: Payot, 1931), 43.

104. François Weil, *Les Franco-Américains, 1860–1980* (Paris: Belin, 1989), 30–34.

105. Jean Heffer, préface to Weil, *Les Franco-Américains,* 5.

106. Gilbert Chinard, *Les Réfugiés Huguenots en Amérique* (Paris: Belles Lettres, 1925); Charles W. Baird, *History of the Huguenot Emigration to America* (New York: Dodd, Mead, 1885); John Mack Faragher, *A Great and Noble Scheme: The Tragic Story of the Expulsion of the French Acadians from Their American Homeland* (New York: W. W. Norton, 2005); E. Wilson Lyon, *Louisiana in French Diplomacy, 1759–1804* (Norman: University of Oklahoma Press, 1934).

107. See David G. Haglund and Justin Massie, "*L'Abandon de l'abandon*: The Emergence of a Transatlantic 'Francosphere' in Québec (and Canada's) Strategic Culture," *Québec Studies* 49 (Spring/Summer 2010): 59–85. Also see Georges Vattier, *Essai sur la mentalité canadienne-française* (Paris: Champion, 1928); and the preface written by Élisabeth Nardout-Lafarge, "Histoire d'une querelle," in Robert Charbonneau, *La France et nous: journal d'une querelle* (Québec: Bibliothèque québécoise, 1993), 7–26.

108. See C. Stewart Doty, "'*Monsieur Maurras est ici*': French Fascism in Franco-American New England," *Journal of Contemporary History* 32 (October 1997): 527–38; Guy Fritsch-Estrangin, *New York entre de Gaulle et Pétain: les Français aux États-Unis de 1940 à 1946* (Paris: La Table Ronde, 1969); and Gaston Henry-Haye, *La Grande Éclipse franco-américaine* (Paris: Plon, 1972).

109. For those religious controversies during the Third Republic, see Gérard Cholvy and Yves-Marie Hilaire, *Histoire religieuse de la France contemporaine, 1880–1930* (Toulouse: Bibliothèque Historique Privat, 1986); as well as Adrien Dansette, *Histoire religieuse de la France contemporaine* (Paris: Flammarion, 1965).

110. In particular, see Lubell, *Future of American Politics,* 132–36.

111. For a recent restatement of that case against the interventionism of a century ago, see Michael Kazin, *War against War: The American Fight for Peace, 1914–1918* (New York: Simon & Schuster, 2017).

112. See Manfred Jonas, *Isolationism in America, 1935–1941* (Ithaca, NY: Cornell University Press, 1966).

113. See Leland V. Bell, "The Failure of Nazism in America: The German-American Bund, 1936–1941," *Political Science Quarterly* 85 (December 1970): 585–99; and Timothy J. Holian, *The German-Americans and World War II: An Ethnic Experience* (New York: Peter Lang, 1996).

114. See Stephen C. Fox, "General John DeWitt and the Proposed Internment of German and Italian Aliens During World War II," *Pacific Historical Review* 57 (November 1988): 407–38; John Christgau, *Enemies: World War II Alien Internment* (Ames: Iowa State University Press, 1985); and Allan R. Bosworth, *America's Concentration Camps* (New York: Bantam Books, 1968).

115. Sander A. Diamond, *The Nazi Movement and the United States, 1924–1941* (Ithaca, NY: Cornell University Press, 1974); Leland V. Bell, *In Hitler's Shadow: The Anatomy of American Nazism* (Port Washington, NY: Kennikat Press, 1973).

116. Christopher Caldwell, "Is This the End of French Intellectual Life?," *New York Times,* 7 March 2021, SR4.

117. Or a "named human population with a myth of common ancestry"; see Smith, "Ethnic Sources of Nationalism," 49.

118. In particular, Johnston, *Cultural Realism.*

119. Philippe Roger, for instance, sees the French political employment of *Anglo-Saxon* as representing one more stage in the genealogical development of French anti-Americanism, to such a degree that the British can often find themselves airbrushed out of the picture entirely. As he writes, "one can take energetic aim at the 'Anglo-Saxons' while all the time intending to target none other than the Americans." Roger, *Ennemi américain,* 237.

120. For the Anglo-Saxon oppositional element in French identity construction, see Hayward, *Fragmented France*; as well as Marisol Touraine, "La Représentation de l'adversaire dans la politique extérieure française depuis 1981," *Revue française de science politique* 43 (1993): 807–22.

121. James Holland, *Sicily '43: The First Assault on Fortress Europe* (New York: Atlantic Monthly Press, 2020).

122. Thomas E. Hicks, "Enduring the Rigors of Conflict," *New York Times Book Review,* 20 November 2020, 9.

123. See Reginald Horsman, "Origins of Racial Anglo-Saxonism in Great Britain before 1850," *Journal of the History of Ideas* 37 (July–September 1976): 387–410; and Horsman, *Race and Manifest Destiny: The Origins of American Racial Anglo-Saxonism* (Cambridge, MA: Harvard University Press, 1981).

124. Boyle, "Venezuela Crisis," D1210. For a valuable analysis of British advocacies of "peace through Anglo-Saxonism," see Duncan Bell, "Before the Democratic Peace: Racial Unionism, Empire, and the Abolition of War," *European Journal of International Relations* 20 (September 2014): 647–70.

125. See James Bryce, "The Essential Unity of Britain and America," *Atlantic Monthly* 82 (July 1898): 22–29; and the similarly optimistic Andrew Carnegie, "A Look Ahead," *North American Review* 156 (June 1893): 685–710.

126. Richard Olney, "International Isolation of the United States," *Atlantic Monthly* 81 (May 1898): 577–89, at 588. This article is the text of his Harvard address of March 2, 1898.

127. See John W. Burgess, "Germany, Great Britain, and the United States," *Political Science Quarterly* 19 (March 1904): 1–19.

128. Finley Peter Dunne, *Mr. Dooley in Peace and in War* (Boston: Small, Maynard, 1898), 53.

129. Particularly energetic in the performance of these definitional calisthenics were Havelock Ellis, "The Genius of England," *North American Review* 204 (August 1916): 211–25; and Madison Grant, *The Passing of the Great Race, or the Racial Basis of European History* (London: G. Bell and Sons, 1919).

130. Another champion of cultural pluralism, Randolph S. Bourne, would have been similarly amazed. Bourne, "Trans-National America," *Atlantic Monthly* (July 1916): 86–97.

131. Rose, "Anti-Americanism in France," 473.

5. Vive la différence?

1. Kelley, *Cultural Pattern in American Politics*, 15.

2. Johnston, *Cultural Realism*.

3. Dueck, *Reluctant Crusaders*.

4. Wildavsky, "Choosing Preferences"; Kaplowitz, "National Self-Images."

5. Kuisel, "Gallic Rooster Crows Again," 1.

6. Reflecting a structural bias is Desch, "Culture Clash."

7. See Perry Anderson, *The H-Word: The Peripeteia of Hegemony* (London: Verso, 2017); and G. John Ikenberry and Daniel Nexon, "Hegemony Studies 3.0: The Dynamics of Hegemonic Orders," *Security Studies* 28 (May 2019): 395–421.

8. See William A. Macdonald, *Might Nature Be Canadian? Essays on Mutual Accommodation* (Montreal and Kingston: McGill–Queen's University Press, 2020); and Ann-Sofie Dahl, "The Myth of Swedish Neutrality," in *Haunted by History: Myths in International Relations*, ed. Cyril Buffet and Beatrice Heuser, 28–40 (Providence, RI: Berghahn, 1998).

9. For illustrative examples, see Seymour Martin Lipset, *American Exceptionalism: A Double-Edged Sword* (New York: W. W. Norton, 1996); Kim Voss, *The Making of American Exceptionalism* (Ithaca, NY: Cornell University Press, 1993); Laurent Wirth, *L'Exception française, 19e–20e siècles* (Paris: Armand Colin, 2000); and Yves Tinard, *L'Exception française: pourquoi?* (Paris: Maxima, 2001). Also see Akira Iriye, "Exceptionalism Revisited," *Reviews in American History* 16 (June 1988): 291–97; Michael Kammen, "The Problem of American Exceptionalism: A Reconsideration," *American Quarterly* 45 (March 1993): 1–43; James W. Ceasar, "The Origins and Character of American Exceptionalism," *American Political Thought* 1 (May 2012): 3–28; Claude Imbert, "The End of French Exceptionalism," *Foreign Affairs* 68 (Autumn 1989): 48–60; and Sophie Meunier, "The French Exception," *Foreign Affairs* 79 (July/August 2000): 104–16.

10. Roger Cohen, "A Smaller Torch, but a Promise Equally Imposing," *New York Times*, 20 June 2021, 4.

11. For this claim, see Pierre Bourdieu, "Deux impérialismes de l'universel," in *L'Amérique des Français*, ed. Christine Fauré and Tom Bishop (Paris: Éd. F. Bourin, 1992), 149–55; and Stanley Hoffmann, "Deux universalismes en conflit," *Tocqueville Review* 21 (2000): 65–71.

12. Kaplan, "France and Madison's Decision for War."

13. Kaspi, *Temps des Américains*, 305.

14. For this latter claim, see Peter J. Katzenstein, ed., "The West as Anglo-America," in *Anglo-America and Its Discontents: Civilizational Identities beyond West and East* (London: Routledge, 2012), 1–30; and John Bew, "Pax Anglo-Saxonica," *American Interest* 10 (May / June 2015): 40–49.

15. See Robert Gilpin, "The Theory of Hegemonic War," *Journal of Interdisciplinary History* 18 (Spring 1988): 591–613; and Gilpin, *War and Change.*

16. For this logic, see Jack S. Levy, "Declining Power and the Preventive Motivation for War," *World Politics* 40 (October 1987): 82–107.

17. Allison, *Destined for War*, 187.

18. Dale C. Copeland, "International Relations Theory and the Three Great Puzzles of the First World War," in *Outbreak of the First World War: Structure, Politics, and Decision-Making*, ed. Jack S. Levy and John A. Vasquez (Cambridge: Cambridge University Press, 2014), 167–98.

19. At the start of the nineteenth century, France boasted a population of 30 million, topped in Europe only by Russia; a century later, four other European lands (including Russia) had a larger population than France. See Goubert, *Course of French History*, 234–36.

20. For one analyst's well-known attempt to quantify relative capability (aka power) as a function of a set of (ostensibly) objective as well as subjective values, see Ray S. Cline, *World Power Assessment 1977: A Calculus of Strategic Drift* (Boulder, CO: Westview, 1977).

21. J. Adam Tooze, *The Deluge: The Great War and the Remaking of Global Order, 1916–1931* (London: Allen Lane, 2014), 23–24.

22. See Michael E. Howard, *War and the Liberal Conscience* (New Brunswick, NJ: Rutgers University Press, 1978); Adler, "War-Guilt Question"; and Lloyd E. Ambrosius, "Wilson, the Republicans, and French Security after World War I," *Journal of American History* 59 (September 1972): 341–52.

23. See Steele, *Ontological Security in International Relations.*

24. Terhune, "From National Character to National Behavior."

25. Gleason, "Identifying Identity"; Stryker and Burke, "Past, Present, and Future of an Identity Theory."

26. Ronald David Laing, *The Divided Self: A Study of Sanity and Madness* (London: Tavistock, 1960).

27. In particular, see Anthony Giddens, *Modernity and Self-Identity: Self and Society in the Late Modern Age* (Cambridge: Polity Press, 1991). On this transformation, see Karl Gustafsson and Nina C. Krickel-Choi, "Returning to the Roots of Ontological Security: Insights from the Existentialist Anxiety Literature," *European Journal of International Relations* 26 (September 2020): 875–95.

28. For this analytical formulation, see Kenneth N. Waltz, *Man, the State, and War: A Theoretical Analysis* (New York: Columbia University Press, 1959).

29. See John H. Herz, "Idealist Internationalism and the Security Dilemma," *World Politics* 2 (January 1950): 157–80; and Robert Jervis, "Cooperation under the Security Dilemma," *World Politics* 30 (January 1978): 167–214.

30. Mitzen, "Ontological Security in World Politics," 360–62.

31. Henri Tajfel, "Social Identity and Intergroup Behaviour," *Social Science Information* 13 (April 1974): 65–93.

32. See Abdelal et al., "Identity as a Variable."

33. Mercer, "Anarchy and Identity," 241–42. Also see Rupert Brown, "Social Identity Theory: Past Achievements, Current Problems and Future Challenges," *European Journal of Social Psychology* 30 (November 2000): 745–78.

34. Tobias Theiler, "Societal Security and Social Psychology," *Review of International Studies* 29 (April 2003): 249–68, at 261.

35. On the phenomenon of "Othering" in international relations, see Neumann, "Self and Other in International Relations."

36. Alexander Lanoszka and Michael A. Hunzeker, "Rage of Honor: Entente Indignation and the Lost Chance for Peace in the First World War," *Security Studies* 24 (October 2015): 662–95, at 667.

37. See Steven Ward, "Lost in Translation: Social Identity Theory and the Study of Status in World Politics," *International Studies Quarterly* 61 (December 2017): 821–34.

38. See David A. Lake, *Hierarchy in International Relations* (Ithaca, NY: Cornell University Press, 2009); and Marina G. Duque, "Recognizing International Status: A Relational Approach," *International Studies Quarterly* 62 (September 2018): 577–92.

39. See Allan Dafoe, Jonathan Renshon, and Paul Huth, "Reputation and Status as Motives for War," *Annual Review of Political Science* 17 (2014): 371–93.

40. See Steven Ward, *Status and the Challenge of Rising Powers* (Cambridge: Cambridge University Press, 2017); and Michelle K. Murray, *The Struggle for Recognition in International Relations: Status, Revisionism, and Rising Powers* (New York: Oxford University Press, 2019).

41. See, especially, Renshon, *Fighting for Status*; Tudor A. Onea, "Between Dominance and Decline: Status Anxiety and Great Power Rivalry," *Review of International Studies* 40 (January 2014): 125–52; and Wohlforth, "Unipolarity, Status Competition, and Great Power War."

42. See Paul, Larson, and Wohlforth, *Status in World Politics*.

43. Jean Daniel, "Anti-Semitism and Anti-Americanism," *International Herald Tribune*, 18 October 2002, 9.

44. Pascal Cuche, "Irak: et si la France s'était trompée?," *Politique étrangère* 68 (Summer 2003): 409–22, at 411–12. Also see Alain Hertoghe, *La Guerre à outrances: comment la presse nous a désinformés sur l'Irak* (Paris: Calmann-Lévy, 2003).

45. The president made this remark to France's consul general in New York, Edmond Bruwaert. Quoted in Lewis L. Gould, "Diplomats in the Lobby: Franco-American Relations and the Dingley Tariff of 1897," *Historian* 39 (August 1977): 659–80, at 679.

46. On these first three periods, see, respectively, Martin, *France and the Après Guerre, 1918–1924;* Wall, The *United States and the Making of Postwar France;* and Vincent Jauvert, *L'Amérique contre de Gaulle: histoire secrète, 1961–1969* (Paris: Éd. du Seuil, 2000).

47. Guéhenno, "Américanisation du monde."

48. Ernst Weisenfeld, "François Mitterrand: l'action extérieure," *Politique étrangère* 51 (Spring 1986): 131–41.

49. Diana Pinto, "De l'antiaméricanisme à l'américanophilie: l'itinéraire de l'intelligentsia française," *Commentaire* 8 (Autumn 1985): 874–79. On this same period, see also Denis Lacorne and Jacques Rupnik, "Introduction: France Bewitched by America," in *The Rise and Fall of Anti-Americanism: A Century of French Perception*, ed. Denis Lacorne, Jacques Rupnik, and Marie-France Toinet (Houndmills: Macmillan, 1990), 1–31.

50. To an English correspondent for the *New York Journal* who contacted him in early June 1897 following the publication of news that he had died, Twain remarked that "the report of my death was an exaggeration." Emily Petsko, "Reports of Mark Twain's Quote About His Own Death Are Greatly Exaggerated," *Mental Floss*, 2 November 2018, https://www.mentalfloss.com/article/562400/reports-mark-twains-quote-about-mark-twains-death-are-greatly-exaggerated.

51. Pascal Ory, "From Baudelaire to Duhamel: An Unlikely Antipathy," in *The Rise and Fall of Anti-Americanism: A Century of French Perception*, ed. Denis Lacorne, Jacques Rupnik, and Marie-France Toinet (Houndmills: Macmillan, 1990), 42–54.

52. A term coined by the philosopher W. B. Gallie; see William E. Connolly, "Essentially Contested Concepts in Politics," in *The Terms of Political Discourse*, 2nd ed. (Princeton, NJ: Princeton University Press, 1983), chapter 1.

53. Kenneth R. Minogue, "Anti-Americanism: A View from London," *National Interest* 3 (Spring 1986): 43–49, at 43.

54. Andrew Kohut and Bruce Stokes, *America Against the World: How We Are Different and Why We Are Disliked* (New York: Times Books/Henry Holt, 2006).

55. Tony Judt and Denis Lacorne, *With Us or Against Us: Studies in Global Anti-Americanism* (New York: Palgrave, 2005), 13.

56. See Antonello Gerbi, *The Dispute of the New World: The History of a Polemic, 1750–1900*, trans. Jeremy Moyle (Pittsburgh: University of Pittsburgh Press, 1973); and Ray Allen Billington, *Land of Savagery, Land of Promise: The European Image of the American Frontier in the Nineteenth Century* (New York: W. W. Norton, 1981). On this transatlantic bilateral polemic from a French and American perspective, see, respectively, Echeverria, *Mirage in the West;* and Howard Mumford Jones, *America and French Culture, 1750–1848* (Chapel Hill: University of North Carolina Press, 1927). More generally, see Sigmund Skard, *The American Myth and the European Mind: American Studies in Europe, 1776–1960* (Philadelphia: University of Pennsylvania Press, 1961); Cushing Strout, *The American Image of the Old World* (New York: Harper & Row, 1963); Arthur P. Whitaker, *The Western Hemisphere Idea: Its Rise and Decline* (Ithaca, NY: Cornell University Press, 1954); and Daniel J. Boorstin, *America and the Image of Europe: Reflections on American Thought* (New York: Meridian Books, 1960).

57. McDougall, *Promised Land, Crusader State*, 9.

58. On British anti-American attitudes as gleaned from survey data, see Webb, "Observing America."

59. Sweig, *Friendly Fire;* Naím, "Perils of Lite Anti-Americanism," 95–96.

60. John Fonte, "Liberal Democracy and Transnational Progressivism: The Future of the Ideological Civil War within the West," *Orbis* 46 (Winter 2002): 2–14.

61. The kind of critique Paul Hollander labels "rational" anti-Americanism. See Hollander, *Anti-Americanism: Irrational and Rational* (New Brunswick, NJ: Transaction Books, 1995).

62. Josef Joffe, "Dissecting Anti-isms," *American Interest* 1 (Summer 2006): 164–70. Also see Joffe, "The Rise of Anti-Americanism," in *Überpower: The Imperial Temptation of America* (New York: W. W. Norton, 2006), chapter 3.

63. Barry Rubin and Judith Colp Rubin, *Hating America: A History* (New York: Oxford University Press, 2004), viii–ix. Also see the typology developed in Peter J. Katzenstein and Robert O. Keohane, eds., "Varieties of Anti-Americanism: A Framework for Analysis," in *Anti-Americanisms in World Politics* (Ithaca, NY: Cornell University Press), 9–38.

64. Thierry Meyssan, *L'Effroyable Imposture: aucun avion ne s'est écrasé sur le Pentagone* (Paris: Carnot, 2002). Revel comments wryly, apropos of the immense readership enjoyed by this book after its publication in March 2002, that it spoke volumes about the credulousness of the French and inspired perplexity about the intellectual qualities of a people often declaring themselves to be "the most intelligent on earth." Revel, *Obsession anti-américaine*, 258–59.

65. One writer claims that the world's "first anti-American riot" occurred in The Hague in 1787. See J. W. Schulte Nordholt, "Anti-Americanism in European Culture: Its Early Manifestations," in *Anti-Americanism in Europe*, ed. Rob Kroes and Maarten van Rossem (Amsterdam: Free University Press, 1986), 7–19.

66. Walter Russell Mead, "Why Do They Hate Us? Two Books Take Aim at French Anti-Americanism," *Foreign Affairs* 82 (March/April 2003): 139–42, at 139.

67. See Portes, *Fascination and Misgivings*. Contemporary works of this fearful genre include Octave Noël, *Le Péril américain* (Paris: De Soye et fils, 1899); and Joseph Ribet, *Le Vol de l'Aigle de Monroë à Roosevelt* (Paris: Ernest Flammarion, 1905).

68. See John Cowper Powys, *The War and Culture: A Reply to Professor Münsterberg* (New York: G. Arnold Shaw, 1914).

69. Duhamel, America the Menace, 18–19.

70. Jean Baudrillard, *Amérique* (Paris: Grasset, 1986).

71. Roger, *Ennemi américain*, 361–62. For the Maginot analogy, also see Alain Minc, *La Grande Illusion* (Paris: Bernard Grasset, 1989).

72. Roger, *Ennemi américain*, 282, 359.

73. Revel, *Obsession anti-américaine*, 238–39.

74. William R. Keylor, "France and the Illusion of American Support, 1919–1940," in *The French Defeat of 1940: Reassessments*, ed. Joel Blatt (Providence, RI: Berghahn, 1998), 204–43, at 222.

75. In addition to Duhamel, *America the Menace*, other titles providing the defensive flavor of "golden age" anti-Americanism include Chastanet, *L'Oncle Shylock;* Romier, *Who Will Be Master*; and Aron and Dandieu, *Cancer américain*.

76. Kadmi-Cohen, *Abomination américaine*, 263.

77. Serge Klarsfeld, *La Shoah en France: Vichy-Auschwitz la solution finale de la question juive en France* (Paris: Fayard, 2001).

78. Salvador de Madariaga, *Englishmen, Frenchmen, Spaniards*, 2nd ed. (New York: Hill and Wang, 1969), 62–66.

79. Sophie Meunier, "The Distinctiveness of French Anti-Americanism," in *Anti-Americanisms in World Politics*, ed. Peter J. Katzenstein and Robert O. Keohane (Ithaca, NY: Cornell University Press, 2007), 129–56, at 155–56. Also see Alain Duhamel, *Le Complexe d'Astérix: essai sur le caractère politique des Français* (Paris: Gallimard, 1985).

80. Christian Julienne, *Le Diable est-il libéral?* (Paris: Les Belles Lettres, 2001).

81. For valuable discussions of what the term actually means in the American context, see Louis Hartz, *The Liberal Tradition in America: An Interpretation of American Political Thought since the Revolution* (New York: Harcourt, Brace, and World, 1955); and Charles Forcey, *The Crossroads of Liberalism: Croly, Weyl, Lippmann and the Progressive Era, 1900–1925* (New York: Oxford University Press, 1961). More generally, see John Rawls, *Political Liberalism* (New York: Columbia University Press, 1993); William Galston, *Liberal Purposes: Goods, Virtues, and Diversity in the Liberal State* (Cambridge: Cambridge University Press, 1991); Will Kymlicka, *Liberalism, Community, and Culture* (Oxford: Oxford University Press, 1989); John A. Hall, *Liberalism: Politics, Ideology, and the Market* (Chapel Hill: University of North Carolina Press, 1987); Edward Fawcett, *Liberalism: The Life of an Idea* (Princeton, NJ: Princeton University Press, 2014); Helena Rosenblatt, *The Lost History of Liberalism: From Ancient Rome to the Twenty-First Century* (Princeton, NJ: Princeton University Press, 2018); and James Traub, *What Was Liberalism? The Past, Present, and Promise of a Noble Idea* (New York: Basic Books, 2019).

82. Alain Laurent, *Le Libéralisme américain: histoire d'un détournement* (Paris: Les Belles Lettres, 2006). Also see James L. Richardson, "Contending Liberalisms: Past and Present," *European Journal of International Relations* 3 (March 1997): 5–33.

83. See Hal Brands, *American Grand Strategy in the Age of Trump* (Washington, DC: Brookings Institution Press, 2018); and Drezner, Krebs, and Schweller, "End of Grand Strategy."

84. See G. John Ikenberry, "American Decline, Liberal Hegemony, and the Transformation of World Politics," in *Coping with Geopolitical Decline: The United States in European Perspective*, ed. Frédéric Mérand (Montreal and Kingston: McGill–Queen's University Press, 2020), 222–50.

85. Ikenberry, A *World Safe for Democracy;* Kagan, *Jungle Grows Back*.

86. For critiques, see Chalmers Johnson, *Blowback: The Costs and Consequences of American Empire* (New York: Henry Holt, 2001); John J. Mearsheimer, *The Great Delusion: Liberal Dreams and International Realities* (New Haven, CT: Yale University Press, 2018); Bacevich, *Age of Illusions;* and Patrick Porter, *The False Promise of Liberal Order: Nostalgia, Delusion, and the Rise of Trump* (Cambridge: Polity Press, 2020).

87. The term *neoliberalism* is considered in English-speaking policy precincts to be a recent qualification of *liberalism*, emphasizing the virtues of a relatively unconstrained global marketplace, but in reality the neologism has its origins in pre–Second World War France. See Gaëtan Pirou, *Néo-libéralisme, néo-corporatisme, néo-socialisme* (Paris: Gallimard, 1939).

88. See Vincent Chriqui, *À qui profite le libéralisme?* (Paris: Édition 1, 2003); Georges Burdeau, *Le Libéralisme* (Paris: Seuil, 1979); and Thierry Leterre, *La Gauche et la peur libérale* (Paris: Presse de SciencesPo, 2000).

89. On the lengthy pedigree of this trope, see Émile Faguet, *Le Libéralisme* (Paris: Société française d'imprimerie et librairie, 1903); and Edmond Demolins, *Anglo-Saxon Superiority: To What It Is Due*, trans. Louis Bert Lavigne (London: Leadenhall, 1899), which despite its title is really an inquiry into liberalism.

90. See Walter Michael Simon, *French Liberalism, 1789–1848* (New York: Wiley, 1972); George Armstrong Kelly, *The Humane Comedy: Constant, Tocqueville, and French Liberalism* (Cambridge: Cambridge University Press, 1992); Roger Boesche, *The Strange Liberalism of Alexis de Tocqueville* (Ithaca, NY: Cornell University Press, 1987); W. David Clinton, *Tocqueville, Lieber, and Bagehot: Liberalism Confronts the World* (New York: Palgrave Macmillan, 2003); Pierre Manent, *An Intellectual History of Liberalism* (Princeton, NJ: Princeton University Press, 1995); Stephen Holmes, *Benjamin Constant and the Making of Modern Liberalism* (New Haven, CT: Yale University Press, 1987); and John Anthony Scott, *Republican Ideas and the Liberal Tradition in France, 1870–1914* (1951; repr. New York: Octagon Books).

91. Mathy, *Extrême-Occident*, 253–54.

92. One such exception being Guy Sorman. See Sorman, *La Solution libérale* (Paris: Fayard, 1984); and Sorman, *Le Progrès et ses ennemis* (Paris: Fayard, 2001).

93. See Celeste A. Wallander, "NATO's Enemies Within: How Democratic Decline Could Destroy the Alliance," *Foreign Affairs* 97 (July/August 2018): 70–81; Henrik B. L. Larsen, *NATO's Democratic Retrenchment: Hegemony after the Return of History* (London: Routledge, 2019); Stanley R. Sloan, *Transatlantic Traumas: Has Illiberalism Brought the West to the Brink of Collapse?* (Manchester: Manchester University Press, 2018); and Ivan Krastev and Stephen Holmes, *The Light that Failed: A Reckoning* (London: Penguin, 2020).

94. Randolph M. Siverson and Juliann Emmons, "Birds of a Feather: Democratic Political Systems and Alliance Choices in the Twentieth Century," *Journal of Conflict Resolution* 35 (June 1991): 285–306.

95. Mark A. Boyer, *International Cooperation and Public Goods: Opportunities for the Western Alliance* (Baltimore: Johns Hopkins University Press, 1993), 121.

96. Risse-Kappen, *Cooperation among Democracies*, 194–95.

97. "One could . . . argue that the North Atlantic Alliance represents an institutionalization of the security community among democracies. While the perceived Soviet threat certainly strengthened the sense of common purpose among the allies, *it did not create the community in the first place.* NATO was preceded by the wartime alliance of the United States, Great Britain, and France, which also closely collaborated to create various postwar regimes in the economic and security areas." Risse-Kappen, *Cooperation among Democracies*, 32 (emphasis added).

98. See David G. Haglund, "The Case of the Missing Democratic Alliance: France, the 'Anglo-Saxons' and NATO's Deep Origins," *Contemporary Security Policy* 25 (August 2004): 225–51.

99. Zeev Maoz and Bruce Russett, "Normative and Structural Causes of the Democratic Peace, 1946–1986," *American Political Science Review* 87 (September 1999): 624–38.

100. Ironically, Moscow *did* know what was being said in the secret trilateral talks of early 1948, but it was because its agents had compromised the *British* delegation to the talks. See Cees Wiebes and Bert Zeeman, "The Pentagon Negotiations March 1948: The Launch-

ing of the North Atlantic Treaty," *International Affairs* 59 (Summer 1983): 351–63; and Wall, *The United States and the Making of Postwar France*, 133–35.

101. For a typical expression of wartime idealism about the meaning of France, see Pierre Maillaud, *France* (London: Oxford University Press, 1942). The idealism was sustained by the claim that de Gaulle's Free French epitomized the eternal France. See Jean-Louis Crémieux-Brilhac, *La France libre: de l'Appel du 18 juin à la libération* (Paris: Gallimard, 1996).

102. See Albert Guérard, *The France of Tomorrow* (Cambridge, MA: Harvard University Press, 1942), xiii–xviii. As for *German* France, its collaborationist zest was so potent as to make even Vichy look, in comparison, like the beating heart of the Resistance. See Pascal Ory, *La France allemande (1933–1945): paroles françaises* (1977; repr. Paris: Gallimard, 1995).

103. The scholarly and other published output on relations between Roosevelt, Churchill, and de Gaulle is enormous. The best starting point is Julian Jackson, *A Certain Idea of France: The Life of Charles de Gaulle* (London: Penguin Books, 2019). On these strained relations both during and following the war, see Simon Berthon, *Allies at War: The Bitter Rivalry among Churchill, Roosevelt, and de Gaulle* (New York: Basic Books, 2001); Aglion, *Roosevelt and de Gaulle;* François Kersaudy, *Churchill and de Gaulle* (New York: Atheneum, 1983); Newhouse, *De Gaulle and the Anglo-Saxons;* Rossi, *Roosevelt and the French;* Viorst, *Hostile Allies;* White, *Seeds of Discord;* Frédéric Bozo, *Deux stratégies pour l'Europe: De Gaulle, les Etats-Unis et l'Alliance atlantique, 1958–1969* (Paris: Plon, 1996); and Constantine Pagedas, *Anglo-American Strategic Relations and the French Problem, 1960–1963: A Troubled Partnership* (London: Frank Cass, 2000).

104. Coker, *Twilight of the West*, 38–45.

105. Higonnet, *Sister Republics,* 273–75.

106. Jacques Godechot, *Les Constitutions de la France depuis 1789* (Paris: Garnier-Flammarion, 1970).

107. René Rémond, *La République souveraine: la vie politique en France, 1879–1939* (Paris: Fayard, 2002), 9–16.

108. Herbert Luethy, *France against Herself*, trans. Eric Mosbacher (New York: Meridian, 1955), 25–26. See also Friedrich Sieburg, *Who Are These French?*, trans. Alan Harris (1932; repr. New York: Macmillan, 1938).

109. David Thomson, *Democracy in France since 1870,* 5th ed. (London: Oxford University Press, 1969).

110. Winock, *Belle Époque,* 14.

111. Daniel Chirot, "The Social and Historical Landscape of Marc Bloch," in *Vision and Method in Historical Sociology,* ed. Theda Skocpol (Cambridge: Cambridge University Press, 1984), 22–46; Zeev Sternhell, *Ni droite ni gauche: l'idéologie fasciste en France,* 3rd ed. (Paris: Fayard, 2000). Also see André Géraud, *Les Fossoyeurs,* 2 vols. (New York: Éd. de la Maison Française, 1943).

112. For a valuable corrective of the conventional view that France during the Fourth Republic was more or less a "failed state," see Jenny Raflik, *La République moderne: la IVe République, 1946–1958* (Paris: Éd. du Seuil, 2018).

113. Georgette Elgey, *La République des illusions, 1945–1951: ou la vie secrète de la IVe République* (Paris: Fayard, 1965).

114. André Kaspi, *La Libération de la France, juin 1944–janvier 1946* (Paris: Perrin, 1995), 368–72; William I. Hitchcock, *France Restored: Cold War Diplomacy and the Quest for Leadership in Europe, 1944–1954* (Chapel Hill: University of North Carolina Press, 1998), 16–18. Also see Isser Woloch, *The Postwar Moment: Progressive Forces in Britain, France, and the United States after World War II* (New Haven, CT: Yale University Press, 2019).

115. Rioux, *Fourth Republic*, 72–73.

116. Hoffmann, "American Social Science." For a critique, see Peter Marcus Kristensen, "Revisiting the 'American Social Science'—Mapping the Geography of International Relations," *International Studies Perspectives* 16 (August 2015): 246–69.

117. A claim made in James Kurth, "Inside the Cave: The Banality of IR Studies," *National Interest* 53 (Fall 1998): 29–40.

118. For Walter Russell Mead, the competing paradigms are Jeffersonianism, Hamiltonianism, and Jacksonianism, whereas for Walter McDougall, the analytical tension is between what he terms "old testament" precepts (roughly congruent with classical European realism) and "new testament" ones, associated with liberal internationalism. See Mead, *Special Providence;* and McDougall, *Promised Land, Crusader State.*

119. See for this postulated predisposition to liberal internationalism, John Gerard Ruggie, "The Past as Prologue? Interests, Identity, and American Foreign Policy," in *America's Strategic Choices*, ed. Michael E. Brown et al. (Cambridge, MA: MIT Press, 1997), 163–99; David C. Hendrickson, "In Our Own Image: The Sources of American Conduct in World Affairs," *National Interest* 50 (Winter 1997/98): 9–21; Daniel H. Deudney, "The Philadelphian System: Sovereignty, Arms Control, and Balance of Power in the American States-Union, circa 1787–1861," *International Organization* 49 (Spring 1995): 191–228; and Daniel H. Deudney and G. John Ikenberry, "The Logic of the West," *World Policy Journal* 10 (Winter 1993/94): 17–25.

120. Martin Griffiths, *Rethinking International Relations Theory* (Basingstoke: Palgrave, 2011), 14. Also see Jennifer Sterling-Folker, "All Hail to the Chief: Liberal IR Theory in the New World Order," *International Studies Perspectives* 16 (February 2015): 40–49.

121. One close observer of French foreign policy notes that "a national strategic culture with deep roots in history and geography is not easily abandoned." Gordon, *Certain Idea of France*, 185.

122. See Brooks, "Duelling Realisms."

123. Quoted, respectively, in Young, *American by Degrees*, 122; and Robert H. Ferrell, *Woodrow Wilson and World War I, 1917–1921* (New York: Harper & Row, 1985), 152.

124. Serge Berstein, *Histoire du gaullisme* (Paris: Perrin, 2001), 294–95. See also Jean Touchard, *Le Gaullisme* (Paris: Éd. du Seuil, 1978); Anthony Hartley, *Gaullism: The Rise and Fall of a Political Movement* (New York: E. P. Dutton, 1971); and Gaetano Quagliariello, *La Religion gaulliste* (Paris: Perrin, 2006).

125. Stanley Hoffmann, *Decline or Renewal? France Since the 1930s* (New York: Viking Press, 1974), 337–38.

126. Brenner and Parmentier, *Reconcilable Differences.*

127. See Michael Dunne, "US Foreign Relations in the Twentieth Century: From World Power to Global Hegemony," *International Affairs* 76 (January 2000): 25–40. But for a send-up of this perspective, see Michael Fitzsimmons, "'Liberal Hegemony' as Straw Man," *American Interest* 14 (May/June 2019): 38–40.

128. See Emmanuel Todd, *Après l'empire: essai sur la décomposition du système américain* (Paris: Gallimard, 2002); and G. John Ikenberry, "Liberalism and Empire: Logics of Order in the American Unipolar Age," *Review of International Studies* 30 (October 2004): 609–30.

129. Mearsheimer, *Tragedy of Great Power Politics*.

130. Ryan Hass, *Stronger: Adapting America's China Strategy in an Age of Competitive Interdependence* (New Haven, CT: Yale University Press, 2021), 75.

131. For that earlier period, when the "h-word" often invited employment its strong sense, see G. John Ikenberry, "Getting Hegemony Right," *National Interest* 63 (Spring 2001): 17–24; and Ikenberry, *Liberal Leviathan: The Origins, Crisis, and Transformation of the American World Order* (Princeton, NJ: Princeton University Press, 2011). Also see Rosemary Foot, S. Neil MacFarlane, and Michael Mastanduno, *US Hegemony and International Organizations: The United States and Multilateral Institutions* (Oxford: Oxford University Press, 2002).

132. For what remains, to this day, the most successful denotative exploration of multilateralism, one that focuses on the liberal norms subsumed in the shared commitment to indivisibility, nondiscrimination, and diffuse reciprocity in all matters related to security and defense cooperation, see Lisa L. Martin, "Interests, Power, and Multilateralism," *International Organization* 46 (Autumn 1992): 765–92.

133. John Gerard Ruggie, "Multilateralism: The Anatomy of an Institution," *International Organization* 46 (Summer 1992): 561–98, at 567–68.

134. See Célia Belin, *Balancing Act: The Limits of Pragmatism in the Franco-American Relationship and the Way Forward* (Washington, DC: Brookings Institution/Robert Bosch Foundation Transatlantic Initiative, October 2018).

135. On this variant of balancing, see T. V. Paul, *Restraining Great Powers: Soft Balancing from Empires to the Global Era* (New Haven, CT: Yale University Press, 2018).

136. Charles Krauthammer, "The Unipolar Moment," *Foreign Affairs: America and the World 1990/91* 70 (1991): 23–33.

137. See David G. Haglund, "Les mythes qui nous font vivre et mentir," in *Les relations transatlantiques: de la tourmente à l'apaisement?*, ed. Arthur Paecht (Paris: Institut Français de Relations Internationales et Stratégiques/Presses Universitaires de France, 2003), 227–36.

138. See in particular Hubert Védrine with Dominique Moïsi, *France in an Age of Globalization*, trans. Philip H. Gordon (Washington, DC: Brookings Institution Press, 2001).

139. William R. Thompson, "Dehio, Long Cycles, and the Geohistorical Context of Structural Transition," *World Politics* 45 (October 1992): 127–52.

140. Léon Daudet, *The Stupid XIXth Century*, trans. Lewis Galantière (New York: Payson & Clarke, 1928).

141. David A. Bell, *The First Total War: Napoleon's Empire and the Birth of Warfare as We Know It* (Boston: Houghton Mifflin, 2007).

142. See Anthony Adamthwaite, *Grandeur and Misery: France's Bid for Power in Europe, 1914–1940* (London: Arnold, 1995).

143. See Jonas, *Isolationism in America;* and Kupchan, *Isolationism.*

144. On misperceptions of Yalta, see Reiner Marcowitz, "Yalta, the Myth of the Division of the World," in *Haunted by History: Myths in International Relations,* ed. Cyril Buffet and Beatrice Heuser, 80–102 (Providence, RI: Berghahn, 1998); and Serhii M. Plokhy, *Yalta: The Price of Peace* (New York: Viking, 2010).

145. Noël Mamère and Olivier Warin, *Non merci, Oncle Sam!* (Paris: Éd. Ramsay, 1999), 12.

146. Kenneth N. Waltz, "Globalization and American Power," *National Interest* 59 (Spring 2000): 46–56, at 54.

147. For one such intrepid advocacy, worthy of Astérix himself, see Henri de Grossouvre, *Paris–Berlin–Moscou: la voie de l'indépendance et de la paix* (Lausanne: L'Age d'Homme, 2002).

148. Simon Collier and William F. Sater, *A History of Chile, 1808–1994* (New York: Cambridge University Press, 1996), 197.

149. Alain Peyrefitte claimed that he learned of the quote indirectly from Vladimir Lenin, who said he got it from reading somewhere that Napoleon had been its author. Peyrefitte, *Quand la Chine s'éveillera . . . le monde tremblera* (Paris: Fayard, 1973). More prosaically (and accurately), Peter Hicks attributes the words to a screenplay written by Bernard Gordon for the 1963 Hollywood film *55 Days at Peking,* starring Charlton Heston, Ava Gardner, and David Niven. Hicks, "'Sleeping China' and Napoleon," Fondation Napoléon, https://www.napoleon.org/en/history-of-the-two-empires/articles/ava-gard ner-china-and-napoleon.

150. See Richard Maher, "Bipolarity and the Future of US–China Relations," *Political Science Quarterly* 133 (Fall 2018): 497–525.

6. Do Leaders Matter?

1. Waltz, *Man, the State, and War.* Also see J. David Singer, "The Level-of-Analysis Problem in International Relations," *World Politics* 14 (October 1961): 77–92.

2. Kenneth N. Waltz, *Theory of International Politics* (Reading, MA: Addison-Wesley, 1979).

3. See Alexander L. George, "The Causal Nexus between Cognitive Beliefs and Decision-Making Behavior: The 'Operational Code' Belief System," in *Psychological Models in International Politics,* ed. Lawrence S. Falkowski (Boulder, CO: Westview, 1979), 95–124.

4. Daniel L. Byman and Kenneth M. Pollack, "Let Us Now Praise Great Men: Bringing the Statesman Back In," *International Security* 25 (Spring 2001): 107–46, at 109.

5. On some of the challenges confronting those who pursue these pleasures, see Elizabeth Colwill, "Subjectivity, Self-Representation, and the Revealing Twitches of Biography," *French Historical Studies* 24 (Summer 2001): 421–37.

6. Jervis, "Do Leaders Matter?," 154.

7. For an attempt to do something similar with respect to the First World War, and to "remove" from the scene not Hitler but the assassinated Austrian Archduke Franz Ferdi-

nand, see Richard Ned Lebow, *Archduke Franz Ferdinand Lives: A World Without World War I* (New York: Palgrave Macmillan, 2014).

8. An insightful argument against the scoffers, E. H. Carr among them, is presented in Daniel Nolan, "Why Historians (and Everyone Else) Should Care about Counterfactuals," *Philosophical Studies* 163 (March 2013): 317–35. Also see Richard J. Evans, *Altered Pasts: Counterfactuals in History* (Waltham, MA: Brandeis University Press, 2013).

9. Levy, "Counterfactuals, Causal Inference, and Historical Analysis," 384–85. Also see Fearon, "Counterfactuals and Hypothesis Testing in Political Science."

10. For sympathetic treatments of Benjamin Franklin, who was sent to France in December 1776 to represent the United States and remained in his post until Thomas Jefferson's arrival, see Claude-Anne Lopez, *My Life with Benjamin Franklin* (New Haven, CT: Yale University Press, 2000); and Bernard Faÿ, *Benjamin Franklin: citoyen du monde* (Paris: Calmann-Lévy, 1931).

11. Meade Minnigerode, *Jefferson, Friend of France, 1793: The Career of Edmond Charles Genet* (New York: G. P. Putnam's Sons, 1928). Also in the category of advertised "friends of France," we find Myron T. Herrick, a former Republican governor of Ohio who went on to become an extremely popular American ambassador to Paris from 1912 to the end of 1914. T. Bentley Mott, *Myron T. Herrick, Friend of France: An Autobiographical Biography* (Garden City, NY: Doubleday, Doran, 1929).

12. Claude Fohlen, *Jefferson à Paris, 1784–1789* (Paris: Perrin, 1995), 13–15.

13. Among the few French scholars who have decidedly *not* forgotten the twenty-sixth president, one has stood head and shoulders above the rest: the late Serge Ricard. See Ricard, *Companion to Theodore Roosevelt;* Ricard, "An Atlantic Triangle in the 1900s: Theodore Roosevelt's 'Special Relationships' with France and Britain," *Journal of Transatlantic Studies* 8 (September 2010): 202–12; Ricard, *Théodore Roosevelt: principes et pratique d'une politique étrangère* (Aix-en-Provence: Publications de l'Université de Provence, 1991); and Ricard, *Théodore Roosevelt et la justification de l'impérialisme* (Aix-en-Provence: Université de Provence, Service des Publications, 1986).

14. See David G. Haglund, "That Other Transatlantic 'Great Rapprochement': France, the United States, and Theodore Roosevelt," in *America's Transatlantic Turn: Theodore Roosevelt and the "Discovery" of Europe,* ed. Hans Krabbendam and John M. Thompson (New York: Palgrave Macmillan, 2012), 103–19.

15. See J. Lee Thompson, *Never Call Retreat: Theodore Roosevelt and the Great War* (New York: Palgrave Macmillan, 2013); and John Milton Cooper Jr., *The Warrior and the Priest: Woodrow Wilson and Theodore Roosevelt* (Cambridge, MA: Belknap Press, 1983). Also, more generally, see John Patrick Finnegan, *Against the Specter of a Dragon: The Campaign for American Military Preparedness, 1914–1917* (Westport, CT: Greenwood, 1974); George C. Herring Jr., "James Hay and the Preparedness Controversy, 1915–1916," *Journal of Southern History* 30 (November 1964): 383–404; and Michael Pearlman, *To Make Democracy Safe for America: Patricians and Preparedness in the Progressive Era* (Urbana: University of Illinois Press, 1984).

16. Russell Buchanan, "Theodore Roosevelt and American Neutrality, 1914–1917," *American Historical Review* 43 (July 1938): 775–90.

17. See Peter Collier with David Horowitz, *The Roosevelts: An American Saga* (New York: Simon & Schuster, 1994).

18. Charles Lyon-Caen, *Notice sur la vie et les travaux de M. Théodore Roosevelt (1858–1919)* (Paris: Firmin Didot, 1921), 91, 142.

19. For French reaction to the 1898 war, see Louis Martin Sears, "French Opinion of the Spanish–American War," *Hispanic American Historical Review* 7 (February 1927): 25–44.

20. On that grand strategy, see Howard K. Beale, *Theodore Roosevelt and the Rise of America to World Power* (Baltimore: Johns Hopkins Press, 1956); and Frederick W. Marks III, *Velvet on Iron: The Diplomacy of Theodore Roosevelt* (Lincoln: University of Nebraska Press, 1979).

21. Horace Dominique Barral [Marquis de Montferrat], *De Monroë à Roosevelt, 1823–1905* (Paris: Plon, 1905), 347, 354–56.

22. Ribet, *Vol de l'Aigle*, 271–72.

23. Hubert Védrine, *Les Cartes de la France: à l'heure de la mondialisation* (Paris: Fayard, 2000).

24. Thomas T. Lewis, "Franco–American Relations During the First Moroccan Crisis," *Mid-America* 55 (January 1973): 21–36. Also see Douglas Eden, "America's First Intervention in European Politics: Theodore Roosevelt and the European Crisis of 1906–1906," in *A Companion to Theodore Roosevelt*, ed. Serge Ricard (Oxford: Wiley-Blackwell, 2011), 350–67; and Aïssatou Sy-Wonyu, "Les États-Unis, la France et la crise marocaine de 1905," in *Relations franco-américains au XXe siècle*, ed. Pierre Melandri and Serge Ricard (Paris: L'Harmattan, 2003), 53–84.

25. Tardieu, *Notes sur les États-Unis*, 370–71.

26. Portes, *Fascination and Misgivings*, 3–6.

27. Albert Savine, *Roosevelt intime* (Paris: Librairie Félix Juven, 1904), 270.

28. Theodore Roosevelt, letter to John St. Loe Strachey, January 27, 1900, in Elting E. Morison, ed., *The Letters of Theodore Roosevelt*, vol. 2, *The Years of Preparation, 1898–1900* (Cambridge, MA: Harvard University Press, 1951), 1143–46. Notwithstanding what he said to this English correspondent, Roosevelt did have English ancestry, his father's mother having been a Pennsylvanian of Welsh, English, German, and Scotch-Irish descent.

29. Savine, *Roosevelt intime*, 3.

30. See Young, *American by Degrees*.

31. Edmund Morris, *Theodore Rex* (New York: Random House, 2001), 393.

32. Nelson Manfred Blake, "Ambassadors at the Court of Theodore Roosevelt," *Mississippi Valley Historical Review* 42 (September 1955): 179–206, at 205.

33. See Zahniser, *Then Came Disaster*.

34. Viorst, *Hostile Allies*, v.

35. See Béziat, *Franklin Roosevelt et la France;* François Kersaudy, *De Gaulle et Roosevelt: le duel au sommet* (Paris: Perrin, 2004); Aglion, *Roosevelt and de Gaulle;* Berthon, *Allies at War;* Newhouse, *De Gaulle and the Anglo-Saxons;* Rossi, *Roosevelt and the French;* and White, *Seeds of Discord*.

36. This is argued in Frank Costigliola, "The Nuclear Family: Tropes of Gender and Pathology in the Western Alliance," *Diplomatic History* 21 (Spring 1997): 163–83; and Costigliola, *France and the United States*, 30–31.

37. John McVickar Haight Jr., "Roosevelt as Friend of France," *Foreign Affairs* 44 (April 1966): 518–26, at 518.

38. Julian G. Hurstfield, *America and the French Nation, 1939–1945* (Chapel Hill: University of North Carolina Press, 1986), 238, 240.

39. Thomas A. Bailey, *The Man in the Street: The Impact of Public Opinion on Foreign Policy* (New York: Macmillan, 1948), 134–37.

40. Mead, *Special Providence,* 322–23.

41. Robert W. Tucker, *A New Isolationism: Threat or Promise?* (New York: Universe Books, 1972), 28.

42. Willard Range, *Franklin D. Roosevelt's World Order* (Athens: University of Georgia Press, 1959), xi. For similar opinions, see James MacGregor Burns, *Roosevelt: The Lion and the Fox* (New York: Harcourt, Brace, & World, 1956); Frank Freidel, *Franklin D. Roosevelt: Launching the New Deal* (Boston: Little, Brown, 1973); and Michael Fullilove, *Rendezvous with Destiny: How Franklin D. Roosevelt and Five Extraordinary Men Took America into the War and into the World* (New York: Penguin Press, 2013).

43. On the impact of revisionism during the interwar period, see Warren I. Cohen, *The American Revisionists: The Lessons of Intervention in World War I* (Chicago: University of Chicago Press, 1967); on FDR's years as an isolationist, see Robert A. Divine, *Roosevelt and World War II* (Baltimore: Johns Hopkins Press, 1969).

44. Waldo H. Heinrichs, *Threshold of War: Franklin D. Roosevelt and American Entry into World War II* (New York: Oxford University Press, 1988).

45. See John McVickar Haight Jr., "France, the United States, and the Munich Crisis," *Journal of Modern History* 32 (December 1960): 340–58.

46. Mead, *Special Providence,* 181. On the early phase of Jeffersonianism, see Merrill D. Peterson, *The Jefferson Image in the American Mind* (New York: Oxford University Press, 1962); Lawrence S. Kaplan, *Jefferson and France: An Essay on Politics and Political Ideas* (New Haven, CT: Yale University Press, 1967); Lance Banning, *The Jeffersonian Persuasion: Evolution of a Party Ideology* (Ithaca, NY: Cornell University Press, 1978); and Noble E. Cunningham, *The Jeffersonian Republicans: The Formation of Party Organization* (Chapel Hill: University of North Carolina Press, 1957).

47. John Lamberton Harper, *American Visions of Europe: Franklin D. Roosevelt, George F. Kennan, and Dean G. Acheson* (New York: Cambridge University Press, 1994), 60. On this Rooseveltian focus on "hemispherism" in the 1930s, see also David G. Haglund, *Latin America and the Transformation of US Strategic Thought, 1936–1940* (Albuquerque: University of New Mexico Press, 1984).

48. Howard, *War and the Liberal Conscience,* 85.

49. See William L. Langer, *Our Vichy Gamble* (New York: Alfred A. Knopf, 1947); Louis Gottschalk, "Our Vichy Fumble," *Journal of Modern History* 20 (March 1948): 47–56; and Béziat, "Réalisme diplomatique à rude épreuve."

50. Maurice Ferro, *De Gaulle et l'Amérique, une amitié tumultueuse* (Paris: Plon, 1973), chapter 2.

51. Kaspi, *Libération de la France,* 237.

52. See David H. Burton, "Theodore Roosevelt: Confident Imperialist," *Review of Politics* 23 (July 1961): 356–77.

53. See Jennifer Pitts, *A Turn to Empire: The Rise of Imperial Liberalism in Britain and France* (Princeton, NJ: Princeton University Press, 2005).

54. William Roger Louis, *Imperialism at Bay, 1941–1945: The United States and the Decolonization of the British Empire* (Oxford: Clarendon, 1977), 28. Also see Martin Thomas, *Fight or Flight: Britain, France, and Their Roads from Empire* (Oxford: Oxford University Press, 2014).

55. Unsurprisingly, the scholarly corpus on French experience with (and enthusiasm for) empire is vast. Good examples include Jean Bouvier, René Girault, and Jacques Thobie, *L'Impérialisme à la française, 1914–1960* (Paris: Éd. de la Découverte, 1986); Nicolas Bancel, Pascal Blanchard, and Françoise Vergès, *La République coloniale: essai sur une utopie* (Paris: Albin Michel, 2003); Raoul Girardet, *L'Idée coloniale en France de 1871 à 1962* (Paris: Hachette, 1979); David Chuter, *Humanity's Soldier: France and International Security, 1919–2001* (Providence, RI: Berghahn, 1996); Tony Chafer and Amanda Sackur, eds., *Promoting the Colonial Idea: Propaganda and Visions of Empire in France* (New York: Palgrave, 2002); D. Bruce Marshall, *The French Colonial Myth and Constitution-Making in the Fourth Republic* (New Haven, CT: Yale University Press, 1973); John F. Cady, *The Roots of French Imperialism in Eastern Asia* (Ithaca, NY: Cornell University Press, 1954); and Conklin, *Mission to Civilize*.

Conclusion

1. Hennessy, "Psycho-Cultural Studies," 47.

2. Hennessy, "Psycho-Cultural Studies," 44.

3. See, for instance, Webb, "Observing America."

Index

Abenakis, 93

Acadians, 142

Acheson, Dean, 24

Adams, Henry, 78

Afghanistan, vii

African Americans, 76

Aix-la-Chapelle, treaty of (1748), 110

Alaska panhandale boundary dispute, 29

Alcott, Louisa May, 128

Algeciras, 212

Algonquians, 93

Allen, Woody, 30–31, 110, 166

Allison, Graham, 81, 158–59

Almond, Gabriel, 64

American Council of Trustees and Alumni, 84

American Expeditionary Force (AEF), 21

American Journal of Sociology, 100

Amnesty International, 85

Andres, Giovanni, 53

Anglo-American relationship: impact of
Irish "question" upon, 125–26, 136–37.
See also special relationships: United
States and United Kingdom

Anglo-Irish Treaty (1921), 107

Anglo-Saxons/Anglo-Saxonism, 67, 90,
145–49, 152; as constitutive feature
of French anti-Americanism, 173; as
cognitive linchpin, 176; Mr. Dooley
definition of, 147; Teutonic origins of,
147–48; Theodore Roosevelt rejection
of, 213 .

anti-Americanism, 167–71, 178; French
variant of, 13–14, 19–20, 35, 41, 99,
149, 152–54, 171–72, 206; as function
of status anxiety, 164; civilizational critique, 172–73; consequences of, 174–75;

waxing and waning of, 165–68. *See also*
Anglo-Saxons/Anglo-Saxonism

Argall, Samuel, 92

Aron, Raymond, 46

Ash, Timothy Garton, 27

Astérix, 176

Athens, 81

Auschwitz, 175

autonomy, 190, 193

Bacevich, Andrew, 95

Balkans, 85, 134

bandwagoning, 211

Barros Luco, Ramón, 194

Baudrillard, Jean, 173

Beavis and Butthead, 84

Benedict, Ruth, 59

Berger, Peter, 88

Berstein, Serge, 187

Biden, Joseph, vii, 11, 19, 223

bipolarity, 56, 192, 194

Blair, Tony, 16

Bloch, Marc, 184

Breda, treaty of (1667), 92

Brinton, Crane, 39–40

Brubaker, Rogers, 120–23, 137

Bulge, battle of the (1944–45), 84

Bush, George H. W., 11

Bush, George W., 16, 22, 31, 32, 82, 201, 211

Byman, Daniel, 201

Caesar, Julius, 176

Californios, 138

Campbell, Charles, 43

Canada, 154, 182

Canadian Corps, 107

Cape Breton Island, 109

Cartesianism, 176

Chicago Council on Foreign Relations, 22

Chicanos, 76, 138

Chile, 194

China, 28, 81, 178, 189, 193, 194

Chinard, Gilbert, 115

Chirac, Jacques, 14, 16

Churchill, Winston, 10, 202

civic nationalism, 86

civilizational rallying, 27–29, 133

Clemenceau, Georges, 39, 137, 160, 187

Cleveland, Grover, vii

Clinton, Bill, 21–22

Cohen, Roger, 16, 154

Coker, Christopher, 183

comparative politics, 63–64, 68

conspiracy theorizing, 171–72

constructivism, 56, 68

contingency, 69, 80, 101, 103, 204–5, 220;
and "shadow of the future," 102;
indeterminacy of, 224. *See also* critical
junctures

counterfactual reasoning, 104; alliance of
1778 as critical juncture, 105, 110; "miracle" counterfactuals, 208; "redirecting"
counterfactuals, 203–4. *See also* path
dependence

critical junctures, 104

Cromwell, Oliver, 92

Cruz, Ted, 6

Cuba, 189, 210–11

Cuban Americans, 121, 142

cultural pluralism, 114; American, as threat
to French interests, 118, 144–45. *See also*
multiculturalism

culture, xii; as ethnicity, 49, 54, 75, 78, 222;
as historical context, 49; as ideas, 49,
54, 75, 222; as symbolism, 55; definition of, 52–53; individual agency and,
221–22

Culture and Democracy in the United States
(Kallen), 76

Daladier, Édouard, 215–16, 220

Daudet, Léon, 191

Deerfield raid (1704), 97

Defense Threat Reduction Agency, 50

de Gaulle, Charles, 19, 25, 28, 42, 167, 183,
187, 201, 207, 214, 219–20

democratic alliance theory, xi, 179–80. *See
also* liberalism

democratic peace theory, 179

de Montbrial, Thierry, 26

Descartes, René, 176

Desch, Michael, 59, 63

Deutsch-Amerikanischer National-Bund
der Vereinigten Staaten von Amerika
(NGAA), 132

Deutsch-Amerikanischen Zentralbundes
von Pennsylvanien, 132

diasporas (ethnic), 76, 113–14, 125–34, 151,
200; denotative qualities of, 120–22;
"Brito-America," 136–39; "Fran-
co-America," 141–43; lobbying (ethnic),
119, 122–24, 136. *See also* First World
War: debate over American entry into

Dickens, Charles, 29, 203

Disraeli, Benjamin, 212

Dittmer, Lowell, 65

Dominion of New England, 109

Doyle, Michael, 9

Drake, Samuel Adams, 95–96

Droysen, Johann Gustav, 58

Dueck, Colin, 152

Duhamel, Georges, 115, 172–73

Dunne, Finley Peter, 147

Durkheim, Émile, 58

Duroselle, Jean-Baptiste, 12, 17, 77, 114,
139–40

Duroselle-Tardieu thesis, 114–19, 134–44

Eliot, T. S., 65

Ennemi américain, L' (Roger), 165

Entente Cordiale (1904), 129

Erbfeindschaft thesis, 70, 77, 82–83, 85–86,
89, 97–112, 151, 205–6

Erlanger, Steven, 33
ethnic conflict, 39; as primordialism, 88;
    between French and Americans, 77, 82,
    85, 94–98; defining characteristics of,
    92. *See also* Erbfeindschaft thesis; King
    William's War; Queen Anne's War
ethnicity: and heterostereotyping, 115, 145,
    152, 164; and historical context, 99; as
    national character/identity, 69; as race,
    76, 147
ethnocultural studies, 75
European Union (EU), 5, 24–25, 47–49
exceptionalism, 154

Faulkner, William, 77
Febvre, Lucien, 88
Fenians, 126. *See also* Irish Americans
Fifth Republic (France), 167
filibustering, 122, 126
First Amendment rights, 119
First World War, x, 21, 60, 81, 107, 121,
    132–35, 158; and debate over Ameri-
    can entry into, 135–36, 217; as "grand
    climacteric" in Franco-American
    relations, 159–60, 209. *See also* power
    transition theory
Fohlen, Claude, 206, 220
Fortmann, Michel, 15
Fourth Republic (France), 23–24, 118,
    184–85
Franco-American alliance (1778), 39–40,
    82, 155, 160
Franco-Prussian War (1870–71), 131–32;
    American attitudes toward, 126–28, 166
francophobia (American), 14–15, 22, 41–42,
    98, 166
Franklin, Benjamin, 206
Freeman, Edward, 53
French Canadian immigration, 141–43. *See
    also* Quebec
Friedman, Jonathan, 78
fungibility, 223
Fyfe, Hamilton, 60, 62

Gaddis, John Lewis, 52
Gallic Wars, 176
Gaullism, 187–88
Geertz, Clifford, 54–55, 64–65
Gerbi, Antonello, 170
German Americans, 119, 121, 126, 128–32,
    140–41, 143–44
German "problem" in IR, 118; of France,
    128–29
Germany, 15, 41, 43, 128–29, 193, 212. *See
    also* Weimar Germany
Giddens, Anthony, 162
Giraud, Henri, 219
Gladstone, William E., 125, 212
globalization, xi, 167, 176
Glorious Revolution, 109
"Goldilocks" perspective: of France, 20–21,
    33, 160–61; of the United States, 23–25
Grant, Ulysses S., 127–28
Gray, Colin, 50, 57–58, 63, 66, 68, 150
Grosser, Alfred, 36, 42, 46, 118
Guizot, François, 212
Guthrie, Arlo, 172

Han Chinese, 137–38
Harcourt, William, 125
Harper, John Lamberton, 218
Harris, Joel Chandler, 19
Hechter, Michael, 100–1
Heffer, Jean, 141
hegemonic war, 156, 158. *See also* power
    transition theory
hegemony, ix–xi, 154, 178, 188–89
Hennessy, Bernard, 61–62, 221–22
hermeneutics, 57
Hexamer, Charles John, 132
Hicks, Thomas E., 146
historical memory, 84, 98, 200
historical sociology, 67, 99
historicism, 73
history, 68; as constitutive of national char-
    acter/identity, 78; as "undead past,"
    77, 82; construed as context, 80;

history (*continued*)
    contrasted epistemologically with
    political science/IR, 73–74, 80, 200–1;
    "lessons" of, 78
Hitler, Adolf, 12, 202, 204, 218
Hobbes, Thomas, 95
Hoffmann, Stanley, 51, 186, 188
Holland, James, 146
Hollande, François, 32
homeland security, 39
Huguenots, 142
Huntington, Samuel, 27–28, 63
Hunzeker, Michael A., 164
Hurstfield, Julian, 215
Hussein, Saddam, 13, 15, 165–66

ideology, 152, 200, 222
Ikenberry, John, xi, 4, 46
Illusion of National Character, The (Fyfe), 60
imperialism, 219–20
Indigenous peoples, 76
INF crisis (1983), 167
Institut de France, 210
intellectual history, 5
Intercolonial Wars (1689–1763), 79, 83,
    105. *See also* King George's War; King
    William's War; Queen Anne's War;
    Seven Years' War
Interpretation of Cultures, The (Geertz), 54
Iraq, 13, 30, 77. *See also* Iraq invasion (2003)
Iraq invasion (2003), 14–16, 29, 82, 165
Irish Americans, 123, 125–26, 144
Irish Free State, 144
Irish "question" in IR, 125
Iroquois, 93, 95–96
isolationism, ix, 136, 143–44, 160, 174, 192,
    216–17
Italian Americans, 143
Italy, 24

Jackson, Andrew, 111
Jay Treaty (1784), 40, 155
Jefferson in Paris, 206

Jefferson, Thomas, 206–7
Jeffersonianism, 218
Jervis, Robert, 202, 206, 221, 223
Joan of Arc, 208
Joffe, Josef, 171
Johnston, Alastair Iain, 52, 55–58, 64–65,
    68, 150, 152
Jones, Alex, 172
July Monarchy, 179
Jusserand, Jean Jules, 129, 141, 213

Kadmi-Cohen, Isaac, 175
Kagan, Robert, 32–33, 48
Kallen, Horace M., 75–76, 136, 148–49
Kandel, Maya, 95
Karr, Alphonse, 224
Kaspi, André, 13, 38, 99, 156, 160, 207
Keene, Jennifer, 117
Kelley, Robert, 75, 150–51
Kerry, John, 32
Keylor, William, 174
King George's War (1743–48), 98, 107–110
King Philip's War (1675–76), 93–94, 97, 108
King William's War (1689–97), 79, 93–97
Kirke, David, 92
Kiser, Edgar, 100–1
Kosovo war (1999), 14–15
Kosovo Polje, battle of (1389), 85
Ku Klux Klan, 75
Kuisel, Richard F., 169
Kupchan, Charles, 29

Lachine raid (1689), 93, 96
Lafayette, Marquis de, 15, 77
La Hogue, battle of (1692), 191
Laing, R. D., 162
Lamartine, Alphonse de, 212
Lanoszka, Alexander, 164
Lantis, Jeffrey, 50
Le Pen, Marine, 194
levels of analysis in IR, 162, 199. *See also*
    Waltzian images
Levy, Jack, 104, 134, 205–7

Liberal International Order, 178: as synon-
ymous with West, 157; threats to, 4–5
liberalism, 67, 152, 176–77; as contrasted
with French realism, 153, 178–88, 219;
as American grand strategy, 186; and
democratic alliance theory, 180–82
Libya, 33
Lincoln, Abraham, 202, 212
Lind, Michael, 121
Lloyd George, David, 137
Locke, John, 88
Louis, William Roger, 220
Louis XIV, 208
Louis XVI, 223
Louisbourg, conquest of (1745), 109–10, 205
Lowell, James Russell, 128
Luckmann, Thomas, 88
Luethy, Hubert, 184
Lusitania, 209
Lyon-Caen, Charles, 210

Macmillan, Harold, 202
Macron, Emmanuel, 115–16; and "An-
glo-Saxon" threat, 145–46, 148–49, 177,
190, 223, 225; and quest for autonomy,
190; invokes strategic culture, 46–47;
calls NATO "brain-dead," 5–7, 19, 47
Maduro, Nicolás, 189
Maginot Line syndrome, 174
Mali, 33
Mamère, Noël, 192
Man, the State, and War (Waltz), 199
Maulnier, Thierry, 44
Maximilian I, 127
May, Ernest, 119
McDougall, Walter, 40, 170
McKinley, William, 166, 210, 213
Mead, Walter Russell, 40, 140, 172, 216, 218
Mearsheimer, John, 189
Mélenchon, Jean-Luc, 194
Merkel, Angela, 6–7
Meunier, Sophie, 175–76
Mexico, 189

Meyssan, Thierry, 172
Miller, John J., 82–83, 85–86
Minogue, Kenneth, 169
Mitterrand, François, 26, 167
Mitzen, Jennifer, 162–63, 187
Mohawks, 93
Mohegans, 93
Montcalm, Louis-Joseph de, 107
Molesky, Mark, 82–83, 85–86
Monroe doctrine, 30
Morocco crisis (1905), 212
Mortefontaine, treaty of (1800), 40
Mouvement républicain populaire (MRP),
185
multiculturalism: as synonym for An-
glo-Saxonism, 146–49; as "threat" to
France, 115. *See also* Macron, Emmanuel
multilateralism, 186, 189, 191
multipolarity, 25, 67, 189, 211; as source
of suboptimal cooperation, 153, 173,
185–93, 200
myth, 67, 78

Napoleon Bonaparte, 40, 191, 194, 202
Napoleon III, 128
Narragansetts, 93
narrative positivism, 69, 223
national character, 37, 59, 101–2, 161, 221–22;
and heterostereotyping, 60; as ethnicity,
74; as "modal personality," 61; defense
of, 59–60. *See also* relational realism
National German-American Alliance
(NGAA), 132–33
national identity, 61–62, 67, 90; as distinct
from national character, 161–62;
American identity shifts, chronology
of, x, 105–10
national interest, 63
Newman, Randy, 170
Nipmucks, 93
North Atlantic Treaty Organization
(NATO): "disarray" of, vii–viii, 5–6,
179; Franco-American wangling within,

North Atlantic Treaty Organization
(NATO) (*continued*)
25–29; temporal origins of, 41, 181;
Ukraine war impact upon, 18–19, 194,
225. *See also* Macron, Emmanuel
Norton, Charles Eliot, 128
Nouvel Observateur, le, 166
Nova Scotia, 109
Nye, Joseph, 75

Obama, Barack, 6, 17, 31–32
Obama doctrine, 33
Obsession anti-américaine, L' (Revel), 165
offshore balancing, ix
"oldest allies" imagery, 16, 31–32, 77, 98,
110, 201
Olney, Richard, 147
Onishi, Norimitsu, 115
ontological security, 13, 26–27, 161–62, 180;
ontological security dilemma on Franco-American relationship, 163–65, 173,
187. *See also* social identity theory
operational code, 201, 217, 222
Operation Torch (1942), 43
Orwell, George, 11
Ory, Pascal, 168–69
Our Oldest Enemy (Miller and Molesky), 82

Paris Commune (1871), 183
Paris peace conference (1783), 40
Parti communiste français (PCF), 185
path dependence: as reactive sequences,
69, 102–3, 113, 203; as self-reinforcing
sequences, 69, 102; historical context,
75, 99, 223. *See also* contingency
Peabody, Dean, 60
Peloponnesian war, 81, 157
Pequots, 93
Perrin du Lac, François Marie, 35, 101, 150,
153–54
"personality-in-culture" approach, 61
Pétain, Philippe, 143, 219
Pierson, Paul, 68–69

Plains of Abraham, battle of (1759), 107
Pocumtucks, 93
Poincaré, Raymond, 160
political culture, 64–65
Pollack, Kenneth, 201
Poltava, battle of (1709), 85
positivism, 56–58, 68. *See also* narrative
positivism
power: as relative capability, 67; definitions
of, 51. *See also* power transition theory
power transition theory, 81; and relevance to
Franco-American relations, 155–59, 165
presentism, 73, 80, 113, 156
prestige, 61. *See also* status anxiety
preventive war, 158
Prussia, 127. *See also* Franco-Prussian War
(1870–71)
Putin, Vladimir, vii, 4, 12, 18, 85, 116, 148,
157, 179, 194–95

Quebec/Quebeckers, 141–42, 225
Queen Anne's War (1702–13), 79, 96–97

Ranke, Leopold von, 53
rational-choice theory, 64, 100
Reagan, Ronald, 177
realism/realists, 56; classical realists, 63;
French realism, 153–55, 181, 185–88;
human-nature realism, 187; relational
realism, 79, 99–102, 112, 152, 161–62,
204, 224; structural realism, 51, 55–56,
155, 187, 199
Redeemed Captive Returning to Zion, The
(Williams), 97
republicanism, 86
Revel, Jean-François, 165–66, 174
Rhineland, occupation of (1918–23), 117
Ribet, Joseph, 211
Risse, Thomas, 180–82
Rodnick, David, 59
Roger, Philippe, 39, 165–66, 174
Roosevelt, Archie, 209
Roosevelt, Edith, 213

Roosevelt, Franklin D., 42, 178, 201, 203, 207–8, 214–20

Roosevelt, Kermit, 210

Roosevelt, Quentin, 209–10

Roosevelt, Theodore, 43, 128–29, 203, 206–16, 219–20

Roosevelt, Ted, Jr., 209–10

Rose, Arnold, 148–49

Rosenau, James, 18

Rubenzer, Trevor, 124

Ruggie, John, 190

Russia, 193–95, 202, 225

Russian "problem" in IR, 80

Saint-Germaine-en-Laye, treaty of (1632), 92

Salem, Massachusetts, 96

Sanders, Bernie, 6

Saratoga, battle of (1777), 82, 105

Sarkozy, Nicholas, 16, 17, 31

Sartori, Giovanni, 123

satisficing, 225

Savine, Albert, 212–13

Schenectady raid (1690), 96

Schoenbrun, David, 23–24

Second Anglo-Dutch War (1665–67), 92

Second World War (1939–45), x, 13, 23, 42, 144, 191, 202, 214

Section française de l'internationale ouvrière (SFIO), 185

security communities, 179, 181

security dilemma, 162. See also ontological security

Sedan, battle of (1870), 191–92

Sedgwick, Robert, 92

September 11 attacks, 14. See also Meyssan, Thierry

Serfaty, Simon, 38

Seven Years' War (1756–63), 106–10

Sewell, William, 55

Sicily, invasion of (1943), 146

Siegfried, André, 17

Simon, Herbert A., 47

Small, Melvin, 124

Snoop Doggy Dogg, 84

Snyder, Jack, 58

social identity theory, 90–91, 163–65. See also status anxiety

social media, 84

soft balancing, 25, 190

Somers, Margaret, 99–101

Soprano, Tony, 81

Soviet Union, 22–23, 25

Spain, 191, 210

Spanish-American War (1898), 210–11

Sparta, 81

special relationships: denotative qualities of, x, 8–12, 209; United States and France, 12–13, 17; United States and Germany, 10; United States and United Kingdom, 10–11, 179

Stalin, Josef, 202

status anxiety, 153, 161, 164–65, 180, 192. See also ontological security

Sternhell, Zeev, 184

strategic culture, xii, 7; as analogous to political culture, 65–66; as cognition, 58, 67, 150–51; as context, 58, 66–70, 223; as national identity, 67; employed as dependent variable, 47–49, 56, 74, 150; employed as independent variable, 49–50, 74, 150; "generations" of, 56, 59–60, 63; Gray-Johnston debate, 56–57, 150

strategy: definition of, 52–53; as grand strategy, viii–ix, 152, 178, 186, 210

suboptimality: and alliance, 111; and cognitive antinomies, 152–65, 176–81; and temperament, 35–36; as "bounded rationality," 44–47, 200, 224; as le différend franco-américain, 99, 155, 200, 214, 223, 225; consequences of, 42–43; in defense and security cooperation, 9, 13, 58, 163, 173; Karr's aphorism, 224

Sweden, 154

symbolism, 55, 65–67. See also political culture

Syria, 32

Tajfel, Henri, 163

Tale of Two Cities, A (Dickens)

Tardieu, André, 36, 38, 39, 114, 116–18, 129, 135, 139, 140–41, 212

Terhune, Kenneth, 161

Theory of International Politics (Waltz), 199

therapeutic crises, 29–30, 111

Thiers, Adolphe, 212

Third Republic (France), 143, 183–84

Thirty Years' War (1618–48), 191

Thomson, David, 184

Thucydides, 81; and "trap" metaphor, 159, 165

Tooze, Adam, 160

transatlantic collective identity, 164, 173, 183

Trump, Donald J., vii, 6–8, 19, 21, 32–33, 177–78, 186, 201

Tufnell, Stephen, 139–40

Twain, Mark, 167

Tyler, Edward B., 53

Ukraine war (2022–), 18–19, 85, 90, 157, 179, 190, 193–94, 202, 224–25

unilateralism, 174, 190–91. *See also* isolationism

unipolarity, 82, 119, 167, 190–91, 193–94, 211

United Nations, 216; Security Council of, 14–15

University of Connecticut Center for Survey Research and Analysis, 84

Van Buren, Martin, 213

Vasquez, John, 134

Venezuela, 189

Venezuela crisis (1895), 29, 111. *See also* therapeutic crises

Viau, Hélène, 15

Vidal, Gore, 84, 98

Vimy Ridge, battle of (1917), 104, 107

Viorst, Milton, 214, 220

Voltaire, 145

Waltz, Kenneth N., 55–56, 193, 199–200

Waltzian images, 199–203, 223–24

Walzer, Michael, 65

Wampanoags, 93

War of 1812, 40, 43, 155

Warin, Olivier, 192

Washington, George, 40, 136, 187, 216, 223

Waterloo, battle of (1815), 191

Webb, Stephen Saunders, 108–9

Weber, Max, 58

Weimar Germany, 218

Weltanschauung, 201

Westphalian era, 191. *See also* multipolarity

Whiggism, 73

White, Elizabeth Brett, 82

Wilde, Oscar, 50

Williams, John, 97

Williams, Raymond, 52

Wilson, Woodrow, 118–19, 121, 135–36, 139–41, 187, 202

Wilsonianism, 186, 218

Winock, Michel, 184

Wisconsin school of history, 53

Wolfe, James, 107

Wolfers, Arnold, 23

Yalta myth, 192

Yorktown, battle of (1781), 84

Zedong, Mao, 202

Zemmour, Éric, 137, 194, 235, 255, 268

Zuboff, Shoshana, 84

CPSIA information can be obtained
at www.ICGtesting.com
Printed in the USA
LVHW052105020523
745892LV00001BA/57